Presidential Seizure

in

Labor Disputes

Presidential Seizure

in

Labor Disputes

John L. Blackman, Jr.

HARVARD UNIVERSITY PRESS

Cambridge, Massachusetts

1967

Distributed in Great Britain by Oxford University Press, London

Library of Congress Catalog Card Number 67-20871

PRINTED IN THE UNITED STATES OF AMERICA

To Patricia

Foreword

Labor-management disputes which constitute a national emergency, or which are judged by some to create such an emergency, have been a persistent theme in public and scholarly discussions over the past two decades. Each work stoppage of national prominence stimulates renewed concern with the adequacy of present national legislation to protect the public interest. The New York City transit and the airline mechanics' strikes of 1966 are the more important recent illustrations. A. H. Raskin reflects this widespread concern: "In many strategic sectors of industry, no remote relationship exists between the capacity or social responsibility of the negotiators and the degree of damage they are able to visit on the economy . . . Labor-management negotiators who ought not be allowed to cross the street without a seeing-eye dog are free to inflict hardship on millions of their fellow citizens through sheer incompetence at the bargaining table. And there is not one thing anyone in the community can do to arrest them for reckless use of a dangerous economic weapon." (*Saturday Review,* February 25, 1967, p. 32.)

In the arsenal of weapons available for the protection of the public interest in labor-management disputes, governmental seizure of industrial property is relatively little known. Yet there have been 71 instances of presidential seizure and temporary operation of industrial property in such disputes over the past hundred years. Transportation facilities have been seized in 21 cases and military suppliers in 32 other cases. Sixty seizures were made under legislation expressly authorizing its use and 11 cases, including the 1952 steel industry, relied on the general or other powers of the president. Some seizures were in wartime, others in reconversion periods, and still others in times of peace. There is great diversity and variety in the experience with presidential seizure.

Professor Blackman's painstaking research over many years has now provided the definitive work on the experience of these 71 instances of presidential seizure. His intensive review of the records of the operations of the facilities during the seizure period, which has varied from two days to three and a half years, is not likely to be repeated by any scholar. This volume and its appendixes will be quickly recognized and cited as the authoritative source of information on presidential seizures in industrial disputes.

Professor Blackman is aware of both the strengths and limitations of presidential seizure as a means to restore or to maintain production and as a weapon to facilitate the resolution of the underlying dispute. There may be legitimate differences of opinion over any appraisal of the experience with seizure compared to other methods of securing operations and settling disputes. But any judgment must be aware of the experience with the various weapons in the government arsenal. The story of presidential seizure has now been systematically presented affording a widespread review of its place among the measures to protect the public interest in labor-management disputes.

This volume will be of interest to all those concerned with the difficult questions of designing procedures and machinery to deal with emergency disputes, including those in labor organizations, managements, various branches of government, and the academic community.

JOHN T. DUNLOP

Author's Preface

This book has evolved through a long period of study of presidential intervention in emergency labor disputes. Although its focus is on the accumulated experience with presidential seizure, it has been extended to include the experience with other coercive measures used by the presidents to keep industrial production going, except for mere "cooling-off" periods. This has permitted the examination of seizure in a wider context—presidential action to require production in emergency disputes—which is then considered briefly as a distinct form of public control in industrial relations.

The need for a study of the nation's extensive experience with presidential seizure was pointed out to me in 1949 by Joseph L. Miller, of Washington, D.C., who had participated in several seizures during World War II as a labor relations adviser. Mr. Miller also directed me to important sources of information and contributed valuable reminiscences. During 1949 and 1950, I obtained special permission from the Departments of the Navy and of the Army to examine their seizure records; and in the period from 1949 through 1953 I spent many days poring over the unpublished reports and correspondence of those agencies. At that time, I also examined at the National Archives the historical files of other seizing agencies, notably the Petroleum Administration for War, the Office of Defense Transportation, and the Department of the Interior. I also benefited from interviews and correspondence with many present and former officials of government departments and business firms who had taken part in some of the seizures.

I cannot begin to thank by name all the persons who so kindly helped me, but I must mention Rear Admiral John B. Heffernan, USN, the director of naval history, and Carl J. McDonald, chief of reference, Naval Records Management Center, Arlington, Virginia, and two officials of the Office of Chief of Military History (OCMH) of the Department of the Army—Dr. Stetson Conn, the acting chief historian, and Israel Wice, chief of the general reference section. For permission to consult certain records of the Petroleum Administration for War in the National Archives, I am indebted to Carroll D. Fentress, executive secretary of the Petroleum Administration for Defense. I have benefited greatly from the kind permission given me by John H. Ohly, formerly with the industrial personnel division of the army service forces, to read and draw upon his monumental but still unpublished study, "History of Plant Seizures During World War II: Emergency Operations of Private Industrial Facilities by the War Department," 1946 (manuscript, 3 volumes of text, 4 volumes of appended documents, in the files of OCMH).

I became convinced from some parallel economic circumstances of our three "total wars" (the two world wars and the Civil War) that "there must have been" a seizure in the Civil War, although none was known to labor historians. When this conviction led me to the discovery of brief allusions to the War Department's seizure of the Philadelphia & Reading Railroad during a strike in July 1864, I was guided expertly to the long forgotten, official records of the case in the National Archives by Miss Valerie Stubbs of the staff of OCMH.

In December 1953, I gave a preliminary report of the seizure investigation before Professor Sumner H. Slichter's graduate seminar in collective bargaining at Littauer Center, Harvard University; and during the two following years I was supported in further research and writing at Cambridge, Massachusetts, by grants from the Jacob Wertheim Committee of Harvard. This support permitted the completion of my doctoral dissertation (1957), from which the present Chapters 2, 3, 4, and 9 were extracted. A further review of the evidence to determine the public standards developed by the seizing agencies was conducted in 1957–1960 while I was at Bucknell University, where I was assisted by a summer faculty research grant. This activity is reflected in Chapters 5, 6, 7, and 8. The plan of identifying and examining all cases of required production other than by seizure was carried out later at the University of Massachusetts and resulted in the comparative treatment of Chapters 1 and 10. In order to update and unify the study, the entire manuscript was revised in 1965–1966. The final typing was supported by a grant from the new Labor Relations and Research Center of the University of Massachusetts.

Although the help of many persons has been acknowledged in the endnotes, I wish to thank several others, not cited there, for informative and stimulating interviews: Louis B. Atkinson, David E. Bell, Kendall M. Barnes, Archibald Cox, William H. Davis, Joseph A. Fanelli, G. F. Foley, Edward F. Hickey, James R. Hoffa, Matthew E. Kearney, the late William M. Leiserson, Robert Mandel, Arthur M. Ross, Carl Schedler, John R. Steelman, and Robert D. Weeks.

Most important, I wish to acknowledge my indebtedness to my teachers of economics and government at Harvard, especially to John T. Dunlop and the late Sumner H. Slichter, both of whom encouraged and supported this study in so many ways. In addition to the influence of the writings, classroom teaching, and personal guidance of both these men, Mr. Dunlop read the entire draft of the dissertation and made numerous suggestions for its improvement. I also wish to thank Mrs. June Hill whose skillful editing of two final drafts has spared the reader many tedious passages.

Finally, an author's acknowledgments are not complete without reference to the patience, encouragement, and self-sacrifice of his family and friends. My parents helped financially when I was a graduate student. My former wife, the late Ruth Appleton (Chapin) Blackman, typed several drafts of the dissertation and some of the later chapters and contributed helpful editorial criticism. My wife, Patricia Chase (Gustafson) Blackman, has supported this undertaking in many ways, including proofreading of the manuscript and galleys, preparing the index, and bearing patiently the long hours of literary widowhood.

JOHN L. BLACKMAN, JR.

North Amherst, Massachusetts
March 1967

Contents

PART ONE

Seizure as a Means of Public Control in Particular Disputes

PART TWO

Standards of Public Policy During Seizure Operations

APPENDIXES

Tables

Key List of Presidential Seizures
in Labor Disputes

(with identifying chronological numbers)

Lincoln

(Civil War)

1. Phila. & Reading R.R. (U)

Wilson

(World War I)

2. Railroads (1917–1920) (U)
3. Wire systems (M)
4. Smith & Wesson Co. (M)

F. D. Roosevelt

(Defense emergency)

5. North American Aviation (U)
6. Federal Shipbuilding (M)
7. Alcoa freighters (U)
8. Air Associates (M)

(After Pearl Harbor)

9. T. P. & W. R.R. (M)
10. General Cable Corp. (L)
11. S. A. Woods Machine Co. (M)
12. F. P. & E. R.R. (U)
13. Coal mines (May 1943) (L)
14. American R.R. of P. R. (U)

(Under WLDA)

15. Atlantic Basin Iron Works (M)
16. Coal mines (Nov. 1943) (L)
17. Mass. leather companies (U)
18. Western Electric Co. (L)
19. Railroads (1943–1944) (L)
20. Fall River textile mills (U)
21. Los Angeles water & power (U)
22. Jenkins Bros. (M)
23. Ken-Rad Tube & Lamp (M)
24. Montgomery Ward (Chicago only, Apr. 1944) (M)
25. Montgomery Ward (Hummer mfg. div.) (M)
26. Phila. Transportation Co. (L)
27. Midwest trucking firms (M)
28. San Francisco machine shops (L)

29. Phila. & Reading Coal (U)
30. International Nickel (U)
31. Soft coal mines (foremen, 1944–1945) (U)
32. Cleveland Graphite Bronze (L)
33. Hughes Tool Co. (M)
34. Twentieth Century Brass (M)
35. Farrell-Cheek Steel (M)
36. Toledo machine shops (U)
37. Cudahy Bros. (M)
38. Montgomery Ward (Chicago & six other cities, Dec. 1944) (M)
39. Cleveland Electric (U)
40. Bingham & Garfield Ry. (L)
41. American Enka Corp. (L-M)
42. Coal mines (1945) (L)

Truman

43. Cities Service refinery (U)
44. United Engineering Co., Ltd. (L)
45. Carter Coal, *et al.* (M)
46. Cocker Machine & Foundry Co. (M)
47. Chicago trucking firms (L)
48. Gaffney Mfg. Co. (M)
49. Mary-Leila Cotton Mills (M)
50. Humble Oil & Refining Co. (M)
51. Pure Oil Co. (M)
52. Scranton Transit Co. (U)
53. Diamond Alkali Co. (U)
54. Texas Co. (U)
55. Goodyear Tire & Rubber Co. (U)
56. Sinclair Rubber (U)
57. Springfield Plywood Corp. (L)
58. U. S. Rubber Co. (U)
59. Illinois Central R.R. (L)

(Reconversion after V-J Day)

60. Oil refineries & pipe lines (U)
61. Capital Transit Co. (U)
62. Great Lakes Towing Co. (U)
63. Meat-packing firms (U)
64. N. Y. Harbor towing firms (U)

Historical information about each seizure, in table form, is in Appendixes A, D, E, and F.

Key to Abbreviations

Seizure precipitated by—

L	Labor non-compliance	18 cases
M	Management non-compliance	24
L-M	Both parties' non-compliance	1
U	Unadjudicated dispute	28
		71

Presidential Seizure

in

Labor Disputes

PART ONE

Seizure as a Means of Public Control in Particular Disputes

I shall always be a friend of labor, but in any conflict that arises between one particular group, no matter who they may be, and the country as a whole, the welfare of the country must come first.

—HARRY S TRUMAN, radio address on second day of nationwide railroad strike, May 24, 1946

CHAPTER 1

Seizure and Other Forms of Control in Emergency Disputes

Presidential seizure and temporary operation of industrial property has occurred 71 times in labor disputes, beginning with the Civil War. The technique has been employed by four presidents—Lincoln, Wilson, Franklin D. Roosevelt, and Truman.

The purpose of these seizures has been to keep production going in the face of threatened or actual stoppages in industries deemed essential for governmental or private use. In most cases, seizure has been employed only after the president has failed to persuade the parties to settle their dispute without a strike or lockout.

Seizure is only one of several means of coercion authorized by Congress or improvised by the presidents in both peace and war to keep production going in emergency disputes, but it is the one that has been most frequently resorted to. Other measures employed during the last 100 years (in a total of 23 disputes) have consisted of: the citation of strike leaders for contempt of antistrike injunctions, the prosecution of strikers under criminal statutes, the use of soldiers or civilians as temporary replacements, the proclamation of qualified martial law, and the adoption of new *ad hoc* legislation. Altogether nine presidents, including members of both political parties, have used one or more of these measures—Lincoln, Hayes, Cleveland, Wilson, Harding, Franklin D. Roosevelt, Truman, Eisenhower, and Kennedy.

Of the instances other than seizure, all but the two cases of *ad hoc* legislation involved the use of powers not expressly granted by Congress for this purpose. In contrast, seizure has been employed 60 times under legislation expressly authorizing its use in emergency labor disputes, and only 11 times under the president's claimed general or other powers.

Many of the seizures are surprisingly little known, despite the fact that they had important consequences upon the history of collective bargaining, upon the national structure of wages and even prices, and upon the personnel practices and corporate forms of several industries. The earliest seizure, for example—that of the Philadelphia & Reading Railroad in July 1864—is not mentioned in any of the standard histories of collective bargaining or of the labor movement, although it adversely affected for many years the rise of the great railroad brotherhoods.

Perhaps our memories are short because all the seizures have been temporary, lasting only until the dispute was settled or until the president decided that government control was no longer needed. The longest seizure extended only for three and a half years (the Toledo, Peoria & Western Railroad); the shortest for two days (Cleveland Electric Illuminating Co.). The median duration has been 95 days.

It is also probable that our unfamiliarity with many of the seizures stems from the fact that 48 were of individual firms, 19 of them having only 1,000 employees or less (six with 300 employees or less). The smallest company was the Twentieth Century Brass Works, of Minneapolis, a foundry with only 55 workers, operated by three partners (1944–1945). The firm was part of the critical foundry industry whose output was considered essential to winning the Second World War; and its compliance with a wage order of the National War Labor Board was deemed necessary for the success of a national program for the peaceful adjustment of labor disputes in wartime. The largest single enterprise to be seized was the Illinois Central Railroad, which had approximately 42,000 employees and provided transportation in 11 states (1945–1946). The operation of this extensive carrier was about to be halted by a jurisdictional dispute between two railroad labor organizations.

In addition to individual firms, the presidents have taken over groups of firms in 23 of the 71 seizures. These have been the more spectacular cases. Yet many are now forgotten. For example, it is seldom recalled that presidents have taken possession of all the major railroads on five occasions (1917–1920, 1943–1944, 1946, 1948, and 1950–1952); that unresolved disputes have led to the takeover of other basic industries such as the telephones and telegraphs (1918–1919), the coal mines (1943–1944, 1945, and 1946–1947), the large meat-packers (1946), many oil refineries (1945–1946), the midwest trucking firms (1944–1945), and the basic steel producers (1952).

Besides the one case of seizure in the Civil War, this technique has been employed in the First World War (three times), the Second World War (51 times), and the Korean War (three times). But seizure has also been used in a period of reconversion from war to peace (eight times between V-J Day in 1945 and December 31, 1946) and in two periods of peacetime rearmament (1941—four times; 1948—once). The occasions for seizure have been periods of military urgency, but its use has by no means been confined to times of formal, declared war.

The use of seizure has also been considered or threatened in other peacetime disputes—by Cleveland in 1894, by Theodore Roosevelt in 1902, by Wilson in 1914 and 1916, and by Kennedy in 1963. In 1902, the mere threat of seizure is believed to have induced the anthracite mine owners to accept binding arbitration by a presidential board. In the other labor crises, other forms of compulsory production were adopted in its place.[1]

Although the alternatives have been used most often in peace (10 cases), they also have been employed in war (three times in the Civil War, twice in the First World War, twice in the Second World War, and once in the Korean War) and again in the economic reconversion from war to peace (four times in 1919, and once in 1946).

The experience with seizure and with the other forms of required production has not previously been studied in its entirety as a distinct form of presidential action in labor-market impasses. Not only have some of the actual instances been overlooked, but the total experience of required production has not been systematically explored in its relationship to national emergency labor disputes. For this reason, it seems desirable to begin the study of this body of experience by placing it in historical context with the other reasons for presidential intervention in labor disputes.

REASONS FOR PRESIDENTIAL INTERVENTION

Historically, the presidents have intervened in particular labor disputes for three purposes: to suppress physical violence; to enforce the continuance of industrial production; or to mediate a settlement.

The first instance of intervention to suppress physical violence was by President Jackson in 1834 when he sent troops to the line of the Chesapeake & Ohio Canal, at the request of the Maryland legislature, to halt a bloody jurisdictional struggle between two rival gangs of laborers.

The first example of presidential action to compel the continuance of production, against the wishes of one or both of the disputing parties, was in 1863 when President Lincoln used soldiers to load and unload government vessels at New York piers during a strike of longshoremen. The first such instance in peace was in February 1877 when President Hayes, through the attorney general, brought criminal proceedings against striking engineers of the Boston & Maine Railroad. (The engineers were found guilty of conspiring to obstruct the mails.)

Presidential mediation to seek a settlement of a dispute was first undertaken in 1902 when Theodore Roosevelt summoned both parties in a long anthracite strike to the White House and induced them to accept binding arbitration by a presidential board.

Although the three purposes of presidential intervention have often coincided in the same cases, each involves a different technique of control, has different effects upon the dispute and upon the national economy, and requires different considerations of public policy. Let us look briefly at the historical experience with each in turn.

Suppressing physical violence. At first, this intervention was only in response to the call of state governments that found the violence accompanying certain disputes too severe for their military forces to control. Later, presidents on their own initiative sent troops to protect federal buildings (such as arsenals and post offices) and to protect federal personnel. They have also sent troops to safeguard private property where the federal government has had a financial interest (as in the manufacture of military equipment), or where the property was in federal receivership. However, such intervention has neither assured the public a continuous supply of goods and services nor guaranteed the parties an early (or an equitable) settlement of their controversy.

The history of intervention to preserve order has been the subject of several extensive investigations, from which the following lessons have been learned: the policy standards under which the military policing is conducted will affect, and possibly determine, the outcome of the private controversy; the standards followed may reflect the special interests of one side unless the president gives clear directives and keeps control of the troops out of the hands of state or local governments and private organizations.[2]

The crucial questions of public policy appear to have been: Should the strikers be allowed to block entry by nonstriking employees? Should the companies be allowed to import strikebreakers from other areas? If the answer to both questions is impartially "no," the strike becomes a test of strength between the management and the union members—a form of collective bargaining, policed but tolerated by the federal government. If the answer to the first question is "yes," the company is badly handicapped in the bargaining. If the answer to the second question is "yes," the strike becomes a competitive struggle between two rival groups of workers, and the union usually loses.

When President Jackson sent soldiers to the line of the Chesapeake & Ohio Canal, then under construction, their "presence" was said by the president of the company, John H. Eaton, to have aided him in dismissing "troublemakers," meaning the leaders of a violent strike against the company's employment of a second (and rival) group of laborers.[3] In this case, the importation of strikebreakers was, in effect, permitted, and the company was thereby assisted. With quite different results, Wilson's despatch of troops to the Colorado coal fields in 1913–1914 was accompanied by a ban on the importation of strikebreakers, enabling the miners ultimately to win some improvements in working conditions.[4] But neither action brought an early resumption of production, for the troops in the first case permitted the company to suspend work (a lockout), and in the second permitted the continuance of the strike.

Required production. Intervention by the presidents to require the resumption or continuance of industrial production goes back fully a century. As we have seen, nine presidents have acted to require production over the resistance of one or both of the disputing parties. Although these instances have been infrequent, they nevertheless constitute a distinct class of executive action aimed at the preservation of industrial order. Originally intended to prevent the breakdown of industrial services urgently needed by the government to conduct its operations in war and peace, they have been extended to cover services essential to the general functioning of private commerce.

The concept of compulsory production consists of presidential actions to require an uninterrupted flow of goods or services in a particular firm or industry, regardless of the existence of a labor dispute and in spite of resistance to such a flow by some of the participants in the firm or industry. Such actions either explicitly or implicitly withdraw the right to strike and to lock out in negotiations for the settlement of the particular dispute. The requirement of uninterrupted production continues until the dispute has been settled or until the urgent need for such production has ended, whichever occurs sooner.

This type of presidential intervention is clearly to be distinguished from action merely to investigate or to mediate a dispute in a major industry. It is also to be distinguished from action simply postponing stoppages of production for a given number of days, whether by voluntary agreement of the disputing parties or by the compulsory means provided in the Taft-Hartley Act and in the Railway Labor Act. Under the so-called emergency provisions of those acts, strikes and lockouts can be delayed for 60 or 80 days but are entirely lawful at the end of the cooling-off period. Although these measures have proved helpful adjuncts to public investigation and to high-level mediation of important labor disputes, they do not assure the uninterrupted flow of the particular industrial service.

Under the definition of required production used here, there have been 94 instances in approximately 100 years—71 of them using seizure and 23 using other means. The instances are identified in Appendixes A and C.

The earliest known instance of required production (June 1863) was intended specifically to protect government operations in wartime. Lincoln's use of soldier-prisoners (deserters) and civilians hired in the open market (volunteers) was confined to loading and unloading government vessels at the New York piers. The government was concerned with keeping military supplies moving to the front, but carefully avoided interfering with the longshoremen's strike insofar as it tied up privately operated shipping. As a result, the longshoremen soon won a reasonable wage increase.[5] This was a case of required partial operations.

The next instance of required operation was also aimed at safeguarding the transportation of military supplies. It came about at the urging of the employer, however, and was conducted in a most one-sided manner. When the newly organized Brotherhood of the Footboard, fresh from organizational victories in the midwest, struck the country's largest coal-carrying railroad, the Philadelphia & Reading, on July 1, 1864, shutting it down completely, the president of the company, Charles E. Smith, induced the War Department to furnish 160 train crewmen from the military railways and to take over formal possession and operation of the road to assure an adequate supply of coal for the army and the navy.[6]

Within a week after army operation of the railroad began, the strikers capitulated, more than half of them were discharged, and the rest were reinstated without the increase in pay they had been demanding.[7] Within another month, the Brotherhood of the Footboard, reeling from this defeat as it met in second annual convention, voted to change its name to the Brotherhood of Locomotive Engineers, dropped from office its founder and first "grand chief engineer," William D. Robinson, and elected as his successor a nonmilitant, Charles Wilson, who discouraged strikes and established the Locomotive Engineers' Mutual Life Insurance Association.[8]

After a decade of Grand Chief Engineer Wilson's moderate administration, he, too, was removed in another reversal of the organization's policy. A special convention of the BLE voted to replace Wilson with P. M. Arthur after Wilson had publicly denounced a strike against a wage cut by the engineers of the Pennsylvania Railroad.

Thus it came about that Arthur led the engineers into a strike which became the first known case in peacetime of presidential intervention to keep operations going over union resistance. In February 1877, when the BLE struck and closed down the Boston & Maine Railroad, President Hayes, as we have seen, through his attorney general, directed the arrest of its local leaders on a charge of conspiring to obstruct the mails. The men were tried in federal court, found guilty, and punished.[9] The railroad replaced the striking engineers and resumed operations. Thus a strike was treated for the first time as a federal crime, in this case by presidential interpretation of an old statute.

In these few cases, we find the beginnings of a federal policy which has been continued for 100 years—a refusal of the government (despite its general toleration of strikes) to permit its essential operations to be interrupted by industrial stoppages, either in war or peace. Lincoln's discreet use of soldiers on the New York docks has been repeated several times by presidents of both political parties.[10] Hayes's resort to an early statute forbidding obstruction of the mails has also been adapted to many labor disputes, although it clearly was not intended originally as a law to govern labor relations. The weakness of this approach was its indirect outlawing of a particular strike without furnishing any substitute method by which the employees could be assured of equitable treatment. As a labor measure, it asserted public control of the dispute without establishing any standards of labor policy. It proved, in practice, to be biased against union labor.

Similarly, the seizure of the Reading Railroad assured the continuity of rail operations without establishing any standards of labor policy. The action was taken under the unchallenged authority of a congressional statute and of a very broad presidential executive order, permitting the War Department to seize any railroad needed for military purposes; but again this statute clearly was not designed for the control of emergency strikes.[11] Yet it was this very technique of seizure which became, a half century later—under the guidance of a socially conscious president (Wilson) and a similarly minded secretary of war (Baker)—an instrument of public control in which policy standards were developed that assured the employees and unions of equitable consideration and at the same time assured the public that price and cost elements would likewise be controlled. This is not to be construed as a general endorsement of all the Wilsonian policies in conjunction with the seizures of World War I, but is intended as a historical recording of the additional dimension given by Wilson to presidential measures requiring the continuance of production.

It has not been generally appreciated to what extent the presidents' actions to compel production have been based upon the need to protect the government's own operations rather than to protect private industry. The latter has been, to some extent, an incidental benefit of the former. Until 1894 government operations appear to have been the sole reason for such intervention, whether in war or peace: the movement of federal troops and their supplies; the manufacture and delivery of military items; the government's responsibility for the mails; the operation of property in federal receivership.

Then in 1894, during the Pullman railroad strike, President Cleveland advanced the concept of federal responsibility for the protection of interstate commerce from interruption by labor disputes.[12] This view reflected the new national economic policy of federal regulation of commerce, expressed in the Interstate Commerce Act (1887), in the first Railway Labor Act (1888), and in the Sherman Antitrust Act (1890). Even so, Cleveland continued to emphasize the government's need to be able to move troops and the mails and (perhaps most important of all) to maintain official communications with the Pacific coast.

The new concept of federal protection of private commerce was repeated and expanded by President Wilson in December 1916 when he vainly sought authority from Congress to seize and operate the railroads if, in time of peace, they should be halted by a strike or lockout. In his fourth annual address to Congress on the state of the union, December 5, 1916, Wilson took the position that railroad labor conditions as a whole could

not be determined by "concerted action of organized bodies of men," but
in cases of such threatened action would have to be investigated and determined by public agencies. He said, in part:

> I would hesitate to recommend, and I dare say the Congress would hesitate
> to act upon the suggestion should I make it, that any man in any occupation
> should be obliged by law to continue in an employment which he desired to
> leave. . .
>
> But the proposal that the operation of the railways of the country shall not
> be stopped or interrupted by the concerted action of organized bodies of men
> until a public investigation shall have been instituted which shall make the
> whole question at issue plain for the judgment of the opinion of the nation is
> not to propose any such principle. It is based upon the very different principle
> that *the concerted action of powerful bodies of men shall not be permitted to
> stop the industrial processes of the nation,* at any rate before the nation shall
> have had an opportunity to acquaint itself with the merits of the case as
> between employee and employer, time to form its opinion upon an impartial
> statement of the merits, and opportunity to consider all practicable means of
> conciliation or arbitration. I can see nothing in that proposition but the justifi-
> able safeguarding *by society* of the necessary processes of its very life.[13] (Italics
> added.)

Here we find a president clearly stating that a transportation strike
which would halt "the industrial processes of the nation"—that would shut
factories as well as stop railroad or other transportation facilities—would
constitute an intolerable form of social disorder, an excessive use of
"concerted action" or market power.

So we find that presidential use of force to keep industrial production
going was introduced in wartime by Lincoln to protect the government's
military operations and in peacetime by Hayes to protect the government's
postal services, and then was extended successively by Cleveland and
Wilson to assure the continuity of interstate commerce. It is significant that
for each of these purposes, the immediate requirement was the maintenance
of some form of transportation.

Subsequent experience shows that transportation has been the industry
most frequently requiring presidential intervention to protect government
operations and/or the civilian economy. Little noticed next to transportation has been the manufacture of military and naval equipment and sup-
lies. The other basic industries, like fuel and power, have required coercive
action much less often. This may be seen from Table 1, in which the 94
cases of presidential action have been classified by industry.

To further clarify the concept of coercion, we should contrast it with the
voluntary renunciation of the right to strike and to lock out by representatives of labor and management in agreements with the president. Such

TABLE 1
CASES OF REQUIRED PRODUCTION BY INDUSTRY

Industry	Seizure cases[a]	Nonseizure cases[b]	Totals
Transportation			
Railroads (nationwide)	5	6	11
Railroads (individual companies)	8	1	9
Shipping and stevedoring	3	7	10
Trucking	2	0	2
Urban transit	3	0	3
Total	21	14	35
Military and naval equipment and supplies	32	6	38
Basic industrial services			
Coal	7	1	8
Petroleum	6	0	6
Electric power	2	0	2
Steel	1	1	2
Total	16	2	18
Miscellaneous	2	1	3
Grand total	71	23	94

[a] Appendix A.
[b] Appendix C.

agreements have been reached in particular disputes since the anthracite strike of 1902. They also were in force for broad categories of disputes in both world wars, in the atomic energy industry from 1949 to 1953, and at missile bases and atomic test sites since 1961. They are to be classed as voluntary public arbitration.

While there are some similarities between the voluntary and the compulsory arrangements, there is an important difference. The voluntary arrangement is a trade between the parties and the government—the parties continuing (or resuming) production in return for government settlement of their dispute. Although the parties yield up their normal market power vis-à-vis, they save face by doing this in the national interest at the president's request, and by obtaining neutral third-party determination of the issues. In contrast, the coercive arrangement involves no trade of this kind—the government withdrawing the right to strike and lock out in the particular instance without the parties' consent.

This difference needs to be further explored. Although in both cases the nature of collective bargaining is altered and government control of the affected labor relations is, in some degree and manner, established, the parties in the voluntary case have negotiated and agreed to the procedure of adjustment and the kind of pressures that will be substituted for the stoppage; while in the other case they have not. In required production, these details are left up to the president, Congress, and the courts.

In historical experience, the presidents have used coercion only as a last resort in three circumstances: when they have believed that they have lacked the power to settle a dispute by mediation or arbitration (chiefly prior to 1902); or when their plea for a voluntary agreement waiving the right to strike or lock out has been refused; or when one of the parties to a voluntary agreement has objected to the adjudicated settlement later (considering itself the loser) and has stopped production. While the national experience with the voluntary agreements has been carefully reported and evaluated by students of collective bargaining,[14] the experience with required production has not heretofore been gathered and examined as a distinct form of public control in particular disputes.

Mediating settlements. The attempt to induce settlements in particular labor disputes by direct presidential mediation dates only from 1902, during the so-called progressive era or era of reform. In keeping with the political temper of the times—with the awakening public interest in the social problems arising from industrialization—Theodore Roosevelt intervened in the long anthracite strike of 1902 in a manner that not only helped to bring the strike to an end but also to assure the miners of reasonable improvements in their working conditions.

In this first use of presidential mediation, the measures taken differed from ordinary mediation in ways that set new patterns for most later instances of action by the White House. There were three significant stages. In the first, President Roosevelt directed his commissioner of labor, Carroll D. Wright, to investigate the dispute. Wright did so, and, in his published report, recommended a reduction in hours from 10 to 9 per day, and the establishment of a joint grievance procedure.[15] Here was fact-finding with recommendations, an action in which a presidential appointee took a public position on the merits of the controversy, committing the government, in effect, to a position based on industrial equity, not neutrality. However, Roosevelt and the union soon discovered what so many subsequent presidents have also learned, that such recommendations are almost certain to be rejected by the loser unless both parties have agreed in advance to accept them, or the president enforces the recommendations with coercive means. In this case, the mine owners said "no."

As a next step, or second stage, President Roosevelt broke precedent by recognizing the union—the United Mine Workers of America, led by John Mitchell—which the mine operators and their banking allies refused to do. In the absence of any legislation recognizing collective bargaining in the coal industry, the union gained in prestige when the president invited representatives of both parties to the White House for a conference, and both came. But that was the sum of the union gains at the conference. Roosevelt, having been warned by Attorney General Knox that he lacked power to do anything about the strike (then four and a half months old), contented himself with terming the continuance of the stoppage "intolerable" and urging the parties to resume work "on some basis." But the parties were as far apart as ever, except that, oddly enough, each urged the president to intervene in a different way. The union wanted him to appoint a board of arbitration. The companies wanted him to send federal troops into Pennsylvania, arrest the union leaders, and prosecute them under the antitrust laws.[16]

Thus the conference failed, despite the prestige of the presidency, as so many later labor-management conferences have failed under the same eminent auspices. Yet it did not entirely fail, for it introduced an important new element into national policy toward emergency disputes. Basically, Roosevelt appears to have supported the Cleveland doctrine of 1894 that strikes might become, in some instances, "intolerable" to public welfare, but he was not willing to use the antitrust laws as Cleveland did. Moreover, to this doctrine Roosevelt added what amounted to a corollary that when the government objects to the continuance of a stoppage, it should assist the parties to settle their dispute, while voicing, in behalf of the public, concern over the hardships of industrial workers and sympathy for collective bargaining. This corollary or new element was immediately endorsed by former President Cleveland himself, who wrote confidentially to Roosevelt, offering to serve on an arbitration panel.

The weakness of the conference, therefore, appears to have been, not in the new policy standards of the president, but in the lack of any means of coercion with which to force an end to the deadlock between the two giant market forces—the wealthy coal barons and the new nationwide union of the miners. Roosevelt proceeded to remedy this defect with a third stage of novel moves.

The president now kept most of his actions behind the scenes. He prepared to use coercive measures, if necessary, but devised a plan that would enable him not merely to obtain a resumption of mining but also to enforce equitable terms of labor that would be recommended by a board of arbitration which he would appoint. The plan, as is now well known, was to have the army seize the anthracite mines in northeastern Pennsylvania, dispossess the owners, and run the mines as "a receiver" under orders that would come exclusively from the president. The award of the board of arbitration would be effectuated.[17]

With this as a trump card, to be held in reserve, Roosevelt proceeded to induce the parties in private negotiations to accept in advance, as final and binding, the terms of a presidential arbitration board. The use of force never became necessary, but its availability gave firmness to the president's tone and, in the view of some historians, was known to the major mine operators and their financial advisers. In the negotiations, Secretary of War Root first secured the support of J. P. Morgan and then, through Morgan, the consent of the major coal operators, including George F. Baer, president of the Philadelphia & Reading Railroad, then one of the largest owners of anthracite or hard coal mines. The concurrence of the union president, Mitchell, was more readily obtained, as he himself had proposed arbitration.[18]

The third and final stage of this first instance of presidential mediation was a smashing success. In the arbitration award, the miners received the reduction to a nine-hour day and the creation of a permanent board of conciliation, which Commissioner of Labor Wright had recommended to the president, together with some lesser gains. The event is now recorded in every history of American labor and, more than that, in nearly every general American history. But the keys to its success need to be carefully noted: namely, that here was a new kind of mediation that no one except the president could possibly conduct; that this new mediation was neither neutral nor passive but involved the government in a commitment to influence the terms of settlement in a manner equitable to the workers and favorable to collective bargaining; and that if the public interest required a withdrawal of the right to strike and to lock out in the particular case, then the government would substitute other pressures for those of the market to assure an early settlement on terms consistent with the government's commitment.

Although the use of force was not necessary, it is evident that political and personal pressures were brought to bear upon the disputing parties by the president, and it is probable that the preparations for force were intimated in the discussions with management. In the subsequent cases of presidential mediation, those presidents who have taken a stand on the merits of a particular dispute have found it equally necessary to apply political and administrative pressures to win the acquiescence of the losing party. Studies of these cases by various scholars have shown that the mere issuance of public recommendations by presidential appointees, or even by the president himself, has been insufficient, in most peacetime cases and even in some cases during war, to induce their acceptance by economically powerful groups, either in labor or in management.[19] The appeal of patriotism, the prestige of the White House itself, and the much-touted "weight of public opinion" have generally been inadequate pressures. Hence, in practice, some of the presidents have developed a variety of more effective pressures and inducements, employing the federal government's vast powers of procurement, of taxation, and of subsidy, in support of their mediation efforts—a development in public administration which is only now beginning to receive the attention of scholarly investigators.[20] Often the presidents have had to go further and threaten coercive measures to terminate (or avert) the stoppage and, incidentally, to support the government's terms. These threats have been either to request special legislation from Congress or to seize and operate the firms under existing legislative authority (or even without such authority). Often these threats have induced acceptance of the president's terms and immediate settlement of the dispute. When the threats have not been effective, however, the presidents have been obliged either to carry out their threats, stepping over the brink from voluntarism to compulsion and converting the case into one of required production, or else to abandon their positions on the merits of the controversies.

It is clear, therefore, that presidential mediation differs from the traditional forms of mediation in two important respects: the parties are subjected to official, governmental pressures and inducements to reach an early agreement, preferably without exercising their perfectly lawful right to strike or to lock out; and the president, in many cases, perhaps in most, indicates some concern over the actual content of the settlement agreed to, either by announcing certain guidelines or by appointing an investigating panel with power to recommend terms of settlement.

The second of these differences has become more crucial as the presidents have added to their public commitments about collective bargaining and the plight of industrial workers a further commitment to the public's need for protection against inflationary union-company agreements. The first cases of this kind appear to have been the railroad shopmen's and bituminous coal disputes of 1919, in which President Wilson urged the parties to agree on terms which would not add to the cost of living. The president's public plea was accepted by the railroad shopmen but was ineffective in the soft coal mines until he had supplemented it with two coercive measures—a revival of wartime price controls, and an antistrike injunction.[21]

This and other experiences show why mediation by the president or his personal representative can seldom be neutral as in ordinary mediation, nor can it generally be consistent with a completely free operation of the private market. First, when a labor dispute reaches the White House, it is usually a case which involves the public interest in one or more ways— possibly in the terms of settlement, probably also in the continuity of production. Second, the president as the head of government and the elected representative of all the people, must act in behalf of the govern-

ment and of the whole people, not necessarily in behalf of the stronger of
the disputing parties. Third, if the parties voluntarily waive their right to
halt production by the strike or lockout, at the president's request, then
they are entitled to an equitable (that is, a government-controlled) substitute procedure for resolving their differences in lieu of the decisions of the
market. Hence the president is virtually required in almost any mediation
to investigate the merits of the dispute, to take a position on some aspects
of it, and to apply some pressures in support of his position.

The historical experience with presidential mediation suggests that its
difference from required production is becoming less. Mediation by the
White House involves varying degrees of pressure up to the point of
compulsory operation. Its great value lies in this flexibility, in the varying
degrees of public control required, in the government's frequent ability to
obtain settlements of emergency disputes without having to require production.

At the same time, in the cases of required production, the procedures
have been becoming more like those under presidential mediation. In the
First World War, Wilson accompanied each instance of forceful operations
by the imposition of terms of employment reflecting the government's
viewpoint of industrial equity. This was a natural development from
Theodore Roosevelt's policy standards of 1902, a big advance over the
biased, pro-management results of the Reading Railroad seizure in 1864
and of the criminal trials on the Boston & Maine in February 1877. This
was public control moderated by standards of policy. The final development in this sequence came in 1941 when Franklin Roosevelt required
that, in cases of required production, the government would continue its
efforts to mediate agreements satisfactory to the parties, provided these
agreements were consistent with the public interest.

So we find two converging trends in presidential intervention in critical
labor disputes: mild but increasing pressures against labor and management
to reach agreements without halting production; and in cases of required
production, continuing mediation in an effort to obtain agreements satisfactory to both parties and consistent with national economic policies.

This volume represents a tentative effort to study as a separate phenom-
enon of industrial relations those disputes in which the presidents have
intervened with coercive measures to keep production going over the protest
of one or both parties. We shall examine not only the 71 cases using seizure
but the 23 cases using other means of control. The emphasis will be upon
the seizure cases, but all will be examined from the same standpoints: How
extensive was presidential control over the labor relations and other economic activities of the disputing parties in each case? What standards of

labor policy and of public administration were observed during the period of control?

This will amount to selecting the most intractable disputes in which the presidents have intervened during the past century of industrial growth. Other disputes which the presidents were able to settle with mere threats of coercive action or with still milder pressures of one kind or another deserve similar analysis as to the nature and degree of pressures applied, the extent and form of presidential influence upon the terms of employment finally agreed to; but these are the less extreme cases. The ones to be studied here reveal the outer limits of presidential power in the history of industrial disputes.

MEANS OF COMPULSION USED

Let us begin by identifying the specific means of coercion, or forms of public control. Although the presidents in many cases have employed two, three, or more forms of coercion simultaneously or successively, it seems desirable here to sort out the primary form of control used in each case, to determine the frequency with which each was used, and then to name the legal basis relied on in these controls. This will complete the historical setting for an analysis of the experience with each type of compulsion.

The primary forms of control used have been: seizure—71 cases; troops or civilians supplied as temporary replacements for strikers—nine cases; prosecution of union leaders for contempt of federal courts which had issued antistrike injunctions—four cases; qualified martial law—four cases; criminal prosecution for violation of federal statutes, other than statutes relating to physical violence—three cases; cancelation by the War Department of a procurement contract—one case; enactment of a special statute writing the terms of settlement into permanent legislation—one case; and enactment of a special statute creating an *ad hoc* board of arbitration whose award would be compulsory—one case. (The specific instances are identified in Appendixes A and C.)

It will be noticed that the list indicates a tendency to experimentation, except for the heavy reliance upon seizure. However, there is a historical bunching of the seizure cases among four presidents out of the nine, that is, among our war presidents. Seizure has clearly been the mainstay in war, but there has been no corresponding tendency in the data toward any one means of coercion in peace. The distribution of the 15 peacetime cases has been: seizure—five; injunctions enforced by contempt proceedings—three; criminal prosecution—three; special legislation—two; temporary replacements—two.

The experimentation has been both legislative and administrative. In some instances the presidents have adapted a law not expressly intended for use in emergency labor disputes. These are the cases which some critics of the presidency have labeled "usurpations" of presidential power. The remaining cases, by our definition, are those that were effected under specific delegations of power by Congress for this purpose. The number of cases under improvised or adapted authority has been 32, the number under express legislation 62.

Delegated powers. Let us look first at the authority relied on in the 62 cases in which the presidents acted under legislation expressly authorizing coercion in emergency disputes. This relates to 60 seizures and two non-seizures. The record suggests a strong preference in Congress, in the past, toward the use of seizure. The two nonseizure cases were governed by the Adamson Act of 1916, which legislated the eight-hour day for train operating crews (39 Stat. 721), and the Railroad Arbitration Act of 1963, which settled the work-rule dispute (Public Law 88–108). The authority for the 60 seizures lay in four statutes: The Transportation Seizure Act of 1916 (39 Stat. 619, at 645)—18 cases; the Joint Resolution of July 16, 1918 (40 Stat. 904)—one case (the telegraphs and telephones); the War Labor Disputes Act of 1943 (57 Stat. 163)—41 cases; and the Emergency Powers Interim Continuation Act of 1952 (66 Stat. 54, 96, 137, 296)—two cases (extensions of the rail seizures of 1950–1952).

It is one of the paradoxes in the history of presidential intervention that these cases of delegated powers evoked more litigation to test the constitutionality of the presidents' actions than the improvised cases. Each of the six statutes named above, except the last, was tested in the courts. The presidents' actions were upheld in every instance.[22] Nevertheless, many of the emergency measures were delayed for several months by the court proceedings.

Several theories have been relied on by Congress and the Supreme Court in authorizing and upholding the use of seizure in labor disputes:

(1) *Requisitioning of military supplies:* the National Defense Act of 1916, and the Selective Service Acts of 1940 and 1948, including amendments to the 1940 act embodied in the War Labor Disputes Act of 1943. According to Professor Clinton Rossiter, "An interesting if little-known precedent for emergency delegation [of power] was the action of the Continental Congress in granting temporary powers of requisition, recruitment, expenditure, and summary arrest to General Washington."[23] (See Appendix A of this study for the specific authority relied on in each seizure and Appendix B for further information on particular statutes.)

(2) *Receivership:* Of the railroad seizure of 1917–1920, Justice Brandeis wrote, in behalf of the court: "The situation was analogous to that

which would exist if there were a general receivership of each transportation system." He likened the director general of railroads to a "receiver."[24]

(3) *Power of eminent domain:* In another suit, Justice Brandeis wrote of the same 1917–1920 rail seizure: "The government was operating the railroad not as a lessee but under a right in the nature of eminent domain."[25]

(4) *Regulation of interstate commerce:* the Food and Fuel Act of 1917. Professor Archibald Cox has written, "If one looks to the reality rather than the words, the requisite constitutional authority [for seizure] resides in the commerce clause."[26]

Improvised measures. Now let us turn to the 32 emergency disputes in which improvised procedures were adopted. This refers to 11 seizure cases and to 21 nonseizure cases. The basis for each seizure has been carefully designated by the presidents, but the authority for some of the nonseizures unfortunately remains obscure to the lay observer.

Here is a layman's view of the authority relied on in the nonseizure cases. The government's contractual powers in military procurement were used to cancel one contract (Scotch Woolen Mills, Chicago, 1918), and to furnish temporary replacements to other contractors in nine disputes, with their permission. Military commanders used their authority to proclaim qualified martial law in theaters of war in three cases, and a similar authority relating to civil disorders in one other (Gary, Indiana, 1919). The contempt cases were based on antistrike injunctions obtained by the Department of Justice under a variety of pretexts: federal receiverships of railroads (July 1877); the Sherman Antitrust Act of 1890 (railroad disputes of 1894 and 1922); the Transportation Act of 1920 (rail dispute of 1922); and the Food and Fuel Act of 1917 (soft coal dispute of 1919). Criminal prosecutions were conducted for conspiracy to obstruct the mails (Boston & Maine in 1877, and the rail dispute of 1920), and for violation of the mutiny statute of 1790 together with the Merchant Marine Act of 1936 (S.S. *Algic*).

This variety of legal approaches emphasizes the lack of a statute for coping with emergency strike situations, and the reluctance of either the presidents or Congress to adopt one, since it would inevitably involve some restriction upon the right to strike.

The convenience of seizure in such cases has led the presidents in 11 situations to seize property even without the authority of laws expressly intended for use in emergency labor disputes. They have relied on other available legislation or general executive and military powers:

1864. Philadelphia & Reading Railroad. Railroad and Telegraph Control Act, approved January 31, 1862 (12 Stat. 334). This act authorized the president to take possession of any railroad or telegraph lines "when in his judgment the public safety may require it." The lines were then to be operated as a post road and as part of the military establishment of the United States. President Lincoln redelegated authority to make seizures to Secretary of War Stanton and to the general manager of military railroads, Brigadier General Daniel C. McCallum. In this case the company formally requested seizure.

1918.   Smith & Wesson (pistols). Sec. 120 of the National Defense Act, approved June 3, 1916 (39 Stat. 166, 213). This act authorized the president to place compulsory orders for military supplies and to take possession of any company refusing to fill the orders. In this case, Secretary of War Baker attached to the compulsory order a requirement for compliance with recommendations of the National War Labor Board, and the company refused to fill the order.

1941.   North American Aviation; Federal Shipbuilding & Dry Dock Co.; and Air Associates. "Pursuant to powers vested in me by the Constitution and laws of the United States, as President of the United States of America and Commander in Chief of the Army and Navy of the United States." (Ex. Order 8773.) Federal Shipbuilding had formally offered its property to the Navy Department for seizure and government operation.

1941.   Three freighters of Alcoa Steamship Co. Sec. 902 of Merchant Marine Act, approved June 29, 1936 (49 Stat. 1985, 2015). This section authorized the Maritime Commission to requisition any vessel documented under the laws of the United States during any national emergency declared by proclamation of the president. The president had declared an emergency because of the war in Europe.

1942.   General Cable Corp.; and S. A. Woods Machine Co. "By virtue of the power and authority vested in me by the Constitution and laws of the United States, as President of the United States and Commander in Chief of the Army and Navy of the United States." (Ex. Order 9225.) The War Department strengthened its position by condemning the Woods properties under the Second War Powers Act (56 Stat. 176).

1942.   Fairport, Painesville & Eastern Railroad. Because President Roosevelt was "unavailable" on short notice, Secretary of War Stimson had to act without an express executive order in order to prevent the destruction of equipment in important continuous-process chemical plants on the line of the struck railroad. Stimson relied on Ex. Order 8972 of December 12, 1941, which authorized him to establish military guards and patrols and to take other appropriate measures to protect from injury or destruction national defense materials, premises and utilities. If the president had been available, an executive order could have been issued under the wartime Transportation Seizure Act.[27]

1943 (May).   Coal mines. "By virtue of the authority vested in me by the Constitution and laws of the United States, as President of the United States and Commander in Chief of the Army and Navy." (Ex. Order 9340.) Congress showed its overwhelming approval of this seizure by enacting, during government possession, the wartime seizure bill that President Roosevelt had been requesting for nearly two years (part of the War Labor Disputes Act—the Connally part of the so-called Smith-Connally Act). The seizure resulted in a suit by the Pewee Coal Co. to recover under the Fifth Amendment for the total operating losses sustained during government possession. The Court of Claims awarded $2241; and the Supreme Court, in 1951, sustained the judgment—a result which, in the view of Professor Edward S. Corwin, "implied the validity of the seizure."[28]

1952. Basic steel industry. "By virtue of the authority vested in me by the Constitution and laws of the United States, and as President of the United States and Commander in Chief of the armed forces of the United States." (Ex. Order 10340.) Congress expressed its disapproval of this seizure in several "nuisance" riders attached to routine legislation, and in a resolution urging the president to use the 80-day injunction procedure of the Taft-Hartley Act. When the steel companies challenged the constitutionality of the seizure, the Supreme Court upheld them and declared the seizure unlawful on the grounds that Congress had not expressly authorized such action and had instead provided an alternative means for handling emergency disputes (the 80-day injunctions).[29]

So when it came to improvising procedures for bringing stoppages forcefully to an end, without special statutory authority, the presidents used seizure in 11 cases, and a variety of other administrative, military, and court procedures in 21 cases. In all these circumstances, the presidents acted on their own best judgment, without consulting Congress or public opinion; but their actions have been subjected to public discussion afterward and to appeal, in some cases, to the courts or to Congress. Of the nonseizure methods, none was ever vetoed by the other branches of government.[30] Of the 11 seizures, only one was questioned in the courts, but this one was resoundingly overturned by the highest tribunal. This was the steel mill seizure of 1952. President Truman promptly returned the mills to their private owners, and a 53-day strike ensued. In the end, the long dispute was settled only by renewed presidential mediation, accompanied by governmental pressures and inducements falling just short of compulsion.

SUMMARY

The presidents in the twentieth century have evolved a vague but fairly consistent national policy of confining their intervention in bargaining disputes (that is, in labor-market impasses) to exceptional cases, chosen by them under the restraint of a possible legislative or judicial veto, and then of applying a rising scale of minimal pressures and inducements in support of the public interest, normally stopping short of the brink of compulsion.

The cases in which production has been required differ from those of ordinary mediation and the suppression of violence in that the government has tacitly or explicitly withdrawn the right to strike and to lock out, requiring the settlement to be reached without these market pressures. The compulsory cases somewhat resemble voluntary public arbitration, in which the parties waive the right to strike and lock out, but are different in that the government unilaterally determines and imposes the mode of settlement and the forms of pressure to be substituted for the market forces. Such action, although taken only as a last resort, constitutes a distinct category of public control. Its continued availability and occasional use have established it as a backstop or ultimate sanction for the lesser degrees of presidential intervention. In this extreme category of presidential intervention, seizure has been the most frequently used and most systematically developed form of public control.

CHAPTER 2

The Resistance of Labor and Management to Seizure Control

There has been a widespread belief that the seizure of property by the president in the face of a strike or lockout, and the raising of the American flag above it, has been sufficient to induce the disputing parties to terminate the strike or lockout at once (if started); to induce them to call off any strike order or embargo that may have been issued for future dates; and to induce them to accept (although reluctantly) the terms of employment recommended by the president's disputes-settlement agencies.[1]

This has not been the usual case. The willingness of those who have created labor-dispute emergencies to pursue their economic goals to the bitter end, to turn their economic weapons against the president in an effort to obtain his aid against their opponents, and to interfere deliberately with presidential measures to maintain uninterrupted production under terms consistent with the nation's emergency policies, has been a characteristic of the majority of federal seizure operations.

In 46 of the 71 seizures (or approximately 65 per cent), some or all of either labor or management rejected the president's authority for at least part of the time, bringing coercive pressure against him as well as against the other disputing party.[2]

Resistance has usually arisen at the beginning of seizure operations, but it has also arisen later during the period of government possession, and it has even occurred shortly before the expected return of the property to private hands. In 38 of the 71 seizure cases (or approximately 53 per cent), some portion of either labor or management (or both) refused to accept the president's interim authority at the outset and tried to obstruct his operational control of the business.[3] In seven of the same seizures, additional instances of resistance occurred later during government possession; and in eight other seizures, resistance with respect to the main dispute arose during the course of government operations after all parties had agreed initially to cooperate.

Resistance has been offered by all the employees of a seized plant or industry in solidarity, or by only a portion of them, for the dispute may have involved rival unions, rival factions within a union, or anti-union hostility. Resistance has also been offered by the top executives of a seized company in unanimity, but occasionally it has come from a divided management or divided board of directors. Frequently subordinate officials have been most cooperative. In the industrywide seizures, resistance of company executives sometimes has been confined to a few of the seized companies.

Another important variable in situations of resistance is that while most of the instances of resistance have been related to the main dispute which brought about the seizure, a number of others have been due to unrelated controversies that arose coincidentally during government possession, especially in the multifirm seizures. These incidental disputes were mostly strikes or threatened strikes by other unions or by the same unions over issues other than those in the original dispute. A few were due to the objections of management to orders to change production methods: for example, the compulsory pooling of services with a competitor. These coincidental disputes were often confined to a single firm in a multifirm seizure.[4]

The use of seizure by the government has forced the disputing parties to develop rather ingenious forms of pressure against each other and against the government, although fundamentally they adhere to the familiar classifications of economic, judicial, and political pressures. The economic pressures are perhaps the most significant because they constitute a modification of the normal processes of collective bargaining and require changes in the government's usual procedures for regulating collective bargaining; but the judicial and political resistance also merit attention because they have required a remolding of the judicial procedures and legislative enactments to fit specific bargaining situations.

In this chapter, we will divide the economic resistance into two classes: stoppages of production, and insubordination against presidential orders. These two forms of resistance are aimed deliberately at two of the interim objectives of seizure—the maintenance of uninterrupted production, and the support of the government's program for peaceful determination of the terms of employment through interim observance of such terms. Thus, we have a total of four classes of obstruction to examine—two economic, one judicial, and one political.

A comparison of the relative usage of the four classes of obstruction shows that the most frequently used has been the stoppage of production, occurring in 31 of the 46 seizure cases which involved resistance; that the next most frequent class of obstruction has been insubordination to the president's orders—21 seizure cases; that the third has been political agitation against some aspect of the seizure—18 cases; and that the least frequent has been resort to court proceedings—15 cases. Of course, there

TABLE 2
FORMS OF RESISTANCE TO PRESIDENTIAL AUTHORITY IN 46 SEIZURES

Category[a]	Seizures involving resistance		Proportion of all 71 seizure cases
Stoppages of production	31	67%	44%
Other insubordination	21	45	30
Appeals to Congress	18	39	25
Court proceedings	15	33	21

[a] More than one form of resistance occurred in some of the 46 seizures.

is some overlapping of these classes of obstruction in the same seizures. Comparative data is shown in Table 2.

STOPPAGES OF PRODUCTION

The most obvious form of resistance to the government during seizure is the stoppage of production. This form of obstruction thwarts the principal objective of seizure—the uninterrupted production of essential goods or services during a period of national emergency. This weapon has been employed principally by the employees and unions but has been used also in a few seizures by the company management.

The record shows that employees and unions have refused to call off strikes and resume production at the time of seizure in 20 cases;[5] have refused at the time of seizure to cancel plans already announced for later strikes in four cases,[6] and have commenced new strikes during government possession in 14 seizures.[7] There have been 51 instances of such new strikes, most of them concentrated in a few lengthy industrywide seizures.

Some of the strikes were major, industrywide shutdowns, and others involved only single plants. Five of the score that went on in the face of seizure were virtually industrywide—four in coal and one in meat-packing; three of the strike plans which were not rescinded were industrywide—one in coal and two in railroads; six of the 51 new strikes started during government possession were industrywide affairs—four in coal, one in steel, and one in the telegraphs. Others, of course, were very small, being confined either to one of many seized plants or to one of numerous departments in a single plant. Nevertheless, even these were usually tests of strength with the government which might have spread to the entire seizure operation if not quickly overcome by the seizing agency.

The above figures add up to a total of 75 strikes (large and small) that actually are known to have occurred during government possession in 31 of the 71 seizure cases. The term strikes as used here includes sit-downs but not slowdowns.

The corresponding record by company managements shows a total of nine attempted lockouts (of which five are known to have been effective for a time) in eight out of 71 seizure cases.[8]

STRIKES AND SIT-DOWNS

Turning now in more detail to the employees and labor unions, we find that they have preferred the strike weapon as a means of bargaining pressure against the president and seizure officials because it is their only weapon of any real significance. The employees, generally speaking, are not in a position to observe or to refuse to observe the president's managerial directives—these are normally matters for the company management and ownership to accept or reject.

The new problems confronting the employees and unions in striking in seized businesses as compared with striking against private management have been: how to establish the legality of such strikes; and how to make them effective against the formidable array of economic, military, judicial, and legislative sanctions available to the president. These problems have been given careful thought and considerable experimentation by the top officers of several national unions, particularly the United Mine Workers of America and the railroad brotherhoods, during the course of various seizures, especially those that were industrywide. By contrast, the so-called "wildcat" strikes and other local stoppages, which attracted much notoriety during World War II, have been conducted virtually like strikes against private management and have been almost always unsuccessful in forcing concessions from the government.

The greatest weaknesses of the local strikes in seizure cases have been the lack of financial resources, the lack of skilled leadership, the active opposition of the national leaders of their own unions, and the relative ease with which so small a number of strikers can be replaced temporarily by the government. This last factor has been especially marked in those industries in which the armed forces have large numbers of trained personnel normally engaged in the same type of work and readily available for temporary replacements. We might mention transportation (by rail, bus, truck, ship or aircraft), communication (by wire or wireless), and power (from combustion, falling water, or atomic fission). The use of technically trained troops has broken very stubborn local stoppages in seized businesses.

In an effort to cope with the unusual problems of seizure cases, the striking unions have developed the following major techniques: extending the strikes to the unseized firms of the same region or industry, or to the unseized plants of the same company; confining the strikes to only a small portion of the seized industry or firm; refusing to call off strikes ordered before seizure but avoiding any overt acts in their support during government possession; calling new strikes during government possession but disguising them as "spontaneous" cessations of work by individual employees; postponing the strikes to other specific dates.

Extending the area of stoppage. This has two advantages. It increases the total bargaining pressure of the union against the government and against the opposing party (usually management), and it hits a point where the government is not in control. The second of these advantages can be countered by the president, but not the first. The president can take possession of the additional struck firms, thus extending whatever powers he may be exercising to the entire field of the union's jurisdiction. But this step adds to the costs and burdens of seizure and does not reduce the size of the union's total pressure unless the entire strike be overcome.

This method has been employed or threatened in eleven seizures,[9] but has seldom succeeded in forcing any concessions from the government, and would appear to have no advantages over striking the entire region or industry at once if the dispute is industrywide or can be made so. The two disputes in which the unions forced concessions from the government by vastly extending the scope of the stoppages were both local matters initially. Hence this may indicate that this weapon is most effective when the union's demands are localized. The first instance was the complaint of telephone workers in the wire systems seizure of 1918–1919 against Postmaster General Burleson's order to discharge phone girls who engaged in "wildcat" strikes lasting more than 24 hours. When the Brotherhood of Electrical Workers (AFL) took a nationwide strike poll, and set a strike date, Mr. Burleson quickly backed down and rescinded his order. The second instance was a jurisdictional dispute between two rival unions in the Electric Auto-Lite plant in Toledo. When the striking union, the Mechanics' Educational Society of America, called out all its mechanics in Toledo and Detroit and threatened also to strike those in Cleveland, the War Department brought the two rival unions together and insisted upon a compromise settlement.

Contracting the area of stoppages. The second union technique devised in seizure cases—confining the strikes to only a small portion of the seized firm or industry—may be considered the reverse of the first method. Its object is to make the stoppage so insignificant economically that the government will be unable to justify the use of emergency measures to forbid it, and yet to choose a group of strikers so strategically placed that they will bring strong pressures against the president and the private companies.

The most interesting examples of this occurred during the Korean emergency of 1950–1953. When hostilities broke out, the Switchmen's Union of North America (AFL) called off its strike against four out of five railroads and continued it against only one—the Rock Island. Nevertheless, President Truman seized the one struck railroad, and obtained an injunction against the strike which the courts upheld.

Two years later, during a long dispute between the railroad brotherhoods and Truman which had resulted in a prolonged seizure of all the major railroads, three of the brotherhoods suddenly started a small walkout against the strategically placed St. Louis Terminal Railroad and the New York Central Lines West. The Army Department quickly suppressed this walkout by obtaining another injunction.

Perhaps the most important aspect of these two episodes is what happened afterward in each case in the federal courts. The unions in each case protested that the injunctions denied them constitutional rights, since the interference to transportation from these stoppages was relatively minor. The federal judges found in both cases, however, that the president was acting under a federal law—the transportation seizure statute of August 29, 1916—which gave him full discretion.[10]

This technique—the small strike—involves a difficult dilemma. It attempts to devise a strike small enough to be lawful, even against the government, and yet so strategically placed as to be a powerful economic weapon in collective bargaining. So far the government has succeeded in satisfying the courts that the strategic effectiveness of the strike justified its suppression. A further difficulty is the question of the propriety of any strike during government operation.

Refusing to cancel preseizure strike orders. This technique was developed expressly to thwart a section of the War Labor Disputes Act of 1943 (the Smith-Connally Act) making a strike in a seized mine, plant, or other facility a crime. The act had been passed by Congress during an industry-wide shutdown of the coal mines with the avowed purpose of preventing further stoppages of this sort during the rest of the war; but the adroit John L. Lewis soon found a way around this new restriction with the apparent acquiescence of President Roosevelt and Attorney General Biddle, and later also of President Truman and Attorney General Clark.

The method thus developed by Mr. Lewis, and adopted by several other union leaders, was simply to order a strike prior to presidential seizure—when the order obviously was lawful—and then, after seizure, to avoid overt action of any kind in support or encouragement of the strike. The miners merely remained out, or went out at the time set, in response to the prior directive, and awaited word from the union leader that their dispute had been satisfactorily settled. No picketing was needed or conducted. No strike speeches were offered or required. The strike had been officially ordered before the government took possession. It remained as a form of pressure against the government and against the private management, either as an actual stoppage or as an imminent strike date.

This device was extremely effective in the hands of John L. Lewis in three industrywide coal seizures—those of November 1943, April 1945, and May 1946—in each of which Lewis not only avoided prosecution during the continuance of the prearranged strikes but negotiated outstanding wage gains with the government under the pressures of the stoppages. Under these pressures, the government either made extensive concessions to the miners in the interim terms of employment—to be effective during government operations—or gave assistance in the negotiation of a final settlement with the owners. In either circumstance, the mine owners were required to make the approved concessions in order to get their mines back.

It is curious that no other labor leader was able to use this device effectively, although many tried.[11] The others who tried it also succeeded in avoiding criminal prosecution under the WLDA, but not in gaining their economic ends. Perhaps this was due in most cases to the small size of the unions involved. But when the leaders of two powerful railroad brotherhoods, A. F. Whitney and Alvanley Johnston, also tried it, they, too, failed; and in failing they provoked President Truman to develop new statutory and judicial means of thwarting this device.

The loophole in the War Labor Disputes Act, which protected union officers from criminal prosecution in these cases, was a proviso which read: "No individual shall be deemed to have violated the provisions of this section by reason only of his having ceased work or having refused to continue to work or to accept employment." This proviso was interpreted by the Department of Justice as protecting the strikers and union officers during government possession and operation of war plants so long as they did not engage in speeches, meetings, or other overt actions intended to encourage the strike.[12] Hence Attorney General Francis Biddle prosecuted only persons who openly advocated the strike, and the department's interpretation was never tested in a court case.

This view, which almost nullified the criminal sanctions provided by Congress in seizure cases, weakened the authority of the National War Labor Board and forced President Roosevelt and his seizing agencies to turn to indirect economic and military sanctions as a means of enforcing NWLB decisions.[13] In the end, it drove President Truman to revive the hated antistrike injunction, which had been outlawed since 1932.

It should be noted that several leaders of "wildcat" strikes, who ignored the congressional ban on overt acts and conducted their strikes with speeches and picketing just as they would have against private management, were arrested and punished under the War Labor Disputes Act. This included officers of several locals of the United Mine Workers and the leaders of a rank-and-file strike committee in the Philadelphia streetcar operation. In some other cases, the seizing agencies referred overt acts to the Department of Justice for possible prosecution, but the department decided that no prosecution was warranted.

It was probably inevitable that, sooner or later, some union, in exercising this special technique for striking in seized businesses without incurring criminal prosecution, would arouse the country and even the White House against it and bring this loophole in the War Labor Disputes Act into public notice and disfavor. This finally occurred in May 1946, when Mr. Whitney, of the Brotherhood of Railroad Trainmen, and Mr. Johnston, of the Brotherhood of Locomotive Engineers, shut down virtually the entire national railroad system during government possession, relying on this technicality to save them from arrest and from public wrath.

It did save them from arrest, but only because they backpedaled quickly and called off the strike in the nick of time. It did not, however, save them from the public wrath nor from the presidential wrath, which proposed new devices for dealing with such stoppages and for plugging the leak in the seizure law. Their hasty retreat saved them from personal penalties, but it did not save their successors and the leaders of other unions from the effect of the new devices when adopted in later seizures.

In accordance with the policy of the Department of Justice, President Truman at first assured the two brotherhood leaders that the prearranged strike would be legal. His turnabout a week later, after the strike began, shows that in great crises the president may be compelled by public opinion to take a stand for the national good against even the most powerful special interests.

Initially the president had personally overruled his seizing agency (the ODT) to assure the unions over the telephone that the act of postponing their scheduled strike for five days would not be an overt act prosecutable under the WLDA and that the strike itself would be legal on the later date if no settlement had been reached. The unions were at first incredulous and termed this "a long way to go." Still wondering, they immediately "leaked" the fact to the press that the president had assured them of the strike's legality despite the WLDA. When the president later reversed himself and took action to suppress the strike, the union chiefs then released to the press the full record of the telephone conversations. These not only revealed the brotherhoods' plan to avoid prosecution by taking no overt actions after seizure but showed that this had been the practice of John L. Lewis and the mine workers in the major coal seizures.[14]

Meanwhile, however, the extraordinary national stoppage of railway service had induced the president to submit a bill to Congress designed, among other things, to remove the loophole under which strike leaders could escape by taking no overt steps in support of a strike during government possession. Although President Truman did not prosecute Messrs. Whitney and Johnston for violating the WLDA, he urged Congress to amend the act so that unions and union officers could be prosecuted if they did not take affirmative steps to end strikes in seized businesses. Under this amendment, inaction by union officers in strikes, far from assuring them of immunity, would have become a crime. They could have been prosecuted for not taking overt steps to halt the strike. Although Congress did not complete action on the amendment, both houses separately approved the proposal, and it remains for future consideration in seizure legislation.

By far the most serious effect of this nationwide railroad shutdown was the fact that President Truman was led to introduce the concept of the antistrike injunction into seizure cases as one of the weapons in his proposed arsenal of additional sanctions. He asked Congress to amend the WLDA to permit him to send his attorney general into the federal courts for injunctions forbidding strikes in seized plants or industries. This was the first suggestion by a U.S. president that the antistrike injunction, which Congress had virtually eliminated in private labor disputes in 1932, should be used in disputes between unions and the government over stoppages in seized businesses. Little notice has been paid in the literature of injunctions to the fact that both houses of Congress separately approved this remarkable suggestion. Since the crisis soon vanished, with the ending of the strike, and the two houses differed on other details of the proposed law, the plan was never formally approved. The importance of this episode is seen, however, in the fact that a few months later President Truman obtained an antistrike injunction in another seizure case (bituminous coal) without the express authority of Congress, and the Supreme Court sustained him.

The Truman proposal for antistrike injunctions in the rail crisis called not only for amendment of the War Labor Disputes Act of 1943 (57 Stat. 163) but also for amendment of the Norris-LaGuardia Act of 1932 (47 Stat. 70) which limits the use of injunctions in labor disputes. It is evident that Congress was quite willing, at that time, to modify the Norris-LaGuardia Act to permit injunctions to be obtained by the president in seizure cases. The case in which the Supreme Court ruled (by a vote of 5 to 4) that injunctions actually were not barred in seized properties by the Norris-LaGuardia Act was *U.S.* v. *United Mine Workers of America and John L. Lewis,* 330 U.S. 258 (March 6, 1947).

Thereafter, the antistrike injunction became the most important means of curbing defiance by big unions in seizure cases, and so forced the unions to seek new means of disguising their concerted stoppages in vain efforts to avoid penalty.

"Spontaneous" stoppages by individual employees. This is a generic term introduced to describe several specific disguises for illegal strikes. The disguises are not unique to seizure cases but have been carried over into seizure operations from earlier union experience with unlawful stoppages when a private employer obtained an antistrike injunction or when the union's contract was interpreted by the employer as barring strikes.

The adoption of this technique in seizure cases has had two principal stimuli: the need for a means to disguise strike calls issued during government possession and operation—the need for a supplementary device to the preseizure strike call; the need for a means to cope with the presidentially obtained injunction, which after the expiration of the War Labor Disputes Act on June 30, 1947, had the effect of outlawing even strikes called prior to the government's taking possession.

The forms of "spontaneous" work stoppage that have been employed in seizure cases are: the simultaneous "resignation" of individual employees; the use of "code words" by union officials such as "contract terminated" and "memorial holiday"; and the simultaneous reporting "sick" of numerous individual employees. These devices have usually been accompanied by the crocodile tears of union officials "deploring" the stoppages and "urging" the individual employees (unsuccessfully) to return to work.

The object of the "spontaneous" stoppage is plainly to obtain the benefits of a bargaining device—the concerted withdrawal from work—without sustaining the penalties of an unlawful action. The effectiveness of the maneuver appears to depend largely upon the verbal ingenuity of the union officials and their lawyers against that of the government attorneys and the federal judges. Apart from the legal complexities involved, the essence of the union argument apparently is that, while the dispute remains unsettled, the members naturally recognize the importance of keeping up the pressure and need no leadership to tell them when to stay home. Thus a "spontaneous" stoppage is a natural economic event. The logical weakness in this argument, however, would seem to be that the negotiations with management are conducted by the leaders of an organization to which the employees belong. So the stoppage hinges upon the action of an organization from which they expect to receive economic benefit.

The device of group "resignations" was used during the government's operation of 74 bituminous coal mines as the result of organizing strikes by the mine foremen in August and September 1944. When the Department of the Interior refused to recognize the foremen's union, although the foremen had returned to work, 18 foremen at the Rochester & Pittsburgh Coal Co., McIntyre, Pennsylvania, handed their "resignations" to the federal manager on September 6, preventing production workers from entering the pits. They "withdrew their resignations" on September 9, after Acting Secretary of the Interior Fortas still had refused to grant recognition and had urged them (by telegraph) to return to work. No one was prosecuted under the WLDA, and no concessions were granted.[15]

The use of "resignations" is obviously a weak, though possibly legal, substitute for an illegal strike. It involves, if the "resignations" mean what they say, the voluntary yielding of all rights to a particular job, including seniority and pension rights. It may have the advantage of saving the employee from jail, but it has the disadvantage of depriving him of an increasingly valuable economic status. In continuing to bargain over the terms of employment, he can only do so, by his own admission, as a prospective new employee. Indeed, putting strikers into this status by discharging them has been one of the coercive sanctions occasionally threatened by the president.[16]

USE OF "CODE WORDS"

The use of "code words" to disguise a strike call has been a standard practice of John L. Lewis and the United Mine Workers for many years. The phrase "no contract," "contract dishonored," or the equivalent is a well-known signal to the miners to lay down their tools, pending union-company negotiations. It avoids overt conspiratorial acts almost as surely as the preseizure strike order. It was raised to a new peak of notoriety in November 1946, when Lewis used it as a means of circumventing the War Labor Disputes Act and summoning an industrywide strike in government-operated soft coal mines in order to bring pressure against President Truman and Secretary of the Interior Krug in renewed bargaining over the interim terms of employment.

Mr. Lewis could have applied for a further wage increase for the miners through the regular procedures of the War Labor Disputes Act (sec. 5). This would have consisted of an application to the National Wage Stabilization Board. But he evidently wanted more than the stabilization board could have approved under existing policies. The strike, therefore, was designed to bring pressure upon the government to change the stabilization policies. It may also be, as President Truman has charged, that the move was timed to embarrass him politically on the eve of new congressonal elections. In any event, Mr. Lewis chose to strike, and to do so he had to circumvent the WLDA.

In order to accomplish this, he adopted the plan of finding fault with the Krug-Lewis interim agreement, which had been signed at the White

House just six months before, then of terminating the agreement unilaterally, and finally of allowing the notice of the contract's termination to serve as a strike call to the 400,000 bituminous coal miners. The notice to the government went out November 1, 1946, that to the miners on November 15, and the effective date of the contract's "termination" was November 20. On that date, virtually all the soft coal miners quit work in a strike against the government.[17]

President Truman accepted the challenge of these illegal tactics and ordered "a fight to the finish," before Lewis' plan was well under way. Through members of his cabinet, the president attacked Lewis' notice of termination from two directions: First, the government asserted that the Krug-Lewis contract covered the terms of employment in the mines for the duration of government possession, and was still valid. Second, it asserted that Lewis' letter to the miners was in reality an illegal strike order. Then it petitioned the U.S. District Court to hold hearings and rule on the validity of the contract, and meanwhile to require Mr. Lewis to rescind his notice of termination. The court agreed immediately that "this notice was a cease work or strike notice," ordered it rescinded, and set dates for hearings.[18]

The court order was historically momentous. It was the first antistrike injunction ever obtained by a president in a seizure case; it was the first injunction obtained by a president in any labor dispute since the passage of the Norris-LaGuardia Act in 1932; it was issued under the authority of existing law, not by reasons of a special act of Congress such as the president had vainly requested in the railroad strike six months earlier.[19]

Mr. Lewis' plan for renegotiating his interim contract with the government under the pressure of an industrywide strike was seriously threatened by these measures, and Lewis himself was caught in a trap of his own making. If he should recall the notice, he would be weakened economically and politically; if he did not recall it, he faced prosecution for contempt of court. If prosecuted, however, there was the possibility that he might wriggle out of it by contending that the Norris-LaGuardia Act had forbidden court orders of this kind. So he chose to carry on and to risk prosecution.

The plan required no further overt action by Mr. Lewis. He sat tight. The miners walked out when the contract "terminated." Mr. Lewis did not even move in court for the dismissal of the government's complaint. He simply reported to Judge T. Alan Goldsborough that the notice to the miners remained "unchanged," and attacked the legality of the order calling for the notice's withdrawal and forbidding a strike. Therefore, on December 3, the court found Lewis and the union guilty of civil and criminal contempt of court; and on December 4 Lewis was fined $10,000 and the union $3,500,000.[20] On December 7, Lewis ordered the miners to return to work until March 31, 1947, "to permit the Supreme Court" to hear his appeal from the contempt verdict "free from pressure." The Supreme Court on March 6, 1947, found that Lewis' notice had indeed "amounted to a strike call" and that his refusal to rescind it, as directed by the lower court, had been civilly and criminally contemptuous of that court. The Supreme Court also found by a vote of five to four that the Norris-LaGuardia Act was not a bar to an injunction obtained by the president in properties seized and operated by the federal government. The chief justice pointed out that the labor dispute here was between the union and the government, as Lewis himself had emphasized, and not between the union and the private owners of the mines, for the dispute was over the interim—not the final—terms of employment. The court also declared that Lewis' postponement of the strike from December 7, 1946, to March 31, 1947, was not yet a genuine retraction of the strike notice nor a satisfactory compliance with the lower court's order, and directed him to comply in full. It reduced the fine of $3,500,000 to $700,000 only if Lewis fully complied. He did.[21]

Thus the device of calling a strike by using a "code word," namely, that the miners had "no contract," failed the first time it was tried in the middle of a seizure operation. It failed to win any improvements in the contract; and it failed to save Lewis and the union from prosecution and punishment. Indeed, having been found guilty of willful refusal to halt a strike which he had called, Lewis probably also could have been prosecuted under the WLDA for having illegally begun a strike in seized facilities. The courts had plainly regarded his notice to the miners as an overt strike action during seizure.[22] But he was allowed to escape this additional punishment. Probably the union had suffered sufficiently with the $700,000 fine.

On one other occasion, Mr. Lewis used a "code word" to launch a strike in the seized mines. This was on March 29, 1947, when he notified all local unions that he had designated the week of April 1 to 6, 1947, as a "memorial period" or "week of mourning" to honor the 111 miners killed four days previously in the tragic explosion of the Centralia Coal Co.'s mine No. 5 at Centralia, Illinois. Although the miners' contract contained a provision for the designation of memorial periods, this one was generally regarded as a strike in which Lewis was seeking to draw attention to the lack of enforcement of mine-safety laws and codes, and to pin the blame for the terrible Centralia disaster upon the seizing agency's insufficient concern with the mine-safety problem.

The nearly industrywide shutdown was only partially effective. Secretary of the Interior Krug kept 518 of the mines closed until they could be federally inspected. Two congressional committees conducted investigations, and eventually a law was passed requiring federal inspectors to submit reports to Congress on unsafe mines (61 Stat. 725, approved August 4, 1947); but no real teeth were put into the law.[23] Mr. Lewis was not prosecuted under the WLDA, nor was an injunction sought.

While Lewis' criticisms were vituperative and personal, he was essentially right. The seizing agency, the Department of the Interior, missed a great opportunity to demonstrate the effectiveness of a federal mine-safety program having teeth. The seizing agency had real power under the seizure law. It did draft a fine new "mine-safety code," but left the enforcement up to the miners and the union. This did not work because the miners as well as the operators lose money if the mines are shut down to take safety measures. The only workable program will be one that is nationally uniform and compulsory, thus raising the costs of mining similarly for all firms in this competitive industry.

"SICKNESS" STRIKES

The third form of disguise used to call illegal strikes in the midst of seizure operations has been the simultaneous reporting "sick" of large numbers of individual employees. This differs from the use of "code words" in two respects: the individual employees, instead of remaining away without authorization, attempted to legalize their absences by reporting "sick," and the union officers, instead of merely pretending to take no overt action regarding a strike, issued crocodile pleas and requests to the employees to return to their jobs. Despite such "pleas," many of the men remained out until the union officers added the equivalent of "now, we really mean it" to their "urgings."

This disguise was not unique to seizure but was introduced by the Brotherhood of Railroad Trainmen in the long railroad-seizure operation of the Korean War when the War Labor Disputes Act no longer was in effect but court injunctions had become customary to make strikes illegal on the government-operated railroads. The brotherhood called strikes in this way on December 13, 1950, and January 29, 1951, in key railroad terminals—both times as negotiations for a final settlement of the national dispute were being conducted.

The device was effective the first time in winning additional concessions from the railroads in negotiations mediated at the White House by Dr. John R. Steelman; but it failed completely the second time because not only the railroads but the government clearly felt that the labor organizations were unjustified in repudiating the "White House agreement" and in "coming back for more." In neither case did the yardmen or their brotherhood officers convince anyone that they were not striking. But by repeating the maneuver within a month after its first success, they brought upon themselves numerous penalties ordered by President Truman, including a trial for contempt of court. The brotherhood's arguments in a week-long trial before Judge Michael L. Igoe in Chicago failed to shake this tough-minded jurist from the plain fact that the brotherhood had contemptuously defied the federal court injunction.

The trial showed that no one—not even the union—took the "sickness" part of the disguise seriously. The BRT attorney, Walter N. Murray, declared in court that the members were "sick in body and soul" because of the delay in obtaining the railroads' agreement to a satisfactory contract.[24] And Joseph W. O'Hearn, the brotherhood's general chairman on the Peoria & Pekin Union Railroad, while denying that the men were on strike, testified: "I said they were sick—sick of conditions as they are, and sick of waiting 21 months for some kind of answer from the railroads."[25]

The more serious aspect of these two stoppages in important railroad centers was the contention of the BRT officers, including the president, William P. Kennedy, that the strike was "an unauthorized stoppage"—that is, unauthorized by the brotherhood—which they were helpless to terminate. The inference was that the labor organization lacked control over its members in their bargaining activities, and that the leaders were being repudiated by rank-and-file actions. The BRT also argued that the strikers included men who were not members of the brotherhood.

Although such uncontrolled action by the rank and file and by local union leaders has occurred in several seizures, it does not appear to have been the case here. The points made by the BRT officials were contradicted by three types of evidence given at the trial: testimony by several members of the BRT that they had been told by their general chairmen to "go out sick and stay out"; evidence that the only railroads in Chicago, out of 28, on which there was no stoppage of work were the two not represented by the Brotherhood of Railroad Trainmen (the Rock Island and Chicago Great Western); and the relationship of the stoppage to the bargaining situation. Judge Igoe emphasized the third type of evidence. He pointed out that the strike of December 13, 1950, had begun during bargaining negotiations and had continued, despite the injunctions, until the railroads had agreed to make additional concessions in a proposed final settlement. He concluded that the brotherhood members must be held responsible as a group for the actions they had taken as a group in their own economic interest. Since such action was in defiance of an order of the court, on railroads that were in government operation, the action was contempt of court.

While the judge had misgivings as to the sincerity of the brotherhood officers in trying to end the walkout, he "gave them the benefit of the doubt" and acquitted them. But he found the Brotherhood of Railroad Trainmen guilty of civil and criminal contempt of court, and fined the organization $25,000. The brotherhood did not appeal. Instead, it subsequently took the almost unprecedented step of acknowledging its guilt in two other federal jurisdictions (District of Columbia, and Cleveland) and was fined an additional $75,000 and placed on one year's probation.[26]

Postponement. The innocent-looking fifth device keeps the president and the opposite party (usually private management) under continuous, even increasing, pressure from an impending stoppage of production. The effect is similar to that of a strike date set prior to seizure, which the union refuses to withdraw after the government takes over—an overhanging, but not immediate, shutdown. It differs, however, in two respects: It provides a temporary easing of an intense pressure—a return to work for a limited time, or a temporary deferment of an actual stoppage—giving it a spurious appearance of union cooperation with the president when it actually represents continuing defiance; it is a form of "hit-and-run" tactic, a means for alternately relaxing and intensifying the economic pressure upon the president in a continuing "war of nerves"; for as each new deadline approaches, the president must decide whether to prepare further coercive measures or to yield to the union and grant some or all of its economic demands. Saul Alinsky has described this type of union tactic as "the hit-and-run type, short strikes with interludes of unbearable tension between," adding that "in this war of nerves," the miners' union believed the government, preoccupied with grave military problems, "would of necessity have to break first."[27] The use of such a series of deadlines by a labor union in a seizure case does not assure uninterrupted production; it is the very opposite of such assurance. The postponement of a shutdown to a later date is not the voluntary acceptance of the president's temporary control of the business, but a clear effort to bargain with him over terms of employment.

President Roosevelt took this view of John L. Lewis' use of the postponement tactic. When asked by the press on June 25, 1943, whether he would "accept or recognize" Lewis' "deadline of Oct. 31"—the date which Lewis had set as the latest to which the miners would work for the government without an improved contract—Mr. Roosevelt replied, "No."[28]

The act of seizure manifests a governmental decision that the stoppage should be forbidden for the duration of the emergency period—not merely deferred during a mediatory or bargaining "truce." A principle of seizure is that the government will remain in possession and control of an essential business that has experienced (or been threatened with) a shutdown until either the dispute has been settled or the emergency ended, whichever occurs sooner. Under this rule, the parties must postpone the shutdown either indefinitely or until the government relinquishes possession. If they adopt the latter, this forces the government to retain possession until the emergency has ended, but it does not subject the government to bargaining pressure—threatening the continuity of production—as the postponement to another specific date does.

The postponement device was introduced into seizure cases by John L. Lewis in an effort to dodge the coercive measures of President Roosevelt and President Truman, while still subjecting them and the coal operators to recurring pressures. It was highly successful in its first usage in 1943 when Mr. Lewis by its means forced President Roosevelt, the NWLB, and the coal operators to acknowledge the principle of portal-to-portal compensation and to grant the miners a substantial increase in take-home pay. It failed, however, three years later when Mr. Lewis again tried it in a vain effort to thwart President Truman's history-making use of an antistrike injunction against him. On this occasion, the Supreme Court not only upheld the president's use of the injunction in a government-operated industry but found that Lewis' postponement of an industrywide soft coal stoppage from December 7, 1946, until March 31, 1947, had been only a partial compliance with the antistrike order of the lower court, and required him to cancel his strike order completely, rescinding the postponement (which he did).

Mr. Lewis appears to have been the only labor leader to try the postponement device as a deliberate pressure tactic. Two of the railroad brotherhoods also deferred a scheduled industrywide shutdown for five days in May 1946, but this was at the specific suggestion of President Truman to permit further negotiations of the dispute. The delay resulted only in a new mediatory offer by the president, which the brotherhoods regarded as no better (and perhaps worse) than the emergency board had previously recommended.

The five forms of strike tactics in seizure cases described above do not exhaust the list of bargaining pressures devised by employees and unions in seizure cases, but they are the ones which have caused the greatest difficulty for the government. The sit-down seems to have lost popularity and has not been effective so far in seizure cases. Sit-downs were conducted by a group of checkers at the Federal Shipbuilding & Dry Dock Co., were threatened by anti-union employees at Air Associates, and were conducted by two small groups of rubber workers at Goodyear. All were overcome promptly. The slowdown, which does not halt production but curtails output, failed once but has been used successfully three times to gain concessions during federal possession.[29] Other tactics have been tried, and others doubtless will be developed.

LOCKOUTS

Turning now to the company managements, we find that they have attempted on only a few occasions to prevent the resumption of production after seizure occurred or to halt production during the course of presidential operations. There have been five instances in the first of these categories, and four in the second, making nine lockouts or attempted lockouts in all. Most of these instances of obstruction occurred in seizures resulting from company noncompliance with labor-board decisions (six of the nine instances), but one occurred in a seizure resulting from labor's noncompliance, and two others in a case that had not been adjudicated prior to seizure.

This type of resistance to the president's control has been relatively infrequent because of the serious costs to business management of shutdowns in boom periods, such as wars and the cold war. In periods of rising product prices, it is in the interest of the owners to maintain production at peak levels, without interruption, under the old factor prices, insofar as this is possible. Hence management is more apt to resist the president's seizure authority by refusing to observe the new terms of employment ordered by the federal board while continuing operations without a halt.

Another possible reason for the infrequency of open defiance is the ease with which the government can remove insubordinate executives and take over direct control. Of the nine instances referred to, the government responded by removing the company presidents in five and was on the point of removing one in a sixth when the firm capitulated. The defiant managements have tended to look for more subtle means of obstructing federal control in the hope of avoiding such drastic reprisals. The company presidents, even when ousted, have proved that they still have some influence over the seized firms, however, for in several instances they were able to threaten virtual shutdowns of government operations through special, indirect means. It should not be overlooked, moreover, that such displacement of company executives and assumption of direct control by seizing agencies adds to the expense of seizure and to the time required of high government officials in a time of national emergency. The attempted stoppage of production by defiant executives, therefore, may be an effective means of troublemaking for the government and country.

The forms of lockout employed in the nine instances cited above have included the conventional laying off of employees (six instances) and the less familiar withdrawal of company executives or supervisors in the attempt to obstruct operations (the other three instances). We will discuss each of these forms of lockout in turn.

Laying off all employees. Seized companies have refused to reopen their plants when federal officials took possession, and have sought instead to bargain with the government over the terms of federal operation. In one instance—the Federal Shipbuilding & Dry Dock Co., a subsidiary of the United States Steel Corp.—the company wished to negotiate the terms of compensation for sale or use of its property, and to work out such details as the method of taking inventory, before resuming production. When the federal officer in charge, Rear Admiral Harold G. Bowen, told the company president, Mr. Lynn H. Korndorff, in salty navy language, that these matters could be taken up later, and that the first task was to reopen the shipyard, the company president replied: "Why are you Navy boys trying to open the plant up immediately? Are you trying to show how good you are?" The admiral's firm insistence upon immediate and unconditional resumption of shipbuilding was supported a few minutes later by the undersecretary of the navy, James Forrestal, who arrived unexpectedly. After consultation between the shipyard and Washington, Secretary of the Navy Knox relieved Mr. Korndorff of his authority and reopened the shipyard with only one day's delay.[30]

In another instance of company refusal to resume operations, a majority of the soft coal operators of Iowa in May 1946 refused to resume mining as the government took over unless assured that they would be given compensatory price relief for the higher labor costs required by the Krug-Lewis agreement.[31] While the exact method of handling this situation is not known, the requested assurance actually was given to the whole government-operated soft coal industry.[32] Such assurance probably would have been forthcoming, as a matter of policy, even if the Iowa mines had not sought to compel it. In Kentucky, a year earlier, three small mines remained closed despite government seizure, but little is known of the circumstances.[33]

In addition to the above situations, seized companies have closed their plants during government possession in two cases, laying off all employees. Each of these lockouts marked an effort by company management to bring bargaining pressures against the union and employees without consulting the seizing agency. Each of these shutdowns involved major steel plants.

In the first instance, Admiral Ben Moreell, president of Jones & Laughlin Steel Corp., shut down his big Pittsburgh steel works as a means of forcing the seized Monongahela Connecting R.R., a J. & L. subsidiary, to lock out its employees in a wage dispute with the Brotherhood of Railroad Trainmen. This indirect lockout of a seized railroad by its chief customer (also its owner) continued from March 10, 1951, until March 23, 1951, when the assistant secretary of the army, Mr. Karl Bendetsen, sent word that the railroad must raise the pay of its trainmen and engineers and resume operations by 4:00 P.M. that day or the railroad president, Mr. A. L. Hutchinson, would be replaced. The railroad complied, and the big steel company reopened the next day. The lockout followed a long slowdown by the railroad's operating employees—a slowdown which the company claimed had created a hazardous condition in its blast furnaces and hot-metal trains—but the army's action was directed solely against the company.[34]

The other lockout by big steel mills occurred at the conclusion of the three-day strike called by Phil Murray in the seized steel industry after Judge Pine had ruled the seizure unconstitutional on April 29, 1952. With Judge Pine's ruling temporarily stayed, pending appeal, Murray sent the men back to work; but several steel companies refused to reopen immediately, unless given guarantees by the union against further stoppages.[35] Among these were the United States Steel Co., J. & L. Steel Corp., and two subsidiaries of National Steel Corp. The U.S. Steel Co. further delayed the reopening of its Pittsburgh plants because of a dispute with the Brotherhood of Locomotive Engineers on the Union Railroad, an unseized subsidiary. When the army began considering whether to add the Union Railroad to its group of seized steel company subsidiaries, U.S. Steel resumed operations. All plants were back in operation by May 5, without any assurance from the union so far as was publicly announced.

Withdrawing management from the premises. The top executives of two firms seized during World War II withdrew from their plants to unannounced or inaccessible locations, and sent word that the seizing officials would run the company's equipment only "at their peril," meaning subject to suit for damages. This was the equivalent of a "strike" by the company executives. It appears to have been intended to persuade the seizing agency—the War Department—that direct operation without company cooperation would be impossible. The War Department met the challenge by bringing in army officers who had had business and engineering experience, and by drawing heavily upon the cooperation of the regular employees, foremen, and junior executives. With this aid, the operations were never interrupted. The two concerns were Ken-Rad Tube and Lamp Corp., Owensboro, Kentucky, and Gaffney Manufacturing Co., Gaffney, South Carolina, controlled by Deering-Milliken Co.[36]

This technique was somewhat more effectively employed by James W. Carter, president of the Carter Coal Co., of McDowell County, West Virginia, in 1947. Mr. Carter had refused to observe the terms of the Krug-Lewis agreement during government operations, and so had been discharged by the coal mines administration on December 31, 1946. Direct control of operations was then assumed by the CMA. When Mr. Carter later threatened to withdraw key supervisory officials from the mine—a low-volatile mine requiring specialized knowledge of safety techniques—the government was faced with the possibility of having to close the mine. In the absence of government officials or others qualified to direct such dangerous operations, the government granted some of the concessions requested by Mr. Carter.[37]

An indirect means of obstructing presidential operation of seized plants, even when the government had removed the company presidents, was through the company's continuing control of certain departments not directly involved in the labor dispute and therefore not taken over by the seizing agency. This division of company control between the old private management and the government managers enabled the former to create considerable trouble. In most instances, the government solved the problem rather simply by extending control to the remainder of the company. But in the Montgomery Ward cases, the legal uncertainties over the president's authority to be in possession of even part of the property led the government to hesitate to extend its control. This weakness Ward's chairman Sewell Avery shrewdly exploited for several months.

Mr. Avery refused to pay the War Department for orders filled by the government from the seized mail-order houses, although he controlled the central accounting office and had the money received from the customers. The War Department, finding that this was costing the government nearly $1,000,000 a week, retaliated on August 1, 1945, by refusing to fill any more orders at the fashion mail-order house in Chicago. The employees were left idle although at work and being paid. The army resumed filling orders the next day but took the drastic step of preparing to take possession of the rest of Ward's nationwide system of properties. Mr. Avery then agreed to pay for goods shipped by the government.[38]

While discussing management interference with production in seized plants, a final word may be said about Sewell Avery's famous sit-down in his Chicago office. While it is true that Mr. Avery refused to leave his office and was carried out by two soldiers at the instance of Undersecretary of Commerce Taylor, no stoppage of production would have resulted if Mr. Avery had been allowed to remain. Nor did the government gain genuine control of the business by removing him. Mr. Avery continued to direct the business from another building. The episode, therefore, has little significance except for Mr. Avery's political campaign attacking the NWLB and the Roosevelt administration.

INSUBORDINATION

The second general method of resistance to the president's control during seizure is the refusal to observe his interim directives, while keeping production going without interruption. This class of resistance has been found in 21 of the 71 seizures. It may take the form of a broad refusal to acknowledge the president's authority to make any changes (or to forbid any changes) in the terms of employment or in the operational methods of the firm or industry. Or it may take the narrower form of resistance to certain specific orders of the president or seizing agency, without objecting to other orders or to his interim control generally. As previously mentioned, this class of resistance has been offered largely by the executives and owners of seized firms and only rarely by employees and unions.

The experience with seizure shows that company executives have refused to accept the president's authority in at least some operational matters in 18 seizure cases.[39] In addition, some of the production employees have refused to obey such directives in six seizure cases.[40] In only three of the latter—a small segment of the first national railroad seizure, the Hummer manufacturing division of Ward's, and the San Francisco machine-shop cases—was resistance clearly instigated by union officials; and in the first two of these the obstruction was aimed basically at other unions, not at the government or at the private employers. In the three remaining labor cases, the resistance was by individual employees who were anti-union and who may have been secretly encouraged by the old private management. Thus we find that management has made three times as much use of this general class of obstruction as has labor (18 seizures to six). While this refusal to observe the president's interim orders does not interfere directly with the continuity of production, it has in a few cases been accompanied by deliberate stoppages of production, and in certain other cases has induced an early abandonment of presidential possession and a return to private economic warfare.

Thus, insubordination has been accompanied and supported by deliberate attempts to interrupt production in seven of the 21 seizures in which it has occurred, and by threats of stoppages in two or three others. Such attempts have succeeded, however, in only three of the 21 cases—resulting in one day of delay in the resumption of production at Federal Shipbuilding, in a strike of several days in one of the 104 San Francisco machine shops, and in a lockout of unknown duration in certain Iowa coal mines. This form of resistance also has contributed to the early abandonment of presidential possession followed by new outbreaks of strikes in two of the 21 cases— Federal Shipbuilding and the first Montgomery Ward seizure.

Such defiance of the president's managerial directives is in itself a bold continuance of economic bargaining pressures during government possession and, whether accompanied by attempted stoppages or not, is a form of civil disobedience intended to induce either: a settlement during seizure reflecting these one-sided pressures; or temporary operation by the government under terms reflecting these same pressures; or relinquishment of the property by the government and a return to normal collective-bargaining procedures.

In the face of such tactics, it is not sufficient for the seizing agency merely to maintain production without interruption. For if the obstructing party achieves a coerced settlement or forces the government into modifying its interim directives, this means the government has failed in its secondary objective of upholding the prestige of its emergency program of peaceful disputes-settlement, and may also have failed to hold the line of its wage-and-price stabilization standards. In the second of these alternatives, the seizing agency also has failed to treat the disputing parties impartially. Neither is it sufficient for the president to let go of the business suddenly. For if the obstructing party accomplishes the third of these objectives—the return of the property to private operation without settlement of the dispute —then the government has fallen down in its principal objective, the maintenance of uninterrupted production.

The only rule consistent with all the objectives of public policy is for the president to maintain production under terms of employment set by him (preferably through the disputes-settlement board or the seizing agency) without coercion from either of the parties. This implies firm support for the interim directives, including the use of sanctions when necessary in their enforcement. It also implies the president's retention of possession until the dispute has been settled without one-sided pressures, or until the emergency has ended, whichever happens sooner.

Company executives. The refusal by company executives to observe the president's directives in the seized plants took various forms, but we may group them into two categories: the general refusal of all cooperation with the seizing officials, based upon the contention that neither the president nor the seizing officials were acting lawfully in asserting possession and control; and the refusal to carry out certain specific orders of the president or seizing agency, while obeying other orders, this refusal occasionally accompanying a reservation as to the president's right of possession but generally marked only by an attack upon the specific directives named.

All these moves are forms of civil resistance and, if successful, would prevent the execution of policies which the president believes to be in the national interest; but the first group is the more flagrant challenge to federal authority and prestige. It meets the total assertion of national control with total resistance to it; and if the government is uncertain of its legal position or timid in its action, it may be routed by such bold maneuvers. But the company executives taking such a stand risk all by their uncompromising attitude, and may in the end bring upon themselves not only failure to obstruct the seizing officials but public disapproval as well.

There have been 10 known instances of the general refusal of all cooperation with the president and his representatives by the officials of seized companies. These refusals have taken the form of oral statements but have been supported by various forms of obstruction, other than attempted stoppages, ranging from the physical denial of admittance at the seized property to an insistence on preliminary negotiations over the "terms" of the seizure. In five instances the company officials refused physical access to their books, records, and funds, while in two others they made the books available but walked out of the plants without a word of explanation of the operations. In seven instances, they took action in court aimed at having the seizure ruled unlawful. None of these forms of resistance interfered with production in any direct way.[41]

In nine of the 10 instances of general defiance, the seizing agency responded by removing the uncooperative company executives from further managerial control and responsibility. By this means, the government officials gained full and prompt control of six of the 10 seized establishments and proceeded to operate them in accordance with the president's orders, the defiance proving completely ineffectual.

In two cases, however, the great energy and skill of the industrial leaders, the wealth of their corporations, the soft and inept policies of the federal seizing officials (none of whom was from a military department), and the existence of doubts within the government itself as to the legality of the seizures, resulted in the complete defeat of the federal representatives. The two instances were the Postal Telegraph-Cable System (one of the wire systems taken over in July 1918), and the Chicago properties of Montgomery Ward & Co. (seized in April 1944).

The two successful private executives in these instances were Clarence Mackay and Sewell Avery. Their obstruction was so effective that the president of the United States in each instance returned the properties to their private owners unexpectedly, without having settled the labor dispute and without having established full interim control of the businesses. Even Mr. Avery was able to do this only once, however. When he tried it again eight months later, the same tactics failed completely. He lost control of the records, funds, and operations of his stores and mail-order houses in seven cities to the more experienced and adroit personnel of the War Department.

The two remaining cases of successful defiance among the 10 instances of general refusal of cooperation were also large corporations. In these cases, the government overcame the initial opposition of the companies to federal control but ultimately relinquished possession of the properties without having enforced the recommendations of the disputes-settlement boards to which the companies had objected. The effect on the government's program of semivoluntary dispute-settlement was therefore the same as in the instances of Mackay's and Avery's defiance. These two remaining cases were the Federal Shipbuilding & Dry Dock Co. and the Humble Oil &

Refining Co. In the latter case, the initial defiance was overcome by court proceedings rather than by displacing the company executives.

These four cases of the government's failure to observe the terms of labor cited by the president in ordering the seizures occurred in the administrations of three presidents—Wilson, Franklin Roosevelt, and Truman. All were marked by renewed strikes as the employees and unions realized the extent to which the seizing agencies had "let them down." Two of the returned properties were reseized when the stoppages occurred (Ward's and Humble Oil) but in only one were the contested terms of labor then effectively imposed—Ward's.

The second group of situations in which company officials refused to carry out directions of the president and seizing officials differs from the first only in degree. These are seizures in which the resistance was less than total. In only one of these situations did the officials deny the president's right to take possession of their property (the Carter Coal Co. in May 1946). In 11 other situations, the companies accepted the seizure as lawful but objected to some or all of the interim labor terms that the president directed should be observed. The record shows that the company executives were no more successful in these instances of partial resistance than in those of total resistance. In nine of the 12 situations (including Carter Coal Co.), the defiant private managers were removed, and the objectionable orders of the president or of the seizing agency were put into effect. In the other three situations, no disciplinary measures were taken by the government, and the defiance apparently served its purpose effectively.

The instances of successful refusal to obey certain specific orders of the government (while obeying others) were: the Western Union Telegraph Co. in the wire systems seizure, July 1918; five railroads in the industrywide takeover of May 1946; and a majority of the coal mine operators of Iowa in the bituminous coal seizure of May 1946. Only the first of these was of major importance. Here the seizing agency (the Post Office Department) was out of sympathy with the policy it was supposed to enforce—forbidding the discharge of employees for membership in a union. Besides, Postmaster General Burleson himself was no match for the shrewd business executives he faced. Hence, the orders he issued on this subject were circumvented throughout federal possession by the tacitly approved device of laying such discharges to "insubordination." This resulted, after nearly a year, in a nationwide strike of telegraph operators against the timid seizing agency and the giant corporation headed by Newcomb Carlton that was manipulating it. But the company had so successfully ferreted out those employees who joined the union (the Commercial Telegraphers, AFL) and had so relentlessly discharged them, that very few were left to join the strike, and it failed.

In all the situations of company refusal to observe the president's interim directives, the private managements were encouraged in their defiance by the very fact that seizure deprived the employees and the unions of the right to use the strike weapon. This gave the private managements a new sense of security from the pressure of employee stoppages. That they should now be confronted with a new pressure—the demands of the government to control and change the interim terms of employment—seemed to them most objectionable. What good was seizure to them if it merely substituted government pressure for union pressure? What good if it freed them from strikes, only to fetter them in their traditional freedom of action regarding managerial policies? Hence their reluctance to turn interim control over to the president of the United States and to the seizing agencies.

Yet we must remember that these companies were the exceptional ones— the rugged individualists, large and small, who wanted either to continue normal economic warfare against the unions even in the midst of global wars, or to accept a temporary truce only if it tied the unions' hands without tying managements'. They were often willing, as a matter of improving their bargaining strengths, to accept that part of the national program for the peaceful settlement of disputes that ended strikes, but not the part of it that settled the disputes. Hence, the only way to save the national program was to enforce both aspects of it against the obstructionists. This is what seizure did when it was handled by government officials who not only maintained uninterrupted production but enforced the terms of employment recommended by the federal agencies charged with peaceful adjustment of disputes.

Employees and unions. A refusal to observe the president's interim managerial policies while keeping production going has seldom been undertaken by unions because: the control of working conditions is largely in the hands of management; and the bargaining pressures open to employees, other than striking, are not powerful weapons. For these reasons, we find that only eight examples exist of this kind of resistance (in six seizures); that not one of the eight situations was instigated by a national union; that all were sponsored either by union locals in conflict with other union organizations or by anti-union individuals; and that four of the situations even showed plainly the hand of private management as an inspiration or support of the obstructive action. This brief record contrasts with the 74 strikes conducted by production employees in 32 of the 71 seizure cases, many of them sponsored by national unions.

It is obvious that whenever wage rates ordered by the president are unsatisfactory to labor, a strike is the only coercive remedy. However, the eight instances of obstruction dealt with here show that individual employees do have within their control several matters outside the wage area.

The eight examples included: a refusal to work overtime beyond 48 hours a week; the urging of other employees to refuse certain work assignments; the direct refusal to accept certain work assignments; the reporting of conditions in a plant to officials of the former private management (termed "spying" by the new government-appointed managers); and a refusal to continue the payment of dues to the union. All of these are matters requiring the cooperation of individual employees for their successful operation.

Probably the most serious of these acts of insubordination was the refusal of Lodge 68, International Association of Machinists (AFL), to agree to the working of emergency overtime hours beyond 48 a week (or eight a day) in the San Francisco "uptown" machine shops during World War II. Prior to seizure the business agents of the lodge, backed by union penalties, had induced about 3,000 machinists to refuse to work extra hours, when requested to do so by their employers, despite an order of the National War Labor Board and despite the disapproval of the lodge's stand by the national officers of the IAM and AFL. Even after seizure, close to 500 machinists reported for work one hour late in order to avoid the extra hour posted in certain shops by order of the seizing agency (the Navy Department).[42]

The inability of the lodge, because of the War Labor Disputes Act, to support this resistance by overt action, once seizure had occurred, weakened its position. The lodge, while refusing to yield its basic opposition to overtime work, nevertheless withdrew its penalties against individuals who worked overtime in the seized shops and carefully refrained from any public word or deed urging noncooperation with the government. Attorney General Biddle, who investigated the situation on the spot, ruled that the criminal provisions of the WLDA were inapplicable, just as they had been in the coal mine seizures, unless conspiratorial acts of an overt nature were committed.

The seizing agency was obliged, therefore, to apply the new indirect economic sanctions, with the formal approval of President Roosevelt, in order to bring this individual disobedience to an end. The citation of 58 machinists of draft age to their draft boards, and the discharge of several older men without the right of referral to other war work, ended the resistance in about a week. The action of the draft boards, which had begun to induct the cited men, was then suspended.

There is evidence that the officers of Lodge 68 believed, prior to seizure, that the government had no lawful means of punishing individual employees who refused to carry out an order of the president of the United States in the seized plants. They had able legal advice. But they overlooked the obvious right of the president, as the new employer, to discharge insubordinate individuals; and they overlooked the extensive wartime controls over employment opportunities, and also the rule that occupational deferment of draft-eligible men is a privilege bestowed at the government's convenience and not an individual right. The lodge successfully avoided criminal prosecution under the WLDA, but it failed to prevent enforcement of the emergency overtime rules.

This was the most important example of union and employee resistance without striking. Two instances of refusal to accept particular work assignments, and of urging others to refuse, stirred up more excitement at the time than seems understandable at this distance. Neither situation interfered seriously with production or influenced the interim terms of employment set by the government. The first—the case of the railroad tugmen—resulted, however, in important litigation which forced the government into more restrained use of the economic sanctions. The railroad tugmen's insubordination in the seizure was unusual in that it amounted to a secondary boycott—a refusal to handle goods furnished by another union despite orders of the seizing agency (the Railroad Administration). About 16 tug captains and their crews (112 men) were laid off by the seizing agency when they refused to tow coal and grain barges in New York harbor manned by members of the Tidewater Boatmen's Union (International Longshoremen's Assn., AFL), who had settled with the private boat owners for a compromise wage increase; whereas the Masters, Mates and Pilots of America, and one or two other unions (all AFL), were still holding out against the private boat owners for a more substantial increase. The railroad tugmen were not involved in the dispute, since the government had granted them their maximum demands to assure uninterrupted operation. They joined in the fray, however, to help their striking compatriots on the private tugboats. In the end, their compatriots surrendered by agreeing to equally bad compromise terms.[43]

The second instance—the action of the two machinists of Lodge 68, IAM—who urged other employees to refuse certain work assignments, was met by the seizing agency (the Navy Department) with the prompt discharge of the two men and their blacklisting for all other government or war work. They and the lodge responded with suits against various high government officials alleging "involuntary servitude" and "cruel and unusual punishments." In the end, the government backpedaled slightly by limiting the penalties to 60 days' duration.

Another example of insubordination by individual production employees —and almost the only one resulting in some sucess—was the refusal to continue payment of union dues. This peculiar form of obstruction occurred in three seizure cases (Federal Shipbuilding; Hummer manufacturing division of Montgomery Ward; Hughes Tool Co.)—all of them seized originally because of management's defiance of a dispute board's recommendations for compulsory maintenance of union membership. These operations soon became paradoxical. The seizing agencies overcame the company's opposition and were in position to enforce the objectionable orders by simply discharging the employees who did not "maintain" their union memberships by keeping up their dues payments. But it was found that large numbers of employees were delinquent in their dues, despite the fact that they had joined the union voluntarily and despite the government's orders. Closer inquiry disclosed a new union organization springing up in each case and attracting the members of the older union. The new organizations were independent local unions in two cases, and a group threatening to secede from an AFL into a CIO union in the third. The seizing agencies found themselves confronted with employee opposition in company non-compliance cases. The obvious fact was, of course, that the employees were divided, and that private management was indirectly encouraging the insurgent group.

The government's complete control of the operations was scarcely adequate for these intricate internal problems. If the seizing agency were to discharge the delinquent employees under the maintenance-of-membership order, it would lose the services of hundreds of irreplaceable skilled workers in essential production. If it did not discharge them, it would weaken the prestige of the national disputes-settlement program (particularly the maintenance-of-membership policy); and it might also face a protest-strike by those employees who remained loyal to the older union. In either event, production would suffer.

The first seizing agency to deal with this problem (the Navy Department in 1941) sidestepped it. Secretary of the Navy Knox refused to discharge any delinquent employees of Federal Shipbuilding, thus giving the rival, uncertified union (and the company management) a full triumph over the federal program of disputes-settlement. The next seizing agency to deal with it (the War Department in 1944–1945) tackled it head-on. Undersecretary of War Patterson compelled the employees in the Hummer case to pay up, after threatening discharges and actually suspending four employees. In the Hughes Tool case, his representatives induced the older union (the United Steelworkers, CIO) to petition the NWLB to modify its order from maintenance of membership to compulsory check-off of dues; and Secretary Patterson personally warned the NWLB of the impossibility of enforcing both maintenance of membership and uninterrupted production. The NWLB then changed its order as requested. This gave the independent union a partial victory, for all past delinquencies in dues were canceled, and the check-off was applied only to future payments by the CIO members.

The only remaining case of employee insubordination is the reporting of conditions in a seized plant (S. A. Woods Machine Co.) to the former management, who were, of course, still the owners of the property. Such behavior indicated a divided loyalty, and the culprits were fired, but it is believed that information was still made available by others to the former management.[44] It would seem that some provision ought to have been made for the authorized inspection of the plant by the owners, so that this devious method need not have been employed.

Perhaps the most interesting aspect of the entire record is that the only examples of successful obstruction by employees, other than by striking, were in situations where the obstructing employees were a faction supporting the stand of the private management.

In concluding this survey of resistance to the president's managerial directives by both executives and employees of seized firms, we may note that this type of disobedience has been less dramatic and less directly menacing than a stoppage of production, since it relates only to the day-to-day control of labor conditions and not to the continuity of output. It has often gone unnoticed in the press, for example. But it has been accompanied frequently by attempts to stop or delay production, and it has provoked the opposite party on some other occasions to interrupt production. Even without this, however, it has been injurious to respect for lawful federal procedures, and to the authority of the government in seizure operations.

LEGAL RESISTANCE

The third general class of resistance to the president's seizure and control of essential businesses in labor-dispute emergencies is the commencement of legal proceedings asking for court injunctions to restrain members of the president's cabinet or other seizing officials from taking or keeping possession of a firm or industry.

Such proceedings have been initiated at least 27 times—17 times in an attempt to prevent seizure by the president's representatives, and 10 times during government possession in an effort to terminate seizure.

This has been, therefore, a frequent device for trying to upset the government's disputes-settlement programs. It has been confined almost entirely to management, however, since the unions and individual employees have preferred to strike for this purpose. Of the 27 proceedings referred to above, 26 were initiated by company managements and only one by a union. The legal moves have related to 15 of the 71 seizures, and to five other cases of noncompliance that did not end in seizure.

Of course, the right of individuals and organizations to resort to the courts for protection against unlawful actions of the executive branch of the government is fundamental; and in the case of coercive, semimilitary action such as seizure, this right is especially important. There are two qualifications which must be added, however: The right of appealing to the courts may be abused by employing it merely to delay and obstruct the government's disputes program as a means to enhance a bargaining position against the opposite party. The individual rights of economic conflict in a given bargaining dispute may be less urgent and less important in time of war than nationwide economic mobilization. There is, therefore, a basic conflict of rights in wartime between the individual's normal freedom of action and the temporary necessity to coordinate the entire national effort around the achievement of an early military victory.

The results of the legal actions brought by disputing parties against the president's disputes-settlement program may be viewed in two lights. Legally, they have been unsuccessful in nearly every case; but as an indirect means of economic resistance (that is, as a delaying action) they have been frequently effective. Only one of the 27 suits ever gained a final verdict holding the presidential action complained of to have been unlawful (the steel-seizure case of 1952), although several suits were left dangling because the emergency ended while the litigation was still pending, and the courts were able to avoid making a judgment; but the actions have succeeded, thanks to the judgment of some of the lower courts, in delaying the enforcement of the wartime control-program for labor disputes and in causing the president political embarrassment.

As indicated, this has been accomplished through injunction suits of three types: suits to prevent the enforcement of the NWLB orders by seizure or any other means—proceedings which effectively deferred the enforcement of NWLB orders for as long as 14 months against certain business concerns and forestalled it indefinitely against several others; suits to compel federal officials to relinquish possession of seized property—in which the interim orders of the courts proved even more significant than their final judgments; and suits and motions to restrain seizing officials and other federal agencies from carrying out specific managerial policies in seized businesses—resulting in interruptions of the policies for several weeks in a few cases. Let us look at the delaying power inherent in each of these types of legal resistance.

Preventing seizure. 17 suits by 11 company managements in World War II were for the admitted purpose of preventing seizure and the enforcement of NWLB decisions that the companies had refused to comply with. They were decisions, of course, that the companies had lost before the NWLB. There were no suits to prevent the enforcement of NWLB decisions that the companies had won. The attitude of business management toward seizure depended, like that of labor, on whether the purpose of seizure was to enforce a decision against it or for it. Of the 11 companies which brought these suits, six later were seized, but five successfully avoided seizure.

Since one of the companies was seized three times (Montgomery Ward), these suits relate to eight seizures.[45]

The 17 actions to prevent seizure were remarkably unsuccessful legally. Only one resulted in an order of a lower court forbidding the government to take possession of a plant; and this order was reversed on appeal (Humble Oil).[46] This legal victory of the government was weakened, however, because it was due partly to a policy of legal avoidance based on the refusal of the NWLB to enforce its orders by seizure or any other means while such suits were pending. This policy enabled any company that so desired to delay seizure—if not to prevent it—by the mere filing of a suit asking an injunction forbidding the seizure. No interim order of the court was necessary.

The War Labor Board and the Department of Justice took the position that the orders of the NWLB were merely advisory to the parties and to the president of the United States, and that any coercive steps taken by the president, such as seizure, were independent of the board's decisions. This view was successfully urged upon the courts and adopted by them.[47]

In order to conform to this position, however, the board had to refrain from "threatening" seizure against any of the firms that brought action in court. The board's restraint included the withholding of any recommendations to the president that he "take appropriate action" in these cases. In fact, the board filed affidavits with the courts in such suits declaring that the labor disputes had not been referred by the board to the president nor to the director of economic stabilization. In such circumstances, the appellate courts (and sometimes the district courts) dismissed the suits on the ground that no one was threatening anyone, and so there was no cause of action.

A pertinent statement from the NWLB on this aspect of seizure was that of Lloyd K. Garrison, a public member of the board, before a special committee of the House of Representatives in January 1944: "The [Montgomery Ward] Company has a lawsuit pending here in the District of Columbia, and so has the Gypsum Company, and we have been hesitant, while those lawsuits are pending, to attempt to refer the cases to the president, or anything of that sort."[48]

So it is clear that the mere commencement of proceedings acted to stay the NWLB from reporting the case to the president; and in the absence of such a report, the president took no seizure action. But the ultimate legal victory by the government was achieved at an economic cost of delayed enforcement of the war program for labor-disputes settlement. These circumstances did not prevent the enforcement of the program against noncomplying unions, that is, against unions which had lost the decision and then gone on strike. The NWLB went ahead and reported such cases to the president for seizure action, much to management's delight. But the little group of rugged manufacturers and one chain retailer, who was willing to defy the government in the midst of war, successfully protected themselves for a time against the unfavorable NWLB rulings. They could not, of course, protect themselves in this way against stoppages of production if their employees became impatient at the nonenforcement and struck. To have done this, they would have needed seizure.

Generally speaking, this series of court actions interrupted the enforcement of the government's program for peaceful disputes-settlement against noncomplying (and suing) managements from September 1943 until November 1944—a period of about 14 months at the height of the war. This was the time required to obtain a final decision in a "test" suit—the case of *Montgomery Ward & Co.* v. *National War Labor Board.*[49] However, during this period the NWLB made exceptions when the employees, who had won the decisions, struck in protest over the nonenforcement. In four such cases, the NWLB asked for and obtained seizure despite the managerial objections.[50] In two other cases the NWLB also obtained seizure, although suits were still pending, after the employees voted to strike without setting a strike date.[51] A different legal situation permitted the president to proceed in one other case which had been long delayed by the company's suit. Here seizure was effectuated, not because a strike occurred, but because the company was found guilty of unfair labor practices by the National Labor Relations Board, which had statutory powers of enforcement. The War Department then took possession, although the company's appeal from NLRB had not been finally adjudicated.[52]

The ablest practitioner of this form of resistance was Sewell Avery, who as chairman of Montgomery Ward & Co. staved off the seizure of stores in Detroit, Denver, and Jamaica, New York, for 15 months (from September 1943 until December 1944) until his "test case" was heard and argued at all judicial levels and decided against him; and who as chairman of the United States Gypsum Co. completely forestalled seizure of any of the company's plants by pressing parallel litigation.[53]

The next best user of this form of obstruction was a latecomer to the scene, Humble Oil & Refining Co., a subsidiary of the Standard Oil Co. (New Jersey). Humble obtained the only temporary restraining order and preliminary injunction ever issued to prevent a labor seizure. These orders restrained the NWLB and a list of about 80 other federal officials and agencies from taking possession of the Humble plant in Ingleside, Texas, to enforce the NWLB order. Although the orders were soon overruled by a higher court, the company obtained further delay by not appealing immediately to the Supreme Court. Finally, under pressure from the union, which had voted to strike over nonenforcement, President Truman seized the plant, whereupon the company immediately filed its appeal.[54]

The other suits of this kind were less significant but contributed to the force of the delaying action.

Terminating seizure. Ten legal moves (nine by company managements and one by labor organizations) were made during the president's actual possession of business property in the attempts to have the courts rule such possession unlawful and to have them order the property returned to private hands. In addition, the government itself began two suits that were intended to establish the lawfulness of its possession and to obtain court orders restraining the company executives from interfering with federal operations. (The two government suits, both against Montgomery Ward & Co., were, of course, opposed by the company.) Altogether, therefore, there have been 12 legal moves (during 10 seizures) in which the primary issue has been the continuance or termination of government possession.[55] In addition, the government has had to defend the lawfulness of seizure in several other cases in which the point was raised incidentally to other legal issues.

The object of the companies and labor organizations that participated in the 12 cases involving possible termination of seizure by the courts was (with one exception) to prevent the enforcement of terms of employment reached through the government's program for peaceful adjustment of disputes, and to bring the disputes back into the arena of private economic warfare. The winning party in each of these cases, of course, was fully satisfied to have seizure continue. The one exception among the 12 cases was the Commercial Cable Co., a subsidiary of the Mackay Companies, whose suit for an injunction to terminate seizure arose from the efforts of the seizing agency to consolidate its cable services with those of its competitor, Western Union, rather than from efforts to enforce the labor recommendations of the first NWLB.

Only one of the 12 cases resulted in a final determination by the Supreme Court that the seizure was unlawful. This was the suit of the steel companies against Secretary of Commerce Sawyer in 1952.[56] The ruling, although unique, had important consequences. It resulted, first, in relinquishment of possession by President Truman, followed by an industrywide strike and the granting by the companies of most of the concessions the Wage Stabilization Board had recommended. It resulted, second, in the refusal of Congress to continue the disputes-settlement powers of the president's Wage Stabilization Board, and before long in the abandonment of even the stabilization functions of the board. In summary, the steel companies' suit appears to have gained them a political victory at the cost of a 53-day shutdown.

The other suits and motions seeking to terminate seizures either were not appealed after dismissal in the district courts or they were declared moot because the economic issues had been settled before the courts could reach a final determination of the legal issues. The latter circumstance is quite significant. The judicial process is generally too slow to yield final solutions in emergency periods. Either the emergency will come to an end, or the parties will reach some other solution before the lawyers and judges can complete their consideration of the relative merits of the conflicting rights involved.

In these circumstances, it is not surprising that the primary interest of the disputing parties, and of the executive branch of the government, too, has been in the initial decisions of the lower courts and in the interim arrangements approved by the courts at any level, pending appeal of the initial decisions. There have been, so far, five initial decisions that specific seizures were unlawful.[57] There have been three initial decisions upholding the legality of the seizures.[58] No matter which way the decision went, however, the losing party has asked for an interim "stay" of the order, and the winning party has often come back with a request for "modification" of the "stay." The point to watch, therefore, the real focus of interest, has been the courts' decisions as to the interim terms of employment and the interim powers of the seizing agency during the lengthy litigation.

The reasons for this concentration upon the intermediate arrangements may be understood in terms of economic pressures. The bargaining dispute is inevitably between one party who desires a change in conditions of employment and one who opposes it. The dispute is given urgency by the fact that general economic conditions are rapidly changing (as always occurs in periods of war, or of mobilization, or of demobilization). But there is another and even more important element of pressure. Congress and the executive agencies are endeavoring to stabilize and control the rate and nature of economic change. The seizure is aimed at enforcing a rate and kind of change believed by the president and executive agencies to be equitable and in the national interest. It is important to effectuate this program before economic conditions get out of hand and the program loses its largely voluntary support. It will be too late to apply war controls after the war has ended.

One other significant element in these interim orders is that the plea before the court is that of a single private organization to hold up the government's program because the petitioner has lost a decision under that program. It is not a suit between the original private disputants, but an appeal to one branch of the federal government to delay the work of another branch at a time of national economic crisis—often at a time of grave military peril.

This explains why some of the courts in both world wars and in the Korean emergency have refused to grant interim orders interrupting the president's program of wage stabilization and peaceful disputes-settlement while hearing complaints against the program; and why some courts also have stayed orders issued by the courts below. Several judges have authorized the seizing agencies to proceed in full control of the interim operations of the seized businesses, while the legal issues were being argued and decided in court. Under such orders, the economic interests of the plaintiffs have been regarded as protected by the constitutional guarantee of "just compensation." Other courts, however, have issued preliminary or interim orders that directly curbed the seizing agencies and halted the federal program of wage stabilization and peaceful settlement of disputes.

As already noted, five seizures were held to have been unlawful by the district courts. Two of these were allowed to proceed without any court interference, pending further consideration of the legal issues—T. P. & W. R.R. and Fox Coal Co. This leaves three seizures in which the orders of the lower courts immediately curbed presidential control, on the plea of private management, pending final decisions as to the validity of the seizures —Montgomery Ward, Humble Oil, and basic steel. Two of the latter were interim rulings leaving the seizing agency in possession of the business but forbidding it to make any changes in the terms or conditions of employment. These orders were in effect at Montgomery Ward's facilities in seven cities from January 27 to June 26, 1945 (a period of five months) and in the seized steel mills from May 3 to June 2, 1952 (a period of one month). In the steel mill case, a more liberal view almost prevailed. On May 1, the court of appeals of the District of Columbia refused the companies' request to forbid the president to make unilateral changes in terms of employment, pending the appeal, but, on May 3, the Supreme Court adopted the conventional view freezing the pre-existing terms.

The third ruling that disrupted seizure control was an *ex parte* restraining order that forbade the seizing agency's representative to have possession of the business at all. This was in effect at the Ingleside, Texas, refinery of the Humble Oil & Refining Co. from June 6 to June 22, 1945.

In these three cases, the courts, in effect, required the employees and the unions to bear the hardships of delay, while the companies continued to enjoy the arrangements they desired. This was known as "maintaining the status quo." That this was advantageous to the companies is shown by their strong pleas for these arrangements.

Ward's, in June 1945, although seeking to terminate government possession, nevertheless urged the court of appeals to let the army continue in interim possession, in order "to insure against recurrence of labor disputes," while also begging the court to keep the five-month ban on changes in terms of employment (imposed by the lower court), since the changes would be very costly to Ward's. This argument asked the court of appeals to use the seizure power, which Ward's condemned, to enforce Ward's own maximum bargaining demands against the union—terms already rejected by the NWLB and by the president of the United States as contrary to the public interest in wartime. Such an interim arrangement actually had given Ward's, for five months, more than it could have obtained by winning the suit. The court of appeals, taking into account all the equities, rejected the plea.[59]

Seven years later, in another but less serious war situation, the steel companies urged almost identical arrangements upon both the appeals court and Supreme Court, stating frankly that the interim changes which President Truman was expected to make would not only be costly but would alter the relative "bargaining positions" of labor and management to labor's advantage. On this occasion, the Supreme Court overruled the appeals court and granted the steel companies' request.[60] Both Ward's and the steel companies urged these arrangements in the name of "maintaining the status quo"; but, as someone has remarked, everything really depends on *whose* "status" is being maintained—capital's, labor's, or the public's.

That the suits seeking to terminate the seizures were merely adjuncts of bargaining is indicated by the fact that seven of the nine companies involved refused to observe any orders of the president or of the seizing agency from the moment of seizure. The company executives were insubordinate without waiting to learn whether the seizure was lawful or not. Neither did they wait for the courts to issue interim orders. From the beginning of seizure, they enforced in their plants, by economic means, the conditions of employment they sought to establish in the courts as a matter of right. This was perhaps because the mere bringing of these suits during seizure did not halt the enforcement of the control-program, as did the bringing of the preventive suits prior to seizure. Hence, the economic resistance was begun as a kind of private restraining order that would be immediately effective.

But the three restraining orders actually issued by the courts during seizure, which we have mentioned, did paralyze the federal seizing agencies at once, and added to the delay already caused by the preventive suits. These orders left the president's representatives in nominal possession of great industrial properties but without any control over them. The "status quo" order at Montgomery Ward's, for example, added another five months to the 15 months of delay already caused by the company's preventive actions in the federal courts. This was a remarkable feat of obstruction, which not only postponed the application of the federal labor-control program at Ward's through most of a long and desperate war, but weakened the program elsewhere by raising doubts as to the legality and even the propriety of its use against management. The feat is the more notable in view of the fact that the program which it weakened had been supported initially by the representatives of major business and labor organizations and had been ratified subsequently by Congress in the War Labor Disputes Act.

Mr. Avery evidently found a loophole in the WLDA as effective as the one John L. Lewis had found. Mr. Avery's loophole was the claim that his company was not important to the war effort and should be exempted from the war-labor program; but he used the occasion to attack the program itself as it applied to the management of any firm or industry. There is no question that the companies in these legal actions had political as well as legal objections to the entire control-programs, and that through these interim orders they achieved more than they could have achieved through favorable, final decisions of the courts.

But this is not all that the status quo orders did. They also affected important changes in the seizure process itself which are of particular interest in our study of seizure. The orders forbidding the seizing agency to make any interim changes in the seized business—issued specifically in the Ward and steel cases, and even more broadly in the Humble case—effectively shifted the interim control from the seizing agencies to the courts. The civilian and military personnel at the plants, although subordinates of the president, were thereafter expected to carry out the courts' interim orders, and to disregard specific orders of the president. It is a remarkable fact that the two presidents against whom these interim orders were directed—Franklin D. Roosevelt and Harry Truman—accepted them immediately and required their subordinates to comply with them completely.

The presidents have not always shown such complacence in the face of court interference. President Lincoln refused to recognize the writ of habeas corpus issued by Chief Justice Taney during the early military crisis of the Civil War. President Theodore Roosevelt instructed Major General John M. Schofield to pay no heed "to any authority, judicial or otherwise; except mine," if it should be found necessary for him to take over the operation of the anthracite mines toward the end of the five-month strike of 1902. President Franklin Roosevelt countered the Supreme Court's overruling of his reform legislation by a proposal in 1937 to retire superannuated justices and to enlarge the court.[61]

Yet F.D.R. acquiesced in the policy of delaying the enforcement of his wartime program of disputes-settlement so long as the prevent-seizure suits were being argued and weighed in the federal court. After Mr. Avery had lost his preventive suits, however, President Roosevelt reseized Ward's properties and assigned the administrative task to the War Department. The latter quickly overcame Mr. Avery's economic resistance. But when Mr. Avery won the preliminary round of a new legal battle, and the district judge not only ruled the seizure unlawful but froze the status quo, Mr. Roosevelt was en route to Yalta. In his absence, the government bowed to the vague and oral economic command of the court, and so nullified the

War Department's achievement of managerial control. We can only specu-
late as to whether the president would have decided any differently if he
had been in Washington and in health. As it was, he returned from Yalta
ill and died before the circuit court of appeals acted to restore the War
Department's—and the president's—authority at Ward's.

Two episodes in which the seizing agencies showed certain signs of
independence with respect to judicial behavior should be noticed in this
connection. One incident occurred in Roosevelt's administration, and one
in Truman's. So far as we know, the matters were never referred to the
White House, but were decided at the cabinet or little-cabinet level in
Washington. Both were instances in which the seizing agencies refused to
comply with *ex parte* restraining orders issued against them (or their
representatives at the seized properties) by federal district judges. In the
first instance, Secretary of the Navy Forrestal, Chairman McNutt of the
WMC, and Chairman Davis of the NWLB II, were forbidden to continue
certain economic sanctions in force in a seized machine shop in San
Francisco (Judge Michael J. Roche, September 20, 1944); and the second
was the order, already referred to, in which Judge T. M. Kennerly forbade
the district representative of the PAW from taking or maintaining possession
of the Ingleside refinery of the Humble Oil & Refining Co. (June 6, 1945).

In the San Francisco case, the general counsel of the Navy Department is
said to have advised the seizing officers that the court's *ex parte* order had
been issued without justification and should not be complied with; and it
was not. Instead, the U.S. attorney at San Francisco reportedly obtained
an informal understanding with Judge Roche that the order would not
be enforced and would be considered merely as a rule to show cause.[62]
In the Humble Oil case, the PAW refused to remove the notices of seizure
it had posted on the refinery bulletin boards, and took the position that
the court order restrained only its district representative and not the PAW
itself. Even so, the agency sent no one else to the plant until Judge
Kennerly had held hearings on the matter and had set aside the writ.[63]

The most momentous situation in seizure history, from the constitutional
standpoint, was, of course, the steel-seizure case of 1952 in which President Truman claimed to have seizure powers which neither Congress nor
the courts could take from him.[64] The crisis receded, however, when Mr.
Truman not only complied with the Supreme Court's interim order forbidding any changes in the terms of employment in the seized industry but
announced that he would abide by the final decision of the court no matter
which way it went.[65] When the court ruled the seizure unlawful, he faith-
fully and promptly relinquished possession. While the Truman decision
avoided any constitutional issue over the relations between the executive
and judicial branches of the government, his attitude toward the legislative

branch in this situation was anything but acquiescent. Telling his aides he intended to put the cat on Congress's back, he went personally to the Capitol and asked them to provide a remedy for the industrywide steel strike which followed the resumption of private control.[66] When Congress replied by voting down two seizure bills and "requesting" instead that he meet the steel-production emergency by using the Taft-Hartley Act's injunction procedure, he firmly refused; and there the issue rested.

But the status quo order had still another effect upon seizure: it converted a presidential seizure into an old-fashioned strikebreaking operation. It not only retained the ban against stoppages, but also ruled (for an indefinite period) in favor of a continuance of the terms of employment favored by management. This made the seizure no different from an injunction, Taft-Hartley type or otherwise, except that its duration was not specified but continued until the court changed the order or finally disposed of the case. Such an order prevents the adjustment of wages and working conditions either in the interests of efficient production, or of equitable treatment of the employees. It removes the most distinctive feature of seizure—the assumption of the role of temporary employer, and the managerial responsibilities that go with it, by the executive branch of the government.

President Truman said in his *Midyear Economic Report,* July 19, 1952 (p. 13): "Any action by the government requiring resumption of operations, without touching upon the issues at stake, is an intervention regardless of the merits on the side of that party which desires no change."

This point was the very basis upon which the majority of the Supreme Court discriminated between a presidentially obtained injunction without seizure and one obtained with seizure in the United Mine Workers' case (330 U.S. 258). The court unanimously condemned the injunction without seizure as forbidden by the Norris-LaGuardia Act (47 Stat. 70); but a majority of the justices held an injunction with seizure to be lawful because seizure made the government the temporary employer of the miners, responsible for the interim terms and conditions of employment, whereas an injunction alone would have forced the men to work at terms fixed (and desired) by the private management.

Looking now at the Supreme Court's unanimous order in the steel-seizure case (*Youngstown* v. *Sawyer,* 343 U.S. 937) enforcing the terms desired by private management in the government-operated steel industry, as an interim measure, one wonders if the court has abandoned the careful discrimination of the United Mine Workers' case between just and unjust forms of judicial restraint. Has the court now dealt the Norris-LaGuardia Act a more severe blow by forbidding the president to exercise the responsibilities of a just employer during seizure? If the interim order in the steel-seizure case becomes a precedent, private employers could convert any seizure into the equivalent of an old-time injunction by bringing an equity suit against the seizing agency and requesting an interim order enforcing the status quo.

In view of these considerations, we may see why the bringing of injunction suits against the president's seizure representatives became a significant weapon of management in the bargaining struggle over the terms of employment, and why the interim orders of the courts became more important than their final judgments.

The latter point may be further clarified. The suits attacking seizure offered the possibility of an immediate order freezing the status quo, and of an ultimate order returning the business to private control. Of the two, the interim order was clearly the more valuable, since it granted more than the total relief prayed for. The interim order approved the maximum bargaining demands of management and enforced them with the full might of federal power. The ultimate order, if it granted all that management asked for, would merely return the property to private hands and the dispute to collective bargaining. Management would have to negotiate with the union thereafter. This was illustrated in the steel mill case, where the interim order guaranteed the steel companies their full bargaining demands for an additional month, whereas the favorable final order resulted only in the return of their property, followed by a two-month strike and the yielding by the companies to most of the union's demands.

We may also see in these experiences one reason why the National War Labor Board of World War II successfully urged Congress not to provide for judicial review and judicial enforcement of its orders. The board believed that peaceful settlement of labor disputes was indispensable in wartime, and that this could be achieved only through government provision of a swift and equitable means of adjusting the disputes that the parties could not settle by negotiations. The chairman of the board, William H. Davis, wrote to a member of Congress on June 9, 1943:

It is the unanimous opinion of the industry, public, and labor members of the war labor board that, if the board's proceedings are to terminate in court, its utility will be seriously impaired. We are authorized by the secretaries of war and navy to state on their behalf that the delay consequent on judicial review of the board's decisions would substantially and seriously impair the production of munitions of war.[67]

A system of judicial review and enforcement of board orders would have required more lengthy and formal proceedings by the board itself. It also would have required—whenever the losing party appealed from the board's decision—a further series of hearings and decisions in the regular courts. The board hoped to avoid this by keeping its decisions purely "advisory," and by leaving any enforcement against noncomplying companies or unions up to the president. But although Congress complied with the board's request, the board did not altogether escape judicial review and delay. We have just seen how the management of several large corporations improvised a method of delaying the enforcement of board orders by applying for court injunctions, either before or during seizure, against the president's representatives.

The use of court proceedings by Montgomery Ward, United States Gypsum, Humble Oil, and the steel industry to obstruct seizure proved to be a more effective form of interference than refusal to cooperate in the plants. Although the president can replace insubordinate executives in seized businesses, he cannot replace uncooperative judges; nor can he disregard judicial orders without raising grave political and constitutional issues. Thus, there seems to be no satisfactory escape from this form of resistance if wealthy corporations choose to employ it in war crises. But we can build certain defenses against such obstruction.

The first requirement of a wartime labor program, if it is to be armored against the attacks of some future Sewell Avery, is that it should be written into a law that is unequivocally applicable to all major industries. The law should not exempt half the economy from participation in the war effort, leaving one half controlled and the other half engaged in industrial warfare.

The next requirement would be either a wider voluntary adoption by the courts of the role described above of protecting the status quo of the war program, during litigation over it, instead of protecting the status quo of the corporations' collective bargaining positions; or if the courts reject this role, Congress could authorize the president, in seizure cases, not only to put into effect the decisions of a wage board or disputes-settlement board, but to continue the decisions in effect during the pendency of any litigation, until and unless the decisions should be found to be unlawful in a final decree of the Supreme Court.

There is also the possibility of making any future war-labor program (or emergency-disputes program) enforceable and reviewable in the courts. The government's experience with the Montgomery Ward case led many federal officials to believe that court enforcement would be more effective against Mr. Avery than seizure had been. It induced President Roosevelt to order the drafting of a bill along this line. But the public members of the NWLB urged simply an amendment of the National War Labor Act to bring firms engaged in "distribution and transportation" under the same seizure provisions as those engaged in "manufacture, production, or mining" (sec. 3). This would have closed Mr. Avery's loophole without opening new channels of court delay to his battery of skilled attorneys. President Roosevelt, at the time he signed the executive order for the second seizure of Ward's retail properties (December 1944), directed the attorney general's office to prepare a bill for introduction in Congress that would amend the WLDA to make decisions of the NWLB judicially enforceable and reviewable. Further impetus was added to this assignment when Judge Sullivan ruled the Ward seizure unlawful on January 27, 1945. The draft was not completed, however, until after Mr. Roosevelt's death on April 12, 1945. The proposed bill was submitted to an interagency conference presided over by Fred M. Vinson, director of OWMR, on May 3, 1945, and was unanimously approved. But nothing further was done at once, and on June 8, 1945, the Seventh Circuit Court of Appeals overruled Judge Sullivan (by a vote of two to one) and held Ward's seizure legal. The plan thus petered out.[68]

Some corrective action by the Truman administration undoubtedly would have been taken if the appeals court had invalidated the Ward seizure, but the two to one decision of the appellate body that the seizure had been legal under the WLDA as it stood (the word "production" being stretched by the court to cover Ward's business activities), and the ending of the war soon thereafter, took the steam out of official efforts to strengthen the WLDA. The administration's proposed bill was not even presented to Congress. However, if we are to learn anything from the World War II experience, we ought not, in any future crisis, to re-enact such legislation without securely plugging the loopholes through which Sewell Avery and John L. Lewis attacked the national disputes-settlement program during that lengthy war.

In reviewing these cases, one gains the impression that the crucial element is how much force Congress wishes the president to exercise in seizure cases. The ability of the president to maintain production in seized businesses, and to observe the terms of employment which have been established by federal authority, depends to a large extent on the existence of a clearly written seizure law embracing all industries, giving the president control of the terms of employment, and containing adequate penalties. In the absence of such a law, individual citizens, unions, and corporations rightfully expect the courts to protect them as they endeavor to win the labor disputes through private bargaining without interference from the White House.

It is a heartening fact that the courts remained open for such purposes in the midst of the greatest war in American history. Yet the task of prosecuting such a war successfully, with the least possible sacrifice of individual economic freedom, requires the energies and ingenuity of all branches of the government, and the cooperation of all elements of the people. When Congress is timid about spelling out the necessary individual sacrifices, the president and the executive agencies are naturally impelled by the war urgencies to do it themselves, thus enlarging the area of personal government. Then the irate individuals rush to the courts and seek to have seizure ruled unlawful, or at least delayed indefinitely; or they seek to have specific orders of the president concerning the seized properties ruled unlawful, or at least stayed during protracted litigation, perhaps until the end of the war; and so the courts find that they, instead of Congress, have the responsibility of working out the details of the compromise between war urgency and individual freedoms.

POLITICAL PROTESTS

Under our government of divided powers, there are two forms of appeal against the decisions of the president. One is to the courts; the other is to Congress. As we have seen, the courts are available for complaints that the law has been improperly administered in a particular case or that the law itself is unconstitutional. Likewise Congress is available for complaints that the law is bad or weak and should be changed in the public interest or that the law has been misinterpreted by both the president and the courts and should be clarified.

In the history of seizure, both labor and management have appealed to Congress on a number of occasions against presidential actions—frequently with success. The normal pattern is for the party which has lost the decision before the presidential disputes-settlement board and then has lost the routine appeal to the president himself to appear before a congressional committee and complain that it has been unjustly treated and that there should be a new law. This complaint sometimes accompanies the filing of a suit in court; sometimes it is an alternative to court action. In one curious case, a group of business firms appealed to Congress to pass a law compelling the president to seize them—and Congress did.

The appeal to Congress is, in effect, the appeal to public opinion. It is not a technical complaint, as in court litigation; it is an appeal to the public's sense of justice and national policy. Hence the losers in seizure cases have usually publicized their views through speeches, interviews, and printed literature. Their intention clearly has been twofold: to bring pressure upon Congress to act in their behalf, and to prepare the way for a possible electoral change in the political complexion of Congress or of the presidency.

Political action of this sort is the constitutional right of every individual and group. It differs from the economic and judicial forms of obstruction that have been discussed previously in that it relates to broad public policy as well as to the specific equities of a particular dispute. The protesting party must generalize from its own situation and show that its adverse position under seizure is not mere economic misfortune, but the result of an unjust feature of existing law. To obtain corrective legislation, it must convince the public and Congress (or at least Congress) that the employment of seizure in its case represents a general policy that is either too strict or too lenient for the national good.

Fortunately, the right of political protest has remained virtually unimpaired even in our most serious wars—the Civil War and two world wars. The government's conduct of these wars and its policies toward the civilian population, including labor, has been subject to searching scrutiny in Congress, in the press, and from the platform, during the height of hostilities. In the Civil War, Congress had its "committee on the conduct of the war"; in World War I, several investigating committees; and in World War II, the Truman committee and others. The findings of these committees, and of the public, often resulted in important changes in military and economic policy by Congress and the president. Moreover, national elections were held in each of these wars, at the normal intervals, with the opposition candidates only slightly less insulting to each other than in normal, peacetime campaigning. In one of these wars (World War I) a change in party control of Congress was voted near the end of hostilities (November 8, 1918), and during a lesser struggle (the Korean War) a complete change of administration was voted well before the shooting ended (November 1952).[69]

In the presidential seizures that occurred in these wars, the losing party freely voiced its complaints by one means or another. And in eight of these seizures, it gained at least some measure of relief against the president through the help of that independent branch of the government. (See Table 3.) For reasons that may become clearer as we go along, most of these political successes were by business managements rather than by labor unions.

The methods of agitation employed when the protesting party has been management have included the issuance of pamphlets and press releases, the insertion of ads in newspapers and magazines, the writing of special articles for magazines and newspapers, and the distribution of circular letters to stockholders, customers, and suppliers. In the field of spoken communication, they have included speeches before the National Press Club (Washington), at business organizations and stockholders' meetings, and over the radio and television. Some of the printed and oral material has suggested that the public send its protests to members of Congress. The political methods of management have also included direct communication with members of Congress by telegram and letter as well as testimony before congressional committees. The methods employed by the unions have been similar, except that they have appealed particularly to their own memberships and to other labor organizations for political support. A resounding forum for labor protests on one occasion was the annual AFL convention (June 1919).

Among the unions, political protests have been directed most often against presidential abridgements of the right to strike in wartime. It has been only in wartime, of course, that any general curtailment of this right has been imposed; but it is in wartime that labor is in most demand and that its bargaining position is strongest. Hence union leaders have turned angrily to Congress for help when they have believed that the presidents were assuming control of labor disputes without adequately meeting union requirements. Their protests have taken the form of demands that Congress should continue (or restore) the right to strike, even under war conditions. Such demands have been presented to Congress by important unions in three wars—the Civil War, Second World War, and Korean War. Nevertheless, these demands, in each case, have been ineffective, with the important exception of delaying for two years, in the Second World War, the adoption of antistrike (seizure) legislation.

The protests of large unions against all legal restraints upon the right to strike have placed Congress between the cross fires of national and special interests. No matter what it does, Congress cannot please everybody. The opposition of both the AFL and CIO unions to seizure legislation in 1941 led President Roosevelt to suggest to Senator Tom Connally (D), Texas, that the seizure bill be handled through the Judiciary Committee, of which Senator Connally was chairman, rather than through the Labor Committee which the president regarded as union dominated.[70] Through this strategy, the Smith-Connally bill (or War Labor Disputes Act) was passed at last in June 1943, after two years' delay, authorizing the president to seize mines and war plants in labor disputes, and making a strike in a seized facility a crime. Even then, the act came under constant attack from union officials (as well as from Sewell Avery), and was subject, as we have seen, to several forms of evasion. After V-E Day, several unions began a new drive to repeal the act; but Congress refused to alter it, and the law remained on the books, as originally intended, until the end of the hostilities was proclaimed by President Truman on December 31, 1946.

The other failures of labor leaders to obtain repeal of seizure legislation in wartime occurred in the Civil War and in the Korean War. In both wars, the railroad brotherhoods were incensed at the president and the War Department for using wartime railroad-seizure legislation to break strikes and to deny (or limit) wage increases on the railroads. Their political protests, however, failed to induce Congress, in either case, to modify or to repeal the seizure act. Indeed, in the Korean War, Congress repeatedly extended the duration of the act to make sure no strike occurred.

The only real political victories of the unions in protest against presidential actions in seizure cases relate to peripheral matters: the defeat of President Truman's request for extreme penalties to be added to the Smith-Connally Act during the two-day shutdown of all the railroads in May 1946, and the directing of congressional attention to mine-safety enforcement during the bituminous coal operation of 1946–1947. The entire labor movement united to prevent enactment of the first; and the United Mine Workers successfully obtained the adoption of mildly remedial legislation in the second.

On the whole, Congress appears to have recognized the strength of public opposition to strikes in wartime, and to national transportation strikes at any time. But in deference to the unions, it has often added provisos to antistrike (seizure) statutes, stating that nothing shall be done by the president under these statutes "inconsistent" with the permanent labor laws guaranteeing the right to strike. This legislative equivocation has added to the uncertainties of administering the statutes, has prolonged strikes, and has left the president, as we have seen, helpless at times to aid the unions themselves against noncomplying managements. Leaving the reconciliation of conflicting clauses to the president, to the seizing agencies, and to the courts, has simply added to industrial anarchy in times of national crisis.

On management's side, the protests against presidential action have followed two lines of thought: protest against restraint of the right to engage in economic warfare with their employees in resisting the employees' demands; or protest against unsatisfactory financial compensation and damages for the period of government control. Three specific examples of the first and four of the second are identified in Table 3.

The protests of business management have been more often acceptable to Congress than those of the unions. Probably this is because in four of seven cases of management's protest, the company executives showed that their resentment over the higher wages imposed by the president would be considerably placated by a compensatory rate (or price) increase, and/or by a liberal settlement of claims for damages and government "use" of their property. For example, in World War I, the compensation arrangements made by the government for the seized railroads were so generous that 855 independent "short-line" railroads protested to Congress at being left out of the seizure. Congress brought them in, over the protests of President Wilson. As the war came to an end, the railroads and the seized wire systems protested that President Wilson appeared to be offering them the alternatives of nationalization or immediate return to private operation.

TABLE 3
PROTESTS TO CONGRESS AGAINST SEIZURE ACTIONS

Emergency	Issue	Source	Result[a]
	Labor		
Civil War	Right to strike over wage demands	Railroad train crews	Lost (R)
World War II	Right to strike over wage demands	Coal miners, some machinists, truck drivers, etc.	Lost (D)
Postwar II readjustment	Moderation in seizure penalties	Railroad train crews	Won (D)
Postwar II readjustment	Federal mine-safety enforcement	Soft coal miners	Won (in part) (R)
Cold war & Korean War	Right to strike over wage demands	Railroad train crews	Lost (R) (D)
	Management		
World War I	Just compensation and continuation of seizure	Short-line railroads	Won (D)
Postwar I readjustment	Just compensation and termination of seizure	Major railroads	Won (R)
Postwar I readjustment	Just compensation and termination of seizure	A.T. & T. and Western Union	Won (R)
World War II	Right to engage in economic warfare with employees	T.P. & W. R.R., S. A. Woods Machine Co., Montgomery Ward & Co., etc.	Lost (D)
Postwar II readjustment	Right to engage in economic warfare with employees	Steel companies owning coal mines (foremen issue)	Won (R)
Postwar II readjustment	Just compensation after termination of seizure	Midwest trucking firms	Won (R)
Korean War	Right to engage in economic warfare with employees	Major steel companies	Won (D)

[a] R = Republican; D = Democrat (Congressional majority).

The giant utilities wanted neither of these frightful choices. What they wanted was a temporary continuance of government control—fully protected against strikes—while they obtained from Congress additional benefits on rates and guaranteed earnings to tide them over the postwar readjustment. Through skillful political maneuvering, they obtained this very result. The protests of 103 midwest trucking firms after World War II were no less generously answered by the Congress.

One obvious explanation of these political victories for business management is that Congress could please the companies without displeasing the unions. The guaranteed rates and earnings did not eliminate the wage increases but offset them. The only economic losers in these arrangements were the consumers, who paid the added costs either in higher charges for essential services or in higher taxes for the federal subsidies.

Congress had a more delicate problem in those other protests in which management asserted the right to deal with their employees through individual or collective bargaining—regardless of the stage of war mobilization (that is to say, without seizure). The legislators appear to have solved this problem according to the seriousness of the war emergency. In those protests which arose during active hostilities in World War II (such as Montgomery Ward), Congress made no concessions in the law. However, in those arising in lesser emergencies—the readjustment after World War II and the truce-negotiation stalemate of the Korean War—Congress sided with management against the president and recommended full freedom of action for the companies.

In all these problems, there is a temptation to accept a much simpler explanation of congressional response. This explanation would be that Republican Congresses always granted the appeals of business management, while the Democratic Congresses always granted the appeals of labor. While this is partly true, it is not wholly true; and to the extent it is true I would question its significance. A glance at Table 3 will show that Republican Congresses have supported all the protests of business management against the presidents, and that they have rejected two appeals of labor while granting only one. But the record of the Democratic Congresses is not so neatly converse as one might expect to find it. The table shows that the Democratic Congresses also have rejected two appeals of labor while granting only one; and that they have supported two of the protests of business against the president (including the major steel companies in 1952) and rejected only one.

The really significant question would seem to be: Would Congress really have done differently under the same circumstances if the other party had been in control? In my judgment, the particular circumstances, especially the degree of national mobilization then in effect, has been the major influence upon these congressional decisions. We may notice that during the periods of active hostilities of both world wars the Democratic Party was in control, whereas in the periods of readjustment immediately afterward the Republican Party was in control. This fact alone introduces a correlation between party and emergency that would reduce the significance of any seeming correlation between party and policy.

If, then, we leave aside partisan considerations, we may summarize the results of 12 political appeals to Congress against the president's seizure actions as follows: Congress supported eight of the 12 appeals—two out of the five from labor and six out of the seven from management.

It now remains for us to see what the effect of this congressional support on the seizure operations was. What was the reaction of the presidents to the repudiation of their seizure policies by Congress? The answer is that the presidents acquiesced in the congressional "veto" of their policies in four cases but refused to do so in four others. In four of the protests the presidents signed the bills Congress had passed and thus frankly shifted their positions; in two others the presidents vetoed the bills, but in the latter two instances Congress repassed the bill over President Truman's veto (the Taft-Hartley bill).

The remaining three examples of presidential reaction involved more serious resistance than vetoes. The reactions of the presidents in these cases at least partly nullified the intent of Congress. In the first—the "short-line" railroad case of 1918–1920—President Wilson played political leapfrog with Congress for three years and apparently won in the end. Wilson's director general of railroads, William G. McAdoo, had announced at the start of the railroad takeover that the government did not intend to extend its guarantee of profitable earnings to the hundreds of short-line railroads, most of which had been impoverished by the rising costs that accompanied the war. Three times, however, Congress passed legislation to require the same generous public treatment for these lines as for the major railroads, and each time Wilson nimbly leaped over the legislation, once by a veto and twice by supplying his own interpretation to the short-line clauses of the laws.

In the second case of presidential evasion of a congressional seizure decision, President Truman applied against John L. Lewis and the United Mine Workers one of the penalties which Congress had failed to give him earlier in the year for possible use against the railroad and maritime unions. This was an antistrike injunction. When the soft coal miners struck in November 1946, Mr. Truman did not repeat his request to Congress for seizure penalties. He asked the federal courts for an injunction, and they gave it. However, it should not be overlooked that the two houses of

Congress had each separately approved the use of the injunction in seizure cases as a result of Mr. Truman's earlier appeal.

The third presidential evasion of a congressional seizure decision occurred in the steel industry case of 1952. While President Truman scrupulously complied with the Supreme Court's ruling that the seizure was illegal and relinquished possession of the steel mills, he refused to carry out Congress's explicit "request" that he appoint a Taft-Hartley fact-finding board and obtain a Taft-Hartley 80-day antistrike injunction and conduct a Taft-Hartley vote among the employees on the industry's last offer. He firmly refused to reintervene with an injunction in behalf of the steel companies. Instead, he returned the dispute to collective bargaining and allowed the union and the companies to fight it out in the free market. This obviously meant that the steel industry accomplished only half its objective. The industry did not wish to settle the dispute in the free market any more than the union did; but each wished to have the government intervene on its side. The views of the steel companies, as presented to the Senate Labor Committee by John A. Stephens, vice-president in charge of industrial relations of United States Steel Co., included opposition to a continuance of seizure and the substitution for seizure of an indefinite antistrike injunction.[71] The end result, therefore, might well be considered a draw.

In sum, it appears that the "losing party" in presidential seizure cases has several times successfully appealed presidential decisions by political agitation. The appeal to Congress has been successful in eight instances; but, of these, the president has evaded the congressional intent (at least in part) in three. The right of political protest, nevertheless, remains an important and fundamental right—a safeguard against possible presidential abuse of seizure power. Those who protest in this manner, however, have the burden of proving that what they propose in lieu of the president's actions will be more truly in the national interest—that it will not merely improve their bargaining or financial position at the expense of others but will be better for the nation.

CHAPTER 3

Methods of Overcoming Resistance to Seizure Control

Seizure has been subject to contradictory myths. One, dealt with in the last chapter, held that the mere proclamation of government seizure and operation of industrial property in a labor dispute automatically ended the dispute and any work stoppage. Another has been the exact opposite, claiming that presidential seizure was a mere "paper tiger," a pretense of power, in which labor and management have been left as free as ever to bring pressures against each other through interruptions of essential production. The experience with seizure runs between these extremes.

Although the presidents and their subordinates have encountered serious resistance from the parties in conducting some of the seizures, they have devised face-saving and coercive means of overcoming this resistance. Contrary to the "paper tiger" view of seizure, the president's occupation of a firm or industry in an emergency dispute—if done with the support or acquiescence of Congress and the Supreme Court—puts the government in a strong position to resist economic pressures from special interests. To be sure, this governmental strength does not manifest itself automatically; but the record shows that the presidents have developed, in their temporary role of combined industrial manager and military commander of seized enterprises, unique and powerful instruments of both persuasion and compulsion. They have used these instruments to obtain the cooperation or reluctant compliance of interests which had defied the national wage stabilization and disputes-settlement programs.

SAVING FACE FOR THE DISPUTING PARTIES

The presidents and seizing officials have developed concepts and practices designed to induce the prompt and voluntary acceptance of presidential control by all the parties in a dispute, in order to avoid the necessity (insofar as this is possible) of applying coercive measures such as economic and military sanctions.

The government officials have relied, first, upon the natural patriotic appeal and face-saving effect of seizure brought about by the government's assumption of responsibility for the continuity of production and for the interim terms of employment, pending an agreement or the ending of the emergency.[1] The compulsion of seizure gave the disputing parties a face-saving pretext as well as an obligation for yielding extreme positions and for accepting government mediation or arbitration of their differences.

Warnings. The public has become familiar with the measures normally taken at the start of every seizure to warn the disputing parties of the fact of government possession—the posting of notices, the raising of the flag, the issuance of statements to the press and over the radio and television. It is less familiar, perhaps, with certain other steps which have necessarily been taken privately, and with some that have been taken only in special circumstances.

The first step taken by the seizing agency designated by the president has been to notify the owners of the property. In single-plant seizures, the seizing agency has usually sent a high-ranking official to the plant with credentials and notices. In two seizures the Navy Department was embarrassed because it had not been supplied with any written order by the White House (the Federal Shipbuilding and General Cable cases). Secretary of the Navy Knox was obliged to send Rear Admiral Harold G. Bowen to these important firms with oral orders only. Later, the admiral obtained copies of the presidential executive orders from the newspapers.[2]

The seizing official has served the notices upon the highest company executive available, usually the president, asking if the management would cooperate with the president of the United States throughout the government's possession. In cases where the seizure was the result of the private management's defiance of an order from the war labor board or from the president of the United States, the answer to this question was generally "no," whereupon coercive measures had to be taken. In cases where labor had been defiant, the answer from the company management was almost invariably "yes."

In multiplant seizures, the means of notifying the owners has varied. Often the seizing agency has sent junior officers around to each plant with official papers. In the oil refinery seizure of October 1945, it appears to have taken nearly two weeks for navy officers to arrive at all 53 plants.[3] Usually, the seizing agencies have merely sent telegrams to the heads of the numerous companies. This was the practice in industrywide takeovers, such as coal.

In two smaller cases (midwest trucking and San Francisco machine shops), the government assembled representatives of all the companies in meeting halls and explained the policies to be followed, both asking and answering questions. Despite the hostility of the trucking firms, which had been seized because of management noncompliance, the ODT obtained assurance of cooperation from all of the 103 seized companies as well as from the union. Later, however, three of the firms refused to execute the orders of the ODT, making coercive measures necessary. In the San

Francisco machine-shop case, the management of the 104 seized companies cooperated throughout government possession, although the union did not.

The next step by the seizing officials was almost always to confer with strike leaders and with the union officers even when there was no strike. This was usually done by sending the labor-relations specialist on the seizing officer's staff. Occasionally, the top government official would receive the union chieftains in his office. In multiplant seizures, the director of the seizing agency either conferred in Washington with the officers of the national union or sent telegrams from Washington (occasionally the telephone was used) to the union's national headquarters. On one occasion, Secretary of War Stimson addressed all the railroad employees by radio (December 27, 1943). In every case, the union representatives were asked if they would cooperate fully with the president of the United States throughout the period of government possession.

When the seized plant had been shut down for several weeks, it was generally necessary to communicate individually with strikers who lived at a distance or who were out of the city. Despite the wonders of the modern press, radio, and television, there were always some who did not "get the word." Then, too, in some types of plants, it was necessary to bring in the foremen and maintenance crews ahead of the operating personnel in order to clean, repair, and prepare the machinery for resumption of operations. These key personnel usually were notified by telephone.

In taking these steps, the seizing officials have tried to make it clear that seizure was not a nominal or token affair but an exercise of federal control. They have included in many of the posted notices and in some of the telegrams and personal interviews a reminder that the federal law forbade interference with government operation of the seized plants by strike, lockout, or other obstruction. They have frequently included a summary or quotation of the penalty provisions of the law, together with a warning that "all legal and proper measures and sanctions available" will be taken if obstruction is encountered. In nearly all the cases cited in this section, the action of the seizing agencies was followed by the full cooperation of all the parties throughout federal possession.

Most helpful to the seizing authorities in these situations have been the efforts of national officers of the unions involved to convince the local union leaders and the union members that they should honor their contracts and their "no-strike" pledges and accept the jurisdiction of the government's disputes-settlement procedures.

A more serious form of warning has been the appearance of agents of the Federal Bureau of Investigation or of the intelligence division of one of the armed services in the communities affected by the stoppages of production. These agents have interrogated strikers and company executives in numerous seizures (just before and just after the takeover) to find out the nature of the dispute, the attitudes of those involved, and (in the cases of the FBI) the possible occurrence of any violations of law, and (in cases of the military investigators) the possible need for troops to preserve order.

The most formidable warning, of course, has been the actual preparation for the use of troops. While this is implicit in every seizure conducted by the president as the "commander in chief of the armed forces," and while the use of troops usually has been directly authorized in the president's seizure order, the actual movement of the soldiers close to the seized plant has shown in several cases that seizure was more than just a formality. In six seizures, the alerting or moving of troops occurred without the need for their use. The use of troops as a coercive sanction in cases of actual resistance to presidential authority occurred in 13 other seizures.

Very elaborate preparations were made by the army in two seizures which were entrusted to it directly in the winter of 1943–1944—the nationwide railroad takeover of December 1943, and the seizing of the water and power department of the city of Los Angeles, at the request of Mayor Fletcher Bowron, in February 1944. In both these situations, the army alerted troops for two purposes—not only to preserve order but also to operate the seized equipment. The troops were not needed for either purpose, however, since the employees and unions involved called off their strikes and cooperated fully with the War Department.[4] How far this readiness of the army to meet any continuance of the strike during government possession contributed to the calling off of the strikes is impossible to estimate. An unknown factor is how well known the army's preparations were to the union leaders. In certain other cases, it is clear that the strike leaders underestimated the army's capabilities.

Troops were deployed in strength in the seizure of the Cities Service refinery at Lake Charles, Louisiana, in April 1945. Armed soldiers were stationed both inside and outside the refinery to prevent damage to equipment and a recurrence of the mass picketing and blocking of highways that had marked the stoppage prior to seizure. It is pleasing to report that, with the arrival of the troops, the pickets immediately were withdrawn; and, after a mass meeting conducted by seizing officials of PAW and army officers, the workers resumed production.[5]

Two other cases ought to be referred to briefly in which troops were employed or made ready. One of these was the novel use of two naval shore patrolmen at each of the 53 seized oil properties in October 1945 to raise the flag each morning and to lower it at night in strict military manner, thus emphasizing the patriotic aspects and coercive possibilities of seizure. The other was the moving of a military police battalion into South Park,

Pittsburgh, 11 miles from the track of the Monongahela Connecting R.R., when the road was seized in June 1946. In both cases, all the parties cooperated fully throughout government possession.[6]

The kind of warnings described, combined with the forms of assurances which follow, served to convince even the parties who believed they were the losers in the seizures that they should cooperate with the president and seizure officials in 25 of the 71 seizure cases. The losers in these cases appear to have been convinced that they would have lost more by a test of strength with the government than by accepting the seizure and making the best of it.

It is worth noting that of these 25 cases of full cooperation, 21 involved stoppages of production in effect on the day of seizure, three had stoppages scheduled soon to begin, and only one involved no immediate threat of a stoppage.

Assurances. The assurance of justice in the interim operation of seized properties and in the concurrent mediation of the related disputes is the saving grace of the seizure method. Without it, presidential seizure becomes merely the executive equivalent of a court injunction. While seizure has been used occasionally in a one-sided manner merely to suppress a strike without consideration of the workers' demands or merely to coerce the business management into accepting the workers' demands before terminating the strike, there has been a considerable tradition built up by the seizing agencies of scrupulous regard for the rights of both disputing parties. This has been especially true of the War Department (now the Department of the Army), which has handled about half the seizure cases for the president (34 out of 71 cases).

The evolution of seizure policies that have safeguarded the rights of both disputing parties while fulfilling the primary purpose of protecting the public interest in uninterrupted production has come slowly through seizure experience in four wars and several lesser crises. A series of such rules has been developed and made standard procedure by the more experienced federal agencies. These rules have been incorporated into the executive orders of the presidents in the later seizures. They show the unusual capacity of seizure as an emergency technique for establishing just economic relationships as well as for suppressing private industrial warfare. This capacity for the equitable direction of a private business for a temporary period has not been found in the antistrike injunction or in the criminal arrest of strikers. On the other hand, we should remember that the best social machinery cannot give justice unless it is operated with wisdom and impartiality.

The earliest forms of equitable and face-saving assurances given by seizing officials were to the stockholders and managers of seized firms.

This should not be surprising. The suppression of strikes had been practiced by government without apology; but the forceable seizure of industrial property, even as a war measure, so shocked the general public as to draw the most solicitous statements from our presidents and the most generous provisions from Congress regardless of political party.

The earliest forms of such assurance were: The government regards itself as a trustee for the owners of the property, promising to return it to them in as good or better condition than it was received and with just compensation for its use. The assurance to the owners that they would be fully protected against damage and loss of revenue due to government use is probably a derivative of the constitutional requirement that private property shall not be taken for public use without "just compensation" (Amendment V). Such assurance is contained in the earliest known statute authorizing seizures, the Railroad and Telegraph Control Act of January 31, 1862 (12 Stat. 334), which was used in the first known labor seizure, that of the Philadelphia & Reading R.R. in July 1864. The act provides for the appointment of three commissioners by the president "to assess and determine the damages suffered, or the compensation to which any railroad or telegraph company may be entitled." The earliest theoretical expression the author has found that the president and the seizing agency were virtually trustees for the owners is in the statement of President Wilson when taking possession of the railroads in December 1917: "Investors in railway securities may rest assured that their rights and interests will be as scrupulously looked after by the government as they could be by the directors of the several railway systems." The government will interfere as little as possible with the normal functions of management in cases where management accepts the president's authority in labor matters. These two concepts were developed by the Lincoln administration during the Civil War, and were extended by the Wilson, Roosevelt and Truman administrations in World Wars I and II.

Such assurances were balanced by the Wilson administration in World War I with the following pledges directed to the employees and unions: The government recognizes its obligation to the employees of the business to see that they are compensated adequately and treated justly in return for their services to the government. The government will modify the existing practices of collective bargaining as little as possible beyond requiring that there shall be no interruptions of production. These policies were continued in World War II by the Roosevelt and Truman administrations.

Then, in World War II, even more sophisticated forms of face-saving assurances were added to the list by Roosevelt and Truman: The government will protect its employees against physical violence at their place of work, going to and from work, and in their homes. President Roosevelt, upon taking possession of the North American Aviation plant at Los Angeles in June 1941, said, "The Army has been directed to afford protection to all workers entering or leaving the plant, and in their own homes."[7] The government may approve specific procedural arrangements, not affecting the merits of the dispute, to protect and preserve the basic positions of the parties pending either an agreement or the ending of the emergency, whichever occurs first. The government offers to the disputing parties, in disputes not previously adjudicated, a peaceful and just method for the settlement of their dispute through government mediation or arbitration. The government accepts responsibility for the interim terms of employment during its possession and for the enforcement of peaceful means of adjustment for the balance of the emergency; hence it assures both parties that in acquiescing in these arrangements they are not prejudicing their basic bargaining positions, but are remaining free to reassert these positions when the emergency is over and to resume the use of economic weapons against each other.

Some of these forms of assurances have had especial significance with respect to seizures that were due originally to noncompliance with a disputes-board decision. For example, when seizure was intended to enforce compliance by a defiant group of employees, management needed to be convinced that its normal activities would be interfered with as little as possible; otherwise seizure would have penalized the party that had been cooperating with the president as well as the one that had been defying him. The reciprocal of this was needed in the case of a seizure due to managerial defiance of a labor-board decision; then labor needed to be assured it would not be penalized for its cooperation by having its normal collective-bargaining rights modified by the seizing officials beyond the necessary minimum.

A more difficult problem arose in trying to find means to reassure the defiant party in noncompliance cases—the dissatisfied party, which considered itself the "loser" of the decision. The government assured these parties on several occasions that the accommodation required of them was purely temporary—for the duration of the emergency only—and without prejudice to their initial (extreme) bargaining position. They were advised that after the war or emergency had passed, they would be free to resume the normal methods of industrial warfare, including strikes and lockouts, in support of their original demands.

This concept is quite logically derived from the semivoluntary, emergency nature of seizure, and appears to have been a major influence in enlisting the cooperation of several noncomplying managements and unions in World War II. It exemplifies the underlying fact that seizure does not compel a basic settlement, although it frequently induces one. Seizure is neither compulsory arbitration in the usual sense nor a compulsory final settlement in any sense. Seizure is semivoluntary in that the parties are urged but not required to reach a permanent settlement, and in that if any arrangement is imposed upon them it is temporary and without prejudice to their basic positions.

Nevertheless, these assuring facts about seizure left more than half the noncomplying parties unsatisfied; and they refused to cooperate with the seizing officials by resuming production. Some of the counterarguments that figured in this continued resistance were: once a change has been adopted in wages or union security, it cannot easily be reversed; the "temporary" sacrifice asked of them was excessive; and wage issues are always related to current economic conditions and so are not deferrable.

Turning to seizures that occurred in unadjudicated disputes, we find that all the above assurances have been useful, and that they have obtained the cooperation of management and/or of labor more frequently than in noncompliance cases. The problem in stoppages of this kind, where no government decision on the merits has yet been given, is to convince the parties that all the arrangements during seizure, including those for the adjustment of the dispute, will be sufficiently equitable to justify their acceptance without a struggle.

Such assurances have gained management's cooperation in virtually every case, but have failed often with the employees and unions. Probably this is because seizure's first effect is to ban the strike—labor's best weapon—without injuring management either in its bargaining position or its property rights; whereas the employees, if they agree to give up the strike weapon, become subject entirely to the adjustment procedures and interim terms adopted by the government.

Artificial face-saving devices. One of the forms of assurance mentioned was the granting of a specific procedural concession to one of the parties, not affecting the merits of the dispute, to protect further the party's basic position against the possibility of permanent compromise during federal control.

The forms of procedural arrangements, granted to labor by the government, have been: a promise that any wage increase mediated or arbitrated during government possession would be retroactive, at least to the date of seizure; discharge of substitute employees (strikebreakers) who had been hired by private management during the strike preceding seizure and reinstatement, without discrimination, of the regular employees who had struck prior to seizure; an interim compromise between rival unions to protect their positions until the proper government agencies should decide the representation dispute.

Those granted to management have been: discharge of employees who had engaged in violence prior to seizure during the strike against private management; permission to the company to withhold its labor-relations records from the seizing officials on the ground that such data are "privileged and confidential"; an agreement that no official of the seized company would be required to take any step to effectuate the order of the National War Labor Board, but that all such steps would be taken exclusively by seizing officials.

Such artificial arrangements require special attention because they are easily confused with certain other actions of the government during seizure.

First, they can be confused with the interim terms of employment. The artificial devices genuinely protect the relative bargaining strengths of the contending parties, pending either an agreement or the end of the emergency; whereas the government's choice of interim terms of employment prejudges the dispute and directly influences the relative bargaining strengths of the parties.

Second, these procedural devices, although frequently agreed to by the government before a resumption of production by the parties, are also to be distinguished from the substantive concessions (bearing upon the merits of the dispute) that were sometimes granted by the presidents and seizing agencies—concessions that were considered to indicate a lack of full governmental control. While both these concessions were granted under "pressure"—that is, prior to the requesting party's promise to cooperate with the president—the procedural concessions differ from the substantive ones in that they do not compromise the government's wage-price policies, nor do they injure the bargaining position of the opposite party.

The effectiveness of these arrangements, like that of the coercive penalties also used by the presidents, is difficult to measure because so many other influences were brought to bear upon the parties before they decided to accept or to reject presidential control. All that we can compute factually is the number of these concessions that were followed by the cooperation of the party they were granted to. By this test, we find that 10 of the 20 procedural concessions granted to labor were followed by the cooperation of the employees and unions involved, and that two of the three concessions given to management were followed by management cooperation. Since two of the labor concessions were made in the same seizure case (Toledo, Peoria & Western R.R.), we may modify the first figure to say that the procedural devices used to protect the basic position of labor were followed by labor's cooperation in nine out of 19 seizure cases.

Possibly a more helpful analysis could be made by examining the record of each device separately. This suggests that the discharge of strikebreakers hired prior to seizure by private management and the temporary freezing of union representation disputes have been useful devices on a number of occasions contributing to the cooperation of unions and employees during seizure; that a couple of rather remarkable concessions to management have served to appease them in the seizures of two giant corporations (without granting any substantive demands); but that the much-heralded and much-used promise of retroactive pay was frequently ineffectual in gaining the cooperation of labor during seizures.

The use of retroactivity in seizure as a means of obtaining the cooperation of labor pending an agreement or decision on the merits of the dispute calls for some discussion, not only because of the frequency of such use (in 14 seizure cases) but because of its somewhat analogous use by National War Labor Board II in settling many hundreds of dispute cases.[8] The two uses, while the same in principle, were somewhat different in application and effectiveness. Its use by NWLB II was under a system that amounted to voluntary arbitration by the majority of firms and unions of the country. The board could effectively promise that any wage increase would be made retroactive to the date the board took jurisdiction because representatives of management had agreed to abide by all decisions of the board. The seizure cases, however, were ones in which one or both of the parties had rejected the jurisdiction of the board, and in which voluntary compliance was lacking.

In considering the use of retroactivity in seizure cases, therefore, we should distinguish two problems: the question of what to do about prior awards of disputes-settlement agencies directing retroactive wage changes; and the question of what to do about wage disputes in which no such awards had been made. The latter has led to presidential promises that any wage increases mediated or arbitrated during government possession would be made retroactive at least to the date of seizure. It may be said briefly here that the payment of wage increases that had accrued prior to seizure was at first refused by the seizing agencies and later, on direct orders of President F. D. Roosevelt, was carried out only if the "net operating revenues" of the seized companies were sufficient. These restrictions prevented the payment of retroactive sums in several seizure cases.[9]

The promise of retroactivity in connection with wage disputes that were unsettled at the time of seizure appears to have been frequently unsuccessful as a face-saving device. Out of the 14 cases, labor refused (when asked at the start of seizure) to withdraw its strike pressures and to assure the government of uninterrupted production in six, and it interrupted production in three others after first agreeing to work.

An examination of the cases in each of these categories discloses some interesting facts. The six cases in which labor refused to cooperate at the start were all instances of labor's noncompliance (prior to seizure) with disputes-board decisions—cases in which the avowed purpose of the strikes was to induce the government to reconsider its decisions and to grant more favorable terms to the unions. The three in which the union's cooperation was only temporary consisted of one case of labor's noncompliance, one in which no previous disputes-board decision had been made, and one in which a previous disputes-board decision had been accepted by the union but rejected by the companies. The strike in the last was, of course, to bring pressure upon both the government and the industry to enforce and to accept the disputes-board decision or something close to it. The five cases, in which labor cooperated from start to finish, consisted of two cases in which the unions sought enforcement and acceptance of prior disputes-board decisions satisfactory to themselves; two in which no previous disputes-board decisions had been made; and one in which labor had rejected the recommendations of a presidential emergency board. In the latter case, President Roosevelt had agreed to review the recommendations of the emergency board before the seizure occurred.

The above record appears to indicate that the employees and unions accepted the assurance of retroactivity and resumed work in seizures in which the government already had ruled satisfactorily to them or in which they expected a satisfactory ruling; whereas they disregarded the retroactive promise and turned the strike pressure against the government in seizures in which the government already had taken a position unsatisfactory to them or in which they were unsure of the government's favor. Surely labor knew that the value of a promise of retroactivity depends upon the size of the wage increase ultimately adopted, either as an interim federal order or as a final settlement. Certainly they were also aware that a promise of retroactivity is irrelevant and inapplicable to many noneconomic issues—union security, for example. Unions that have carried their disputes to the point of requiring presidential seizure are apparently not generally willing to yield up the right to strike—even against the government—in return for a mere promise of retroactive wage payments in an otherwise unsatisfactory settlement.

COERCIVE MEASURES

When one or more of the disputing parties refuses to accept the face-saving opportunities of seizure, as a substitute for normal industrial warfare, the president has available an arsenal of more serious measures that he may use to "enforce industrial peace" among the resisting parties.

It should be observed that the mere assertion of government possession in a presidential order or proclamation is not coercive until and unless implemented, but it establishes the government's new position in that plant or industry. It may be said, by way of analogy, that the American Declaration of Independence was an assertion of power which had to be effectuated by forceful measures.

These additional measures have been termed "coercive" to emphasize that they are intended primarily as pressures, not as punishments. They are intended to bring about acceptance, however reluctant and belated it may be, of the peaceful procedures under the control of the president.

When the president and his subordinates apply these additional pressures, they continue to emphasize the warnings and assurances that had been given previously and that will continue to save face for the offending group and so make its ultimate acquiescence easier. Whether the new measures are added a few at a time or applied all at once in a crushing blow, the object of the government remains the same—to induce acceptance of peaceful procedures.

The coercive measures may be aimed at gaining control of the physical property and its operations, or at inducing a final settlement of the dispute. We shall be concerned in this chapter only with the first of these objectives— interim control of operations.

The various coercive measures available to the presidents for inflicting loss or social humiliation on defiant parties during seizure are summarized below under the headings of moral, economic, military, judicial, and legislative sanctions. This array of measures at the president's disposal suggests the flexibility of pressures—both as to degree and kind of pressures—that have been brought to bear against obstructive parties in labor seizures.

Moral sanctions: Presidential warnings and assurances.
Economic sanctions:
  a. Imposed directly by the seizing agency
     1. Discharge, demotion, or temporary replacement of strikers, executives, or other employees.
     2. Control of interim terms of employment.
     3. Control of funds of the company; control over the payment of dividends; control over production, sales, advertising, procurement, and investment policies.
     4. Extension of possession to additional property of the same or another company.
  b. Imposed with the cooperation of other executive departments of the federal government
     1. Manpower sanctions: denial of clearance; denial of referral to other jobs; blacklisting.

2. Withdrawal of vacation privileges and union-security privileges previously granted by federal disputes-settlement boards.
3. Cancellation or transfer of a company's procurement contracts.
4. Development of alternative means of services and supply.

Military sanctions: Imposed with the cooperation of the Department of Defense, the armed forces, and the selective service system

1. Occupation of buildings; possession of equipment, books of account, and funds; exclusion of unauthorized persons.
2. Protection of seized property and of the persons therein; policing of adjacent areas and workers' residential areas.
3. Recall of reserve personnel to active duty in specialized industrial tasks; direct commissioning of experienced civilians.
4. Cancellation or modification of individuals' draft exemptions and deferments.
5. Drafting of employees for noncombat military duty at the seized plant.

Judicial sanctions: Imposed with the cooperation of the Department of Justice and the federal courts

1. Criminal prosecution for statutory violations.
2. Antistrike and other court injunctions with prosecution for contempt.
3. Condemnation of private property for public use (either temporary or permanent).

Legislative sanctions: Imposed with the concurrence of Congress

1. Presidential recommendations for *ad hoc* procedural or substantive legislation.
2. Presidential recommendation for new, but applicable, general legislation.

Of the five classes of penalty, three come directly within the authority of the president as chief executive and commander in chief. These are the moral, economic, and military sanctions. The presidents, therefore, have placed principal reliance upon these measures in instances of obstruction during seizure operations. The other two classes of penalty, the judicial and legislative, require the cooperation of the other major branches of the federal government—the courts and Congress. So the presidents have turned to them only when the executive measures have been insufficient.

The moral, economic, and military measures have provided a remarkably flexible combination of mild, moderate, and formidable pressures at the president's immediate command. All three have been combined and blended in varying patterns in every seizure. It is the economic measures, however, that have been the most appropriate, the most frequently relied upon, and, generally speaking, the most effective.

Of the economic sanctions, the following have been the most important in inducing the cooperation of recalcitrant individuals and groups with the president:

(1) *The power to hire and fire.* This ancient strikebreaking weapon has been employed against company executives as well as against striking employees under the following rules: When the defiant parties have withdrawn voluntarily from the operation, they have been replaced (whenever possible) until such time as they consented to return and to accept the president's authority, or until the end of the emergency, whichever occurred sooner. When the defiant parties have continued at work but refused to obey presidential orders, they have been discharged and replaced by those who would carry out such orders. In some cases, those discharged have returned and offered to obey presidential orders, if reinstated; they have usually been reinstated without penalty (though initially on probation). The government service has proved a considerable reservoir of temporary replacements for both management and labor.

(2) *Control of the interim terms of labor.* This includes salaries of executives, wages and working conditions of other employees, and the status of unions. Control has been exercised as follows: consideration of changes requested by the obstructing parties has usually been delayed until the obstruction ceased; changes unfavorable to the obstructing parties have been made on several occasions as a further means of pressure.

These economic measures have been particularly appropriate for dealing with an economic dispute and for suppressing a kind of private warfare which (although contrary to the public interest in wartime) consists solely of exerting bargaining pressures against one another. The suppression of industrial warfare in time of national emergency poses a special problem, since such warfare is entirely legal (and indeed is considered a proper expression of the freedom of private contracts) in time of peace.

Seizure enables the president to turn the bargaining weapons of noncooperating individuals and groups against themselves, without necessarily stooping to bargain with the defiant party (though this has sometimes been done). The president's use of the removal power and replacement power under seizure and his control of the terms of employment involves no arrest, no violence, no imprisonment, no stigma of criminality. It does act coercively, however, by causing loss of income, personal inconvenience, and social humiliation. When successful in the president's hands, it results in a bargaining defeat for some especially hard bargainers. It thus makes the "punishment" fit the "crime."

The primary economic weapons have been supplemented occasionally by other economic sanctions, such as the manpower penalties used in a half dozen seizure cases: workers who had been deferred for military service because of their war work and who were discharged by the seizing agency were reclassified by selective service and inducted for combat duty. Since this was always preceded by a warning, the effect was to offer to the youthful workers a choice of remaining in war industry under the president's terms or of entering the army. This was known in both world wars as the "work or fight" principle. This choice or penalty was never applied to company executives, although it was contemplated in one or two cases. Many executives were above the draft age. Workers who were not eligible for military service and who were discharged by the seizing agency were denied clearance and referral to other war work by the United States Employment Service. Since this, too, was preceded by a warning, the effect was to offer to the older workers a choice of remaining in war industry under the president's terms, or of moving into nonwar work, or of retiring from the labor force altogether. This device was always joined with the "work or fight" principle, although it actually contradicted it, for it allowed and even encouraged obstructing employees to withdraw from the war effort entirely. It was applied in this form to individual production workers, but several company executives were, in effect, also given the choice of cooperating or of withdrawing thereafter from the war effort. The company executives, who were discharged by the seizing agency, were removed from the war effort; many of them devoted themselves thereafter to attacking the government's war policies politically.

These manpower sanctions, although generally coercive, offered remarkable escape clauses to individuals who conscientiously disapproved of the nation's labor policies. This was comparable to the consideration shown to conscientious objectors.

Company managers and owners. When the company executives have offered physical resistance to the representatives of the president, these gestures have soon been overcome, although in such operations tact has proven as important as tactics on the part of the government officials.

The spectacle of armed soldiers physically carrying out the chairman of a nationwide mail-order company aroused more sympathy for the defiant executive than disapprobation. The same objective was accomplished unobtrusively in other seizures, including a later one of the same mail-order house.

Success in this method was demonstrated by the War and Navy Departments, not by civilian agencies, in the few cases where company executives either withheld their funds, keys, and books, or personally interfered with operations by staging sit-downs or by giving obstructive orders and advice. In the Federal Shipbuilding case, the company president was asked to move his offices to another floor, and, since he was slow in acting, the change was made one evening while he was out. In the S. A. Woods case, the company president was simply not readmitted to the plant on the third day of possession.

The blundering order to remove Sewell Avery by force was given by Undersecretary of Commerce Taylor, on the advice of Attorney General Biddle, not by any official of the War or Navy Departments. His removal failed to gain control of the company's records for the government because the employees continued to obey Mr. Avery (who communicated with them by telephone).

Mr. Biddle, in his memoirs, acknowledged that this had been a tactical mistake. In a frank reassessment of the episode, he pointed out that the show of force had given Mr. Avery a "melodramatic" incident to use in his political campaign against the war-labor program, without having induced any of the employees to acknowledge the authority of the Department of Commerce in the mail-order operations.[10]

The Ward failure was not repeated, however, because President Roosevelt gave responsibility for the second seizure to the secretary of war, not the secretary of commerce; and Secretary of War Stimson with the help of Undersecretary of War Patterson, "captured" Ward's books and funds in seven cities on the fifth day of the takeover by a well-planned, surprise maneuver in which not a single armed soldier was used and no arrests were made.

When Mr. Avery gave the same blunt refusal to the War Department that he had given to the Commerce Department, the War Department made secret preparations over a holiday weekend to gain control of the retail operations. At the opening of business on January 2, 1945, according to a War Department historian, John H. Ohly, a team of carefully selected, unarmed army officers and enlisted men appeared at each Ward store or mail-order house then in government possession. One of the officers took custody of the cash and changed the combination on the safe. Another (an accountant) took possession of the books and cut them off at the time of their seizure. The officer in charge (an experienced businessman in private life) summoned the store manager and asked him to work for the government, taking orders only from the United States Army. The officer warned the manager that if he refused he would be discharged and asked to leave the premises.

For several hours the Ward executives appeared stunned by the blitz. They asked for time, presumably to consult higher company authority in Chicago. Then one by one they came to the War Department representative and announced that they would have to refuse to work for the government. Each manager was then discharged and left the store.

According to Ohly's narrative, other supervisory personnel were then assembled and told that the manager had been discharged, that full government operation was under way, that they must obey government instructions, and that if they refused they, too, would be discharged. Moreover, they were warned the penalties would not stop with their discharge. Sanctions in the form of criminal prosecutions under the WLDA, the cancellation of draft deferments, and blacklisting by the WMC, would be invoked. By nightfall, most subordinate executives had indicated their willingness to cooperate— apparently on orders from Mr. Avery—and had accepted appointments as War Department employees.[11]

The army gained control, not with bayonets, but by a combination of the economic pressures available under seizure and the threat of criminal arrest under the seizure statute.

Later, in the coal mine seizure of 1946, when the owner of a small mine in West Virginia refused to yield the keys of his office and threatened to barricade the mine entrance, the naval officer in charge warned that he would remove any barricades and force open any locked safes; whereupon the owner yielded.

In general, however, company resistance has not been of the physical type, but has consisted of outwardly welcoming the seizing officials while firmly refusing to carry out any of their orders. The obvious response to this has been the discharge of such company officials for the period of government possession, and their replacement by other executives borrowed either from the government service or from private business.

Such officials—usually including the company president—have been replaced in 16 seizure cases (or 76 per cent of the 21 seizures in which company resistance to the president's authority was encountered). This includes the two situations in which the top company officials "walked out" just prior to the arrival of the government officials—a kind of management strike (Ken-Rad Tube & Lamp Corp. and Gaffney Mfg. Co.). The assignment at the very beginning of government officials experienced in the type of businesses being taken over has assured the failure of such "strikes" as these.

The generally small number of company executives makes their replacement relatively easy compared to the replacement of larger numbers of skilled and striking workmen. This is a weapon that defiant companies have not been able to counter successfully, except where the president's seizure authority has been uncertain or his seizing representatives unskilled. Occasionally, certain lesser penalties have been used against company executives: a reduction in salary (Twentieth Century Brass); or transfer to less responsible positions (American R.R. of Porto Rico); but these were special circumstances.

The president's economic weapons are supportable by both military and judicial sanctions. Armed soldiers actually have been used for police purposes in only three instances of managerial resistance (Air Associates, S. A. Woods Machine Co., Montgomery Ward). The judicial sanctions have included the obtaining of two court injunctions forbidding interference with the government's possession and control of the business. A temporary restraining order was obtained against 17 officials of Montgomery Ward & Co. in April 1944; and an injunction was made practically effective a year later in the new Ward seizure after the government's application was approved by the circuit court of appeals and the court refused to limit federal control pending appeal to the Supreme Court.

The application of criminal laws to company managers was contemplated in several instances, but never used—with one tactless exception. In the first seizure of Ward's, the Commerce Department went so far as to arrest the assistant to the operating manager of the company and to charge him with "intent to steal" a government notice which he had removed from the wall of the company's offices; the case was dismissed as moot after return of the property. This is the only known case of the arrest of a company executive in a labor seizure.

The president also has coercive weapons which he may use against obstructing ownership as well as the salaried executives. (In very small firms, the same persons may be both owners and executives.) One is his power to control the funds of the company and to influence new sources of funds, including advance payments on the government compensations under procurement contracts. Akin to this is the power to withhold payments of dividends to stockholders. These collateral economic weapons can be devastating in their effectiveness against small, family-owned businesses with limited financial resources; but they are not so significant against giant corporations.

The big weapons against big corporations are the basic ones of hiring and firing employees, including the top executives, and control of the terms of employment, together with the general control of other operational policies, including purchase of materials, production methods, sales methods, and investment in new plants and equipment. When a government official takes over these responsibilities and powers, even the largest corporations know they have lost the economic struggle with the president and are helpless, except for political or legal protests.

The overcoming of managerial opposition is more difficult, from an economic standpoint, when management is supported by some of the production employees. Then the president may have to overcome a strike or even physical violence as well as surmounting the noncooperation of company officials. In the case of Air Associates, for example, President

Roosevelt had to keep troops at the plant for several weeks because of threats of violence and threats of a sit-down by a group of nonunion workers sympathetic to the old private management.

The president may even be faced with a situation wherein if he enforces a labor-board order against management, one group of employees will strike in support of management, while, if he fails to enforce the order, another group of employees will strike in protest. This was the case at Hughes Tool Co., where the employees were divided between two rival unions. The seizing agency (the army), using the greatest tact, obtained a modification of the original order from the war labor board and managed to win the cooperation of all parties in observing the revised order.

Still another problem of special difficulty for the president and his subordinates is operating an entire industry in which management's co-operation is partly withheld. This has occurred in three instances: the rail-roads, 1918; the midwest trucking firms, a regional group, 1944; and the steel mills, 1952. The opposition was overcome in the first instance by discharging the president of every major railroad and then appointing a federal manager for each road—sometimes the former president, sometimes a subordinate executive of the road. The appointment of regional directors of the railroads also strengthened the government's control. In the next case, the managers of three out of 103 trucking firms were discharged for noncooperation; and in the last case, the president of the United States failed to sustain his right to be in possession when challenged in the courts.

Employees and unions. When the employees of a seized facility refuse to cooperate with the seizing officials, the problem is proportional to the number of employees resisting. A major factor is whether the resistance is supported by national union officials, or only by local union officials or rank-and-file committees.

The immediate objective of the seizing agency has two phases comparable to those found in cases of company resistance: to gain and assure access to the property, protect employees who wish to work, and exclude those who are interfering with operations; to obtain a resumption of operations, either with the regular employees or with temporary replacements.

The first phase of the problem relates to the overcoming of picketing, sabotage of company property, and attacks upon workers either at home, en route to work, or at work. The tactics employed have been those of any restrained, well-disciplined police force, deploying men as plant guards, transport guards, street patrols, and mobile reserves. In addition, the army has leaned heavily on the principle that a massive concentration of forces— a great show of strength—will prevent rather than provoke clashes.

The police tactics, executed with the relatively high discipline found in the federal forces (army, navy, air force, and marine corps) and with the restraint assured by civilian control, have been successful in every case. They have been applied in citywide tieups of streetcar, bus and subway-elevated lines (Philadelphia) and of trucking companies (Chicago). They have been used successfully in strikes of individual railroads, a bomber plant, an oil refinery, a group of towboats, and a single coal mine. All have been effectuated without a single serious injury.

The largest scale of police action was in the Chicago trucking strike in June 1945. In that case, the seizing agency (the Office of Defense Transportation) obtained the cooperation of the War Department and brought 12,000 soldiers into Chicago to serve as guards. The troops were quartered in parks, at a race track, and at five high schools. They rode on trucks and guarded terminals. Strikers who were seen slashing tires or throwing bricks through windshields were turned over to the city police. Full protection was assured, after a few days of confusion, to all drivers and dockers, whether civilian or military.

In this case, and in all the others, the police problem was restricted to a single city or region; and in all, except the New York towboat case, the solution was facilitated by the support given the government by national leaders of the union. Moreover, in the Chicago trucking and the Philadelphia transit strikes, resistance was weakened by division of the employees into rival factions, with leaders of one group urging a return to work for the government while leaders of the other urged continuance of the strike against the government.

Thus it should be noted that the country has never actually experienced the police problem involved in attempting to resume operations in a full industrywide shutdown over the opposition of national union officials. What would occur in such a case can only be speculated.

In the second phase of the problem, the principal means of coercion used by the presidents and their representatives to induce a return to work have been: a refusal to consider or promise any changes in the terms of employment until the men have returned to work; and the use of temporary replacements borrowed from other government departments or from civilian life until the strike is ended. These measures have been supplemented on several occasions by the citation of youthful strikers to their draft boards for reclassification and induction for combat duty; also by citation of older workers to the war manpower commission for denial of referrals to other war work. Another supplementary method has been the development of alternative means of service and supply, such as the use of government-owned transport.

In addition to these economic measures, President Roosevelt on a few occasions turned to the arrest and trial of "wildcat" strike leaders who had urged men to strike and so had interfered with the operation of seized facilities under the War Labor Disputes Act. This technique was limited to situations in which local union leaders or a rank-and-file strike committee flagrantly persisted in urging continuance of the shutdown despite contrary advice of the national union leaders. It was never used against a national officer of a union.

The effectiveness of those measures has virtually paralleled that of the police measures just described, and for almost the same reasons. The principal limiting factor again is the number of employees on strike, but a secondary factor is the kind of skills of those requiring replacement. In the Hughes Tool Co. case, the threat of a few hundred machinists to strike was a greater problem for the War Department than the noncooperation of the top executives of the firm—or than the strike of a far larger number of truck drivers in Chicago—even 14,500 of them. The key to breaking the strike is the government's ability to obtain temporary replacements; and this has proved most practical in the field of transportation (land, sea, and air) because of the large numbers of trained transport personnel in the armed forces. Finally, in most of the cases where the strikes were successfully broken, the strikes did not have the support of national union officials; hence many of the employees had returned voluntarily to work.

Within the limitations described—a single city or group of cities, and a divided union leadership—these measures have been successful in inducing, first, a resumption of production with the substitute workers and non-strikers, and second, the return of the strikers as soon as the effectiveness of the government's measures has been demonstrated.

These limitations, however, explain why the presidents have faced a different and more difficult problem when the national officers of a labor organization have threatened, or brought about, a strike during government possession of an entire industry. When the labor organization has a membership embracing most of the industry, and when a significant part of the work is skilled work, the president clearly is not able, under the scarce labor conditions of an emergency period, to find temporary replacements for the entire group. Thus the economic balance of power will lie with the union whenever it can control most of the supply of one type of skilled labor in a period of high demand.

This kind of problem has developed into actual stoppages in seized industries only once during the "shooting" phase of a major war—the strikes called by John L. Lewis in the coal mines in 1943—but it has been one of the principal economic phenomena of postwar readjustments following each world war. The nation has had several close calls from industrywide strikes during war. In the Civil War, troops had to be maintained in the anthracite fields because of recurring strikes and disorders, but President Lincoln rejected demands that he seize the mines. In World War II, the railroad brotherhoods set the date for a nationwide shutdown (December 30, 1943), but were dissuaded from this by President Roosevelt's seizure of the roads. At about the same time, stoppages in the steel mills became widespread, and President Roosevelt only prevented these from being made official by threatening seizure and intervening in the policies of the National War Labor Board.

CHAPTER 4

The Effectiveness of Seizure
as a Means of Control

In view of the resistance frequently offered by some of the disputing parties to the president's authority during seizure, and of the necessity for full control of industrial operations in order to effectuate congressional purposes, an attempt has been made to evaluate the presidents' success during the 71 seizure cases.

In practice, the seizing agencies consider that they have achieved effective control when the following requirements have been met: the president and his subordinates have unrestricted physical access to the property; a normal number of employees are at work—either the regular force or permanent replacements; the president's orders are being observed throughout the property; there are no threats of later stoppages; and government possession is not subject to termination at a specified date but to cessation when the dispute has been settled or the emergency ended.

This implies that control was not achieved until any strike or lockout had been overcome, terminated, or postponed indefinitely, and until the company management either was carrying out all presidential directives or had been replaced by managers who would do so.

The seizing agencies, of course, did not invent this concept of control; they were merely translating into enforceable terms the basic principles of the statutes as they had been modified or sustained in court litigation. Their duty was to execute the congressional purpose of placing the president temporarily in a combination of military and managerial authority over the physical property, personnel, and industrial operations. To do this, they employed the face-saving and coercive measures that we have examined. Then this control permitted the president to assure the continuance of production on terms that he considered to be equitable and in the public interest; or, alternatively, to mediate an agreement on terms consistent with the public interest. But the uses to which the control was put, and the standards observed in its application, are a separate topic to be examined later.

CASES OF FULL CONTROL

Adopting the above definition, we find that the president and his subordinates achieved full control in 57 of the 71 seizures (80 per cent). In 25 seizures (35 per cent), the president obtained control through the immediate and continued acceptance of his authority by both disputing parties for the duration of government possession.[1] In 32 other seizures (45 per cent), the president overcame acts of resistance by one or more of the disputing parties with coercive measures without granting any concessions or support under pressure to the aggressive party.[2]

Both parties fully cooperating. This concept has been strictly defined, so that any situation of resistance caused by one of the disputing parties during presidential possession excludes that party from the category. The rule has been applied so that a seizure in which a small sit-down occurred among a dozen employees has been scratched from the list of those in which labor fully cooperated, just as surely as one in which all the employees of a plant or industry went on strike. Again if either party accepted the president's authority initially but later reneged, that case, too, is left out. Also a seizure in which the company management went into court and sought an injunction declaring the seizure unlawful has been excluded even though the company may have acquiesced in governmental possession "under protest" pending the outcome of the litigation.

Our observation that 35 per cent of the seizures have been fully cooperative indicates a rather high degree of immediate and voluntary acceptance of federal authority by all the elements of labor and management. Although this percentage is only a little more than one-third, it is the test of perfection from which some of the other cases deviate only in minor respects. It measures the full success of the face-saving principle—the attainment of cooperation by the various warnings and assurances by the president without the actual use of force; but it also indicates the limits of the effectiveness of the face-saving element, because in a substantial majority of the cases coercive measures became necessary.

The record is especially revealing when examined in two parts: (1) the cases known as noncompliance cases, in which one of the parties had precipitated the seizure by refusing to accept the recommendations of the president (or of some presidentially appointed board); and (2) the remaining cases, in which the disputes had not been adjudicated on their merits by any government agency prior to seizure.

In the 43 noncompliance cases, the major problem was obtaining the cooperation of the losers. It was easy enough to obtain the cooperation of the winners. For example, management cooperated fully in every single case of labor's noncompliance. Even so, the record shows the cooperation of about one-third of the losers among both labor and management; and in seven other cases, certain elements on the losing side cooperated fully, reducing the scale of the coercive measures required.

In the 28 unadjudicated cases, no one, of course, was either the winner or the loser at the moment of seizure. We do find an important tendency, however, in that the management has given its full cooperation in 23 of these cases and has also cooperated initially in three other cases. Management has been found to accept presidential control in these unadjudicated controversies because such control takes away the bargaining weapon of the employees and the union—the right to strike. Management either is unaware that seizure also may take away its own control over the terms and conditions of labor, or else it is hopeful that this power will be exercised only in its favor. In three of the cases, some or all of management withdrew its initial cooperation with the president after finding that he was changing the terms and conditions of employment in a manner objectionable to them.[3]

It should not be surprising, then, to find that labor's record of cooperation in these unadjudicated cases is poor. In fact, the employees and union cooperated fully in only 13 cases. In three others the employees and unions cooperated initially, but certain groups later conducted strikes. In the 12 remaining unadjudicated cases, labor withheld its cooperation at first and tried to "bargain" with the president over the terms of its employment.

Resistance overcome. More than one situation of resistance occurred in some of the seizures. This resulted variously from: obstruction by some elements of both labor and management; renewal of obstructive tactics later by the same disputing party; and outbreaks of obstruction by several different elements of labor or management, especially in multifirm seizures of long duration. The latter may involve resistance by employees of different unions or executives of different companies, while those of other unions and companies are cooperating.

Resistance to presidential control by labor (employees and unions) is considered to have been overcome when a strike call has been rescinded or indefinitely postponed by those who called it; or, alternatively, the strike leaders have been arrested, or otherwise discredited, and the regular employees have returned to work in normal numbers; or the government has obtained permanent replacements in the open market. A strike which has merely been postponed to another (announced) date is considered not to have been called off, and is treated as a deliberate interference with presidential control of a seized property.

In cases of obstruction by company executives, the obstruction is regarded as having been overcome when the uncooperative officials have ceased their obstruction or have been replaced by others (private or governmental) who are willing to cooperate with the government during presidential possession; or a court order obtained by company attorneys against seizing officials has expired or been nullified by a higher court. A lockout order or a walkout by company executives is considered ineffective as soon as the company executives have been replaced by others.

Under the above definitions, the effectiveness of the president's use of coercive measures in overcoming obstruction to his control may be summarized like this:

(1) 72 out of 105 situations of resistance that have been identified (or approximately 70 per cent) were brought successfully under control by the presidents through the use of coercive measures. These 105 situations of resistance occurred in 46 of the 71 seizure cases; and 32 of the 46 were brought finally under the president's control (or approximately 70 per cent).[4]

(2) The situations of resistance caused by management were more frequently overcome than those caused by labor. Of 29 situations in which management obstructed the president's control, 24 were overcome by firm measures (approximately 83 per cent). Of 76 situations in which labor obstructed the president's control, 48 were overcome by forceful means (approximately 63 per cent). This is a significant difference between seizure's effect upon management and labor, but it will be noticed that even labor's obstruction was overcome in nearly two-thirds of the situations.

(3) The resistance encountered in relation to the main disputes—the controversies that led to seizure—were more frequently overcome than the resistance arising coincidentally in the course of federal operation in connection with other matters (day-to-day labor relations and production problems). Of 69 instances of resistance related to the main disputes, 51 were overcome by coercive measures (approximately 74 per cent); whereas of 36 instances of resistance related to coincidental disputes, only 21 were overcome (58 per cent).

The degree of success being examined here measures the power of seizure when directly challenged. It is not a measure of the effectiveness of seizure as a whole. It is an attempt to reduce to figures the success of federal coercive measures in overcoming deliberate acts of interference with presidential authority in seized enterprises.

The most important figures in the above summary are those showing that 70 per cent of the resistance situations (72 out of 105 situations) and 70 per cent of the seizure cases marked by instances of resistance (32 out of 46 cases), were brought successfully under the president's control by coercive measures. The test of effective control in seizure cases has been that every situation of resistance has been overcome without yielding concessions—not only situations of resistance related to the main disputes but any arising coincidentally in connection with other matters.

We should remember that these figures do not indicate the extent of seizure control, but only the effectiveness of seizure in one of its two methods of achieving control. The other is the face-saving method resulting in voluntary cooperation "under protest," as previously examined. By adding the two methods, we get a means of estimating the degree of success of the presidents in obtaining uninterrupted production under their interim control. Adding 25 to our 32 seizures, we obtain a figure including both coerced and voluntary acquiescence in the president's seizure power, showing that seizure has enforced peaceful procedures under the control of the national government in a total of 57 cases out of 71 identified seizures. This gives us a percentage of 80 as a measure of the effectiveness of seizure in obtaining such control.[5]

THE TIME CONSUMED IN GAINING CONTROL

The duration of each situation of resistance encountered by the seizing agencies is measured in this section by days, then averaged and classified according to the number of weeks involved.

The interval of obstruction measured will be either from the time of arrival of seizing officials at the property—the moment of actual seizure—to the termination of the obstruction; or from the commencement of obstruction arising during government possession to the termination of the obstruction, as the case may be. In either event, if the obstruction continued until the termination of government possession, then of course it was not overcome; and the latter date will be taken as the date of termination of the period of partial uncontrol.

The specific forms of obstruction to federal authority measured will be those described in Chapter 2, except for the political protests. The obstruction measured will include, therefore, all stoppages of production (strikes, lockouts and sit-downs), serious threats of stoppages, refusals of management to cooperate with the government, refusals of either labor or management to carry out specific orders of the government in the operation of the business (wage changes, union security, overtime work, and so forth) and court proceedings brought by either management or labor in an attempt to restrict or deny the president's control.

All these forms of resistance to the president's assumption of control will be lumped together and measured by only one dimension—time. No distinction will be made as to the kind of resistance or the proportion of employees or executives participating. This is in accord with the practice of the seizing officials of treating each act of resistance by a group of any size as a challenge to their effective control of the business operations in the seized property. They measure their effectiveness by the number of days required to overcome the act of resistance, and so will we in this chapter.

Some of these acts of resistance will be considered to have been overcome in "zero" days. This is a convenience for handling those situations in which defiant management was immediately replaced and also those in which hostile court proceedings resulted in no orders restricting the seizing officials.

In accordance with these definitions, the *cumulative* time record of the seizing agencies in overcoming deliberate acts of resistance in 105 situations is: 39 (37 per cent) overcome in one week or less; 47 (45 per cent) in two weeks or less; 55 (52 per cent) in three weeks or less; 72 (70 per cent) ultimately (including 11 that took more than three weeks and six for which the time is unknown); 33 (30 per cent) never overcome.

The *average* time required to gain control in 66 situations that were "ultimately overcome" (for which data exists) is: five days (median time), 25 days (mean time), and a range of zero to 395 days.

Similar data have been compiled with respect to the time required to gain full control of each seizure case, as distinct from individual situations of resistance. The rule followed has been that no seizure case is considered fully controlled until every situation of resistance therein has been overcome. So the times shown may reflect the longest of several situations of resistance occurring simultaneously or the total of several situations occurring successively.

The *cumulative* time record in gaining full control in 46 seizure cases is: 22 (50 per cent), one week or less; 25 (54 per cent), two weeks or less; 28 (61 per cent), three weeks or less; 32 (70 per cent), ultimately; 14 (30 per cent), never controlled.

The *average* time in 32 cases that were "ultimately" checked is: three and one-fourth days (median time); two and one-half days (mean time), and a range of zero to 395 days.

We may now combine our data on the time required to overcome resistance to presidential control with the data, given previously, as to the number of seizures in which both parties cooperated voluntarily with the president. This will give us the total time record of all seizure cases in establishing uninterrupted production under the interim control of the president.

The *cumulative* time record of 71 cases is: 25 (35 per cent) controlled immediately through voluntary cooperation alone; 47 (66 per cent) in one week or less through coercive measures or voluntary cooperation; 50 (70 per cent) in two weeks or less; 53 (75 per cent) in three weeks or less; 57 (80 per cent) ultimately; 14 (20 per cent) never fully controlled.

The *average* time in 57 cases that were controlled "ultimately" after either voluntary cooperation or resistance is: zero days (median time), 12 days (mean time), with a range of zero to 395 days.

The above data show that the time required to gain control was remarkably short in two-thirds of the seizure cases. Full control was gained immediately in one-third of all presidential seizures through the voluntary cooperation of both parties (the face-saving effect). Full control was obtained in another third of all the seizures within a single week through the application of coercive measures by the seizing agencies with the assistance of other government departments. Hence we may conclude that seizure accomplished its major purpose—gave to the government not only continuous production of essential items but the enforcement of its policies regarding labor-dispute adjustment and wage-price stabilization—either at once or in a very few days—a week at most—in two out of every three uses (47 out of 71 seizures, or 66 per cent).

The record is no less impressive when we see in the data above that the median time required to overcome resistance in 32 seizure cases was only three and one-quarter days—three days or less, in 16 of the cases. The mean time of 21½ days is misleadingly high because of two or three extreme situations.[6] Actually, 29 of the 32 fell below the mean. When we include the cases of voluntary cooperation, as well as of resistance (25 plus 32 equals 57), we find the median time to assure control is "zero" days, that is, immediately, and the mean time is only 12 days despite the same extreme situations.

In analyzing this time record, an interesting point has been a comparison of the time required to overcome situations of management obstruction and situations of labor obstruction. This comparison shows first that management obstruction usually has been overcome more quickly. The median time required among 24 instances of management obstruction was three days, whereas the median time among 36 instances of labor obstruction was seven days. On the other hand, the mean time required showed an opposite result, with the mean labor-resistance situation requiring 28 days and the mean management situation 37 days.

The shorter duration of most management-resistance situations has been because of the relative ease of replacing a few managers who were uncooperative compared to the difficulty of replacing large bodies of skilled workmen who were on strike. The opposite effect, the higher mean time for overcoming management than for overcoming labor resistance, is due to a half dozen extreme resistance situations which raised the average. These were of two types: those in which the government vacillated a long time before ousting defiant company executives, and those in which the companies succeeded in obtaining court orders restraining seizing officials from executing the presidential directives.

Another comparison throws light on the time required to overcome resistance to the president's authority—a comparison of those situations in which resistance arose at the start of the takeovers and those in which resistance arose later during government operations. This comparison shows that the situations of initial obstruction were usually overcome more quickly, the median time among 30 such situations being five days, whereas the median time among 34 resistance situations arising later was seven days. Similarly, the mean time for overcoming situations of initial obstruction was 27 days, while the mean time of overcoming later situations of obstruction was 40 days.

We may conclude, therefore, that seizure gave the government full control of the affected industrial enterprises in 57 of the 71 cases (or 80 per cent), and gave this control swiftly, that is, in one week or less, in 47 cases (82 per cent of the 57, or 66 per cent of the 71). In the remaining 14 cases, the national interest was successfully defied in varying degrees as the presidents either gave up the control attempts or granted certain economic concessions to the defiant parties in order to achieve partial control.

PARTIAL CONTROL

The seizing authorities very early adopted the rule that they would not consider demands submitted by the disputing parties while the latter were on strike or were in any other way exerting economic pressure upon the government. In other words, the seizing agencies, while usually willing to consult with labor and management, would not bargain with them in return for essential production. The War Department officials, who took over the Philadelphia & Reading Railroad in the Civil War, did not even consult with the striking employees, let alone bargain with them. They simply restored railroad operations with their own crews, and left negotiations to the old private management. A definite rule against bargaining with strikers was first formulated and announced by the federal managers of all the railroads and the wire systems in World War I. With some notable exceptions, this rule was observed by them, apparently with the approval of President Wilson.[7]

This policy stemmed from the early view of the government that such presidential bargaining with one of the parties, would put the government in a position of less than full control of the operations of the seized firm or industry. It would subject the government and the nation to impositions by special interest groups either at the expense of the other party or at the expense of the national interest in peaceful procedures and noninflationary settlements or both.

While the official policy of the government has continued in this vein, several minor departures occurred in World War I (none bearing upon the main disputes that led to seizure, however). Then in World War II, the bitter struggle between President Roosevelt and John L. Lewis over the structure and level of wartime wages led to serious departures from the policy, beginning about October 1943. The precedents then established for yielding concessions to striking employees in seized facilities, although maintaining the outward appearance of government "control," were followed on at least three later occasions by President Truman.

Although the government never granted such concessions to management under pressure, it did on several occasions ignominiously abandon the seizure operation without overcoming management's resistance. While only minor instances of this occurred in World War I (none relating to the main disputes), the contest between President Roosevelt and Sewell Avery in World War II over union security was marked by the government's hasty withdrawal from Montgomery Ward & Co. at one stage to regroup its forces (May 1944).

In view of the official government position that seizure is an assertion of public control in a particular dispute, the 33 departures from this position (occurring in 14 seizures) have been grouped in three principal types and assembled for discussion in this section.[8] The main characteristic of all of them is that control has been partially yielded by the president (and his seizure representatives) because of economic or legal resistance by one or more of the disputing parties. The differences relate to the manner in which the presidents conceded part of their authority.

Presidential bargaining over interim terms. One method by which control was partially yielded under pressure from a disputing party was the granting of some of the union's interim demands, while the employees remained on strike or stood ready to strike—the negotiation of favorable terms of employment to be effective during the government's possession until a final agreement was reached between the original disputants (labor and management, or two rival unions) or until the emergency was ended.

Such concessions on the terms of employment gained the union's promise to return to work for the government, at least for the time being, but the government had to remain in possession in order to fulfill its side of the bargain. The return to work may have appeared to some observers as a victory for the government. It may even have seemed a vindication of federal authority by force. Was not the flag flying over the seized plant, and were not posters proclaiming, "This property is now in the possession of the United States"? The use of troops may have been hinted at, and members of the president's cabinet probably figured in the "successful negotiations" with the union officers. Most impressive of all, perhaps, was the undeniable fact that the government was in possession, and production was again under way.

Yet the whole procedure was misleading if the president (or his subordinate) had agreed, under pressure of one of the parties, to terms or procedures which the government otherwise would have rejected as unfair to the other party or as contrary to the public interest. This is true whether the established methods for the peaceful adjustments of disputes simply had been disregarded, or whether the seizing authorities also had conceded interim terms, under pressure, that they themselves (or another federal agency) believed to be unjust or inflationary. Under these circumstances, industrial warfare was not being eliminated but merely redirected; the president was not coercing but being coerced; and federal authority was not vindicated but weakened.

The author's records indicate 21 examples of this type of presidential concession under pressure, occurring in 10 seizure cases. 19 of the concessions were made to labor, and two to management. However, only eight of the situations related to the main disputes which led to seizure. The other examples were in disputes arising coincidentally during the long government possession of major industries.

The principal examples in main disputes were in the industrywide coal seizures of 1943 and 1946, especially the Ickes-Lewis agreement of November 3, 1943, and the Krug-Lewis agreement of May 29, 1946, both negotiated between a member of the president's cabinet and the United Mine Workers during industrywide shutdowns of the government-operated mines. Other concessions on interim arrangements made under strike pressures (and involving main disputes) were: cancellation of fines for a preseizure strike by Pennsylvania and Ohio soft coal miners, May 7, 1943; indefinite deferment of fines for an industrywide strike during the same coal seizure, June 1943; modification of an NWLB order for maintenance of membership at the Hughes Tool Co.; and a government promise to effectuate the recommendations of a fact-finding board in the meat-packing seizure, January 1946. In addition, interim concessions were probably granted to the Iowa coal operators and to the Carter Coal Co. of West Virginia in the coal seizure of 1946–1947 as a result of threatened lockouts by the company managements.

Presidential bargaining over final settlement. A similar comment may be made regarding the second method by which control was partially yielded under pressure of a strike. This method was the negotiation of a final settlement between labor and management, while labor remained on strike or held the threat of an imminent strike over the negotiations, the settlement being followed shortly by the return of the property to private operation.

This method not only brought about production but settled the dispute and quickly re-established private operations. The president appeared to some persons to have taken over the property by force, to have required them to agree, to have ended the stoppage of production, and to have pulled out promptly. The federal policy of requiring a peaceful settlement of disputes appeared again to have been dramatically vindicated.

Yet the procedure here, too, was a mere pretense of force and a deception of the public, if the agreement was reached because the government allowed the union to use the strike weapon exactly as it would have used it in peacetime, and the government added its own pressures to those of the union against the company management or rival union to accept the striking union's demands. Under these circumstances, the president was coercing not the defiant party but the cooperating party; and industrial warfare, instead of being restrained in behalf of higher production, was being indulged.

Two major examples of this have occurred: the bituminous and anthracite coal settlements of 1945, and the "White House agreement" of December 21, 1950, in the rail seizure of 1950–1952, both negotiated during strikes. A minor example was the settlement of the Toledo machine shop dispute involving rival unions in November 1944.

The forms of pressure that may be brought by the government against the cooperating party (that is, against the owners and managers, or against a rival union) in support of the defiant party (the strikers) include threats of putting the strikers' demands into effect for the period of government possession until the owners or rival union accept the terms or the war ends, whichever happens first; promises of government aid if the owners accept the union's demands—aid in the form of price relief, or additional cost allowances in government contracts; and promises of favorable intercession by the seizing agency with other government agencies, such as the National Labor Relations Board. It should be noticed that these pressures are not the sort to be given wide publicity. A clue to the occurrence of such methods, however, is the settlement of the dispute while the strike is still going on, or while a strike is being threatened. When this occurs, the government clearly is allowing the strikers to bring normal collective-bargaining pressures against the other party, in violation of the peaceful procedures established by Congress or by voluntary agreement of other representatives of labor and management; and the chances are that the government also is exerting additional pressures of its own in behalf of the strikers. In any event, one may be sure that full control is being pretended when it really has been partially yielded.

Return of property without control or settlement. This method differs from the two preceding types in that it involves no concessions or assistance to the defiant party under pressure; but it is the same in that it represents a failure to overcome situations of resistance to federal authority.

In the past, this policy has maintained the appearance of successful governmental coercion. The property was either returned to its owners with the bland (but untrue) assertion that "production has been restored to its normal efficiency," or it was retained until the end of the emergency in a state of pretended (but only partial) observance of the president's orders. In fact, the first of these methods returned the dispute to the field of normal, peacetime collective bargaining without having settled it, thus assuring an early resumption of the very industrial warfare which had led to seizure in the first place. The second of these methods merely tolerated for the balance of the emergency a situation in which one of the disputing parties was interrupting production or refusing to observe presidential directives, although the government nominally was operating the business.

Three examples of the first method—the premature relinquishment of possession without having achieved either a settlement or full control—are the coal mine seizure of May 1943, relinquished in October 1943; the Montgomery Ward seizure of April 1944, relinquished in two weeks; and the steel seizure of April 1952, relinquished in June 1952, on orders of the Supreme Court. An example of the second method—retention of possession through the end of the emergency, without achieving either a settlement or control—is the Postal Telegraph phase of the wire seizure of 1918–1919. There were three other instances of successful resistance, without governmental concession, but these affected only disputes arising incidentally in long seizures. Of the four cases involving main disputes, three were triumphs for management, one for the union (Lewis' United Mine Workers in the summer of 1943).

We have now examined three methods by which the presidents have yielded partial control to one of the disputing parties in some 33 situations in 14 of the 71 seizures. To this, a postscript should be added about three of the situations in which concessions were yielded to powerful unions, situations in which the favored unions came back for second helpings and found the president and the seizing agencies ready with coercive measures instead of with more concessions. Two of these were situations in which favorable interim terms had been granted to striking employees: one in an incidental dispute in New York Harbor in 1919, affecting the employees on railroad-owned harbor vessels; and the other in a main dispute—the bituminous coal seizure of 1946–1947. The third was a situation in which presidential support for a favorable final settlement had been given to railroad employees during a strike: the industrywide railroad seizure of 1950–1952. In all these situations, the second-round demands of the unions were refused, and their resistance overcome by force (although the concessions initially granted were continued). In one, however, a third strike-effort by the union resulted in the granting of additional interim concessions: New York Harbor, 1919.

SUMMARY

Seizure, therefore, has proved to be neither a "paper tiger" nor an instrument of absolutism. Its effectiveness as a means of public control in particular disputes has depended primarily on: the concurrence of the three branches of government in its use (no vetoing of presidential action by Congress or the Supreme Court); legislation clearly applicable to the industry in question; and administration of the seizure by one of the armed services (or by a civilian agency equally committed to impartiality between unions and management). In addition, we have noted that control has been more easily and quickly established in cases of management defiance than of union or employee defiance. The most difficult cases have been those instituted by the leaders of large national unions such as the Mine Workers and the railroad brotherhoods—cases which President Truman likened to "insurrection."[9] But Truman himself—by the adroit combination of seizure with the antistrike injunction and with control over the terms of employment—developed the means to maintain national authority in such cases.

PART TWO

Standards of Public Policy During Seizure Operations

There is nothing arbitrary or unjust in it [presidential seizure and operation of the railways] unless it be arbitrarily and unjustly done. It can and should be done with a full and scrupulous regard for the interests and liberties of all concerned as well as for the permanent interests of society itself.

—WOODROW WILSON, annual address
to Congress, December 5, 1916

CHAPTER 5

Keeping Production Going

The forcible withdrawal of the right to strike and to lock out in a particular dispute, without generally denying this right, places the government under the obligation to use this power responsibly. In insisting upon the continuity of production in a particular firm or industry, the government is, in fact, altering the procedure for the determination of wages and other costs in the particular market, without legislating these changes for a whole class of industry. It cannot, therefore, escape the responsibility for the economic consequences of this discriminatory interference with normal market behavior.

The record of seizure experience shows the development over the years of a set of standards of administrative policy by which the presidents and seizing officials have sought to protect the employees, unions, and owners of seized firms from economic loss or social inequity as a result of government operation.

These administrative standards have evolved from provisions in the statutes authorizing seizure, from details in the presidents' executive orders and in their supplementary letters and public statements, from legal opinions of the attorney general, and from decisions of the Supreme Court.

In each seizure, the labor relations and operational problems have been different. Moreover, the presidents have distributed the operational responsibility for labor seizures among 11 different departments and agencies, some of which were quite unprepared for this specialized assignment. Hence the administrative policies followed were often improvised initially over the long-distance telephone between seizing officials at the plants and their superiors at Washington, with occasional reference of an important issue to the White House, provided the president was not out of the country or otherwise preoccupied. Such improvised decisions might then be formalized in the executive order of a subsequent seizure.

In spite of the varied requirements and the administrative inexperience of many officials, a consensus of public policy appears to have developed among the administrators, aided to a large degree by the systematic approach of the department most frequently called upon to operate seized plants and facilities, the Department of the Army, which carried the burden in 34 of the 71 seizures. In World War II, the department (then known as the War Department) concentrated its seizure responsibilities within the labor branch of the industrial personnel division of the army service forces. The experienced industrial relations officers of this branch drew up a set of procedures which they published as a *Seizure Manual* and which they made available to other agencies which were chosen from time to time for seizure responsibilities. The Navy Department, which was given charge over seven labor seizures and several similar operations resulting from procurement problems, also systematized its practice by setting up an "emergency plants operation section" within the office of the assistant secretary of the navy.

So we find that, despite the wide differences in details, several fundamental standards of public policy emerged to guide seizure administrators as they sought to reconcile the requirements of public policy with the various private interests in each dispute while assuring the uninterrupted operation of the seized firm or industry. These standards were closely related to the assurances usually given to the disputing parties by the president at the start of a seizure operation.

The following is an attempt to formulate the principal standards of public policy which appear to have governed operations in the majority of the more recent seizures:

(1) *Keeping production going, without unconstitutional coercion.* To make production mandatory has meant permitting no strikes or lockouts or suspensions of work or organized slowdowns and no willful interference with operations even by individuals; but seizure, in practice, has been neither involuntary servitude nor confiscation of property. Although the government has the right to draft workers under its militia powers in war or other emergencies, seizure has not been a form of national service; the seizing agencies have allowed individual employees to obtain work elsewhere, except when they would have been frozen in their jobs anyway by war manpower controls. Although the government has the power to take property by eminent domain, subject to just compensation, seizure has involved only temporary public use of private facilities, with the owners protected against any loss or damage to physical property and against any loss of income attributable to seizure, and fully compensated for the government's temporary use.

(2) *Enforcement of terms and conditions of employment as found to be equitable and in the public interest by presidentially appointed boards, subject to final review by the president himself.* Such enforcement has been effectuated, in some cases, through the president's interim control over the terms of employment during his possession, and in other cases through his influence upon the terms of settlement that were finally agreed to. But in still other cases, the president has either refrained from taking a position on the merits of the controversy or has modified his position through the process described in the next paragraph. This procedure has amounted to a form of government regulation of wages and industrial relations on a

semivoluntary, case-by-case basis. Although much latitude has been left for collective bargaining, the overall effect, in many cases, has been the imposition of labor standards adopted at the White House.

(3) *Intensified effort to induce a voluntary agreement, on terms mutually satisfactory to the parties and consistent with the public welfare, before the termination of possession.* This goal has been pursued by means of mediation or voluntary arbitration marked by two special requirements: (a) a ban on strikes and lockouts, and (b) representation of the public interest in the terms of settlement during the negotiations. In these negotiations the terms agreed to by the parties and the president have occasionally constituted a modification of the terms proposed initially by a presidentially appointed board; but the standard has nevertheless been an accommodation of all interests, public and private. The rule has been followed that government possession would not be terminated until either the dispute had been fully settled on terms satisfactory to the president, or the need for uninterrupted production had ceased. Thus seizure has combined elements of mediation, voluntary arbitration, and compulsory arbitration without being properly classifiable as either.

(4) *Operating the property in such a manner as to minimize the interference with the normal operations of private management, of collective bargaining, and of regulation by state and federal agencies.* Although the paramountcy of presidential authority during seizure has been affirmed by the Supreme Court, this authority has been exercised with moderation. The presidents and seizing agencies have treated employees as civilian, not military, personnel, and as special government employees, not under civil service. Although the presidents have frequently changed wages and working conditions during government possession, they have ordinarily continued the fringe benefits established by private management and collective bargaining, protected the existing bargaining rights of unions, and permitted state and federal regulatory agencies to carry out their normal functions. However, the exceptions to these generalizations have been sufficient to warrant the conclusion that seizure has not been a paper proceeding but a form of public control. A technique of designating the previous management of the seized firms as managerial agents of the government has been a recent development intended to minimize (but not eliminate) governmental interference with normal managerial authority. In practice, the seizing agencies have fully controlled the labor relations, personnel practices, wages, and working conditions of the seized firms, and in a number of cases also have changed some of the marketing, financial, and operating practices. The rule has been to seek to fulfill the purposes of public policy without showing bias toward either disputing party, without permanent impairment of the rights of employees, unions or property

owners, and without permanent sacrifice of any of the normal standards of
the regulatory agencies of federal and state governments.

These four standards of seizure administration relate, of course, to
important problems of industrial relations and industrial production and
so bear upon the effects and effectiveness of seizure as an instrument of
public control in emergency labor disputes. In Part Two, we examine the
application of these standards in the 71 labor seizures.

THE FREQUENCY OF STOPPAGES

The first standard to be considered in connection with seizure will be
the ability or inability of the disputing parties to strike or to lock out; or,
in other words, the continuity of production. The measure to be used here
will be the number and duration of work stoppages during the government's
possession. This measure will need to be distinguished from those used in
Part One, for it does not indicate, as they did, whether the president has
achieved full control of the industrial operations. It does not show us
whether the government is in a position to carry out such requirements of
public policy as just interim terms of employment, the use of maximum
pressures to induce a settlement, and the enforcement of public standards
of wage stabilization. It will show us whether production is under way,
not who is directing the production.

The data used will be the instances of actual interruptions of production,
measured in days and classified by time dimension only. No distinction will
be made between a shutdown of a single department of a seized factory
and the shutdown of an entire plant or of most of an industry. The subject
being measured is the frequency and duration of work stoppages, regardless
of size or causation. The stoppages may relate to the main dispute that
induced seizure or to another labor dispute that coincidentally came to a
crisis during government possession.

This measure should indicate the extent to which labor and management
or rival unions used the work stoppage during government possession to
bring bargaining pressures against one another or against the government;
and the extent to which they suspended the use of this economic weapon
under the face-saving or coercive influences of seizure.

The stoppages measured include strikes, lockouts, and sit-downs, but
not slowdowns. The time covered is only that part of any stoppage continuing after seizing officials arrived at the property and posted notices of
possession.

Under these definitions, the following data indicate the frequency of
work stoppages during government possession:

(1) 68 stoppages have been identified as occurring during presidential possession. This includes 63 strikes or sit-downs and five lockouts. The stoppages occurred during 31 of the 71 seizures. There were therefore no stoppages in the other 40 seizures, or in about 56 per cent of them.

(2) The stoppages were distributed among 11 seizures that had resulted from labor's noncompliance, five that had resulted from management's noncompliance, and 15 that were initially unadjudicated.[1]

(3) In 12 other situations of resistance to presidential authority, stoppages were threatened by one of the disputing parties but were averted by the seizing agencies through coercive measures or bargaining concessions. These situations occurred during seven seizures. In three of these seizures, strikes were threatened but averted, and in four seizures lockouts were threatened but averted. Two dozen other situations of resistance have been identified which involved no stoppages or threats of stoppage, but instead involved such pressures against the government and the opposite party as management's refusal to cooperate with seizure officials, institution of court proceedings by management against the seizing officials, slowdowns by employees, and nonpayment of union dues (despite an NWLB maintenance-of-membership order).[2]

If it seems surprising that stoppages did occur in 31 seizures, we should note that more than half the stoppages (39 out of 68) were concentrated in only seven of the seizures—seven long industrywide ones (railroads, coal mines, wire systems, and steel mills).

Although almost two-thirds of the stoppages during government possession were terminated within a week, and more than four-fifths were terminated within two weeks, the longer stoppages, although few in number, deserve special attention because they represent the least successful seizures from the standpoint of keeping production going. If we look, therefore, at the stoppages which continued longer than two weeks (15 days or more), we find 11 such situations.

Most interestingly, the stoppages of longest duration turn out to have occurred in the same seizures in which the largest number of stoppages were concentrated. Of the 11 which exceeded two weeks, all but one (Western Electric) occurred in major industries—rails, coal, wires, steel. Three of these were over incidental issues arising after seizure began. Two of the rest were wildcats (the railroad shopmen's walkout of August 1919 and the Pennsylvania bituminous coal wildcats of July 1943). The remaining five were bitter struggles between the president (or seizing agency) and large national unions (Commercial Telegraphers' Union in the wire seizure of 1918–1919; United Mine Workers in two shutdowns in 1943 and one in 1946; Brotherhood of Railroad Trainmen in the yardmen's "sick" strikes in 1951). The five strikes by national unions occurred during postwar readjustments when the wartime urgencies had been (rather unfortunately but generally) relaxed.

CONSTITUTIONAL SAFEGUARDS

The use of compulsion to obtain the continued operation of a firm or industry understandably arouses the fear of excessive intrusion by the government into the operations of the private market. The word "seizure" itself is disturbing in connotation. Even more alarming to many persons is the sight of the president, under either his general powers or under a grant of authority from Congress, taking personal possession of particular firms which he has designated and directing their industrial operations in such details as the hiring and firing of executives and workers, the banning of strikes, and the fixing of rates of pay. Are there any constitutional safeguards to protect the owners of property, the employees of seized firms, and their unions, from the abuses of executive discretion? Have any standards been established in the experience with seizure?

In general, the experience with seizure has shown that the president cannot proceed far without the concurrence of Congress and the Supreme Court. There are legislative and judicial vetoes as well as executive vetoes under our system of divided powers. In a previous chapter, we have encountered more than a dozen actions of Congress in response to protests from either unions or managements of seized plants. We have also noted that the courts have remained open, even in wartime, to complaints that the president or his representatives acted illegally. However, the greatest safeguard against abuse of the seizure power has been a free political system. In three national elections, seizure has been one of the issues that led voters to give the conservative opposition a majority in Congress— 1918, 1946 and 1952. While each of these elections clearly reflected public weariness with a lengthy war, each also involved dissatisfaction with some aspect of seizure, such as the government's direct operation of the railroads in the First World War, the apparent coddling of some unions in the reconversion period after the Second World War, and the bungling of the steel industry case during the Korean War. It seems unquestionable that a free press and free elections tend to restrain the president both in the frequency of his use, and in the manner of his use, of the government's power of seizure.

Duration of seizure. The question of how long production should be made compulsory by seizure has been of direct concern to Congress in its adoption of seizure legislation. In the Civil War and the two world wars, its grant of authority to the president has been explicitly limited to the duration of the war. In peacetime legislation, the authority has been limited to the continuance of emergency conditions as determined by the president. (See Appendix B.) Since the peacetime arrangement opens up the possibility of indefinite government possession, some proposals have been introduced setting specific time limits on seizure or making any seizure's continuance subject to summary termination by Congress at any time. Although none of these proposals has been adopted, the experience with seizure suggests that the latter plan would be the more practical. The other—setting arbitrary time limits—would convert seizure into merely another "cooling-off period," assuring neither settlement of the dispute, nor continuance of production.

During the Civil War, the only seizure was terminated within a few days, immediately upon settlement of the dispute. In the First World War, by contrast, the government was unable to settle the three disputes that led to seizure, and so it retained possession in each case for the war's duration. When seizure was again employed, during the "defense emergency" of 1941, President Roosevelt introduced a policy of seeking to terminate each seizure "as soon as possible," but only if the dispute had been settled or a procedure of peaceful settlement had been accepted by the parties. In subsequent seizures, as explained more fully later, this policy was formalized into retaining possession until one of two conditions was met: either the parties agreed to continue operations without interruption (having either settled their dispute or agreed to a procedure for settlement), or the war, or other emergency requiring uninterrupted production, had come to an end.

In practice, seizure has never been employed merely as a means of postponing a strike or lockout. The rule has been to assure the continuance of production so long as the essential public need for it existed. (The rule has hastened some settlements and discouraged others.)

No involuntary servitude. The enforced continuance of production has created two problems of individual rights which have perturbed both employees and employers. Since both rights are guaranteed by the Constitution, they have been given considerable attention by Congress, the presidents, and the courts. They are: freedom from involuntary servitude (amendment XIII) and protection against the taking of private property for public use without just compensation (amendment V). The first has been a subject of controversy in nearly all cases of government action to terminate strikes, but the second has been an issue only in seizure.

In virtually every instance of presidential action to require production—from the Civil War to the present—the strikers and the leaders of organized labor have protested that the president's action, in effect, forced the employees to work for a private employer against their will and so constituted involuntary servitude. This has been charged in stoppages that were ended by qualified martial law, by court injunctions, and by compulsory arbitration, as well as by seizure. However, the unions raised this point in the courts in only a few seizure cases; and in only one of these was the union mildly successful. This was the case, described earlier, of an individual in the San Francisco machine-shop seizure, who was indefinitely denied referral to other war work. When litigation was begun, the seizing agency and the War Manpower Commission modified the penalty by limiting it to six months. The court then approved.[3]

The weakness of the union position on involuntary servitude seems to stem from the following considerations. In form, the work requirement is not so much a compulsion to perform certain tasks as the prohibition of a concerted withdrawal from work in a dispute with an employer over the terms of employment. Provision has usually been made for individuals to retire from the labor force or to shift to another employer, provided this was not a concerted movement for bargaining purposes. The power to regulate commerce clearly includes the power to forbid combinations in restraint of trade. In substance, moreover, the government has traditionally had the power to compel individuals to perform services that were socially essential, such as jury duty, work on rural highways, enlistment in the *posse comitatus,* and training, reserve duty, or active service in the militia.[4]

There is an additional consideration in seizure cases: that the strikers are employees of the government, working at terms fixed by public authority. These powers are applicable in peace as well as in war; they are established powers of the government as a whole, not simply war powers of the president.

Nevertheless, the availability of the thirteenth amendment, which was adopted during the Civil War to effect the abolition of Negro slavery, has probably been a valuable influence in assuring due process in the drafting and administration of antistrike legislation. Its frequent citation by the unions in political protests against actions by the presidents has probably limited the number and scope of antistrike actions, and has induced special efforts to protect individual employees from illegal restrictions on their mobility.

The most notable effort of this kind was made by Congress in enacting the seizure provisions of the War Labor Disputes Act of 1943. In section 6, which outlawed any actions to induce, encourage or assist any strike, lockout, or slowdown in a seized plant, there was this additional sentence: "No individual shall be deemed to have violated the provisions of this section by reason only of his having ceased work or having refused to continue to work or to accept employment."

To some congressmen and some observers, this clause was merely an assurance to individual workmen of their right to retire or to change to another employer during government possession of their plant; it did not permit concerted stoppages for the purpose of bargaining with the president over the terms at which they would work. Nevertheless, Attorney General Biddle, noting that the act nowhere made it unlawful to "strike" or to "participate" in a strike, but merely unlawful to induce or to lead others in striking, refused to prosecute strikers or union leaders during seizure unless they engaged in overt acts of calling or assisting a concerted withdrawal from work.[5] As explained in Chapter 2, strikes that had been "called" prior to seizure were allowed to continue; and "spontaneous" mass walkouts were tolerated. This enabled the miners' union and the railroad brotherhoods to maintain strikes during seizure until President Truman, with the assistance of another attorney general, Tom Clark, caught the miners' chieftain, John L. Lewis, in an overt action—in "what amounted to a strike call"—and punished him and the union with severe fines.[6]

Individual workers were thus protected in many instances from prosecution for remaining away from work without valid excuse in seized plants and mines; and the government was obliged to turn, in stoppages other than on the railroads and in the mines, to various indirect sanctions, such as the use of soldiers as temporary employees, the cancellation of draft deferrals, and the withdrawal of gasoline rationing coupons. As we have seen, the government was ultimately able to overcome all stoppages in seizure cases except in the two industries we have named; but the lesson of this episode was surely the need for a clearer statement of congressional intentions in seeking to protect individual rights while restricting strikes in government-operated firms. The confusion arose over the wording of the statute, not over the meaning of the constitutional amendment. Seizure does not appear to have involved any irreconcilable conflict with the constitutional ban on slavery and involuntary servitude.

"Just compensation." The owners of industrial property taken by the federal government to ensure continuity of operations have the same constitutional guarantee of "just compensation" for the public use of their property as do the owners of land taken for a new superhighway. In practice, the industrial owners have been reimbursed under a number of technical formulas, all of which have amounted to reimbursing them not only for any damage to (or loss of) physical plant during government operation but also for any loss of income resulting specifically from increased labor costs imposed by the government, and also for the fair rental value of the property.

It is one of the anomalies of presidential seizure that while some businessmen have protested strongly over the imposition of a union in a seized firm which had a nonunion history, it is hard to find any instance of businessmen protesting that they were not adequately compensated for the financial burdens imposed in seizure. If the seized firm was dissatisfied with the terms proposed by the seizing agency in conjunction with the department of justice, it has been permitted to bring suit in the federal courts, and, if the result of the suit proved unsatisfactory, it could carry its appeal to Congress which could then enact special legislation. This ultimate remedy of legislative relief has been used in three cases—the railroad and wire seizures of 1918 and the midwest trucking case of 1944.

The assurance of the fifth amendment, therefore, is plain, although the details of its application remain to be clarified. The guarantee has been effective regardless of whether the seizure resulted from noncompliance by the seized firm with the recommendations of a presidential emergency board or whether it resulted from union defiance of such recommendations (which the company already had accepted) or from a strike that occurred without any prior adjudication of the dispute by the president. Compensation has not been given or withheld in accordance with the company's cooperation or lack of it. The payment is a right, which, incidentally, is not available in this form in cases of minimum wage legislation or of compulsory arbitration.

The history of the settlements has never been surveyed. In view of the unsettled state of opinion on this subject, a review of the practice may be of interest.

Of the 71 seizures, 63 have been settled by the exchange of mutual releases from claims by the United States and the seized companies, thereby leaving the owners in possession of the actual profits earned during government possession and operation. In some cases, the profits were substantial sums; in a few, they were negative (that is, losses). It is not to be inferred, however, that these 63 operations were merely "nominal" takings of property in which the government exercised no control. As will be described more fully in a later chapter, the private management was actually ousted in ten of these cases, and government officials directly supervised production. In the remainder, company officials served as agents of the government, carrying out government orders, but were subject to removal at the president's discretion. Since some of the company officials were removed at the start of the seizures while others were removed after serving as "managing agents" for some months, it seems clear that their tenure as government agents was highly uncertain. Indeed, the cause of removal in every case was refusal to effectuate the orders of the President of the United States. This circumstance led the Supreme Court majority in two cases to hold that such seizures—regardless of whether company officials were ousted or not—were genuine although temporary takings of private property for public use, entitling the owners to just compensation under the fifth amendment.[7]

In seven of the 63 mutual releases, there was an exception to the complete waiver of claims: the seized firms reimbursed the government for some or all of the government's out-of-pocket administrative expenses. In no case, however, has the government collected a fee for the value of its supervisory or protective services.

The willingness of most managements to accept the actual profits as full settlement of all claims suggests that this arrangement has fully satisfied the seized firms that they were being reimbursed for any damages to physical property and for its fair rental value and, in those cases where the president had imposed wage increases over the firms' objection, for the imputed effect of this upon earnings. In considering the equitableness of the wage cases, it should be recalled that in some of these the government provided a different kind of compensation in the form of increased price ceilings, higher utility rates, larger cost allowances for government contractors, and in one case an additional price subsidy. These measures greatly affected the actual profits. Moreover, as will be elaborated later, the president's decisions on retroactive wage increases also influenced the profit level.

There were eight other seizures in which mutual waivers were not agreed to, and some other formula was adopted. In the railroad and wire seizures of the First World War, Congress guaranteed the companies their normal peacetime rate of earnings, and subsequently appropriated more than one billion dollars to supplement the actual profits of these utilities. In several seizures, agreement was reached upon a fair rental value of the property. In one, the Alcoa Steamship Company, the United States Treasury recovered a net profit of $17,761 after allowing the company to retain $142,256 as compensation for use based on time-charter rates together with a fee for acting as managing agent for three requisitioned voyages.[8] This appears to have been the only case in which a net profit was actually recovered into the treasury. In the Montgomery Ward seizures, the government paid the firm $480,000 for "damages" allegedly inflicted upon the business by the seizure operation,[9] but the statute of limitations was allowed to expire without any further terms of settlement being agreed upon. Hence, in effect, Ward accepted the actual profits as just compensation. In the midwest trucking cases, Congress enacted a special formula that inflated the fair rental value of the trucks and terminals, and, later, to make payment under this formula, Congress appropriated $9,875,000 to supplement the actual profits earned.[10]

The central problem about just compensation, therefore, is not whether the employers are adequately reimbursed in seizure cases, but rather what formula (or formulas) are most appropriate for determining compensation. This is partly a legal and partly a political matter. The Supreme Court, in its latest opinion, split three ways, then subsequently refused an opportunity to clarify its position in the midwest trucking case.[11] The legal problem is essentially whether the government has justifiable claims to offset some of the company's claims. At present, the majority view of the court is negative. The political issue is whether the government should agree, in any cases, to leave the actual profits earned in possession of a seized firm. Although there have been cases where this arrangement seemed unduly generous, there are two situations in which mutual waivers of claims probably have been advantageous to the government. One is the typically short seizure, lasting six months or less, in which accounting and inventory tasks are costly and accumulated earnings small. The other is the seizure of firms with normally small earnings which would not yield a profit to the government under a fair rental formula.

It may be concluded, therefore, that sufficient standards have been developed in seizure practice to prevent it from becoming a means either of drafting labor or of confiscating property.

CHAPTER 6

Enforcing Presidential Labor Decisions

One of the unusual aspects of the seizure experience has been its use as an adjunct of semivoluntary systems of disputes-settlement and wage stabilization—as an instrument for enforcing the decisions of presidentially appointed wage and disputes boards. The experience is unusual because seizure has been administered differently from either of the other major forms of required production—from the antistrike injunction, under which public recommendations for terms of settlement have almost always been ignored, when rejected by one of the disputing parties; and from compulsory arbitration, in which such recommendations have been effectuated automatically.

In the experience with semivoluntary systems, backed by seizure, a practice was adopted which fell between the contrasting policies referred to above. In cases where one of the parties had defied the recommendations of a presidential board, the recommendations were submitted to the president himself for review, after which they were either fully enforced, modified or disapproved. In the reviewing process, the disputing parties usually also were given a further opportunity to submit an agreed recommendation to the president.

The record consists of 43 seizures which occurred after one of the parties had refused to accept terms of settlement proposed by the president or an impartial board (called noncompliance cases), and 28 in which no government ruling had been made upon the merits of the controversy (referred to as initially unadjudicated cases).

In the noncompliance cases, the question that naturally arose was: should the proposals of the presidential boards be enforced? But in the other cases, a different question was faced: should the president (or a presidential board) investigate the merits of the dispute and make public recommendations? In practice, such recommendations actually were made in 17 of the initially unadjudicated seizures. But then came an additional question: if these recommendations are not accepted, should they be made compulsory?

The answers to these questions constituted the administrative standards developed in the seizure experience. Two elements of public policy were involved in arriving at the needed answers. First there was the prestige of the president and his disputes-settlement and wage stabilization boards. Unless the contested decisions were taken seriously and generally upheld, the ability of these boards (and of the president himself) to induce voluntary compliance in future cases would be gravely weakened, and the government's effectiveness as a mediator and keeper of industrial peace would wane. Secondly, the public interest was affected by the contents of any agreements finally reached, for the wage policy adopted affected the stability of the currency, the costs of government procurement, and the balance of international payments. Hence the government's role as regulator of the economy was involved.

Before examining the record of enforcement, it will be useful to note the 22 seizures in which no enforcement problem arose. While seizure has played a very significant role as the enforcing arm of semivoluntary systems of disputes-settlement and wage stabilization, it also has served as a means of keeping production going in the 11 initially unadjudicated cases where the government continued to take no position on the merits of the controversy,[1] and in 11 others in which the government's position, not formulated when seizure began, was accepted by the parties as soon as it was prepared by the appropriate disputes agencies.[2]

This leaves us with six seizures, which were initially unadjudicated disputes, and which became enforcement cases during presidential possession because a presidential agency made public recommendations that were rejected by at least one of the parties. We have, therefore, a grand total of 49 seizures available for study in which enforcement of contested emergency rulings was an issue. (The cases are identified and classified in Appendix D.)

THE CONTESTED RULINGS

The enforcement of contested emergency rulings during presidential seizure falls into two stages: the interim observance, during government possession, of the terms of employment recommended or ordered by the emergency boards, and the attempted mediation of settlements, during government possession, in line with the terms of the rulings.

The two stages are interrelated, since the interim terms become an element in the pressures affecting the final terms of settlement, but each is important in its own right—the interim terms as a means of obtaining controlled conditions of employment during a period of emergency, and the final settlements as evidence of ultimate compliance with the government's semivoluntary control program by private labor and industry.

The achievements and failure of both types are recorded in Appendix D. The data are slightly complicated by the fact that more than one ruling was made in some of the 49 disputes (that is, the 49 seizures) in which noncompliance occurred; but the enforcement policy, with a few exceptions, seems to have been virtually uniform for each dispute. Where the policies were inconsistent within the same seizure, the less significant ruling (policy) is disregarded in the comparisons.

It should be emphasized that the rulings considered here were entirely on the merits, and so included no orders merely to resume production. While some preliminary orders of this type were issued by the second NWLB on assuming jurisdiction of a dispute, and were occasionally defied, they were not rulings on the terms of employment but on procedures of adjustment.[3] Although such defiance was frequently termed "noncompliance" at the time, these cases are not included because they relate to the maintenance of uninterrupted production, not to the enforcement of rulings upon the actual terms of employment. The rulings under study either adjusted specific grievances or determined the provisions of union contracts, or they set up final procedures to do this.[4]

The rulings examined here originated with 10 different types of emergency boards, each appointed for a temporary period, to meet a special crisis in labor relations. In some cases, more than one board participated in the same ruling; hence, the number of participations exceeds the number of rulings. The following list of participations is derived from Appendix D.

National War Labor Board I (1918–1919)	2
Railroad Wage Commission (1918)	1
National Defense Mediation Board (1941)	2
National War Labor Board II, including regional and industry commissions (1942–1945)	40
Fair Employment Practice Committee (1943–1946)	2
Emergency boards under sec. 10 of Railway Labor Act (since 1943)	11
Arbitration boards under sec. 7 of Railway Labor Act (1946)	2
Fact-finding boards (1943; 1946)	2
National Wage Stabilization Board I (1946–1947)	3
Wage Stabilization Board III (1952)	1
President (1919; 1943; 1946)	3

Each of these boards was appointed to meet a special crisis for which the normal regulatory agencies were considered unsuited. Some were intended for a single dispute; others for a broad class of disputes. Some were created under statutory authority, but most under procedures improvised by the White House in the absence of appropriate legislation. It should be emphasized that none was fulfilling a normal regulatory function.

It should be pointed out also that these emergency boards have had a very close relationship with the president. Most were appointed by him, although a few were appointed by members of his cabinet. Only the two arbitration boards were selected by the parties themselves (and this in accordance with law). Therefore, all but the two arbitration boards were, in effect, agents of the president in seeking to effectuate voluntary agreements among conflicting economic interests—agents who naturally reported to him (or to the appointing cabinet officer) when their proposals of settlement were not accepted. Their relation to the president was perhaps comparable to that of a referee or master to the appointing judge, but the issues involved were political and economic rather than legal.

The boards reported even more cases of defiance than the presidents acted upon. For example, NWLB II alone reported 108 cases of defiance, as listed in the *Termination Report,* vol. II, appendix J-39 (a) and J-39 (b). When the president responded by seizure, this did not necessarily mean that he fully endorsed the rulings that were being defied, but the act of seizure did evidence the president's acceptance of the role of reviewing and enforcing authority. The president, in fact, did indicate his endorsement of specific rulings (and his desire for enforcement) in 29 seizure cases by the following methods: in three cases, he issued a public statement indicating approval of the contested rulings; in a number of other cases, of which four are not otherwise classified, his seizure order stated that seizure was due to noncompliance by one of the parties; in 22 cases, his seizure order explicitly required observance of the contested ruling during government possession. At other times, the president indicated by public statements his reservations about the contested rulings and his unwillingness to enforce them without some modification (the railroads 1943; 1946; 1950; and the steel mills 1952). He made no public comment on the specific rulings in the remaining 10 noncompliance cases. Similarly, of the six cases in which rulings were issued during government possession and then defied, the president had personally countersigned the rulings in three (Great Lakes Towing Co.; the meat-packing firms; and the soft coal mines 1946).

Whatever the strong individualists among companies and unions may have thought of the constitutionality of the president's action, there seems little doubt of the high standing and full authority of these boards in the executive arm of the government.

The foregoing list of boards is not a complete directory of the emergency agencies which, in two world wars and the Korean War, took part in wage stabilization and dispute-settlement. There were many others, such as the Fuel Administration, the Spruce Production Corporation, the Shipping Board, the War Shipping Administration, and special agencies of the War and Navy Departments, which also made labor rulings that were at times defied by labor or management; but these agencies met the defiance in other ways—by threatening to withdraw government contracts, by withholding government services, by threatening to seize (without having to do so), and by issuing orders in industries which had already been commandeered for the purpose of operational integration (for example, ocean shipping).[5]

The boards in Appendix D are those whose rulings affected firms that were seized as a direct result of labor disputes.

INTERIM OBSERVANCE

The contested rulings in the 49 seizures were fully observed during the period of government possession in 26 of the cases, about 53 per cent or a little more than one-half. (These are the items marked "yes" or "effectively" in column 6 of Appendix D.) This achievement was a little more notable against management than against labor. The record of full observance against management's resistance was 14 cases out of 24, or about 58 per cent; the record against labor's opposition was eight cases out of 18, or about 44 per cent. Of the six cases initially unadjudicated, the subsequent rulings were observed in four.

The rulings were largely observed in eight of the cases, or about 17 per cent. (This means that some feature of the ruling was never applied, or was applied with modifications, as, for example, the retroactive portions of wage increases.) This policy was followed in four cases of management noncompliance, in two of labor noncompliance, and in two of the initially unadjudicated disputes.

The rulings were not observed during government possession in 15 of the 49 seizure cases, or about 31 per cent. (These are the items marked "no" or "ineffective" in the appendix.) This was the result in six of the management defiance cases, or about 26 per cent; in eight of the labor defiance cases, or about 44 per cent; and in one case in which both labor and management were noncompliant.

Rulings fully observed. In fully observing the rulings of federal emergency boards, the seizing agencies put into effect, during all or part of the period of government operation, the terms of employment recommended or ordered by such boards despite the protests of one of the parties. This resulted either in changes in the existing terms of employment over the opposition of management or labor, or in the prevention of changes which management or labor was seeking.

The changes actually effectuated during government possession, over the opposition of the companies, in accordance with emergency rulings, included the reinstatement of striking or dismissed employees, the raising of wages, payment of retroactive increases, alteration of an occupational wage structure, discontinuance of individual "yellow dog" (anti-union) contracts, check-off of union dues, dismissal of employees for failing to maintain union membership, reference of employee grievances to arbitration, payment of company receipts into a union welfare fund, recognition of a union among a company's foremen and clerical employees (including the signing of a contract between the government and union), and the introduction of standard operating rules. The seizing agencies have obliged employees to work longer hours than they wished to, and to work beside people of a different race, in accordance with rulings of presidentially appointed boards.

The changes denied, despite company protests, have consisted of discontinuance of the check-off of union dues, and discontinuance of maintenance of union membership. The changes denied despite union protests have included certain wage increases, the introduction of "featherbed" rules, and a shift in union jurisdiction.

The compulsory observance of contested rulings during government possession has come about in either of two ways: the seizing agency has employed military, economic, or judicial sanctions (or a combination of all three) to overcome the resistance of the defiant party; or, because of the face-saving effect of seizure, the defiant party has agreed to cooperate in the observance of the contested ruling during the period of government operation. In the latter case, the defiant party has expressly stipulated that it would resume noncompliance as soon as the government withdrew. This second method of obtaining observance of the ruling was developed by seizure officials only after much preliminary experience, and after management (and, to a lesser degree, labor) had witnessed enough seizures to recognize the futility of violent resistance. Of the 26 cases in which the contested ruling was fully observed, coercive sanctions were necessary in 13, or just one-half.

The first full observance of a contested emergency ruling was in 1918 in a case of company defiance (Smith & Wesson, Springfield, Mass.). Both President Wilson and the War Department issued statements saying that the purpose of seizure was to secure compliance with a decision of the National War Labor Board. Because of doubts as to the legality of enforcing the NWLB order under the seizure statute (Sec. 120 of the National Defense Act of 1916, 39 Stat. 166, 213), the War Department set up a dummy corporation, the National Operating Corp., chartered in Delaware, to which it leased the Smith & Wesson plant.[6] President Wilson's references to Smith & Wesson are in his letter to the Bridgeport machinists of September 13, 1918.[7] After removing the company management, the War Department reinstated employees (with back pay) who had been discharged for union activity, discontinued the individual nonunion contracts, raised wages (retroactively), and recognized shop committees of the employees—all in accordance with the NWLB ruling.

The next instance of full observance occurred in 1941 when the War Department again seized a small munitions plant (Air Associates, Inc.,

Bendix, New Jersey), removed the management, and reinstated employees dismissed for union activity. President Roosevelt explained in his executive order directing the seizure that the company had defied recommendations of the National Defense Mediation Board. Similar measures were taken— including the replacement of company executives, and the interim observance of contested rulings of the second NWLB—in four other seizures of World War II (Woods Machine, Ken-Rad Tube & Lamp, Twentieth Century Brass, Gaffney Manufacturing—all of them with small plants).

In the S. A. Woods Machine seizure of August 1942, the War Department again met doubts as to the legality of enforcing the NWLB order by leasing the company's plants to a private corporation (this time not a dummy); but, in the other seizures cited, the War Labor Disputes Act of 1943 was available, and this was considered sufficient authority for direct imposition of the NWLB terms.

In the meantime, however, the possibility of working out a cooperative face-saving arrangement with a noncomplying management, whereby the objectionable ruling would be accepted so long as the government was in possession, was emerging. The Navy Department was possibly the first seizing agency to effectuate such an arrangement. The navy action was taken at the Jenkins valve plant in Bridgeport, Connecticut. Rear Admiral Harold G. Bowen, the officer in charge, directed that all the company's receipts be paid to a navy "comptroller," but otherwise left the existing management free to run the business in the usual way. The navy raised wages and began the accumulation of a reserve from which to pay out the retroactive portion of the wage increase—all in accordance with a NWLB order. The company officials, in effect, were free to carry on with the usual production and marketing policies but were restricted in labor and financial matters.[8]

Soon thereafter, the army worked out an even more cooperative arrangement—more cooperative in that the financial restriction was unnecessary— with a manufacturing plant owned by Montgomery Ward & Co. The company's unexpected willingness to observe the NWLB order requiring the arbitration of grievances, maintenance of union membership, and wage increases, so long as the army remained in possession, apparently stemmed from the fact the plant was making military equipment, and so came clearly under the provisions of the War Labor Disputes Act. The company's contrasting resistance at its retail establishments was based on the claim that these places were not engaged in war production.[9]

Similar face-saving agreements, whereby the company executives were allowed to continue in office as agents of the government during presidential possession in return for their promise to observe the rulings of the NWLB which they had been defying, were made by the seizing agencies in five other seizures resulting from management noncompliance (Farrell-Cheek

Steel, Cudahy Bros., Carter Coal, Cocker Machine, Mary-Leila Cotton—all rather small firms except Carter). In addition, the Department of Agriculture left the existing managements in control in the meat-packing seizure after the fact-finding board recommended a 16-cents wage increase, inasmuch as the companies were willing to observe the department's order to effectuate the increase (although they were not yet willing to sign with the union on it). While the government, in these cases, was thus compelled to retain possession of these plants for many months, it achieved full acceptance of its emergency rulings for this period through merely nominal use of force.

The first case in which a ruling defied by a union was fully observed over the union's opposition occurred in 1943 in the industrywide coal seizure, when Secretary of the Interior Ickes, on orders of President Roosevelt, stood firm against any increase in wage rates for 500,000 coal miners from May until October, in accordance with the NWLB's interim and final decisions. The victory—achieved with the help of the criminal provisions of the War Labor Disputes Act, which came into being during the seizure—was temporary, however. The president and the board yielded to union pressures, and the board issued a much more favorable ruling in October 1943, just prior to the next coal mine seizure.

Nevertheless, the seizing agencies have fully effectuated emergency rulings against labor opposition in several other cases. The War Department put into effect a jurisdictional compromise in the Massachusetts tanneries in 1943, and the next year successfully introduced the employment of Negroes as streetcar operators in Philadelphia, after employing drastic sanctions. In another local transportation case, the ODT, with army help, forced several thousand Chicago truck drivers to agree to an unsatisfactory wage increase.

The Navy Department restored and enforced overtime schedules in 103 San Francisco machine shops—schedules which the companies had discontinued under union pressure—even exceeding the NWLB order by making overtime compulsory when scheduled, not merely optional with the individual workers, and by permitting the scheduling of overtime in excess of that practiced under the expired union contract.[10] The government used the cancellation of draft deferrals effectively in this case. The navy also enforced the continuance of an existing jurisdictional practice in a San Francisco shipyard despite a boycott by the rival union. Last but not least, we should note the spectacular success of Secretary of the Interior Krug, with the full support of President Truman and the Department of Justice, in refusing to change the National Wage Stabilization Board ruling of 1946 (the Krug-Lewis agreement) despite John L. Lewis' adroit moves and bold demands on the eve of the 1946 elections. This case involved the fining of

Lewis' union $700,000 for striking in contempt of court during presidential possession. All the preceding cases of labor defiance required the imposition of sanctions in order to obtain the interim observance of the contested rulings.

On the other hand, the seizing agencies have achieved the full observance of emergency rulings through the cooperation of unions under the face-saving effect of seizure in four instances. The first was in September 1944 when striking foremen of District 50, United Mine Workers of America, continued at work in seized soft coal mines despite the NWLB's refusal to require private management to recognize their union. The next was in 1945 on the Bingham & Garfield Railway when the Brotherhood of Locomotive Firemen agreed to accept a Railway Labor Act emergency-board decision so long as the War Department remained in possession. The third was at Springfield Plywood Corp., Oregon, where the AFL employees bowed to a West Coast Lumber Commission ruling in a representational dispute, and reluctantly joined the CIO union during War Department possession. The fourth was in 1946 when the Brotherhood of Railroad Trainmen returned to work on the Monongahela Connecting R.R., without changes in the work rules, after the seizing agency (Office of Defense Transportation) refused to grant additional concessions beyond the national terms established by President Truman for the major railroads.

So we see that full observance of contested rulings was brought about by the use of coercive sanctions during government possession in six management noncompliance cases and seven labor noncompliance cases; while full observance was obtained through the face-saving effect of government possession in eight or nine management and four labor defiance cases.

These instances of strict observance of contested rulings have led some observers to liken presidential seizure in labor disputes to compulsory arbitration; or, more broadly, to liken the system of informal disputes-settlement and wage stabilization, with seizure at its apex, to compulsory arbitration.[11] But this is an oversimplification. It overlooks the essential economic flexibility and political basis of a system of adjustment centered on the White House.

Under a regular system of compulsory arbitration, the terms of the ruling would, presumably, be applied automatically for a specific period, supported if necessary by judicial sanctions (either contempt proceedings or criminal trials or both). Under seizure, however, the terms of the ruling are first subject to White House review and possible modification; then the resulting ruling is applied by the seizing agency in a manner believed likely to contribute to the mediation of a settlement on a basis of the ruling; that is, it may be observed fully, in part, or not at all. Insofar as sanctions may be required, they are extremely varied, from a mere face-saving arrangement to severe military measures, although the familiar judicial sanctions are also a possibility. Possession and enforcement may continue indefinitely.

In short, the above experience shows that seizure can be used, if desired, to effectuate certain terms of employment for a specific period, just as certainly as a regular system of compulsory arbitration; but that seizure differs from the ordinary compulsory arbitration in its swiftness, its flexibility of application, in its variety of sanctions, its opportunities for mediation, and the indefiniteness of its continuance.

Rulings largely observed. A contested ruling may be described as "largely observed" if the seizing agency put into effect its principal feature during all or part of the period of government operation, but did not effectuate some minor provision. The reason for omitting a provision was frequently the appearance of an unexpected difficulty, not foreseen or allowed for by the emergency board. Here the flexibility of seizure permitted an adjustment. There have been eight seizures of this type—four cases of management noncompliance, two of labor noncompliance, and two initially unadjudicated.

The provisions that caused unexpected difficulties in the management noncompliance cases were either for retroactive pay or for the dismissal of employees under a maintenance-of-union-membership order. In two of the retroactive cases, the seizing agencies were unable to pay the retroactive portion of required wage increases because of insufficient operating revenues (about 75 firms out of 101 in the midwestern motor-carrier case, and plants in several cities in the second Montgomery Ward case). In all other respects, the terms of the NWLB orders were observed during presidential possession. After the termination of the Ward seizure, it appeared that adequate funds might actually have been available from the operating revenues, but by then it was too late.

In another case (Toledo, Peoria & Western R.R.), the seizing agency refused to pay that part of the retroactive sum which related to the period prior to seizure, claiming that services had been rendered to a private employer and not to the government; but the agency observed all the other terms of the NWLB order. Subsequently President Roosevelt clearly authorized various agencies to pay retroactive portions of wage increases for services rendered prior to seizure, but this was never done on the Toledo, Peoria & Western. A similar problem arose in one of the initially unadjudicated cases (Great Lakes Towing) when the management refused to comply with directives of the National Wage Stabilization Board issued during seizure at union request. The seizing agency effected the required current wage increases, but felt powerless to obtain arbitration of the employees' preseizure claims as directed by the NWSB.

The maintenance-of-membership difficulty occurred in Hughes Tool Co., where it developed that discharges of several hundred machinists would seriously handicap war production as well as provoke a strike by the rival union. So the War Department induced the certified union (the United Steelworkers) to ask the NWLB to change its ruling from maintenance of membership to an involuntary check-off, applicable in the future to all employees previously covered by the maintenance provision. The requested modification was granted by the NWLB, approved by President Roosevelt, and successfully effectuated by the army.

Contested rulings also were largely observed in three cases of labor noncompliance, having to do with required wage increases (twice) and with an antisegregation ruling. The latter is especially interesting in the light of later efforts of the government to end racial discrimination. In this case (Western Electric, 1944), President Roosevelt put the power of the executive arm behind a private manufacturing firm which had integrated cafeteria and locker room facilities for white and Negro employees in its Baltimore plant. The firm was engaged almost entirely in war production.

When the white employees protested the company's action and voted to authorize a strike, the NWLB assumed jurisdiction, and the President's Fair Employment Practice Committee adopted a strong resolution opposing renewed segregation in this plant as likely to "lead to discrimination in employment practices."[12] The independent union then pressed its case, asking the NWLB to order the company to restore partitions in the cafeterias and washrooms. The NWLB refused in a unanimous decision; the union struck, and President Roosevelt directed Secretary of War Stimson to take over the plant.

The president's order, however, did not "direct" the secretary of war to enforce the FEPC-NWLB ruling, but merely "authorized" him to take various steps to obtain the "compliance" of the union. The army acted cautiously, employing no troops although some were kept on alert.[13] When the white employees slowly returned to work, and the War Department restored production to normal levels after about two weeks of effort, the department believed it was faced with a choice between remaining in possession "for the duration" or of mediating a compromise.

The War Department obtained the acceptance of all parties to a plan for new and enlarged locker rooms, washrooms, and cafeterias, operated under an informal understanding that white and Negro employees would use opposite ends of the improved areas. This preserved the "principle" of integrated facilities while permitting "voluntary segregation" in practice. The War Department obtained the grudging approval of a representative of the FEPC to this modification of its order, and then withdrew. This was said to be the only order by FEPC against segregation in World War II.[14] It might have become fully operative if supported with the same zeal that the army showed a few months later in introducing Negro operators into the Philadelphia transit system.

Rulings not observed. The failure of the seizing agencies in 15 cases to observe contested emergency-board rulings, during any part of the period of government operation, illustrates once more how far from automatic the process of enforcement has been. This group comprises about 31 per cent of the total of cases (49) in which an emergency ruling was contested.

The nonobservance of the rulings arose from three quite different causes: the indefinite continuance of the status quo by the president and seizing agency as a tactical pressure against the employees and union to induce them to accept the contested ruling as, at least, better than the status quo; the temporary deferment of any change in the terms of employment to facilitate further negotiations by the parties and, in some cases, to permit review of the contested ruling by the president; and the reluctance of seizing agencies, when sympathetic to the managements' point of view, to effectuate changes that were objectionable to management.

The first two causes clearly reflect the government's effort to achieve more than mere interim observance of the contested ruling, namely, its effort to achieve ultimate "voluntary" compliance by the defiant party—a characteristic, not of compulsory arbitration, but of the semivoluntary system of dispute-settlement with which seizure has been employed. The third cause of nonobservance points to a weakness in presidential authority within the executive branch of the government—the lack of truly effective presidential supervision and control.

The seizures in which the government withheld all or part of the directed wage increases as a means of inducing the employees and union to accept the government ruling were the General Cable case; the railroad seizure of 1948; and, after President Truman had first authorized modifications of the emergency board's ruling, the long second phase of the railroad seizure of 1950–1952. At General Cable, the navy withheld the introduction of a three-cent night-shift differential—the only improvement granted by the NWLB—until the employees agreed to accept the ruling. In 1948, Mr. Truman continued the status quo on the major railroads until three brotherhoods agreed to accept a 15½-cent increase. Three years later, Mr. Truman withheld one-half of an approved increase of 25 cents for yardmen and of 10 cents for roadmen until three brotherhoods exhausted all their means of pressure against the White House and then reluctantly accepted the president's terms.

This tactical employment of the power over the interim terms of labor was the opposite of that used against noncomplying managements, against whom the pressure for ultimate compliance was applied not by withholding but by putting into effect the protested wage increase or maintenance-of-membership provisions.

A frequent cause of complete nonobservance of contested emergency-board rulings has been the policy of treating the rulings as not final, but subject to review and modification by the president or by the parties themselves. For this reason, the emergency board's approved changes in terms of employment have been temporarily deferred in seven seizures to allow the parties to resume negotiations over the issues under the mediation of the White House or of the seizing agency. In two cases (Cleveland Bronze, and American Enka), the parties found completely new approaches to the disputes with the assistance of the seizing agency (War Department), and reached settlements which were then approved by the government in lieu of the original NWLB rulings. In three general railroad seizures (1943; 1946; 1950), the emergency-board rulings were found unsatisfactory by the president, after review, leading to new proposals by the president or by his assistant, Dr. John R. Steelman. In the Illinois Central case, on the other hand, apparently neither negotiations nor new proposals ever developed.

Then, in the famous steel industry case, the question of observing or not observing the wage board's recommendations became a central issue in the parties' strategies during seizure, and an issue, too, within the Truman administration. The seizure was handled by Secretary of Commerce Sawyer, who as a businessman and personal friend of some of the steel executives disliked the task and accepted it most reluctantly. Secretary Sawyer deferred the institution of any of the wage board's recommended changes, while he sought unsuccessfully to settle the dispute through renewed negotiations under the pre-existing working conditions—a situation applying maximum pressure upon the union. When these negotiations failed, Mr. Sawyer began preparations to bring about some of the recommended wage increase—a change that would have shifted pressures from the union to the companies—but the change was never effectuated because at that point the Supreme Court intervened with an order forbidding any changes during its consideration of the validity of the seizure. The case remains, however, an outstanding example of the importance of interim terms during any period of government mediation of an emergency dispute—by seizure or otherwise.

Still another explanation for the complete nonobservance of contested emergency-board rulings during some of the seizures has been, as suggested above, the pro-management viewpoint of some seizing officials. Despite explicit statements by the presidents approving the contested rulings, the seizing agencies have failed to observe the rulings in five seizures, all involving the control of large corporations. In the Western Union case of 1918–1919, Postmaster General Burleson, while issuing orders forbidding discriminatory discharges for union activity in accordance with the NWLB ruling, nullified the effect by upholding all actual discharges as justified on "disciplinary grounds." Mr. Burleson, a Socialist, was well known for his anti-union views.

Postmaster General Burleson allowed the defiant company, Western Union, to circumvent his antidiscrimination orders by: establishing a company union whose members received discriminatory benefits; announcing a policy of re-employing, instead of reinstating, those previously discharged for membership in the AFL union (the Commercial Telegraphers' Union); discharging additional CTU members for "insubordination," hence not "solely" for union membership; and requiring "loyalty pledges" as a condition of employment.[15] The discrimination was flagrant enough to cause Felix Frankfurter, then chairman of the War Labor Policies Board of the Department of Labor, to issue a memorandum of protest on Feb. 4, 1919, which Secretary of Labor W. B. Wilson forwarded to Postmaster General Burleson on February 17, 1919. Mr. Frankfurter listed among the justifiable grievances of the telegraph and telephone employees "the failure to enforce the principle against discrimination because of labor union affiliation."[16] Yet Mr. Burleson blandly (or ignorantly) insisted that there was no discrimination.[17]

In 1941 in the Federal shipyard case, where the interests of the United States Steel Corporation were at stake, Secretary of the Navy Knox issued contradictory statements and orders, at first directing that any union requests for discharges under the maintenance-of-membership ruling of the National Defense Mediation Board be referred to the NDMB for approval (which was done), and then putting away in a drawer (unenforced) an official recommendation of the NDMB that four employees be discharged for nonpayment of dues and for leadership of a new rival union.[18] Mr. Knox, in private life, was a wealthy newspaper publisher.

This seizure is another case in which the public was led to believe that the contested ruling was put into effect by the seizing agency. The chairman of the mediation board, William H. Davis, as late as May 22, 1944, thought that the board's ruling had been accepted.[19]

In April 1944, President Roosevelt assigned the seizure of Montgomery Ward & Co. to the Department of Commerce, headed by Jesse Jones, an old friend of Ward's chairman, Sewell Avery. Secretary Jones knew and admired Avery so well that he had proposed him as head of the Continental Illinois National Bank & Trust Co. in 1933. (Avery declined, preferring to remain at Ward's.) Jones considered the seizure "about the most awkward thing the White House asked me to do." He explained: "I was not in sympathy with the move and did not want the responsibility."[20] In the executive order directing seizure, Mr. Roosevelt expressly required that the NWLB order which Avery was defying should be observed during government operation. To effectuate this order (which called for maintenance of union membership and arbitration of grievances), Secretary Jones sent to Chicago his undersecretary, Wayne C. Taylor, who also was acquainted with the Chicago financial world. When Mr. Taylor failed to gain the cooperation of Avery or his subordinates, and was unable to effectuate the NWLB order (despite the spectacular removal of Avery from his office), the president terminated the seizure. The lesson was clear, and in December 1944, when the second Ward seizure occurred, Mr. Roosevelt assigned the task to the War Department.

In 1945, the final year of the war, during two seizures in the oil industry (Humble Oil and Pure Oil), the Petroleum Administration for War was so deliberate in seeking observance of the NWLB rulings on the subject of union security that the war ended before either had been carried out.[21] Although the head of PAW was Secretary of the Interior Ickes, its deputy administrator, Ralph K. Davies, and many of its staff were professional oil men on loan from the major oil companies. The seizures created for them a conflict of interest, for if they employed seizure solely to end a strike, they supported the companies of their own industry against the unions; whereas if they employed seizure to enforce NWLB orders which the companies had defied, they supported the union.

In taking possession of the petroleum facilities, Mr. Davies "emphasized that the agency's sole interest in the matter was to keep the plant in operation," and "made it clear" that the Petroleum Administration had "no jurisdiction for settlement of the dispute."[22] His executive assistant, H. Chandler Ide, expressly disclaimed any responsibility on the part of the agency for enforcing NWLB orders. He said, in an affidavit filed in U.S. District Court in Galveston, shortly after the Humble seizure:

Neither the PAW nor any of its officers or employees has the power or authority to enforce any order of the NWLB, and neither the Petroleum Administration nor any of its officers or employees has taken any action or threatened to take any action with respect to enforcing any directive order of the NWLB against the Humble Co. The full extent of the power and authority of the PAW and its officers and employees with respect to the property of the Humble Oil & Refining Co. is defined in Ex. Order 9276 [presidential order creating PAW] and Ex. Order 9564 [order directing PAW to seize the Humble refinery at Ingleside, Texas].[23]

This apparent disavowal of any intention to observe the NWLB order in operating the Humble Company brought a letter of inquiry from the director of the Office of Economic Stabilization, William H. Davis, who had previously been chairman of the NWLB itself. In reply, the deputy administrator acknowledged that PAW did have a "responsibility under the executive order for the observance of the terms and conditions" of the NWLB orders —both at Humble and at Pure Oil.[24] Accordingly, PAW notified the unions at both companies that the NWLB orders would be observed during government possession. However, hostilities with Japan ceased soon thereafter, and PAW promptly relinquished possession, leaving the NWLB orders still unobserved.

Observance of the maintenance-of-membership provisions of the NWLB orders at the two oil companies, in practice, had to wait until the union locals had submitted certified lists of delinquent members to the seizing agency, whereupon the seizing agency was bound by the executive order of the president to discharge the delinquent members from employment. There was nothing accessible at the National Archives indicating that the union locals had taken this step prior to the termination of government possession; hence some of the delay may have been the fault of the union. At the Pure Oil property, the NWLB order also required the check-off of union dues. Although the seizure took place on June 6, 1945, dues were not checked off at the initial payroll in either July or August. This failure was protested by Charles C. Lipscomb, president of Local 484, OWIU, on August 13, 1945; and on August 22, 1945, Mr. Lipscomb was advised by Glenn A. Campbell, representing the petroleum administrator, that the deductions would be made "henceforth." However, on August 24, 1945, the Petroleum Administration advised the company that it planned to return the facilities to private control "soon." The facilities actually were returned September 10, 1945, without any deduction having been made.[25]

ULTIMATE COMPLIANCE

The second aspect of the enforcement of contested rulings in seizure cases is the attempted mediation of final settlements in line with the terms of the rulings—the attempt to gain ultimate compliance. The object is to bring such pressures to bear upon the defiant parties during government possession that they will cease their defiance and settle the disputes in accordance with the government's recommendations or orders. This enables the president to relinquish possession without resumption of the noncompliance.

Obviously, the converse of this is that if the president does not gain ultimate compliance, he must retain possession indefinitely in order to assure interim observance of the contested terms.

The concept of seeking ultimate compliance is relatively recent in the history of seizure. The Wilsonian idea, for example, was strictly "possession for the duration of the war," with interim observance intended. It was not until the eve of the Second World War in the seizure of Air Associates that an attempt was made during government possession to induce a defiant party to withdraw its defiance and to agree to accept the contested ruling so that the property might be returned to private operation prior to the general relaxation of labor controls.

The seizing agency undertaking this task was the War Department, the company a small aircraft-parts plant in New Jersey. The War Department succeeded after first replacing the company's president with army officers, and then convincing the board of directors that a new president was needed who would comply with the government's labor rulings. The case did much to convince government officials that they had found a better method of enforcement than automatic possession for the duration.

Although the War Department considered the formation of a government corporation to operate the Air Associates plant, if a long seizure became necessary, the department in the end used a threat of withdrawal as a pressure to bring the parties together. This quickly resulted in a signed agreement, and the army did withdraw.[26]

The experience after Pearl Harbor, however, gradually demonstrated that official hopes for using seizure as a means of persuasion and quick withdrawal were overoptimistic, that seizure was not by any means an infallible method of persuading men to change their minds about the wisdom or justice of government decisions in labor matters. Indeed, within a month after Pearl Harbor, President Roosevelt relinquished possession of the giant shipyard of the Federal Shipbuilding & Dry Dock Co., a subsidiary of the United States Steel Corp., without having changed the minds of the defiant steel magnates in the slightest. This quick withdrawal, without compliance, constituted another innovation in seizure history, one equally non-Wilsonian, but far less effective than Roosevelt's earlier innovation, since such quick withdrawals were invariably followed by renewed interruptions of production as well as by loss of prestige for the government's program of peaceful disputes settlement.

Nevertheless, the method of persuasion and withdrawal was successfully used six times under Roosevelt, establishing it as an important new element in seizure technique. It was also used successfully six times under President Truman. This assured ultimate compliance.

The method was first applied to a case of labor noncompliance in August 1942 at the Bayonne, New Jersey, plant of the General Cable Corp. In this seizure, the Navy Department induced a rank-and-file strike committee to go before a meeting of the entire membership of the union local and urge adoption of a resolution acquiescing in the contested National War Labor Board ruling. The membership promptly adopted the resolution, and the navy withdrew.

In the next two months after the General Cable case, Mr. Roosevelt was obliged on two occasions to revert to Wilson's practice of seizure for the duration of the war because of the unrelenting defiance of small employers. In each of these cases, Toledo, Peoria & Western R.R., and S. A. Woods Machine Co., the seizing agency announced publicly that it would remain in possession and control until the war ended in order to assure continued observance of the NWLB orders—a matter of more than three years, as it turned out. The War Department condemned a leasehold interest in the Woods Machine plants.[27] The O.D.T. considered leasing the Toledo, Peoria & Western R.R. to a major railroad but operated it directly instead.[28] Once again, about two years later, a seizing agency made a similar announcement in a seizure resulting from labor defiance, the San Francisco machine-shop case.[29] In other cases of possession for the duration, no specific announcement of the indefinite possession was made.

The experience of 1941–1942 thus demonstrated that persuasion (with early withdrawal) and indefinite possession were alternative policies of seizure, in which the choice was largely up to the defiant party rather than to the president. The noncomplying company or union could compel indefinite possession, if it really preferred this to accepting unpalatable labor terms. This made seizure a more flexible instrument for the enforcement of wage stabilization rulings and dispute-settlements than it had been in the First World War.

Generally, if indefinite possession were preferred, it was because issues of "principle," not of money, were at stake. In one instance, however, some War Department officials believed that Cudahy Bros. Co. preferred indefinite possession to compliance because "the company considers it to be an advantage from the standpoint of labor relations and government assistance on manpower problems to have the army in possession."[30]

In 1943, Congress introduced still another possibility for dealing with defiant parties in seizure cases. In enacting the War Labor Disputes Act, Congress deliberately refrained from authorizing court enforcement of NWLB orders. Instead, it made specific provision for presidential seizure; and, in doing so, established a new procedure for effecting changes in the terms and conditions of labor at seized plants (sec. 5). This procedure permitted either the seizing agency or the employees (directly or through their union) to ask the NWLB to approve changes in terms of labor, including modifications of the NWLB's own rulings. Any such changes were to be mandatory when approved by the NWLB and the president. In one sense, this merely channeled through the NWLB a procedure that had been handled directly by the seizing agencies; but, in a broader sense, it opened the way for a new element in enforcement policy—the practice of reviewing, and possibly modifying, a contested ruling during seizure as a means of achieving agreement between the parties and an early termination of possession.[31] This practice was related directly to the attempted mediation of a final settlement, and should be distinguished from minor changes in the contested rulings made in obtaining interim observance.

Ironically, the War Labor Disputes Act, which introduced this new element of flexibility in enforcement of NWLB orders, was intended by Congress to facilitate stricter enforcement of NWLB orders against the United Mine Workers, led by John L. Lewis. The act did facilitate the interim observance of NWLB terms in the seized mines; but scarcely more than two weeks after the act's adoption, President Roosevelt confessed at a press conference that he was unable to obtain ultimate compliance; as he put it, he was powerless to compel Lewis to sign a labor agreement with the mine owners conforming to the rejected NWLB ruling. At the conference on July 9, 1943, the president was asked if he planned to "compel Lewis to sign" an agreement with the coal operators, in accordance with the NWLB order of June 18, 1943. He replied that he knew of no way of getting Lewis' signature on the contract. He continued, in a sarcastic tone, by asking the reporters what they thought he could do if he sent Lewis a note in longhand on a sheet of pink paper asking him to conform with the board order and Lewis refused.[32] Therefore, in spite of the full interim observance of the rejected ruling, Mr. Roosevelt relinquished possession of the mines the next month, without ultimate compliance.

The miners then ceased work; the NWLB approved new terms embodying the principle of portal-to-portal pay, which Lewis was demanding. Roosevelt reseized the mines. Then Secretary Ickes, as the seizing agent, negotiated terms with Lewis that were mutually satisfactory, although the miners were still on strike, and recommended these terms to the NWLB and to the president, using the new procedure for changing terms of labor in sec. 5 of the WLDA. The NWLB and the president reluctantly gave their approval. Thus, this important new element of flexibility in seizure procedure was introduced under the most adverse conditions, especially in view of Ickes' unfortunate willingness to negotiate with the union while the men were on strike, but the subsequent history of this aspect of enforcement was more effective in the public interest.

The new element of enforcement policy, permitting modification of the contested rulings, after review by the president, was a partial retreat from ultimate compliance, but, when worked out in practice by seizing officials, it permitted adaptation to changed economic conditions or the adoption of new approaches in the final (or seizure) stage of government mediation. It therefore carried to the highest level of the government the original concept of maximizing the element of voluntarism in the emergency program of wage stabilization and disputes-settlement.

The success of the presidents in achieving ultimate compliance may be summarized as follows.

The rulings were accepted by the formerly defiant parties and made the bases of final settlements of the disputes, in 12 of the 49 cases involving contested rulings. This was about 25 per cent—a notably small proportion. (These are the items marked "yes" or "effectively" in column 7 of Appendix D.) These cases of ultimate compliance were more numerous among labor unions and employees than among company managements, both in absolute numbers and in the proportion complying.

The contested rulings were modified, with the permission of the original emergency boards or the president (and then made the basis of final settlements) in 11 of the 49 seizure cases, or about 23 per cent. This policy was followed in six cases of labor noncompliance, in four cases of management noncompliance, in the only case of noncompliance by both parties, and in none of the unadjudicated disputes.

The contested rulings were not accepted at any time by the noncompliant parties, and no agreements were reached during government possession for settlement of the disputes, in 26 of the 49 seizure cases, or a little more than one-half. (These are the items marked "no" in the appendix.) This failure to achieve ultimate compliance came about principally in the management noncompliance cases. The record shows 17 such failures out of the 24 management defiance cases, or about 71 per cent; five such failures out of the 18 labor defiance cases, or about 28 per cent; and four such failures out of the six initially unadjudicated disputes.

Acceptance induced. The seizing agencies have induced ultimate compliance with the contested rulings in only 12 of the 49 cases in which defiance occurred, or a little less than one out of four. Although this is a very small proportion of the total, it is worthwhile to examine the 12 cases in order to see, if possible, why they were successful.

First, we may note that eight of the 12 cases, or two-thirds, were cases of labor noncompliance, suggesting that when the government has demonstrated its determination to enforce the objectionable rulings, labor has been more willing than management to accept defeat and to permit a return to private operations. Doubtless this tendency has been due, in part, to the fact that most of the labor defiance cases were wage cases (five out of eight), which are more readily compromised or deferred than struggles over relative power positions. Nevertheless, two other of the labor defiance cases were union representational disputes (Massachusetts tanneries, and Springfield Plywood). An equally significant factor may be that the return to private operations relieves the union of governmental restraints and restores normal collective bargaining, whereas the acceptance of defeat by management and the return to private operations has usually meant either the beginning of a new period of higher labor costs or the start of a new era of power relationships in which managerial decisions must thereafter be shared more fully with the union.

Next, let us observe that nearly all the successful cases involved firms and employee groups who had only small or moderate resources with which to continue defiance of presidential authority. Three of the defiant firms had no more than 2,500 employees each (one had only 1,000). Six of the employee groups consisted either entirely of rank-and-file employees (with the union leaders supporting the government) or of employees under leadership of local or small independent union officials. The sanctions imposed by the government tended to look rather formidable to these groups. Nevertheless, President Truman's success did extend to two nationwide cases—the big meat-packing firms and three unions in the 1948 railroad case.

So the picture is mixed from either of the above points of analysis, and perhaps one can conclude that the president's achievements depended not only on these circumstances but also on the relative ingenuity and persistence of the particular government officials in applying carrot-and-stick inducements.

The importance of the last-mentioned point is suggested by the strong measures taken by seizure officials during some of the cases cited. For example, the government took control of all company receipts in the cases of Air Associates and Jenkins Bros., and subjected all expenditures to government order.[33] At Air Associates, the government advanced credit only on the condition that the company permanently replace its defiant president. Some of the pressures against employees were equally severe. The government withheld protested wage increases, imposed protested working rules, arrested and tried rank-and-file strike leaders, used troops as strike replacements or to preserve order, and obtained an injunction. These pressures were directed not merely at interim observance but even more at ultimate compliance. However, since the contested orders were not legally binding, the pressures had to have other legitimate objectives, such as keeping production going or improving plant efficiency.[34]

Finally, we should note that the seizing agency, the disputes-settlement board, and sometimes even the president, took action of a mediatory nature that helped, in several cases, to induce compliance. They suggested minor, face-saving concessions (not to be confused with the major modifications of the contested rulings in other cases); they enlisted the aid of interracial conciliation groups, in the Philadelphia transit case;[35] and they obtained adequate price relief in the meat-packing case, not only in higher ceiling prices but in a special congressional subsidy of $10,000,000 to cover the retroactive portion of the directed wage increase.[36]

Rulings modified. In 11 cases, the seizing agencies have obtained the agreement of the parties to a modification of the originally contested ruling and then have relinquished government possession. (See the cases marked "modified" in col. 7, App. D.) This enabled the parties to resume private operations with their disputes settled; it enabled the presidents to avoid the problems of indefinite possession; but it also raised the questions: Did the parties reach their agreements at the public's expense? Did the government yield too much on such policies as stabilization? Does the process of modifying disputes-board rulings weaken the standing of the boards?

Examination of the cases in this group suggests that these questions can best be answered by distinguishing two types of seizures according to the economic scope of the dispute: (1) those in which the wage and other issues were almost exclusively of local interest; and (2) those in which the settlements directly affected the employees of a major industry and indirectly affected the settlements in other industries also. While the difference between these categories is one of degree, the actual cases contrast rather sharply.

Cases of the first type (seven) show, almost by definition, no serious injury to the government's stabilization or other policies.[37] All started with defiance of NWLB rulings, and all ended with modification of those rulings by the board itself; but in the interim the rulings were enforced by the seizing agency against the resistance of the defiant party (except in two seizures where the rulings proved objectionable to both parties), and the changes themselves were mediated while production continued without interruption.

The atmosphere of these seizures, all of which were under War Department control, was one of enforcement, strict impartiality, and uninterrupted production. The department had as its "ultimate objective" either: acceptance of the NWLB order as issued, or the negotiation by the company and union of some other adjustment of their differences which would not be unacceptable to the NWLB.[38] This was no different from the "objective" in the cases listed above in which acceptance was induced. There the parties simply chose the other alternative.

The "objective" of the seizing agency was in conformity with the basic policy of the NWLB of encouraging voluntary agreements wherever possible.[39] The result was one of the characteristics of peacetime bargaining— local variations from the national pattern. For example, under the seizure pressures, two companies gave way a little in their opposition to the union-security provisions required by the board, in return for union concessions on the retroactive wage clause. Another firm (a manufacturing arm of Montgomery Ward) gave way on the wage issue in return for employee concessions on union security.[40] In the other cases of this type, completely new approaches were developed, introducing and settling additional issues or altering the procedure of adjustment, and leaving the labor relations on an improved basis. In all these cases, the parties were assisted by experienced industrial-relations officers from the War Department's "industrial personnel division" headed by James P. Mitchell (later secretary of labor).

The achievement of these agreements for modified rulings required the application of pressures upon uncompromising company and union officials as much as did the achievement of ultimate compliance in the preceding cases. The War Department directly operated two firms (removing the company presidents), and discredited the local union leaders in two others so that one was relieved of his post and the other was virtually superseded. All of which was part of the national effort to persuade a few nonconformists to accept a system of semivoluntary dispute-settlement and wage stabilization which the rest of American industry and labor had accepted immediately after Pearl Harbor.

The other group of cases, in which the government modified its own rulings and then relinquished possession, consisted of four industrywide seizures in which the wage disputes had pattern-setting effects. These were the coal and rail disputes of late 1943, and the rail disputes of 1946 and 1950–1952, which are familiar national dramas.

The significant point is that these cases, while the same in principle as the seven localized disputes, were great enough in scope to threaten the government's anti-inflation programs and to affect the structure of income distribution among the nation's workers.

The problem, of course, was the same in both the national and localized cases—an emergency ruling on the merits that had not only provoked defiance but was considered by the president, on review, to be an impracticable or unwise or soon-obsolete set of government recommendations. For example, the coal ruling disregarded the perennially low earnings of the miners in the depression; the concurrent rail case reflected an unseemly hassle among government agencies over the permissible wage change; the emergency board in 1946 granted less than the existing national pattern; the ruling in 1950 was immediately outmoded by the outbreak of war. Similar difficulties could be cited. In these circumstances, it is not surprising that some method of "appeal" and review developed to permit reconsideration of these cases. Nor is it surprising that the method followed the line of actual practice in decision-making and enforcement—from presidential boards and seizing agencies up to the president.

The differences between the industrywide and local cases were, first, the impact of the industrywide cases (particularly coal) which brought the method of review and modification into being; and, second, the economic importance of these cases that led to two practices, which were not imitated in the localized seizures but which became highly controversial in the pattern-setting ones. Mediation and review was conducted (in three of the four cases) under the pressure of serious strikes, that is, under circumstances in which the president had not yet gained (or had lost) full control of the seized business; and the entire procedure was subjected to the close personal supervision of the president.

Did the great importance of these cases, together with the two unusual practices, result in agreement at the public's expense? Did the president yield too much in the process of modification? Was the standing of the original disputes boards weakened? The line of argument we have been following suggests the following answers: the original rulings clearly needed revision, but the conducting of new mediation proceedings during a strike was equivalent to letting one of the parties put his hand on the scale; the president's close supervision was a necessary exercise of his responsibility under the existing, informal tripartite system of adjustment, but some of his judgments on complex labor-relations issues were made hastily without adequate inquiry through staff advisers; the appeal to the president in major cases is almost inevitable, but the president has seemed in some cases almost to welcome these appeals, whereas a reticence to review particular decisions (and frequent refusals to do so) would do much to support the emergency disputes boards; no great break in the anti-inflation wall occurred, but the wall was seriously weakened in one or two cases; the virtual arbitration of great economic issues at the White House was (and still is) in an experimental stage, but the development of a more systematic procedure for the review of emergency-board findings is desirable.

Rulings not accepted. The seizing agencies have either failed (or not tried) to obtain acceptance of the contested rulings, and so have returned the properties without ultimate compliance, in 26 of the 49 seizures involving such rejected rulings. This is a little more than one-half. (See the cases marked "no" in col. 7, Appendix D.)

Of these 26 unsuccessful cases, 18 were retained in federal possession until the end of the emergency period, after which it was immaterial, from a national standpoint, whether production continued without interruption or whether the government's emergency controls were accepted. The contested rulings were observed during government possession in 16 of the 18 cases.

The reverse of this picture is that the remaining eight of the 26 unsuccessful cases were released prior to the end of the emergency period, without gaining either acquiescence in the contested ruling or agreement upon some modification—an expedient that led inevitably to a new outbreak of industrial warfare and, almost always, to reseizure. These premature relinquishments of possession generally reflected presidential eagerness to get rid of "hot potatoes"—examples being the Federal Shipbuilding case and the first Montgomery Ward case. But the NWLB usually put the "hot potato" back in the president's hand (the second Ward case), and reseizure occurred.

The length of this list of failures will seem less remarkable when we observe that 15 of the 26 represent management refusals to accept disputes-board decisions in favor of some form of union security. This is nearly three-fifths. Here in one package we find the most severe form of resistance to the labor adjustment programs of two world wars and the Korean War—management hostility to union recognition or to any form of compulsory union membership. Moreover, the list contains almost no examples of the type of dispute which we found most easily compromisable—wage disputes; there are only four such cases, although one or two of the union-security disputes also involved wage issues.

This means that in the area of labor defiance, as well as of management defiance, the unsuccessful cases from the standpoint of ultimate compliance were chiefly of the nonwage type. The cases of labor noncompliance that held out until the end of the emergency included one dispute over hours, two over union jurisdiction, and one over workloads.

As a whole, the record of enforcement under seizure has been impressive. By a slight rearrangement of the data derived from Appendix D, we may conclude that the contested rulings were either observed, fully or largely, during presidential possession, or were ultimately accepted as the basis for resumption of private operations, in 42 of the 49 seizures in which enforcement was an issue (or approximately 86 per cent). This can be seen from Table 4.

TABLE 4
CUMULATIVE SUMMARY OF ENFORCEMENT DURING SEIZURE

Disposition of contested rulings	No. of seizures	Per cent of 49 seizures	Cumulative per cent
Fully observed	26	53	53
Largely observed	8	17	70
Not observed but ultimately accepted (10, 42, 68)[a]	3	6	76
Not observed but modified and accepted (19, 32, 41, 65, 69)[a]	5	10	86
Not enforced	7	14	—
Total	49	100	—

[a] Seizure case numbers from Key List and from Appendix D.

The record is clearly as good as that established in successfully keeping production going. For comparison, the data on keeping production going have been arranged in Table 5 in similar cumulative form. This shows that all interruptions of production were overcome in two weeks or less in 62 of the 71 seizures (or approximately 87 per cent).

TABLE 5
SUMMARY DATA ON STOPPAGES DURING SEIZURE

Duration of stoppage	No. of seizures	Per cent of 71 seizures	Cumulative per cent
None after takeover	40	56	56
After takeover, longest stoppage ended:			
In 3 days or less	11	15½	71½
In 3 to 7 days	7	10	81½
In 1 to 2 weeks	4	5½	87
In more than 2 weeks	9	13	—
Total	71	100	—

The record of enforcement shows little if any difference in peace and wartime, although experience in peace has been slight. One cold-war case was marked by full interim observance (Air Associates, 1941), another by ultimate compliance (railroads, 1948), and the third by neither (Federal Shipbuilding, 1941). Of the six cases during reconversion, four had full interim observance, one had ultimate compliance with a modified ruling (railroads, 1946), and one had neither (steel, 1952).

The entire analysis suggests that the terms of employment enforced by seizure reflected in most cases chosen standards of public policy rather than the bargaining demands of the stronger party; in short, a kind of case-by-case government regulation rather than normal mediation. We may conclude, therefore, that seizure has served as a coercive backstop of the semivoluntary systems of dispute-settlement and wage stabilization.[41]

CHAPTER 7

Settling the Disputes

The continued mediatory efforts of the presidents and their subordinates during seizure have received little attention in studies of emergency labor disputes, and occasionally have been dismissed as either perfunctory or impracticable.[1] Yet such efforts, in fact, have been effective in 40 of the 71 seizures studied in this investigation, or approximately 56 per cent. That is to say, the presidents have settled the disputes in 40 seizures and returned the properties to private control without a renewed interruption of production. The other 31 disputes were still unsettled when the president relinquished possession, and strikes occurred soon thereafter in at least 20 of them.

THE DILEMMA OF INDEFINITE POSSESSION

The very nature of seizure involves a specific dilemma. If the primary, or even the secondary, purpose of seizure is to keep production going, then the government can terminate possession only if the parties settle all outstanding disputes that threaten to interrupt production; or the parties give assurance that their dispute(s) will be settled without any (further) interruption of production; or the government becomes willing to accept interruptions of production, due to a change in the urgency of general economic conditions or in the importance of the particular firm or industry.

If the seizure is intended also to enforce the recommendations of a presidentially appointed disputes board, over the resistance of one or both of the parties, additional conditions restrict the president's freedom to relinquish possession. Under these circumstances, the government can terminate possession only if the parties agree to observe the objectionable terms of labor under private operation; or the president is willing, on review, to modify the objectionable terms in a manner satisfactory to both parties; or the government is prepared to relax its economic controls in labor matters, either generally or with respect to the particular firm(s).

These circumstances introduce a dilemma into seizure—that the government must retain possession and control of the seized firms indefinitely unless specific criteria for termination are established (or improvised *ad hoc*). In experience, two criteria have predominated: retaining possession until the emergency (usually a war) is over—which raises the interesting question of when a war is really over; and retaining possession until the dispute is fully settled—which raises other questions as to what really constitutes a settlement, as well as how to induce a settlement in the absence of the pressures of a stoppage. The two criteria were combined in the Second World War and the Korean War.

In addition, some students of labor relations have urged recently that seizure be employed for a limited period only (for example, for 80 days).[2] With a specific deadline of this sort, the strike pressures would merely be postponed for 80 days (as under Taft-Hartley injunctions), and the country would neither be assured of a settlement of the dispute nor of continued production after the 80 days had passed.

The first criterion for termination of seizure—the ending of the economic emergency—has been incorporated by Congress in most seizure legislation, as may be seen in detail in Appendix B. Some of the laws have limited the period of possession to the current war; others to any war; still others have listed a variety of emergencies in which possession would be permissible. In practice, 24 seizures have been terminated, although the disputes were not settled, because the war or other emergency during which they were seized had come to an end.

The decisions in these cases have involved interpretations of the legislative provisions—essentially a definition of when the war or other emergency has really been over. Is a war over the day negotiations for a cease-fire begin, or when hostilities are formally declared at an end by the president or Congress, or when a treaty of peace is finally signed? Or does the war continue, in an economic sense, until the postwar readjustment of industry and labor has been completed?

At the close of the First World War, the army terminated possession of the Smith & Wesson pistol plant just 82 days after the armistice of November 11, 1918, because its contracts with the company for pistols had expired; but possession of the railroads and wire systems continued for many months more while Congress considered and finally passed legislation for the peacetime regulation of these utilities. Proposals for the indefinite retention of these basic industries (and of all wireless stations, too) came from members of the Wilson cabinet (McAdoo, Daniels, and Burleson), but were rejected by the newly elected, opposition-Congress.

A generation later, at the end of the Second World War, the Truman administration determined upon a quick return to normal collective bargaining. Just 11 days after the Japanese government had indicated by radio a willingness to surrender, President Truman issued Ex. Order 9603 (August 25, 1945), directing the release "as soon as practicable" of 22 seized properties at which the labor disputes were unsettled.[3] Within a week, nine such releases were effected. This was from two to five days before the Japanese officials actually surrendered to General MacArthur aboard the *U.S.S. Missouri* in Tokyo Bay (September 2, 1945, V-J Day).

In three of these releases, settlements had been near completion and were then quickly consummated before termination (Cudahy Bros., Goodyear Rubber, and Springfield Plywood); in the others, work had virtually ceased due to expiration of government contracts, or in any case the employees refrained from striking (with the single exception of Hughes Tool Co.). This appeared, for the moment, like rapid and effective reconversion. However, within two weeks the government had ended six other seizures, each with a resulting strike. Of these properties, three (oil refineries) had to be reseized six weeks later in the general refinery takeover; and two more had strikes lasting throughout the winter.

This precipitous release of seized properties, even before American forces had landed in Japan, may have been harmless enough where government procurement contracts were expiring, but where basic industries were involved it overlooked the continuing need for an uninterrupted supply of transportation, equipment, and materials with which to return millions of troops from overseas, to rehabilitate devastated areas and peoples, and to reconvert U.S. industry to peacetime production. For nearly a year after V-J Day, the president found it necessary to make new seizures of basic industries to prevent strike-induced shortages—oil refineries, meat-packing plants, soft coal mines, railroads, and other systems of transportation.

The experience suggests forcefully that the answer to "When is a war really over?" depends, in this context, less on the date of military victory than on the date of completion of the economic readjustment.

The second criterion for terminating possession—seeking to mediate a settlement of the dispute—was introduced in two steps during the seizures that preceded and accompanied World War II. The first step was the decision of President Roosevelt, in the very first seizure of the 1941 defense emergency (North American Aviation), to "get out as quickly as possible" but not until mediation proceedings were effectively operating. On June 10, 1941, the president conferred at the White House with Attorney General Jackson, Secretary of War Stimson, and Sidney Hillman (co-director of the Office of Production Management). According to a memorandum by Mr. Stimson:

The President's views coincided with the other three to the effect that in these cases of taking possession of plants we should keep the practice fluid so as to be adjustable to the different circumstances of each case.

Also, that in this case it was desirable to assume as little of the relationship of direct management to the operations of the company and its labor relations as possible, and that the company should be treated as the agent of the government for that purpose.

Also, that it was desirable to get out as quickly as possible.

Also that it was nevertheless advisable for us to stay in until we had mediation proceedings in train again.[4]

In the official executive order, directing the secretary of war to take possession of North American Aviation, President Roosevelt declared: "Possession and operation hereunder shall be terminated by the president as soon as he determines that the plant will be privately operated in a manner consistent with the needs of national defense."[5] A similar sentence appeared in every executive order issued thereafter by Presidents Roosevelt and Truman in seizure cases.

Congress appears to have approved of this effort to bring seizures to an early termination, for when it adopted the War Labor Disputes Act in 1943, it incorporated a provision that seized plants, mines, or facilities "shall be returned to the owners thereof as soon as practicable, but in no event more than 60 days after the restoration of the productive efficiency thereof prevailing prior to the taking of possession thereof" (sec. 3). This was at first misconstrued to mean that Congress wished the plants returned as soon as the level of physical production had been restored to its former quantity regardless of whether the dispute had been settled.[6] The absurdity of this view was shown in an opinion by Attorney General Biddle, on January 14, 1944, in which Mr. Biddle said, in part:

> To hold that return of possession is required in the face of a threatened recurrence of strikes or work stoppages would compel the government to go through the idle ceremony of relinquishing possession under one executive order and retaking possession under another . . . . The productive efficiency of a mine cannot be determined alone by the physical volume of coal produced at a given time; it is also necessary to consider whether, if the government relinquishes possession, there will be further interferences with production through strikes or stoppages or threats of strikes or stoppages.[7]

Hence the question of when a dispute is really settled needed definition. The validity of Attorney General Biddle's interpretation, from a practical standpoint, was illustrated in the total experience with seizure, in which 20 of the 31 unsettled disputes broke out into a resumption of the strikes when the president relinquished possession. Of these 31 cases, seven were released prior to the end of the emergency, and four of the seven were marked by renewed stoppages of production. (The four were coal mines, May 1943; Montgomery Ward & Co., May 1944; coal mine foremen, 1944; and basic steel mills, 1952. The coal mines and Montgomery Ward were reseized. The reseizure of the steel mills was prevented by Congress and the Supreme Court.)

The effect of releasing the disputing parties from possession prior to the end of the emergency if the dispute were fully settled was to place them under a kind of seizure "parole," by which they were subject to reseizure if any further stoppages occurred. They were released on their good behavior, so to speak. Often the seizing agency, upon terminating possession, would exact pledges from the management and the union(s) that they would not interrupt production again for the balance of the war. (Examples of such no-strike pledges: General Cable seizure by Local 868-B of the International Brotherhood of Electrical Workers (AFL); International Nickel by Local 40 of the United Steelworkers (CIO); Toledo machine shops by the Mechanics Educational Society of America.) Whether or not such pledges were obtained, the effect was the same—the release was conditioned on the parties' ability to maintain production thereafter without interruption. There is no record of any violated "parole" among the 40 cases that were fully settled.

The problem of how settlement was to be brought about was then the key to early relinquishment of possession. In the absence of strike pressures, the presidents have relied on other pressures available during seizure, particularly their control of the interim terms and of the date of release; but it should be pointed out that quite different forms of pressure have been suggested which would cause seizure to operate very differently, and also that seizure can be conducted without any attempt to mediate at all. Indeed, 13 seizures were conducted without any mediation efforts.

The experience with the 13 unmediated cases may throw some light on the proposal that in seizure cases the president should merely keep production going, without intervening in the dispute, leaving the parties to negotiate a settlement through collective bargaining. Of the 13 cases, only one resulted in a settlement (the Reading Railroad case during the Civil War). Of the others, one was prematurely released and had to be reseized (coal mine foremen 1944); the rest were retained for the duration of the emergency.

An example of the above proposal appeared in September 1950 when the Labor Relations Committee of the Chamber of Commerce of the United States declared that if seizure were used in a wartime emergency, "it should be directed solely at resumption of production, and that the government should be forbidden to make any agreement on behalf of the employer or union, but should relegate the parties to bargaining, mediation, and conciliation. During the seizure period, existing terms and conditions of employment should be continued in effect."[8] However, Frank M. Kleiler, in a later review of seizure history, concluded: "The theory that by seizure the government can be neutral and simply ensure vital production or services while disputing employers and unions negotiate their differences and reach

a voluntary agreement, however, really has not had a conclusive test . . .
As a method of maintaining free collective bargaining, [seizure's] success
has not been demonstrated."[9]

Another proposal, more frequently made, is that in seizure cases Congress should designate (or the president should improvise) certain "equal penalties" to be applied to both parties automatically during government possession until they reach an agreement.[10] This would be unlike anything undertaken heretofore. The obvious difficulties with this proposal are that the concept of "equal penalties" is virtually undefinable, and, even if defined and successfully applied, the objective of midpoint solutions is not necessarily applicable nor equitable in all disputes. To impose equal fines upon a wealthy disputant and upon an improverished one would not be equally burdensome. Again, in enforcing the decision of an emergency disputes board, the same penalty applied to the complying party would be patently unfair. Moreover, these proposals ignore the public interest in noninflationary terms of settlement. In short, they appear to confuse equality with equity, and a detached neutrality with impartiality.

In this connection, we should not overlook the fact that any requirement during seizure for rigid observance of the status quo in terms of employment during government possession would not only handicap efficient management of the business but would introduce an automatic bias into the negotiations for settlement in favor of the party which desired to continue the status quo—usually the owners. The absence of any such rigid requirement in the past is one of the principal reasons for presidential success in the 40 cases of mediating settlements acceptable to both parties and to the government as well.

THE RECORD OF SETTLEMENTS

The disputes leading to seizure have been among the toughest in industrial relations history, because they generally involved sturdy individualists used to their own way in giant industries or family-owned firms, or ambitious men contending for supremacy in the union power-structure. They were disputes that the regular or emergency disputes agencies failed to adjust. Hence they frequently reflected defiance of government rulings or competition between union factions rather than conflicts between labor and management.

The most frequent issue in dispute was wages and other matters of compensation, but a close second was union security in its many forms (including union recognition, maintenance of membership, check-off of union dues, and joint grievance procedures). A third was interunion disputes. The wage issues, although bitterly fought, were generally settled during seizure, but the union-security issues were less amenable to compromise and became the chief unsettled issues in seizure cases, as the figures of Table 6 show (derived from Appendixes E and F).

TABLE 6
ISSUES THAT LED TO SEIZURE

Issues	No. of cases fully settled (App. E)	No. of cases not settled (App. F)	Totals
Terms of contract			
Wages	22	8	30
Union security	4	16	20
Hours of work	0	1	1
Work load	0	1	1
Total	26	26	52
Grievances			
Labor-management	6	2	8
Interunion			
Representation	5	0	5
Jurisdiction (work assignment)	1	2	3
Interracial	2	0	2
Total	14	4	18
Secondary boycott			
Housing rentals	0	1	1
Grand total	40	31	71

The principal occasion for disputes leading to seizure has been the negotiation of union contracts. Of the 52 controversies originating in this way, exactly one-half were resolved during presidential possession. A substantial number of seizures arose over grievances under existing contracts, of which more than one-half involved employees at odds with one another rather than with the managements. However, a larger proportion of grievances than of contract disputes was settled during presidential possession—about three-fourths, or 14 out of 18 seizures.

The average time required to obtain all these settlements during seizure ran to 50 days (median) and 108 days (mean), measured by the duration of government possession. This record in which typical settlements required less than two months may be contrasted with the duration of possession in cases that were not settled—215 days (median) and 290 days (mean), typically about seven months. Of course, some issues were settled faster than others, as Table 7 shows (the interunion disputes being the quickest and the union-security issues the slowest).

TABLE 7
TIME REQUIRED TO SETTLE DISPUTES DURING SEIZURE

No. of cases (App. E)	Issue	Median days of govt. possession	Mean days of govt. possession
	Terms of contract		
4	Union security	163	187
22	Wages	56	137
	Grievances		
2	Interracial	54	54
6	Labor-management	51	51
6	Interunion	21	26
40	Total cases settled	50	108

As already mentioned, the settlement of disputes during seizure is made more difficult by the public interest in the terms of settlement—by the necessity of achieving not only an agreement between the parties but terms consistent with national policies of wage stabilization and industrial equity. This has been evident in 60 of the 71 seizures. Rulings of the government agencies upon the merits of the dispute affected not only the 43 cases of noncompliance that resulted in seizure but also 17 of the 28 unadjudicated disputes that resulted in seizure—17 cases in which the government ruled upon the merits after seizure had occurred.

The extent of the public interest in the terms of settlement reached during seizure is suggested by Table 8 showing the outcome of the special mediation efforts in which pressures were applied to induce acceptance of government rulings on the merits of the disputes.

It should be emphasized that the disputes involving management noncompliance were by far the most difficult to settle. Less than one-third of such cases were settled (seven out of 24, or 29 per cent), compared to more than two-thirds of the labor noncompliance cases (13 out of 18, or 72 per cent) and to a similar proportion of the initially unadjudicated disputes (19 out of 28, or 68 per cent).

A complete analysis of each dispute that was fully settled is given in Appendix E, and of each dispute that was not settled in Appendix F.

NONCOMPLIANCE CASES

In 43 seizures, the main disputes had been—at the time of the takeovers—the subjects of rulings upon the merits by emergency disputes boards, rulings which at least one of the parties had refused to accept. The existence of these outstanding rulings has dominated the subsequent negotiations and restricted the mediator's usual freedom of action.

TABLE 8
MEDIATING DURING PRESIDENTIAL POSSESSION

Kind of mediation	Labor non-compl.	Mgt. non-compl.	Both parties noncompl.	Initially unadjudi-cated	Totals
Fully settled during seizure (App. E)					
Govt. rulings accepted	7	3	0	13a	23
Govt. rulings modified and accepted	6	4	1	0	11
Mediation without govt. rulings	0	0	0	5	5
No mediation or govt. rulings	0	0	0	1	1
Total	13	7	1	19	40
Not settled (App. F)					
Govt. rulings not accepted despite mediatory efforts	3	11	0	3a	17
Govt. rulings neither accepted nor mediated	2	6	0	1a	9
Mediation without govt. rulings	0	0	0	2	2
No mediation or govt. rulings	0	0	0	3	3
Total	5	17	0	9	31

a These rulings were issued during seizure in cases not initially adjudicated. Of the 17 rulings, 11 were accepted immediately by both parties; two others were accepted after coercive pressures were applied.

As described in the preceding chapter, and as summarized in Table 8, the government succeeded in inducing ultimate acceptance of the original rulings in only 10 of the 43 cases, but mediated alternative settlements which were approved by the president in 11 other cases. These two groups add up to a total of 21 noncompliance cases, or almost one-half of the total that were settled during seizure and were then returned to private control without a resumption of strikes or lockouts. The average time required in these 21 successful cases was 60 days (median) and 130 days (mean)—a little above the average for all seizure settlements.

The means of achieving settlement may be seen by consulting Appendix E, which shows that defiant parties were induced to accept the original rulings as a result of successful mediation by the following government departments: the seizing agencies, six cases and part of another; the disputes agency, two cases and part of another; and the White House itself, one case (rails, 1948). The table further shows that modifications of the original rulings were accepted by the parties and approved by the president, following mediation by the seizing agencies in eight cases, and by the president or his personal aides in three rail industry cases (1943, 1946, 1950–1952). In some of the rail cases (especially 1950–1952), the National Mediation Board continued to furnish assistance.

In the absence of settlements, it became necessary to retain possession of the properties in 22 noncompliance cases until the country could again afford a resumption of normal collective bargaining; that is, until it could be indifferent to the terms agreed to by the parties and to any temporary shortage of goods and services arising from stoppages during negotiations. Although this rule was followed in theory, not all the properties were released under correct estimates of when the country would be immune to strikes. Four of the unsettled noncompliance cases were released before hostilities ceased, and three others before a suitable economic readjustment had taken place; all required governmental reintervention to mediate the controversies.

INITIALLY UNADJUDICATED CASES

The seizure cases in which no prior ruling had been made on the merits of the dispute by any disputes board have been numerous enough to merit special attention, although they comprise only a minority of the total of seizures (28, or about 40 per cent of the total). Many of the cases drew little public notice because they were single plants, but several were major industries—the railroads (1917–1920), oil refineries, meat-packing firms, and soft coal mines (1946–1947).

It should probably be noted at this point that 12 of the cases classed as "initially unadjudicated" were designated "noncompliance cases" by the second National War Labor Board. The board's terminology, however, confused two separate problems by lumping together instances of defiance of its back-to-work orders with instances of noncompliance with its arbitral rulings on the merits of controversies.[11] In 12 of the 28 cases in this section, the seizure occurred after the board had unsuccessfully ordered the men back to work; but in no case had the board ruled on the issue in dispute. (In the other 16 cases, no disputes board had issued a ruling of any kind.)

The unadjudicated disputes give the mediators a somewhat different task and different opportunities from those presented in noncompliance cases. The principal need in these disputes is to apply the available peaceful procedures, whereas in noncompliance cases the need is to induce acceptance of certain specific terms of settlement or alternative terms equally satisfactory to the government. Another difference is that the mediator has more freedom of action, since the government is not yet committed to a policy and often has no direct interest in the outcome of the controversy. A third difference is that the seizing agencies, who frequently did the mediating, have generally found less resistance to their interim control. When decisions were rendered, they applied to personnel and to property already subject to the moral suasion and physical duress of seizure.

The mediators have tried a variety of techniques, but their efforts can almost all be classified either as directing the parties into available means of arbitration or directly mediating between them. In four cases, no mediation or arbitration of any sort was attempted—with the not surprising result that three of the cases were not settled during government possession.

What agencies did the mediating in the initially unadjudicated disputes? The seizing agencies primarily, according to Appendixes E and F. The War Department, for instance, mediated successfully in five cases and persuaded the parties to arbitrate in four others (once with the help of a NWLB representative). The Navy Department induced arbitration in two cases. The Office of Defense Transportation induced arbitration in one, and mediated in one (with the help of an RWLB representative). The Department of Agriculture persuaded the parties to accept a fact-finding board decision. Next is the NWLB, which helped to induce the use of its own arbitral services in several cases. Lastly we should note several regular agencies of government which participated in mediation once or twice—the Federal Department of Labor, the National Mediation Board and the Maritime Commission. But the point should not be missed that when the regular agencies fail to prevent strike emergencies, and the president intervenes, the responsibility for settlement becomes the president's, and the work is likely to be transferred from those regular agencies to others entrusted with the tasks of emergency supervision.

The record of settlements in these initially unadjudicated cases is rather notable: 19 out of 28 (or nearly 68 per cent), comparing favorably with the 21 noncompliance cases settled out of 43 (or about 49 per cent). And the brief time required to obtain these settlements adds to the impressiveness of the record: a median of 46 days compared to 60 for the noncompliance cases, and a mean of 107 days compared to 126. Yet the better showing is found, on analysis, to be due almost entirely to the relative ease of settling the previously unadjudicated grievance cases, and to the large proportion of such cases among the settlements. In contrast, the problem of inducing settlements in the previously unadjudicated wage cases was often more complex than in the noncompliance wage cases. The emergency disputes boards had to investigate the issues, discuss the solutions, and prepare written orders and opinions—all of which had already been done at the time of seizure in the noncompliance cases.

Grievances. The initially unadjudicated grievance cases have been distinguished by the lack of public interest and also by the general adequacy of regular peacetime procedures to adjust them. Such cases have required presidential action only because the parties have disregarded the available procedures in their contracts or in the various labor-relations acts and have halted production at a bad time. The task of the seizing agencies has been to get the disputes back into the regular peacetime channels of adjustment.

Five disputes, or nearly one-half these cases, have involved union rivalry, and the other six have involved differences between unions and management. The former have proved to be the easier to adjust. The War Department's division of industrial personnel sent officers to the scene who got the disputes back into their normal channels of peaceful settlement.

In three cases, this meant working out some interim arrangement of "peaceful coexistence" between the unions, and then convincing the uncertified group that it should await the outcome of rather distant opportunities for new National Labor Relations Board elections (Massachusetts tanneries, Fall River textile mills, Toledo machine shops). In another case, the army persuaded the National War Labor Board to take over the arbitration of a dispute on a small but critical railroad in place of the National Mediation Board which had failed to prevent the strike (Painesville R.R.). In the fifth case, Secretary of Labor Schwellenbach insisted upon a month's extension of the seizure after V-J Day to give the army a chance to complete its mediation of a dispute involving both interunion and intra-union conflicts (U.S. Rubber).[12]

Of the grievance cases involving differences between the unions and management, three were settled quickly by the War Department's industrial personnel officers (International Nickel, Cleveland Electric, Diamond Alkali). In another case (Goodyear Rubber), navy officers obtained settlement of an accumulation of grievances through the appointment of a special arbitrator chosen by the parties (S. S. Kates), and then set up a permanent umpire system which functioned successfully for years afterward. In this, the navy acted on the advice of the NWLB, which recommended to the parties an experienced umpire (William E. Simkin).[13]

In the above cases, it may be noted that the seizing agencies turned on four occasions to the NWLB, while, in the five remaining cases, they relied solely on their own mediatory efforts. In two of the first group, however, there was interagency disagreement. In the Fall River case, the army at first made substantial concessions to the independent craft unions, which had called the strike, then later withdrew the concessions and acquiesced in an NWLB compromise. In the Goodyear case, the navy and NWLB disagreed as to the best procedure for adjusting the backlog of unsettled grievances, but finally adopted a compromise plan. However, the navy continued to act as final arbiter of new grievances arising during government possession, despite the NWLB's protests.

In addition, the seizing agencies failed to settle two initially unadjudicated grievance cases (P. & R. Coal, and Great Lakes Towing) apparently because the agencies did not undertake any mediatory efforts. Only such a policy would appear to explain the lack of settlement in the Great Lakes case in the face of intensive efforts by other government departments. (The Department of Labor sought vainly to induce the company to arbitrate, and the National Wage Stabilization Board brought pressure against the management by raising wages on the unions' petitions over management's protests.)

Contract negotiations. This class of cases is similar in that the seizures resulted from the breakdown of peaceful procedures of adjustment, not from defiance of government-recommended terms of settlement; but it differs in that the seizing agencies usually found that the normal procedures of peaceful adjustment were not adequate for the resolution of issues in contract negotiations, and that some emergency procedure was needed; and the government did usually have an interest in the terms of settlement to be reached, although it was initially uncommitted as to the degree and nature of such interest.

In these cases, the objective of the seizing agencies was generally to induce the parties to accept the emergency procedures that had been established—the National Defense Mediation Board, the National War Labor Board, the Railway Labor Act emergency boards, or presidential fact-finding boards. By such means, the seizing agencies were able to effect settlement in 10 out of 17 cases—the 10 settlements all being initially unadjudicated wage cases.

In two of the earliest wage cases (North American Aviation, Alcoa Steamship), consideration of the issues by government agencies had already begun, and the strikers were clearly trying to coerce these agencies into prompt and favorable rulings. President Roosevelt ended the strikes with firm measures but agreed to transfer jurisdiction of one dispute (Alcoa) from the Maritime Commission to the NDMB, as the union desired. The decision of the NDMB was mostly unfavorable to the union, which nevertheless accepted it.[14]

In six of the later cases, the seizing agencies coaxed the parties to turn to some form of emergency arbitration of their wage differences. The form of arbitration depended on the applicable legislation. Since the American R.R. of Porto Rico was outside the jurisdiction of the Railway Labor Act,[15] President Roosevelt directed the NWLB to arbitrate the cases. On the other hand, since the Aliquippa & Southern R.R. (a subsidiary of Jones & Laughlin Steel Corp.) was under the jurisdiction of the Railway Labor Act, the NMB induced the parties to accept a special arbitration board under sec. 7 (1951).[16] After V-J Day, because of the absence of applicable legislation, the seizing agencies turned to *ad hoc* fact-finding boards—appointed by the government in two cases (oil, meat), and by the parties themselves in two others (Capital Transit, New York tugboats). In a seventh case, a regional WLB held the threat of compulsory arbitration over the parties, which induced them to negotiate an agreement with the help of an agent of the board (Scranton Transit).[17] The government-appointed boards, in these cases, guarded the public interest in wage stabilization.

One more case of wage settlement remains—an exception to the general use of arbitration. This was the little-known seizure of the Philadelphia & Reading R.R. during the Civil War when the government had neither labor dispute boards nor economic stabilization agencies, but allowed prices to rise unhindered under the influence of wartime demand. When the operating employees of this railroad were persuaded to strike for higher wages by the newly organized Brotherhood of the Footboard, the War Department took possession of the road and restored operations using army employees. This quickly resulted in a settlement described by the president of the line, Charles E. Smith, as the "complete submission of the men"—a solution that reflected the government's abstention from any mediatory or arbitral efforts to offset the effect of its crushing the strike.[18]

The one-sidedness of this policy of forcefully restoring service, without furnishing an equitable means of settling the dispute, is illustrated in the remarkable letter written by Mr. Smith to the commanding general of the troops in Philadelphia, after the end of the strike:

> Philadelphia & Reading Rail Road Co.
> Office 227 South Fourth St.
> Philada. July 18, 1864
>
> Maj. Gen. Geo. Cadwallader [sic]
> Sir
> Our difficulties having terminated by the complete submission of the men, and the discharge of more than one half of them, I avail myself of the occasion to thank you for the prompt support which you rendered to me throughout—especially for your immediate compliance with my request that you should take military possession of the road.
> Your action brought the strike at once to a crisis and hastened a result favorable to us.
>
> Resply, Yours &c
> Charles E. Smith
> Prest.[19]

The great change in seizure policy since that letter was written may be illustrated by contrasting the War Department's aloofness to the terms of settlement in 1864 with its active mediation in the cases of 1942–1952. Not only did the department in the recent cases mediate or induce arbitration, but in one of the cases in 1952 (steel company railroads), it successfully ordered President A. L. Hutchison of the Monongahela Connecting to raise the wages of his operating employees by 12½ cents an hour, although this change was not in accord with the national pattern— about as extreme an incident in the other direction, and as exceptional, as the unmitigated strikebreaking in 1864. Nevertheless, both resulted in prompt and complete settlements.[20]

Except for the Civil War seizure, the government's interest in the actual terms of settlement in these wage cases has been reflected in its effort to guide the settlements, whether in arbitration or in mediation, into terms consistent with the national stabilization policies. This was effective enough in five of the cases to make price relief unnecessary. In two others, the approved wage increases became the basis of subsequent price adjustments, one of them by a procurement agency (North American Aviation), the other by the price stabilization agencies (New York Harbor tugs, 1946).

In still another case, meat-packing (1946), the wage and price decisions were made simultaneously instead of successively, causing an interagency conflict that temporarily delayed a settlement. In the end, the National Wage Stabilization Board and Office of Price Administration, which had wanted to restrict the price increases, agreed with the fact-finding board, the seizing agency (the Department of Agriculture), and the Office of War Mobilization and Reconversion upon a plan which allowed sufficient price increases to cover all the wage increase recommended by the fact-finders. The seizing agency then mediated a settlement in accord with the plan, bringing pressure upon the companies by putting the wage increases into effect in the seized plants (under the terms of sec. 5 of the War Labor Disputes Act). The price increases in the meat-seizure case affected government contracts for meat-procurement as well as the wholesale and retail price ceilings and required a special subsidy to cover the cost of retroactive wage payments.[21]

Thus the government held the line in half this group of cases, but yielded a little in the others, especially in the meat case. However, none of these cases was a major breakthrough; meat, for instance, merely reflected the new wage policy established by a breakthrough in steel (not seized) a few weeks before.

Besides the 10 cases of contract negotiations that were fully settled during seizure, there were seven others which the government failed to settle. These consisted of four wage disputes: the railroads (1917–1920),

Los Angeles Municipal Power Department, Texas Co., and the soft coal mines (1946–1947); together with two union-security disputes: the coal mine foremen (1944–1945) and Sinclair Rubber; and one secondary boycott over housing rentals: Cities Service. Major efforts to mediate settlements were made and came very close to success in the four wage disputes, but no mediation was attempted in the three nonwage cases.

COERCIVE MEDIATION IN THE NATIONAL INTEREST

The technique of mediating settlements during seizure has differed from traditional mediation in three significant respects: the mediators have lacked the pressures of the strike and lockout to bring modifications of extreme positions; they have developed and applied other pressures and inducements available through the special powers of seizure and through the administrative authority of the executive departments; and they have insisted in most cases upon terms of settlement reflecting certain national standards of industrial equity and wage-price stabilization. This contrasts with the normal mediatory practice of seeking agreements upon any terms mutually acceptable to the parties, regardless of the public interest in such terms, while relying upon the economic forces of the marketplace (especially the strike, the lockout, or the threat of a stoppage) to induce compromise and settlement.

As we have seen, the presidents beginning with Wilson have indicated, in all but a handful of cases involving chiefly grievance disputes, certain limits of acceptability with respect to the terms of settlement, although leaving much room for negotiation by the parties. But Wilson, while insisting on certain terms of employment during government possession, undertook no mediation but retained possession for the duration of the war emergency.[22] Later, Presidents Roosevelt and Truman sought to end the seizures quickly by continuing to mediate, by applying coercive pressures, and perhaps also by sweetening the ultimate profit picture, while keeping production going.

In these circumstances, it seems clear that mediation during presidential seizure has been of a new kind that is neither neutral as between the parties nor passive toward the negotiations.[23] The seizing agencies (with a few exceptions) have not been objective outsiders but subjective participants in the negotiations, which have become in effect tripartite. This has been the nature of mediation in the two classes of disputes—noncompliance and initially unadjudicated. In both, the mediators have been expected to uphold national wage guidelines and disputes-board policies without any direct control over the parties' economic circumstances once the dispute has been settled and private operations have been resumed.

Whereas the president's interim position in seizure was marked by strong legal controls balanced against explicitly authorized protections for all the disputing parties—for owners, employees, and unions—his position as mediator carried with it no comparable controls nor protections with which to influence the parties to yield their extreme positions. In mediating, the president and seizing agencies have had no authority to impose terms of settlement, nor could they grant any party explicit compensation for economic concessions made in reaching a settlement. Yet in practice they have developed important pressures and inducements to support their mediation efforts.

The president and the seizing agency have often established areas for maneuvering by the parties through the adoption of policies having the effect of indicating upper and lower limits of acceptability by the government. The highest terms recommended by a government disputes board, as approved or modified by the president, have tended to become the upper limit in the bargaining, because the company scarcely need offer more. The terms actually observed during government possession have tended to become the lower limit—whether these terms are the status quo ante or a change introduced by the government—because the union need not accept less. Each party would find continued government possession preferable to exceeding the limit indicated.

Thus the actions of the disputes board and of the seizing agency have become the two jaws of a pincer, acting to bring about agreement within the limits established by the president. By raising the interim terms, the seizing agency can narrow the spread between the limits; and by reducing the interim terms or by raising the recommendations of the disputes board, the government can cause a wider spread. Generally a narrow spread puts more pressure upon management to settle, since the management is virtually obliged to accept these terms either with or without governmental control. On the other hand, a wider spread puts more pressure upon labor to settle because the union is likely to do better by reaching a compromise agreement with management than by continuing under government control.

In addition to the effects of the interim controls, the president and seizing agencies have devised other pressures indirectly from the regular powers of the executive departments. Some of these have served to compensate the unions and some to compensate the employers for their bargaining concessions. The president has been able to offset union concessions by political patronage and legislative support. He has offset company concessions by tax and price adjustments, by financial subsidies, and by favorable consideration regarding procurement contracts. But the use of these indirect pressures and inducements has not been confined to seizure but has been available and used in other presidential mediation in emergency disputes without the interim controls and pincers effect of seizure.

In view of the obviously unneutral and coercive aspects of mediation in the historical experience with seizure, what has been the effect on the outcome of the disputes? Has mediation in seizure shown any consistent bias toward either labor or management?

An attempt will be made to appraise the effects of government mediation during presidential possession upon the strategic positions of labor and management, classifying the 71 seizures according to the change (or lack of change) in relative bargaining strengths of the parties during government possession. If a noncomplying party was able to gain by its defiance, that is, if it obtained presidential support for terms better than those the government originally recommended, this is treated as a gain for that party—as a shift in its relative bargaining position during seizure. On the other hand, if the terms originally recommended by the government were enforced during seizure, then the noncomplying party gained nothing by its defiance, and neither side improved its position. If the dispute at the time of the takeover was unadjudicated, then the crucial question was: Did either party win substantial concessions from the other during government possession—a gain or shift in bargaining positions? Or did the parties, on the other hand, reach a compromise agreement embodying no significant gain for either side?

The conclusion of this survey is that in 40 of the 71 seizures neither side made any significant gain in bargaining power at the expense of the other; also that the number of seizures in which the union gained at the expense of management (15) was approximately equaled by the number of seizures in which management gained at the expense of the union (16).

The cases of labor gain consist of two types: the noncompliance cases in which the president or the seizing agencies approved better terms for the union than the disputes boards had approved before seizure, thus pressing management to grant more than the government had previously supported— eight cases; and the initially unadjudicated disputes in which the seizing agencies or disputes boards supported terms that were more generous than the companies previously had offered—seven cases. It is noteworthy that 10 of the 15 cases in the category of labor gains involved coal or railroad labor organizations.

The strong position of rail unions during government possession is indicated by the following episode. A complaint was filed by the World Federation of Trade Unions with the International Labour Organization at Geneva during the railroad seizure of 1950–1952, alleging that the railroad employees had been denied trade-union rights, including freedom of

association and the right to strike. The complaint was dismissed as completely invalid by the Committee on Freedom of Association of the ILO,
headed by Paul Ramadier, in March 1952.[24]

The cases of managerial gain comprise two types: noncompliance cases
in which the seizing agencies adopted policies more favorable to management than the disputes boards had approved before seizure—nine cases;
and initially unadjudicated cases in which the seizing agencies supported
terms that were clearly advantageous to management—seven cases. It may
be noted that nine of the 16 cases in this category were powerful corporations in the oil, steel, and public utility fields. However, four of the 16
cases were really interunion disputes in which the government supported
management only in the sense of supporting the existing work-assignment
or representational arrangements; and another favored management only
by suppressing a secondary strike (Cities Service, Lake Charles, Louisiana)
that had sought to induce the company to bring pressure against the owners
of a private housing project with which the company had no connection.

From this evidence, it seems fair to conclude that the pressures brought
to bear upon the parties during seizure have not been mechanically biased
by anything inherent in the seizure technique but have reflected the national
economic policies set by the presidents; and the presidential policies
themselves have not shown any systematic bias in favor of either labor or
management, although a bias toward large organizations among both unions
and companies seems indicated. Of course, different presidential policies
could well introduce a bias toward either labor or management; and
different rules regarding the interim terms of employment could introduce
biased automatic pressures if so ordered by Congress or the Supreme Court.

CHAPTER 8

Minimizing the Interference with Managerial Authority

Although the policy standard developed over the years has been to minimize the changes in the normal day-to-day relationships of employees, unions, and managements, the extent of such interference has been greater than is generally recognized.

In the day-to-day supervision of the seized firms, the seizing-operating agencies have shown a sense of obligation (in the majority of cases) to balance the requirement for continued operation with measures to assure the individual employees of equitable treatment, and to prevent either the union or private management from taking advantage of the situation. In view of the vast powers available in seizure, the restraint shown by the presidents and the operating agencies has been commendable.

Nevertheless, the actual degree of penetration of the managerial responsibilities of the seized firms has been in some cases substantial. In 17 seizures, for example, the private managers of some or all the firms were replaced by government officials who assumed control over all operational matters. These were cases where private managements had refused to effectuate presidential directives. In the remaining seizures, managements were willing to act as agents of the president, and government decision-making was confined largely to labor relations, wages, and personnel practices.

AUTHORITY IN DAY-TO-DAY LABOR RELATIONS

The paramountcy of the president's authority as industrial manager of seized properties has been upheld when tested in the courts. Among the actions validated in litigation have been changes in wages and working rules[1] and the discharge of particular workers.[2]

The only congressional action broadly limiting the power of the seizing and operating agencies in labor relations has been the War Labor Disputes Act; and this act was limiting only in a procedural sense, not in the actual power allowed to the president (57 Stat. 163). The WLDA required in one clause that seized plants, mines, and facilities, while in government possession, "be operated under the terms and conditions of employment which were in effect at the time possession . . . was . . . taken" (sec. 4); but, in the next clause, provided two ways in which these terms of employment could be changed: (1) the employees could petition the National War

Labor Board, either directly or through their union, or (2) the government agency operating such plants could petition the NWLB to approve desired changes (sec. 5).

The effect of these provisions was not to prevent changes in wages and other working conditions during seizure, but to channel them through a central agency. The control of wages and other working conditions in seized plants was thus taken out of the hands of private management by Congress and given to the seizing and disputes agencies jointly, subject to the approval of the president for each change. The method seems to have worked satisfactorily, despite occasional friction between the NWLB and the seizing agencies.

Apart from the above procedural limitation, the presidents and seizing agencies have been free to continue (or to change) existing terms of employment in seizure cases, either in accordance with operational needs, or in accordance with the requirements of the public interest.

It should also be noted that many adjustments in routine personnel administration escaped even the procedural limitation of the WLDA, and were directed by the seizing agencies without reference to the NWLB, because the NWLB ruled that such adjustments were not to be considered "changes in terms and conditions of employment" within the meaning of the act.[3] A contrary ruling would either have swamped the board with decisions over petty details of business operations, or frozen every working rule in seized plants for the duration of presidential possession.

The authority of the seizing and operating agencies in labor relations was usually indicated by the presidents in the executive orders directing the take-overs, but the wording of the orders has varied greatly, while a dozen or more orders have been entirely silent on the interim terms. However, the most striking fact about these orders, when surveyed as a group, is that almost all have allowed interim changes to be made in some way, or have not forbidden such changes. This becomes clearer when we examine the orders which directed the seizing agencies to operate the properties "under the terms and conditions of employment that are in effect at the time possession is taken," and find that even these directions for the status quo have been qualified by some phrase authorizing changes. For example, some orders have stated that operations were to be "subject to the provisions of sec. 5 of the WLDA," or "pursuant to the provisions of the WLDA," or "subject to the applicable provisions of any existing law," all of which meant authority to make changes. In some other cases, the orders for the status quo have been qualified by requiring the observance of specific changes ordered by the NWLB and defied by one of the parties.

Direct operation. The usual classification of seizure controls by the seizing agencies has been in two categories—direct operation and "token" operation—according to whether government appointees replaced the top private managers as full-time supervisors of production and labor matters. Although this classification oversimplifies the great variety of policies actually pursued, it singles out probably the most important government decision affecting the degree of government penetration into managerial affairs.

The terminology of direct and "token" (or direct and indirect) operations has proved more useful than the terminology (also used) dividing seizures into operations for government account and for company account. The latter is ambiguous, unless defined as direct and indirect operations. The term "for government account" suggests the assumption of risks and the supply of funds by the government, but some seizures which began this way were converted at the end to company account, and some that were operated at "government risk" were nevertheless financed with company funds.

Let us examine the direct operations, in which the government has controlled some or all the firms in 17 of the 71 seizures, or in nearly one-fourth of the total, including 12 seizures of individual firms and five seizures of regional or industrywide groups.

Of the 12 individual firms which were directly operated, 10 had defied rulings of emergency disputes boards prior to seizure, and their executives were unwilling, even during seizure, to effectuate the changes ordered by the government. In these firms, management was removed at the outset. Most were small enterprises, usually family-owned and operated, but two were large—the Federal Shipbuilding & Dry Dock Co., a subsidiary of the United States Steel Corporation, with 18,000 employees; and Montgomery Ward & Co., with 72,000 employees, which was seized only in part, thereby creating a difficult operational problem. There were also two seizures of individual firms in initially unadjudicated disputes which were directly operated in order to effectuate arbitral rulings handed down later during government operation (American R.R. of Porto Rico, and Great Lakes Towing Co.). In the first of these, private management was immediately replaced, but in the second it was not replaced until seven months after the seizure had begun (because it refused to act as agent of the government in carrying out the arbitral ruling).

In the regional or industrywide seizures, the government nearly always arranged initially for the existing management to carry on without change as agents of the government, subject to specific orders to be issued by the seizing agency from time to time. These orders often proved objectionable but were generally accepted. The ultimate penalty for refusal to execute such orders was the removal of the insubordinate executives; and this disciplinary step has been taken in certain firms in three industrywide seizures (railroads, 1917–1920; telegraphs and telephones, 1918–1919;

soft coal, 1946–1947), and in one regional operation (midwest trucking, 1944–1945). In addition, the government has assumed full control of operations in one regional case in the short period during which it was supplying all of the personnel (New York Harbor towboats, 1946).

The assumption of direct operation by a seizing agency involved the establishment of federal offices at the seized plant and at company headquarters, and the assignment to the federal offices of production executives, one (or more) labor relations officers, legal and financial advisors, and possibly a public relations man.[4] The number of such appointees depends on whether the government is operating a single firm or a group of firms. For a single firm, as few as a dozen, or 100 or more, have been employed; for an entire industry the number has exceeded 1,000. Much also depends on how far down in the company hierarchy the government has to dip. Usually one echelon has been enough to obtain cooperation.

In direct operations, the government is responsible not only for labor relations but also for production, marketing, and finance. The longer and bigger the seizure, the more such decisions are called for. In some of the railroad seizures, the government has bought new locomotives (rails, 1917–1920, and American R.R. of Porto Rico), built new facilities (rails, 1917–1920, and T.P. & W. R.R.), and consolidated terminals, ticket offices, and routes (rails, 1917–1920). In a long trucking seizure, it has purchased new tractors and has consolidated routes (midwestern case). It has dispensed with company advertising (rails, 1917–1920, and Ken-Rad Tube & Lamp), and dismissed the sales force (Ken-Rad), while in other cases engaging in aggressive sales efforts (T.P. & W. R.R.), and in one seizure retaining the former private management as its sales agent (Carter Coal Co. in the 1946–1947 coal industry operation). Today telephone users still pay a service-connection charge and benefit from the rationalization of long-distance rates, ordered by the postmaster general in the wire seizure of 1918–1919. Similar examples could be cited in the area of finance.

However, our major interest is the government's participation in day-to-day labor relations—in such matters as the interim terms of employment, the status of the union (or unions), the personnel practices, grievance procedure, and coincidental disputes (disputes not related to the basic issues which precipitated seizure). It is here that the seizing agencies have had to supply the employees with equitable working conditions and the unions with protection in their rights of representation despite the ban on striking, while keeping interference with management to a minimum. In the opinion of some legal students, these responsibilities toward the employees are created by "just compensation" as much as the responsibilities toward the owners;[5] but, in any case, the responsibilities toward employees and unions appear to be the natural counterpart of the government's denial of the normal rights of collective action through its forceful insistence upon uninterrupted production. In the opinion of many students of labor relations, the government, having guaranteed the right of collective bargaining by law, cannot equitably withdraw this right from specific groups without providing a suitable substitute for the normal method.

In the direct operations, the seizing agencies have experimented with a variety of substitutes. This is evident by their methods for determining the interim terms of employment. The principal choices have been that the seizing agencies might unilaterally fix the interim terms; or, they might adopt the recommendations of an emergency disputes board; or negotiate bilaterally with the union(s); or turn the matter back to the former private management and the union; or some combination of these.

In the 17 directly operated seizures, the record is diverse and overlapping. The interim terms were fixed by the seizing agencies in six cases, determined by disputes boards in 10, negotiated between government and union in four, and referred back to the original parties in three. While the details of these cases will be discussed later, the mere count of cases at this point shows the extent to which the government displaced private management as a factor in the determination of the interim terms.

In adjusting grievances, the principal issue was whether to permit private arbitration as the final step in a government-operated plant. In the cases directly operated, the seizing agencies enforced the use of private arbitration over the objections of the former managements whenever the disputes boards directed it (T.P. & W. R.R.; S. A. Woods; Montgomery Ward), except for an initial delay in the Woods case. Otherwise, the seizing agencies forbade private arbitration, and took the final step in the procedure; but in either circumstance, the government was clearly calling the tune.

From actual decisions in the 17 cases of direct operation, the reader can see the different policies pursued and the varying degrees of government substitution for private management.

(1) *Railroads* (1917–1920). Labor relations were supervised nationally by a division of labor (headed by a former president of the Brotherhood of Locomotive Firemen and Enginemen) in the office of the director general of railroads. Interim terms of employment were established by directive orders of the Railroad Administration, relying in part on recommendations of a special wage commission. Late in 1919, the RRA signed three contracts with unions over issues other than wages (unions representing shop-crafts, maintenance-of-way men, and clerks). Grievances for all classes of employees on all railroads were handled through a new centralized procedure using bipartite national boards of adjustment, with final decision if necessary by the director general. (Only 10 of over 5,000 such cases had to be referred to the director general.) Grievance procedure was created by

contracts between RRA and 14 national unions. 532 railroads were directly operated by the Railroad Administration, as a result of the RRA's dismissal of the corporations as its agents and appointing federal managers who reported directly to seven regional directors, about five months after seizure began. Although nearly all the federal managers were experienced railroad men, they were forced to sever their connections with the particular companies. Dozens of railroad presidents were dismissed entirely from operational responsibility. Rates were raised by government order. Government authority was upheld in various court actions.

(2) *Telegraphs and Telephones* (1918–1919). No division of labor was created. The Post Office Department issued several orders regarding wages and working conditions, but observance was erratic and sometimes entirely lacking. Postmaster General Burleson modified a contract between the Western Union Telegraph Co. and a new company union, and occasionally mediated labor disputes, but generally urged the companies to negotiate with employees without government assistance. After four months, the Post Office Department merged the land-wire facilities of Postal Telegraph and Western Union over the protests of Postal, professedly to achieve economies, and after another month merged the cable systems of the same companies, discharging top Postal Telegraph executives. Some other Postal Telegraph employees were moved around, and officials sympathetic with Western Union were put in charge. The managements of telephone companies with whom the Post Office Department had the most friendly relations were undisturbed. The department ordered both telegraph and telephone rates increased, an action upheld by the Supreme Court over the protests of state regulatory commissions.

(3) *Smith & Wesson Co.* (1918–1919). The War Department dismissed top company executives and leased the property to a dummy government corporation, the National Operating Corporation, whose officials were army ordnance officers. The government managers set wages and working conditions and adjusted grievances.

(4) *Federal Shipbuilding & Dry Dock Co.,* Kearny, New Jersey (1941–1942). The Navy Department removed the company president, put a navy admiral in charge, and brought in its own civilian labor adviser, who settled major grievances. The only changes in basic conditions of employment were those agreed to by the former company management and the union, but the navy reissued and enforced old plant rules and tightened discipline. Once, on complaint from the union, it revoked severe penalties against two workers.

(5) *Air Associates,* Bendix, New Jersey (1941). The War Department not only replaced the company president for the duration of government possession but persuaded the company's board of directors to obtain new

permanent management. The army employed a civilian labor adviser, who adjusted major grievances. No changes were made in terms of employment until the parties reached an agreement.

(6) *Toledo, Peoria & Western R.R.* (1942–1945). The ODT replaced private management with an experienced executive from another railroad, then issued a new schedule of wages and working conditions for each of 13 classes of employees after a conference with the appropriate labor organization. The ODT claimed that these were not "union contracts" but were instead government schedules supplemented by "memoranda of understanding" between the superintendent and two of the general chairmen.

(7) *S. A. Woods Machine Co.,* Boston, Massachusetts (1942–1945). The War Department replaced private management at first with army ordnance officers, together with a civilian labor adviser, but later leased the company's three plants to a private concern, the Murray Co., of Dallas, Texas. During the first phase, the War Department dealt directly with the local union and made final decisions on grievances as well as a number of job rates. It reinstated three men who had been discharged by the private management for cause, ruling that the offenses had been trivial. It refused to permit arbitration by an outside agency, although directed by the NWLB, since it considered that the employees had become unclassified civil service workers by virtue of the seizure. In the second phase, the new contractor took over. He modified some job rates and fired several veteran foremen for reputedly giving information to the company owners.

(8) *American R.R. of Porto Rico* (1943–1944). The ODT replaced private management with an experienced executive from a mainland railroad. The ODT made a few immediate adjustments in pay for supervisory officers and office employees, and, subsequent to the NWLB award of $100,000 in wage increases for union members, gave a straight 10-per cent increase to all supervisory and office employees. The federal manager forbade arbitration and settled all grievances personally. (About 40 per cent of his decisions went in favor of the union.)

(9) *Ken-Rad Tube & Lamp Corp.,* Owensboro, Kentucky (1944). Private management voluntarily withdrew, and was replaced by army officers, including experienced engineers and labor-relations specialists. The army reorganized personnel practices, adjusted grievances (despite the company's refusal to furnish information on its previous policies), and enforced an NWLB order. A company suit alleging that the government lacked authority to seize the plant and to change the terms and conditions of employment was dismissed by a U.S. district court. It was not appealed.

(10) *Montgomery Ward & Co.,* Chicago, Illinois (1944). Although the Department of Commerce removed Sewell Avery bodily from his office (using soldiers), it found that most of the government orders were dis-

regarded by company employees. One order that was carried out forbade further discharges, without the department's approval. Secretary of Commerce Jones appointed an RFC official, John D. Goodloe, as grievance officer to look into previous discharges and other grievances submitted by the union. Mr. Goodloe obtained answering data from the company, but was unable to hold hearings in the brief period of government possession.

(11) *Midwest trucking firms* (1944–1945). The ODT assumed full charge of unresolved grievance cases when the employers refused to re-establish the old procedure which had broken down and the NWLB failed to establish any new methods despite its announced intention. "Because of the prevailing immunity from strike, there was in any event little or no incentive for the operators voluntarily to organize grievance committees of any kind," wrote the federal manager, Ellis T. Longenecker. (Report of federal manager, p. 29.) The federal manager and his regional managers handled specific grievances in 53 of the 103 seized firms on matters of discharge, seniority, vacation pay, and so forth. Although the federal manager upheld the old union contract, ODT orders regarding maximum use of equipment often conflicted with seniority rights under the contract, and the ODT was able almost invariably to induce employees to concede their rights in such cases. After several months, the ODT discharged the private managers of eight of the 103 firms and began direct operations. In three of the eight companies, this change was because of refusal to carry out orders of the federal manager; in the five others it was caused by financial weakness. In a ninth firm, a warning that the government would assume direct control of operations resulted in compliance with an order of the federal manager. The federal manager assumed control of individual rate policies of all the seized carriers, whether directly or indirectly operated, and in one instance issued direct orders to the publishing agent, over the carrier's objection, to establish an increased rate for the carrier.

(12) *Twentieth Century Brass Co.,* Minneapolis (1944–1945). The War Department retained the three stockholders, who were also its managing officers, in subordinate capacities, but later dismissed one and cut the salaries of the others in half. The army had to handle many business problems such as production scheduling in addition to labor relations.

(13) *Montgomery Ward & Co.,* offices and facilities in seven cities (1944–1945). The War Department discharged plant managers and gained the cooperation of other employees in the seized facilities but was able to obtain only partial cooperation from Sewell Avery who was running the unseized facilities. The Retail Union (CIO) submitted comprehensive demands for changes in terms of employment to the War Department, akin to demands in collective bargaining, but the army stalled and took no action. The army did effectuate the various NWLB orders, except that its authority

was temporarily hampered by a U.S. district court order for about six months. The NWLB settled accumulated grievances from the Chicago facilities, and the army enforced the decisions, reinstating 12 workers and giving pay adjustments to six others. An army decision to furnish wage-rate information to the unions (information not previously furnished by the company) was ruled not a change in terms of employment requiring sec. 5 procedure by the NWLB. The army provided additional training for company supervisors.

(14) *Gaffney Manufacturing Co.,* Gaffney, South Carolina (1945). Top company officials walked out when the War Department officials arrived, and so direct operations became necessary. The army restored the expired union contract, as directed by the NWLB, including its grievance provisions. It also effectuated the "23 Southern Cotton Mills" decision, although Gaffney was not one of the 23 mills, obtaining permission from the NWLB under sec. 5 of the WLDA. The army had to supervise the details of production in one of the South's largest textile mills.

(15) *Great Lakes Towing Co.* (1946–1947). The ODT at first left operations in the hands of private management and even signed a contract assuring management it would not be required to comply with any order that might be issued by the NWLB or other government agency pursuant to sec. 5 of the WLDA. With this assurance, management proceeded to make favorable changes by ignoring various provisions of its existing contract with the union. But sec. 5 was not to be so easily disposed of. Under its provisions the unions obtained wage increases from the NWSB (successor of the NWLB); and when the company refused to effectuate these increases, pointing to its contract with the government, the ODT cancelled the contract, dismissed the company president and took direct control of operations.

(16) *New York Harbor towing companies* (1946). The first phase of this case was one of government operations. The ODT, as seizing agency, called upon the Navy Department and other government agencies to supply tugboats and crews to break the strike of tug crewmen. The result was the establishment of a central despatching office at the Brooklyn Navy Yard, for which the companies supplied "volunteer despatchers" whose activities were coordinated by an executive of one of the companies, "always subject to the immediate supervision of the Navy and the over-all direction of the Federal Manager." (ODT, *Civilian War Transport,* p. 291.) All of the tug crews and most of the boats were the government's (navy, army, and city of New York); so the operation was for government account. The ODT billed those who received towing services and collected approximately $50,000 for the U.S. Treasury. The second phase of the seizure began in about a week when the regular crewmen returned to work. Operations thereafter were by each company in the usual manner.

(17) *Bituminous coal mines* (1946–1947). The seizing agency, the Department of the Interior (assisted by navy officers), negotiated a contract with the United Mine Workers, providing, among other things, for an industrywide welfare fund to be financed by contributions from all mines that had previously had agreements with the UMWA. The agency effectuated this contract as interim terms for the period of government possession (under sec. 5 of the WLDA); but two seized companies refused to contribute to the new fund. The government replaced the top managements of the two recalcitrant companies, seized their funds, and made the required payments into the union's welfare fund. The government closely supervised labor relations in the two firms, but followed the same policy regarding grievances as with the rest of the industry—namely, to act merely for private management in these disputes and to submit any unresolved cases to private arbitration under the industrywide contract. Several disputes between government and union were resolved by arbitration in this way, including one at Carter Coal Co., which was directly operated. A suit by the other company directly operated (Fox Coal Co.) attacked the government's authority to change the terms and conditions of employment. Although the suit was sustained by the district court, it was rejected unanimously by the court of appeals. After five months, the UMWA asked to reopen its contract with the government, but the seizing agency refused. President Truman offered to return the mines to private operation (and so to normal collective bargaining) in two more months, but the union declined this offer and struck against the government. Through court action, Mr. Truman compelled the union to live with the existing interim terms not merely for two months more but actually for eight months more—until the seizure came to an automatic end with the expiration of the WLDA. In the course of the litigation, the Supreme Court appropriately construed the government's position to be that of actual employer for the period of government possession.

Indirect operation. The indirect seizure cases were conducted by the regular private managements as agents of the government under varying degrees of supervision by the seizing agencies. They have been referred to rather inaccurately as "token" operations. The word "token" has been used because the government seldom intervened in the production, marketing, or financial problems in these cases, but confined its controls almost entirely to labor relations; but the extent of intervention in labor relations has frequently been more than a mere formality. The problems and solutions have been similar, in many cases, to those in direct operations.

As explained earlier, this indirect type of seizure operation was developed to simplify the government's administrative burdens, and to minimize its interference with the companies' normal practices, in those seizures in which management was initially in full compliance with the government's emergency labor policies. This concept was formalized by the Department of the Interior in the industrywide coal seizures of 1943. The department entered into written contracts with several thousand mining companies, designating them agents of the government, but reserving control over labor relations for the department's coal mines administration. The chief executive officer of each company was named "federal operating manager." This was later extended to seizures in which neither party was noncompliant (the initially unadjudicated disputes) and even to a few in which management itself was in defiance. In these, managements either agreed to carry out the contested government rulings under the duress of seizure (thus yielding *de facto* without yielding *de jure*) or else wrung a provision out of the seizing agency that only government employees, not company officials, would participate in any enforcement of the objectionable ruling (Humble Oil).

This economical form of seizure operation has been the source of much confusion because, as Professor Cox has pointed out, it leaves "the essential nature" of a seizure action "ill defined." The confusion is because of the seeming contradiction between the language of force used in seizure orders and the administratively simple, cooperative nature of the indirect operation. But this paradox is resolved by the Supreme Court in *U.S.* v. *Pewee Coal Co.* (341 U.S. 114). In the court's view, the government's control in the indirect type of operation was neither fictional nor nominal, but was actual participation "in the mining business." The reasoning was that the government issued orders affecting labor relations during government possession, and was both able to and did remove company managements who refused to carry out the orders.

In these indirect operations, the seizing-operating agencies were able to economize on government personnel, since they had, in effect, waived all responsibility except for labor relations and for keeping a watch on continuity of production.[6] The task of supervision was much greater, of course, in the 10 industry seizures and in the eight regional operations than in the 36 single-firm seizures that were indirectly operated. Yet even in the industrywide operations, much was gained from experience. The War Department, for example, reduced the total personnel required from nearly 700 in the rail seizure of 1943 to not over 50 in the rail seizure of 1950–1952. In the single-firm seizures, the number of personnel needed was much smaller—ranging from a dozen or so down to the solitary figure who manned a lonely desk (at Humble Oil) or one who monotonously inspected daily the length of a small railroad line (Bingham & Garfield Ry.).

The economy of administration in indirect operations does not mean, however, that the presidents and seizing agencies ordinarily overlooked their responsibility to provide an adequate substitute for normal collective bargaining. In most cases, the seizing and operating agencies studied the matter carefully, with the aid of their own labor-relations experts, and often in consultation with the White House. A few of the civilian agencies even borrowed experienced labor-relations officers from the armed forces. The ODT, for example, employed an army officer at Scranton Transit; and the Department of the Interior obtained the services of several navy officers in the soft coal dispute (1946–1947).

Generally the seizing and operating agencies demonstrated their concern for equitable interim terms of labor either by adopting terms recommended by governmental disputes boards or by establishing the terms themselves. In only a minority of the so-called "token" or indirect operations did the agencies turn the issue over to the parties themselves under biased conditions for bargaining (that is, with strikes banned and the terms of labor frozen in the manner private management had established).

In noncompliance cases that were indirectly operated, the operating agencies relied heavily upon the emergency disputes boards for guidance regarding interim terms, effectuating the boards' contested recommendations in 14 seizures, usually at the specific direction of the president in his executive orders. But at times the agencies also showed their independence of the disputes boards, since the boards' recommendations were merely advisory to the president. They effected changes in interim terms in four cases where the boards had recommended continuance of the status quo (specifically the boards had urged the continuance of expired collective-bargaining contracts in the coal mines in May 1943; the San Francisco machine shops; Hughes Tool Co.; and Mary-Leila Cotton Mills); while they maintained the status quo in seven cases where the boards had recommended changes (General Cable; rails, 1943–1944; Humble Oil; Pure Oil; rails, 1946, 1948, and 1950). In some of these instances, they sought (and obtained) the disputes boards' approval for modifications, but in other instances did not even consult the boards.

An illustration of the independence of the seizing agencies is that in the coal seizure of November 1943, when Secretary of the Interior Ickes, acting for President Roosevelt, negotiated an agreement with the United Mine Workers, somewhat exceeding the terms recommended by the NWLB and the President, and then, having obtained the board's reluctant ratification of most of the agreement, went beyond the ratification in the terms he adopted for the duration of government possession.[7] All of which brought cries of protest from the thousands of "federal operating managers"—those so-called "agents of the government" who really were paid by and beholden to the mine owners. Surely, as far as management was concerned, this was a case of having all the trappings of a "paper seizure" but the actuality of federal control.

In the initially unadjudicated cases that were indirectly operated the problem of the seizing agencies was somewhat different from the compliance cases in that there was no contested disputes-board ruling at the outset. The problem, as we have seen in previous chapters, was primarily to get the parties to employ peaceful procedures for resolving their differences, without allowing the strike ban to bias the results toward the side of management. What interim terms of labor would facilitate this result? In several cases, the seizing agencies relied upon disputes boards for guidance in this matter. Secretary of Agriculture Anderson, for example, effectuated as interim terms the changes recommended by a fact-finding board during seizure in the meat-packing case. This put pressure upon the packers to agree to the board's recommendations. Again, the War Department, after effecting temporary adjustments on its own, relied on the NWLB for further recommendations in the Massachusetts leather and textile cases. In a contrasting case, a seizing agency effectuated what it believed was a suitable permanent solution, without consulting a disputes agency. (This was on the Monongahela Connecting R.R. and other rail subsidiaries of the Jones & Laughlin Steel Corporation in 1951.)

In the main, however, the seizing agencies in these initially unadjudicated, indirectly operated seizures, continued the existing terms of employment without change; but this does not mean that they necessarily left the parties free of governmental direction in their labor relations. Either the issues were arbitrated (as in North American Aviation, Alcoa ships, and oil refineries); or they were imaginatively mediated in ways previously described that allowed no advantage to either party from the continuance of the status quo; or the status quo had the effect of upholding the prior rulings of a regular agency (not an emergency board)—the Anthracite Board of Conciliation in the Reading Coal case (1944), and the NLRB in the coal mine foremen's case. Only in two or three instances did the seizing agencies, after setting the status quo, leave the parties to settle their dispute without assistance— with the result that the seizures dragged on without settlement (Cities Service, and Sinclair Rubber).

In the matter of grievances, the question of the propriety of private arbitration arose just as it did in the direct seizure operations. The army required the use of private arbitration as the final step in the grievance procedure in two cases wherein the management had refused to use it, despite NWLB orders—Hummer manufacturing division of Montgomery Ward, and Hughes Tool Co. On the other hand, the navy forbade the use of private arbitration for current grievances in three cases wherein this had either been the normal practice or at least acceptable to management, and named the officer in charge as the final step in the procedure (San Francisco machine shops, United Engineering, Goodyear Tire). The army also made at least preliminary adjustment of grievances in five cases in which grievances had become the main issues, and modified somewhat the usual grievance procedures in three other cases in which the main issue was wages. One civilian agency, the Department of the Interior, set up regional offices to adjust "local grievances which caused or threatened strikes" (coal mines, May and November 1943).

In the matter of personnel practices, the seizing agencies, in the indirect as well as the direct operations, frequently employed their own labor-relations experts (generally at Washington headquarters, but often also at the seized plants), made major suggestions for reform, in several instances supplied additional training for company supervisors, and in two cases encouraged the managements to obtain new directors of industrial relations.

The matter of coincidental disputes was important only in long seizures of firms organized along craft lines, wherein there might be a dozen or more labor contracts not involved in the dispute. To keep renegotiation of these contracts under government control, the navy and army established rules in two lengthy seizures involving numerous craft unions—the 103 San Francisco machine shops in 1944–1945 and the 195 railroads in 1950–1952. Among the navy rules in the machine-shop case was one suspending any provisions that might be agreed upon requiring private arbitration of grievances, or prohibiting the employment of part-time workers, or prohibiting overtime work beyond 48 hours a week.[8] Following a different policy, in the railroad case, the army forbade any changes in working conditions without its prior approval. In at least two instances such approval was withheld. On the other hand, changes that were agreed upon by both the carrier and the labor organization were generally approved.[9]

The two cases just described illustrate a secondary effect of seizure on day-to-day labor relations: that the seizing agencies not only imposed changes upon the private managements but also exercised some restraint upon the changes which the managements normally would have made in the absence of seizure.

CHANGES IN TERMS OF LABOR

As a result of presidential control over the day-to-day labor relations of seized firms, what changes have actually been made in the terms of labor of the employees during government possession? How extensive were these changes? How equitable were they?

In summary, we may say that, although a great deal of lip service was paid to the general rule of continuing in effect the terms and conditions of employment which existed at the time of seizure, there is evidence of important interim changes in more than half the seizures. In fact, the record shows that interim changes were made in 42 of the 71 seizures, and that the seizing agencies employed compulsion in making at least some of these changes in 35 of the 42 seizures, while allowing other changes to be made either at the request of the company or by agreement of the disputing parties in 19 of the 42 seizures (voluntary and compulsory changes often occurring in the same cases).

Changes in interim terms were made in one or more of the following areas: union status, wage rates, basic hours of work, vacation practices, racial integration, or physical conditions of the workplace. Some of the changes were related to the main issues in the disputes which led to seizure; others to secondary issues; still others to problems (not necessarily disputes) arising coincidentally during governmental operations. The changes were concentrated in the areas of union status and wage rates, as Table 9 shows.

TABLE 9
CHANGES IN TERMS OF EMPLOYMENT IN 42 SEIZURES

	No. of seizures		
Changes[a]	Main issue	Secondary issue[b]	Totals
Union status	20	10	30
Wages	14	16	30
Basic hours	2	5	7
Vacation practices	0	9	9
Racial integration	2	0	2
Workplace	0	8	8

[a] More than one kind of change occurred in some seizures.
[b] Or coincidental dispute.

Although 29 seizures brought no change in terms of employment during government possession, the reader should not assume that these seizures were uneventful. For example, in three, the striking employees were replaced temporarily by government personnel; and, in four, the government took over the responsibility for final settlement of grievances. Yet these events were not changes in the actual working conditions of the employees, in the sense used here, but were part of the broader struggle for control of day-to-day labor relations discussed in the preceding section.

Moreover, many of the seizures, in which no changes occurred, were of brief duration; 12 of them were for less than a month, 21 of them for less than 100 days.

Union status. The status of unions was changed in some 30 seizures— in nearly all by compulsion. The seizing agencies imposed a stronger form of union security over the objections of management in 18 cases, and with the concurrence of management in three or four. Specifically, they reinstated employees discharged for union membership or other union activities (five cases), and introduced maintenance of union membership and/or the check-off of union dues (14 cases). In addition, company managements agreed voluntarily with the unions to an extension of union status in one of the preceding cases (Ken-Rad) and in two others (Philadelphia Transportation Co. and a few railroads in 1950–1952), this action being probably not entirely spontaneous on the part of the companies but a response to indirect government pressures. In these voluntary extensions of union security, Ken-Rad signed a contract covering four branch plants which previously had been nonunion; Philadelphia Transportation signed a contract giving a newly recognized union maintenance of membership; and several railroads (in 1952) conceded the union shop to certain labor organizations under newly enacted, permissive legislation.

The government also exercised compulsion in directing certain changes in three seizures involving union rivalries, acting in one case to uphold the NLRB, and in the other two to obtain and follow the advice of the NWLB. The first of these was in the coal mine seizure of November 1943, and was the recognition of the Molders' Union for foundry workers by the Glen Alden Coal Co., in accord with an NLRB ruling. The company claimed it was excused from observing the NLRB ruling by the seizure of its properties, but the seizing agency (Department of the Interior) gave its support to the NLRB, and the courts upheld the seizing agency. In none of these three cases was the status of unionism in doubt or changed in any way, but merely the technical problems in determining the employees' own choice of a representative in collective bargaining. This altered the status of particular unions. On the other hand, as will be pointed out below, there were eight seizures in which the status of unionism indeed was weakened instead of strengthened—five of these being due to government compulsion and three to the seizing agencies' acquiescence in company moves.

In the First World War, President Wilson's War Labor Conference Board unanimously condemned the practice of discharging employees for joining unions, yet a few individual companies felt that their views were not represented by this statement of wartime labor principles and so continued to make discriminatory discharges. A majority of Wilson's wartime disputes board, appointed on the recommendation of the War Labor Conference Board, found two prominent concerns guilty of this practice—the Western Union Telegraph Co. and the Smith & Wesson pistol firm. Pointing out that the industry members of the disputes board had not concurred in the finding, both companies refused to alter their nonunion, closed-shop policies.

President Wilson then backed the War Labor Board by seizing both concerns, assigning one to a department that was as anti-union in policy as the company itself—the Post Office Department. The company, Western Union, continued to discharge telegraphers openly for attending union meetings and for wearing union buttons, and was upheld, although in guarded language, by the postmaster general. At the same time, the president assigned the arms plant to the War Department, which strictly enforced the open shop, reinstating the discharged workers with back pay and dismissing the company's strikebreakers. Meanwhile, on the railroads, which had been seized over a wage dispute, not over discriminatory discharges, the Railroad Administration, by its Order No. 8, forbade discrimination in hiring or firing, and opened the way for the successful organization, on all railroads, of all classes of labor not previously organized—mostly the nonoperating employees. This brought about a very significant change in railroad labor relations.

By the Second World War, the practice of discharging workers for joining unions had been outlawed by the Wagner Act, and diehard anti-union businessmen were opposing the unions more by raising technical obstacles and by stalling over bargaining than by discriminatory discharges. Yet such discharges continued in a few cases, being responsible (in part) for three seizures. At Air Associates, the army met this challenge of the labor law by firing the company's strikebreakers and restoring the discharged union members; on the T.P. & W. R.R., the ODT did the same; at Montgomery Ward, the discharges continued for a time during the first seizure under the Commerce Department, but were halted—and the ousted employees restored—during the second seizure under the War Department.

However, the principal issue over union status in the Second World War was employee responsibility in maintaining membership in good standing after joining. The unions demanded government action to require employees who joined unions to maintain their memberships for the duration of the union contracts; and the wartime disputes boards adopted this principle, despite the objections of the industry members, holding that the unions needed this minimum security in return for giving up the right to strike, and to prevent the dilution of existing membership in the rapid expansion of war employment. An occasional variant or supplementary requirement was the checking-off of union dues by the employers.

Numerous employers resisted this policy and refused to comply with decisions of the National Defense Mediation Board, or its successor, the National War Labor Board. Enforcement of these decisions occurred in 12 seizures and in parts of two others. Despite the resistance that this indicates, a number of other firms acquiesced during the war, some undoubtedly because of the likelihood of seizure if they did not. The total effect was clearly to prepare the way for wider acceptance of these stronger forms of union security in the postwar period.

In enforcing these measures, the government also insisted upon union responsibility, and in several instances withdrew or withheld security privileges from striking unions. In three seizures, the government replaced the union shop (or preferential hiring) with the open shop as a pressure against a striking union (the Seafarers' International Union in the Alcoa freighters case; and Lodge 68, International Association of Machinists, in two San Francisco seizures—the machine shops, and United Engineering). In two coal mine seizures (1943), President Roosevelt personally threatened similar action, namely, to withhold the check-off of union dues, but did not implement the threats.

The government also withdrew union privileges in two cases where the decisions were not punitive but represented the agencies' view of their proper policy toward the unions in direct operations resulting from management noncompliance—Federal Shipbuilding where the union's participation in the grievance procedure was withdrawn, and S. A. Woods Machine Co. where the check-off was discontinued, the latter decision being reversed after a few weeks. In later direct operations of the same sort, the seizing agencies continued the existing union privileges—in one case even extending them. This last was at Montgomery Ward in 1945 when the War Department reversed the company rules against union bulletin boards and other union activity on company property. The War Department also overruled the company's traditional refusal to furnish information to unions on individual wage rates and related matters. However, before taking these steps, the army consulted both the National Labor Relations Board and the National War Labor Board, and obtained their informal assent. The NWLB ruled that the furnishing of wage information to the unions would not be a change in the terms and conditions of employment, within the meaning of sec. 5 of the War Labor Disputes Act, and so would not require formal approval, but the board volunteered that such a policy would be good industrial relations practice.[10]

In indirect operations, when the private managements served as agents of the government, one of the major efforts of seizing agencies was to see that private managements did not take advantage of the protection of seizure to withdraw or reduce the union's privileges. Nevertheless, in two seizures, management did succeed in curtailing some union privileges—at Cleveland Bronze where it tightened up its enforcement of contract provisions regarding the activities of union stewards in the plant, and at Great Lakes Towing where it disregarded some provisions of its union contract, apparently believing the contract was not effective during seizure.[11] In the latter case, the seizing agency (ODT) upheld the union contract in principle, but did nothing to enforce it.

In the Korean War, the White House made a third attempt to gain nationwide support from industry and labor for a program of peaceful settlement of disputes over union status as well as over wages, at least in defense industries. This attempt failed when the industry and labor members of President Truman's National Advisory Board on Mobilization Policy did not agree to give up strikes and lockouts for the duration, and the industry members also refused to accept the decisions of a presidential disputes board on issues of union status. Although the president went ahead and gave the new Wage Stabilization Board authority to hear any disputes which he might refer to it, he drew the line in the end against enforcing the board's decisions on union status.

When the WSB voted, over the protests of its industry members, to recommend a union shop for the basic steel industry, together with a substantial wage increase, President Truman seized the steel mills, as Wilson had seized Western Union and Smith & Wesson; but he hesitated to establish compulsory union membership as interim terms of labor. When another presidential emergency board recommended the union shop for the railroad industry, Mr. Truman also made no move to accept it, although the roads were then in his possession. While the president hesitated, the Supreme Court answered the question for the steel industry by ruling the seizure illegal unless authorized subsequently by Congress.

Some members of Mr. Truman's staff believe he never would have enforced the union shop on the steel industry even if the seizure had been allowed to continue.[12] For one thing, the underlying "no-strike" agreement between labor and industry had not been achieved. For another, despite union complaints, the unions had come a long way since the First World War, when nothing could protect a workman from discharge for wearing a union button except seizure—and not always that.

In addition to making decisions about the status of unions and union members, the seizing agencies often had to choose between rival unions. In some 30 seizures, union rivalries played a part—mostly rivalries between standard unions and independents, but in at least seven cases rivalries between AFL and CIO competitors, and in one case between two AFL unions (the machinists and the boilermakers in United Engineering).

The seizing agencies generally met these delicate situations equitably by following the directives of the NLRB, NWLB, or NMB, as the case might be. Sometimes this meant recognizing a union when the companies were not ready to do so; as when the ODT recognized 13 standard labor organizations on the T.P. & W. R.R., inducing a sharp decline in memberships in the company-type "employee associations," or when the army recognized the United Steelworkers in preference to the Independent Metal Workers at Hughes Tool Co.

On the other hand, the seizing agencies in some cases, whether con-

sciously or unconsciously, encouraged the independent unions in preference to the standard organizations. Two notable examples were the
Post Office Department's acceptance of company unions in the wire seizure
of 1918—a development that was felt through the 1920's and early
1930's—and the Navy Department's nonrecognition of the certified CIO
union at the Federal Shipbuilding plant in 1941, which resulted in a great
loss of membership for the CIO union, a gain for the independent, and
continuing strife throughout the war. These policies, of course, were very
satisfying to the company managements involved. But in a majority of
cases, the seizing agencies hewed to the line of existing procedures for the
settlement of representational and jurisdictional disputes.

Wages. In contrast to questions of union status, the questions of wages
and other compensation are as a rule more easily compromised by the
parties to any dispute; and under war conditions the added costs can
usually be absorbed either through the economies of high volume production
or they can, if government permission is obtained, be passed on to the consumers, private or governmental, in the form of higher prices. This results
in a somewhat better record of voluntary agreements in this area,[13] but
does not prevent the seizing agencies from having to meet difficult wage
problems in many seizure operations.

The record shows that wages have been an issue, either main or secondary, in 46 seizure operations, and that changes in their interim schedule
have been made in 30. This compares with 53 seizures in which union
status was an issue, either main or secondary, among which 30 were
marked by interim changes. (There was an overlapping of interim changes,
of both wages and union status, in 19 seizures.) The interim wage changes
often reflected secondary issues in seizures.

The large number (and large proportion) of wage changes in seizure
cases having wage issues (nearly two out of three) accentuates one of the
important differences in the interim status of employees during a presidential seizure as compared with the period of an antistrike injunction
issued by a court. In the latter case, an interim wage change is very rare—
being normally forbidden by the court or left to the discretion of the private
management which is generally resisting proposed changes.

Among the 30 seizures in which wage changes were made during
presidential operation, compulsion was necessary in 22. Specifically, certain changes were made over the objection of the companies in 19 cases
and over the objection of the unions in three others. (The size of each
change—all of them were increases—is given in Table 10, together with
the number of employees affected in each case.)

In addition to interim changes in wage levels, the seizing agencies
have directed interim changes in the internal wage structures of some

TABLE 10
WAGE CHANGES OVER COMPANY OR UNION OBJECTION

Seizure and date of change	Increase	Employees affected
Company		
Telegraphs, Jan. 1919	5-10% (messengers excepted)	73,000
S. & W., Aug. 1918	15%	over 1,500
T.P. & W. R.R., 1942–1943	35% (av.)	250
Amer. R.R. of P.R., Dec. 1943	10% (av.)	1,700
Coal, Dec. 1943:		
Soft coal miners	$1.50 day	450,000
Hard coal miners	.70 day	80,000
Jenkins, Apr. 1944	.05 hour (.05 shift prem.)	1,450
Ken-Rad, Apr. 1944	.03 hour (.50 minimum)	6,000
Midwest trucking, Aug. 1944	.07 hour (.003 mile)	20,000
T.C. Brass, Sept. 1944	.13½ hour	50
F-C Steel, Sept. 1944	Piece rates	600
Ward's, Jan. 1945	Varied in 7 cities	12,000
Chicago trucking, Aug. 1945	.08 hour	15,000
Gaffney, Aug. 1945	.05 hour (.55 minimum) (.05 shift prem.)	800
Mary-Leila, Aug. 1945	Same as Gaffney	235
G.L. tugs, 1946	15.3%	600
5 meat-packers, Feb. 1946	.16 hour	90,000
Soft coal, May 1946	.18½ hour (welfare fund, .05 ton royalty)	400,000
Mon. Con. R.R., Mar. 1951	.12½ hour	500
Union		
Rails, May 1918	0-43% (range) (increases since Jan. 1916 to be deducted)	1,750,000
Soft coal, June 1943	Tool and lamp charges canceled; vacation pay increased by $25.	450,000
Rails, Feb. 1951:		
Yardmen and yardmasters	.12½ hour	115,000
Road-service employees	.05 hour	150,000
Dining-car stewards	$11.25 month (equivalent to .05 hour)	—

of the same firms, over the objection of either the company owners or the unions; and the compulsory changes have had the effect, in several cases, of altering traditional interregional wage differentials within the seized industries. Besides compulsory changes the seizing agencies have authorized a number of voluntary interim changes in wage scales, as agreed upon by the unions and private managements, or as requested by the managements alone without union objections. In all, the compulsory changes are known to have occurred in 22 seizures, and voluntary changes in six of the same cases and in eight others.[14]

In effectuating the compulsory wage changes, the seizing and operating agencies were by no means merely executing the recommendations or orders of emergency disputes boards. Some of the changes were initiated by the seizing agencies themselves—the application of the NWLB's order in the "23 Southern Cotton Textile Mills" case to a firm which was not one of the 23 (Gaffney Mfg.); or the changes in soft coal in 1946–1947 which included the industrywide welfare fund; or the increases given railroad operating employees in 1951.

Where the changes did reflect wage orders of disputes boards that were outstanding at the time of seizure—and this has been the typical case—the seizing agencies examined such orders independently from the standpoint of their applicability to the particular firms and industries. The seizing agencies had the operational responsibility to determine whether the current income would cover the increased costs and whether the changed rates would create intraplant or interplant inequities that would interfere with the operating efficiency of the employees. In a word, they had to meet the payrolls and keep production going at high levels.

If the seizing agencies found the current income insufficient to meet the interim wage increases, or to maintain normal profits (when this was required by seizure legislation), they frequently sought price (or rate) increases from the appropriate government agencies to offset the deficiencies; and where this, too, was inadequate, they appealed to the president for further aid. In situations where the application of the wage changes was unclear or proved inequitable in operation, the seizing agencies called upon the disputes boards for clarification and modification, or issued orders of their own correcting the difficulties.

As suggested earlier, this independent role of the seizing agencies reflected the lack of legal sanction behind the emergency disputes-boards' decisions, the specific grant of power to seizing agencies in the War Labor Disputes Act, and the nature of seizure as an expression of direct presidential control. Therefore, this is certainly not identical with compulsory arbitration as it is ordinarily conceived—if by compulsory arbitration we mean the action of a board whose award would be enforceable by law. Under such an arrangement, the arbitration board and the courts ordinarily would take over the roles of review and enforcement here exercised by the president and the seizing agencies.

In effectuating the compulsory wage changes in 22 seizures, the seizing agencies found that the current receipts from operations were sufficient in 12 of the cases (or more than one-half) to pay the higher compensation, not only throughout the period of government operation but also in such retroactive periods prior to seizure as were designated by the disputes boards.[15] The operations, whether directly or indirectly controlled by the seizing agencies, yielded sufficient revenues to meet costs of production and to provide a satisfactory profit to the private owners. This is demonstrated by the fact that the firms in the 12 seizures accepted the actual profits earned during government possession as full compensation for the public use of their properties. It seems clear that the added wage costs were largely absorbed by the economies of high-level production and by the partly cost-plus effect of high wartime corporate taxes. It should be mentioned, however, that a few marginal soft coal mining companies were unable to meet the added costs and shut down; they were then released from government possession and control. Another seized firm, the American R.R. of Porto Rico, became bankrupt after the war when business declined.[16]

The financing of compulsory wage increases was more difficult for the seizing agencies—and more costly for consumers and taxpayers—in the remaining 10 seizures of this group.[17] In seven of these cases, the seizing agencies obtained price relief that offset at least some of the increased wage costs. In two more, the government assured the companies an adequate profit by the terms of the final settlements of mutual claims (Smith & Wesson; S. A. Woods). In the tenth (Montgomery Ward), the result was unclear, since the company tacitly accepted the resulting profits as full compensation, but the profit may be considered inflated because the government had withheld the retroactive portion of the wage increase from the employees (totaling over $1,000,000).

The seven cases in which price relief was obtained include several which serve to illustrate two contrasting policies that arose in differing market situations. In one case (midwest trucking), the seized firms were small, numerous, and highly competitive, often operating on small profit margins. The seizing agency (ODT) made strenuous efforts to keep all the weaker firms in operation. In certain other cases, the seized firms included giant as well as small corporations, and competition was of the limited form known as oligopoly. Examples are the railroads, telegraphs and telephones, and meat-packing. The policies of the seizing agencies in these cases, while making special concessions in some instances to the small and weaker firms, centered around guaranteeing normal, high-profit margins for the large firms. In the highly competitive industries, the seizing agency had to beg and urge the firms to get together in support of price rises; but in the closely controlled industries, they had to beg other government bureaus to raise the price ceilings to the levels sought by the large companies.

It should be easy to guess which type of market situation was the more successful in raising prices and passing the higher wage costs on to consumers. In the midwest trucking case, the ODT, while obtaining the elimination of certain depressed volume rates and the institution of higher interstate minimum charges, failed in a year of effort to obtain agreement upon even a modest four-per cent general increase in all interstate charges, owing to persistent opposition. It became necessary for the ODT to lend funds to 28 of the 103 firms, and to take over direct operation of eight in order to keep them in operation.[18] After the war, Congress took pity on these firms and appropriated about $10,000,000 to compensate the entire group with at least normal earnings, but this subsidy came out of taxes rather than higher rates.[19]

On the other hand, the seizing agencies obtained (or permitted) rate increases of up to 20 per cent for the railroads, telegraphs and telephones in the First World War; of 15 per cent for the railroads in the Korean War; and of substantial magnitude for the meat-packing industry after the Second World War. In each case the seizing agency argued with the government stabilization agencies in behalf of the seized corporations. Even after the rate increases had been obtained, Congress added still further to the profits of the seized giants by granting liberal subsidies out of taxes—a fantastic total of $1,123,500,000 to the railroads in 1918–1920; of $14,000,000 to the wire systems in 1918–1919; and of $10,000,000 to the meat-packing firms in 1946. There was also a special increase in the price the government paid for meat procured from the seized packers for the armed forces.

Of the structural wage changes effectuated by the seizing agencies the elimination or reduction of interregional pay differentials was probably the most significant and enduring. The first of these occurred on the railroads in 1918–1919 when nationwide minimum rates were established for each class of labor. These minimums were introduced by the Railroad Administration to correct distortions arising from the sliding scale of percentage increases which it had effectuated at first on the recommendation of a special wage commission. Another major change of this kind was the elimination of the north-south wage differential in soft coal mining. This was achieved in 1941 on the personal order of President Roosevelt in support of a recommendation of the National Defense Mediation Board.

The order was accompanied by a threat of seizure, which, however, did not have to be carried out. The elimination of this differential was continued during later seizures by the seizing agency (Department of the Interior), over the bitter protests of southern operators, through the Ickes-Lewis agreement of 1943 and the Krug-Lewis agreement of 1946. Two similar changes brought about by recommendations of the NWLB were the elimination of a wage differential between motor trucking west and east of the Mississippi River (midwest trucking case), and the reduction of certain north-south pay differentials in cotton textile manufacturing (Gaffney, and Mary-Leila). All these changes, except in cotton textile, were perpetuated after seizure by collective bargaining. It seems likely that these reforms were hastened by their compulsory imposition during wartime in seized firms.

Another reform in the wage structure of industry that was advanced by seizure is the effort to end discriminations in pay and job opportunities between the races and between the sexes. A move in this direction was made by Secretary of the Treasury McAdoo who, as director general of railroads in 1918, ordered equal pay for men and women, and equal pay for Negroes and whites, for the same class of work on all railroads. This change did not establish equality of job opportunities, however. Moreover, not all seizing agencies have even established equal rates. For example, neither the PAW nor the navy did anything to change the rate discrimination between whites and blacks in the Port Arthur (Texas) oil refineries in 1945 (Texas Co. and general oil refining cases). These discriminations were condoned by the dual local union of the OWIU-CIO. In the matter of equal job opportunities, the record is also mixed. Major General Philip Hayes of the War Department, with a smooth combination of tact and firmness, upgraded Negroes to the position of streetcar and bus operators in the Philadelphia Transportation Co., in 1944, in accordance with an FEPC-WMC order; whereas President Truman a year later vetoed a plea of the FEPC to do the same on the Capital Transit Co. in the city of Washington during seizure in a wage dispute. The refusal of President Truman to support the FEPC on this issue resulted in the bitter resignation of FEPC's Charles H. Houston.[20] However, the Philadelphia seizure by President Roosevelt had favorable consequences. The settlement facilitated an early disposition of long-drawn-out negotiations for the employment of Negroes as operators on the Los Angeles Railway. And the employment of Negroes in Philadelphia proved so satisfactory to the company and was so generally accepted by the community that the number employed in operating positions was steadily increased. Nearly a decade later, the company reported 600 Negroes employed in operating positions, some also in bookkeeping, and one in advertising.[21]

In other matters of internal pay relationships, the seizing agencies occasionally have had to order changes. These were mostly to prevent or to correct obvious intrafirm inequities, and so were usually brought about without objection from any of the disputing parties. One such practice has been to assure matching pay increases for foremen and office personnel when increases were given to unionized production workers. Another has been to assure equitable treatment of hourly rated personnel and piece-workers in the same firms when applying increases. On the railroads in 1918, this was done by virtually eliminating piecework. Lastly, we might mention revision of job classifications, among which the most successful appears to have been that conducted by Rear Admiral Harold G. Bowen at Jenkins Bros. through a tripartite committee representing the company, the union, and the navy.

With all this assistance from the government in the more exacting cases, we might expect the payment in full of all the required wage increases, including retroactive portions, to the employees of seized firms. In fact, the record has been very good—almost perfect in such payments from the dates of seizure onward, but marred by failures to pay the retroactive portions of three NWLB-ordered increases which related to periods prior to seizure. The three failures were the amount of $21,000 "owed" to about 100 operating employees on the Toledo, Peoria & Western R.R.; about $700,000 due to some 7,000 drivers for midwest trucking firms; and over $1,000,000 due to several thousand Montgomery Ward employees. In addition, there has been at least one case in which the seizing agency excused a financially weak firm from current payments of a required pay increase. This was the New York, Ontario & Western R.R., which was in receivership, and which the department of the army authorized to "accrue" the 12½-cent increase of February 1951.[22] Reference also should be made to the small coal mines which were allowed to close because of inability to meet the industrywide increases of 1943–1945. Employees in these mines were obliged to seek work elsewhere—a difficulty less calamitous under wartime labor shortages than in peacetime.

The special problem of retroactive wage payments for services performed prior to seizure was solved only as to its legal and administrative difficulties. The financial difficulty—how to obtain the necessary funds if current operating income was insufficient—was explored at the White House level but never solved.

The argument was put forth for a time that the government could not properly pay employees of seized firms for services performed prior to seizure, since such services were not performed for the government. But this view begged the whole question of enforcement. Later, other negative arguments were put forward, claiming that the wording of NWLB orders and of the president's executive orders failed to authorize such payments by seizing agencies.

Finally, after two years of legal wrangling and administrative buck-passing among the disputes boards and seizing agencies, President Roosevelt, in April 1944, solved the legal and administrative difficulties by an executive order and a personal letter to Secretary of the Navy Knox in the case of Jenkins Bros., Bridgeport, Connecticut. In the executive order, Roosevelt authorized the seizing agency (the Navy Department) to "exercise any contractual or other rights" of the seized firm "and to take such other steps . . . necessary to carry out the provisions and purposes of this order and the directive order of the NWLB dated February 9, 1944." This permitted the seizing agency to act in behalf of the firm in connection with services previously rendered to the firm, and authorized any "necessary" steps to enforce the NWLB order, including its retroactive provision. (The executive order was no. 9435 of April 13, 1944, 3 CFR 1944 Supp. 59.) However, the personal letter to Secretary Knox qualified the latter authority by directing Knox specifically to pay the accrued portion of the wage increase out of the current income accumulated during seizure, and if this proved insufficient, to submit a report to the president on the other assets of the firm. The letter was posted on plant bulletin boards but appears never to have been otherwise published.

THE WHITE HOUSE
Washington, D.C.

April 13, 1944

My dear Mr. Secretary:

I have today approved the Executive Order entitled "Authorizing the Secretary of the Navy to Take Possession of and Operate the Plants and Facilities of Jenkins Brothers, Incorporated, at Bridgeport, Connecticut."

Paragraph 1 of that order authorizes the Secretary of the Navy "to exercise any contractual or other rights of the Corporation and to take such other steps as he deems necessary to carry out the provisions and purposes of this Order and the directive Order of the National War Labor Board dated February 9, 1944." Until further direction you will make the retroactive wage payment provided for in the Board's order out of current income accumulated during the period of your operation of the plant and facilities.

I understand that it will take some time to compute the total amount of the retroactive wages due the employees. By the time that is done, however, you should be able to anticipate whether estimated current income will be adequate for that purpose. In the event you should determine that such income will not be adequate, I would appreciate your transmitting to me a report on the other assets of the Corporation so far as they are known to you.

Sincerely yours,
[Signed] FRANKLIN D. ROOSEVELT

The Honorable,
     The Secretary of the Navy.

Acting under this authority, the Navy Department withheld dividend payments and began accumulating a reserve out of current receipts from which to meet the accrued obligations to the employees. Seeing that further opposition was useless, the company agreed to make full payment of $443,321 to 4,875 individuals (some of them no longer employed by the company) for services prior to seizure extending as far back as 17 months, as determined by accountants for the navy.[23]

In later seizures involving wage orders, the president incorporated similar instructions regarding retroactive payments in the executive orders themselves, rather than in accompanying letters. Under one of these, the War Department withheld dividend payments and began accumulating company revenues at the tiny Twentieth Century Brass Works in Minneapolis in order to pay a retroactive wage increase dating back 28 months before seizure. The company then quickly reached an agreement with the union (United Electrical Workers) to pay all current employees their accrued wage increases but to omit such payments to former employees, except those who were in the armed forces. This modification of the original NWLB order scaled down the company's obligation from $42,524 to $23,205. It was approved by the NWLB.[24]

After such clear demonstrations of presidential firmness, the seizing agencies found the companies more willing to carry out orders for retroactive, as well as current, wage increases. Payments dating back six and eight months were made on orders of the seizing agency (the War Department) by Farrell-Cheek Steel and Mary-Leila Cotton.

Nevertheless, in three seizures mentioned earlier, the employees never received the retroactive sums which government disputes boards had said were due them. The failure in the T.P. & W. R.R. case was attributed by the seizing agency (ODT) to lack of authority in the executive order directing the seizure; but it is interesting, and somewhat puzzling, to note that although the executive order was amended twice at the agency's request—once to permit advance payments of compensation to the individual owner of the little railroad—it never was amended in the more than three years of government possession to permit payment of retroactive wages to the operating employees. It may be more than coincidence that this same seizing agency took no steps to ensure payment of either current or retroactive portions of the wage increase due to 15,000 truck drivers in the Chicago trucking seizure until the NWLB intervened near the end of the seizure operation.

In the two other cases mentioned—midwest trucking and Montgomery Ward—the failure to pay the retroactive sums was the result of the financial problem of insufficient current operating income to meet the accrued liabilities, although, in the Ward case, the seizing agency later reversed its initial conclusion and decided (after seizure ended) that funds had been available. This is the problem that we said above was never solved: does the equitable enforcement of wartime wage rulings require that the government supply, out of tax revenues, any funds needed (and not otherwise available) to pay the retroactive portion of the wage increases it requires? That is to say, if the government's cost-plus measures (such as approved price increases) are insufficient to cover the accrued wage increases, should the government directly subsidize this portion of the wage increases? This question was debated in high-level conferences in Washington and in consultations with President Truman late in 1945 in connection with the unpaid sums in both the midwest trucking and the Ward cases. Although some of the government officials argued that the government had a clear moral liability to pay these sums, the conclusion was reached that no existing appropriation could properly be used for this purpose, and that the administration would not ask Congress for a special appropriation.[25]

Nevertheless, the issue could not be evaded so long as seizures continued. The following spring (1946), the problem arose again in the meat-packing seizure. After ordering a 16-cent wage increase for 90,000 employees of the five major companies, the government found that it could compensate the companies only for current and future payments of the increase by lifting the wholesale price ceilings. The wage increase was intended to be retroactive to the start of seizure—six weeks earlier than the price increase; but price increases could not be made retroactive. So the administration went to Congress and asked for a transfer of subsidy authorizations which would permit the Department of Agriculture to compensate the companies directly for the retroactive portion of the wage increase. For this purpose, $10,000,000 was made available. The action drew almost no public attention; but a precedent was thereby set. If seizure is necessary in the future, this issue will undoubtedly reappear, and the government may have to take a public stand. It seems evident to the author that such a stand would have to be in favor of equitable compensation for the employees as well as for the stockholders of seized companies, with the government fulfilling its commitments to the one as surely as to the other.

Working conditions in the plants have occupied the attention of some of the seizing agencies, but with one exception this has occurred only in seizures where wages and/or union security were the major issues. The sole exception was the Western Electric case where the primary issue was an FEPC-NWLB order denying a union request for restoration of segregated cafeterias and locker rooms. In other cases, any changes in the physical conditions of the workplace were regarded by the NWLB II as not being changes in basic conditions of employment requiring NWLB approval under sec. 5 of the War Labor Disputes Act.[26] Hence, the seizing agencies acted on their own to improve sanitary facilities in two cases (Philadelphia Transportation, and Cocker Machine), to improve safety measures in four others (Federal Shipbuilding; coal mine seizures in May 1943, November 1943, and 1946–1947), and to improve company-owned commissaries in one (coal mine seizures in November 1943). Although these changes were carried out cooperatively by the seized companies, the initiative appears to have sprung from the seizing agencies (War and Navy Departments, and Interior Department).

Various changes in the length of the workday and workweek, and in vacation policy, were made in several seizures, but perhaps it will suffice to refer only to one change which was fiercely resisted by company managements when the seizing agency required it, but which the managements later accepted permanently under the pressures of collective bargaining: the change to a portal-to-portal system of measuring time at work in the coal mining industry.

So the conditions of employment have been by no means static in seizures generally. As we have seen, important changes, mostly in wage rates and union status, have occurred in the course of 42 seizures out of 71 or in nearly 60 per cent of the cases. Although in a few cases these changes have come about at the request of private management (without union objection) or by agreement between the company and the union (with the permission of the seizing agency), the majority have been initiated by the seizing agencies—either to effectuate the recommendations of emergency disputes boards or otherwise to establish interim terms of employment which the seizing agencies believed to be equitable for the period of government operation.

Although in the 29 other seizures no major change in terms or conditions of employment occurred, such changes, except in a very few cases, were not forbidden. Instead, most of these operations were too brief to need changes. Despite the emphasis in presidential executive orders, in the War Labor Disputes Act, and elsewhere on the continuation of previous terms of employment unchanged during government possession, the principle of flexibility appears to have been the rule in practice rather than the principle of status quo. Such flexibility (in the face of all the verbal trappings about interim rigidity) enabled the presidents and their seizing agencies to provide, in accordance with their best judgment, equitable working conditions for the employees and efficient operating conditions for the seized companies—even while they were upholding the national interest in continued production and noninflationary wages in these essential firms and industries.

CHAPTER 9

Reducing Conflict with Normal Regulatory Agencies

Presidential seizure and operation of an industrial plant introduces a temporary form of governmental regulation which conflicts, in theory and in practice, with the normal regulatory powers of federal and state agencies. The conflict arises because the seizure is an assertion of public control in the nature of martial rule (although not of martial law), tending to displace other executive agencies (although not the civil courts); and the very occasion for seizure has been the inadequacy of existing regulatory procedures to meet the economic stresses of wartime or peacetime labor crises.[1]

We have already seen in the preceding chapters that seizure has frequently been employed to enforce presidential policies affecting wages and union security (requiring changes or forbidding changes) in particular circumstances of the private labor market; and that this intervention introduced a type of business regulation which was quite different either from statutory minimum-wage regulation or from the unfair-practice procedures of the National Labor Relations Board and the Federal Trade Commission.

Now in the present chapter we will find examples of presidential policies requiring changes or forbidding changes in seizure cases in circumstances where the normal regulatory agencies of the federal or state governments would govern otherwise. This will include cases affecting statutory labor standards (such as social security), the NLRB's administration of collective bargaining, and statutory procedures for the curbing of business monopoly.

The reader will see that the regulatory effect of seizure has been to resolve serious impasses in particular economic situations without permanently reducing any required (statutory) labor standards and without permanently weakening the federal protection of collective bargaining. Indeed, several seizures clearly strengthened collective bargaining by effectuating outstanding orders of the NLRB before they had been finally upheld by the courts. But we will also find that seizure, in several cases, probably reduced the extent of business competition in the seized industries.

In turning now to the conflict between seizure and the normal regulatory bodies of the state and federal governments, we begin by emphasizing the efforts of Congress, the presidents, and the seizing-operating agencies to reconcile the contradictory goals of (1) the paramount authority of the president in the seized firms; and (2) the avoidance of any permanent impairment of the normal standards or procedures of the regulatory bodies, and the minimizing of even temporary modification of these standards or procedures.

In the earliest seizures there was a clear emphasis in both law and presidential policy upon the paramountcy of presidential authority in seized firms. Notice this paragraph from the proclamation of President Wilson, issued upon taking control of the railroads on December 26, 1917.

> Until and except so far as said director [the director general of railroads] shall from time to time otherwise by general or special orders determine, such systems of transportation shall remain subject to all existing statutes and orders of the interstate commerce commission and to all statutes and orders of regulating commissions of the various states in which said systems or any part thereof may be situated. But any orders, general or special, hereafter made by said director shall have paramount authority and be obeyed as such. (40 Stat. 1733.)

The tenor of this order was fully upheld by the Supreme Court on June 2, 1919, in a series of decisions rejecting suits by state public utility commissions seeking to protect their jurisdictions.[2]

By the Second World War, however, Congress had extended normal federal regulation to include the protection of labor standards, including the right of collective bargaining; and in order to make seizure legislation less unpalatable to the unions, Congress wrote into the War Labor Disputes Act of 1943 a proviso that terms and conditions of employment in seized plants should be changed only by a specific procedure and only in a manner that was "not in conflict with any act of Congress" (57 Stat. 163, secs. 4, 5); but Congress offered no advice as to how the president, the National War Labor Board, and the seizing agencies were to reconcile the requirements of a seizure with all the existing acts of Congress. The proviso gave the executive branch a tough assignment.

In practice, the problem was solved largely by a *pro forma* order of the president, which each seizing agency then had to wrestle with as best it could. In the railroad seizure which followed the enactment of the WLDA, President Roosevelt included a paragraph in his executive order evidently modeled on Wilson's but without Wilson's final emphatic sentence.

> Except as this order otherwise provides and except as the secretary [of war] otherwise directs, the operation of carriers hereunder shall be in conformity with the interstate commerce act, as amended, the railway labor act, the safety appliance acts, the employers' liability acts, and other applicable federal and state laws, executive orders, local ordinances, and rules and regulations

issued pursuant to such laws, executive orders and ordinances. (Ex. Order 9412, 8 F.R. 17395.)

A paragraph such as this appeared in most seizure orders issued subsequently by Presidents Roosevelt and Truman. The key phrase was "exceptions" to existing laws as the president or seizing agency might "direct." The seizing agencies thus had to accomplish what the permanent agencies could not under existing law—and do this without transgressing the authority of those agencies.

In seeking to comply with all existing laws, the first question of seizure officials was: which laws? Do the employees in a seized plant or industry become federal government employees, or do they remain purely private employees, or are they in a unique status? Does the seized business become a part of the federal government under direct presidential control, or does it remain a private concern subject to the same federal and state regulatory laws and agencies as before, or does it, too, acquire a unique status?

Such problems as these have been not only legal puzzles but causes of jurisdictional conflict among governmental departments and agencies—federal versus state, permanent versus wartime, and even wartime versus other wartime agencies. The seizing agency has been at swords' points with nearly every other agency, including other seizing agencies. The key question seems to have been: did seizure make the president and the seizing agency supreme in judgment in the seized business, or merely an enforcing agency for other government offices and boards, some of them permanent and some of them temporary wartime agencies; or is the seizing agency a bit of both?

LAWS GOVERNING INDIVIDUAL EMPLOYEES

The seizing agencies got into difficulties in the early seizures by trying to fit the workers neatly into the category of regular federal employees, like those in a naval shipyard or army arsenal. They were forced to acknowledge numerous differences and to make adjustments accordingly. Gradually, some of the government officials came around to the opposite tactic of trying to fit the workers into the category of regular private employees, not subject to government interference at all. This, too, involved obvious incongruities and called for important adjustments.

The problem has been simplified and mastered only by those government representatives who have recognized that the operation is neither public nor private in the normal sense of the terms but is a kind of public trusteeship—the temporary, public custody and control of a private business; and that the extent of interference with normal procedures depends, as in an ordinary bankruptcy receivership, on the degree of cooperation shown to the federal manager by the parties and in the federal manager's judgment of the efficiency of existing practices and personnel.

At this point, we should note two distinct classes of employees in seized plants—that is, distinct with reference to their treatment by the federal managers. One consists of the employees who were on the company payrolls at the time of seizure. The other consists of those who were brought in by the government for supervisory or strikebreaking duties. The second type usually has been personnel lent by regular government departments (both military and civilian), but it has also included military reservists recalled to active duty, civilians borrowed from private corporations, and civilians hired in the open market. The following discussion relates entirely to the first of these two groups.

The first question to be dealt with concerning individual employees was civil service. In the railroad seizure of 1917–1920, Attorney General Gregory ruled that although the employees were controlled and paid by the director general of railroads, they would not be subject to civil service rules.[3] This was a recognition of the realities of seizure operation by a practical-minded attorney general. It was an adjustment from the philosophy expressed by the director general, Mr. McAdoo, to the 1,750,000 employees of the seized railroads on February 18, 1918.

> The government now being in control of the railroads, the officers and employees of the various companies no longer serve a private interest. All now serve the government and the public interest only. I want the officers and employees to get the spirit of this new era.[4]

A few months later the War Department took another step after it seized Smith & Wesson. In order to "free the employees from any restrictions of civil service," as well as to avoid the complications of financing a direct government operation, the War Department went through the legal gymnastics of creating a private corporation in which it held all the stock and then of leasing the seized plant to this dummy corporation for operation as a "private enterprise." Since all the officials of the operating corporation were officials of the Army Ordnance Department, the "private enterprise" was sheer fiction, but it got around the civil service requirements.[5] In World War II, however, the War and Navy Departments reached the conclusion in the earliest seizures that the civil service rules were wholly inapplicable to the employees of seized companies, and this sensible rule was followed by all the seizing agencies thereafter.

The next problem respecting the treatment of individual employees was the question of which laws to observe regarding hours of labor. The "eight-hour law" set maximum daily hours for federal workers in arsenals, naval shipyards, and elsewhere, requiring the payment of time and a half for overtime work. The Adamson Act in 1916 established the basic eight-hour day for railroad operating employees, with straight time required as compensation for any overtime. After 1938 the Fair Labor Standards Act set maximum weekly hours, with time and a half for overtime, for most private employees in interstate commerce. In each war, the question has been: which law is applicable in seizure cases?

In World War I, two opposite solutions were adopted. The railroad administration, although directly operating all the major railroads, observed the provisions of the Adamson Act relating to private employees. It also introduced and extended the eight-hour day to some of the employees not covered by the act. In contrary fashion, the War Department, in the Smith & Wesson seizure, observed the provisions of the eight-hour law as with government workers at army arsenals. In such ways, the government strove to adjust itself to the fact that workers in seized plants were in part governmental and in part private employees.[6]

In World War II, all seizing agencies conformed to the provisions of the Fair Labor Standards Act, regardless of whether the operation was directly controlled by the government or only indirectly operated through the regular company management. The eight-hour law for federal employees was put aside at last, along with the civil service rules, and the provisions for private employees were followed. This was the logical and orderly course of action, since existing practices in this way remained unchanged during the government's temporary custody of the business.

A brief exception to the rule occurred in 1943 because of confusion over portal-to-portal pay. Secretary of the Interior Ickes, while admitting that this method of payment constituted a legal obligation to the coal miners under the law and court decisions, insisted that he was without power as federal operator of the mines to carry it through (seizure of May 1943). On June 20, 1943, therefore, the United Mine Workers agreed to waive such payments from that date until the end of government operation. This meant that portal-to-portal pay was not issued to the miners either currently or retroactively, during the period from June 20 to November 3, 1943. John L. Lewis termed this "a gift of millions" to the coal operators.[7] Inasmuch as agreement was subsequently reached with the operators for the payment of $40 to each miner retroactively in settlement for travel time between March 31 and June 20, 1943, involving a total payment of approximately $18,000,000, this is evidently a conservative estimate. Later in the year, Mr. Ickes changed his mind about portal-to-portal pay, and put the system into effect in the next coal mine seizure (November 3, 1943).[8]

Next, we find confusion arising over the handling of claims for injury to individual employees during government operation. It is obvious that somebody must be liable for these claims; and in view of the sweeping assertions of power made by the president upon taking possession of a strike-affected business, the government can hardly escape the principal responsibility.

The seizing agencies, however, have sometimes taken refuge in the government's immunity from suit (except with its consent) and have made recovery by injured employees or by the widows of workmen killed in the course of their duties extremely difficult. Even when acknowledging the government's liability, the seizing agencies in the early cases were uncertain whether to handle it under state or federal laws. In three seizures involving direct operation by the government, three different methods were followed. In one, the Railroad Administration accepted suits in its own name under the Employers' Liability Act, merely substituting itself for the railroad companies under the existing railroad laws (1918–1920).[9] In another, the Navy Department treated the employees as if they had become government workers in a navy yard, arranging for claims to be handled through the U.S. Employees' Compensation Commission (Federal Shipbuilding & Dry Dock Company, 1941).[10] In the third, the War Department followed the company's practice, using the state workmen's compensation law; it did, however, require all employees to sign cards of authorization, since it had misgivings as to whether this arrangement could legally be continued under federal control (Air Associates, Inc., 1941).[11] With further experience, however, the agencies found that a continuance of the practices followed by private management meant the least confusion and the least expense, and was entirely consistent with the government's primary responsibility during seizure.

This policy was first developed in seizure cases marked by indirect government control (the company management serving as a kind of agency of the government). It was found later that this could also be applied to cases of direct government operation. Under this plan, railroad cases were handled under the Employers' Liability Act, and other cases under the State Workmen's Compensation Acts. As recently as the steel mill seizure of 1952, however, the New York State Workmen's Compensation Board voiced doubt as to whether 50,000 steel employees in New York were federal or private employees. The staff of the board was directed on April 19, 1952, to keep accidents occurring during the seizure period in a special docket in case it should later be decided that they were federal employees.[12]

The most serious cases of government evasion of liability to injured employees occurred in the longest of all the seizures—the three-and-one-half-year operation of the Toledo, Peoria & Western Railroad in 1942–1945.

The Office of Defense Transportation and the Department of Justice denied that the government had any liability for injuries to these employees, despite the fact that the ODT had removed the president of the railroad, had seized all railroad assets, including cash, and was operating it directly. This meant that claimants could not recover either from the federal management or from the former private management. After more than two years of conferences and correspondence, the ODT finally settled such claims out of court, while still denying any liability to do so.[13] In another seizure, the ODT followed a more humane (although equally curious) course. While again denying that the government had any liability, it arranged with an insurance company to accept liability and, of course, paid premiums to the insurance company to meet claims of this sort.[14]

By World War II, a variety of new forms of social legislation were upon the books. Among these were old age and survivors' insurance, unemployment insurance, and corresponding measures for the railroad employees. The seizing agencies appear to have found these measures no problem at all, despite the fact that they related entirely to private employees. All such measures were continued in force. Similar action was taken with respect to the many varieties of private welfare plans that had sprung up, including group life insurance, group hospital plans, and credit unions.

Perhaps "no problem at all" is a little too sanguine. The navy and army did have certain reservations about the applicability of social legislation in the initial seizures of 1941. Secretary of the Navy Knox ordered the social security deductions continued, but set them apart, together with the amount of the employer's tax, in a special deposit account with the United States treasurer, pending a ruling from the Social Security Board as to whether this procedure was satisfactory.[15] Secretary of War Stimson also directed continued deductions but required the employees to sign authorization cards for this procedure as a condition of employment.[16]

So it should be evident from these illustrations that officials representing the president of the United States in the early seizures were as uncertain of their powers to continue things unchanged as of their powers to change them. Not until 1943, after experience with a dozen such seizures, did government personnel lose their evident embarrassment over the paradoxes of seizure control. Only then did orders begin to appear respecting the status of employees in seized plants unabashedly accepting their dual position, making no further efforts to place them wholly in the category of either government or private workers. From mid-1943 onward, the treatment of individual employees followed a more consistent pattern.

Some officials, however, tried to swing the pendulum in the later days of seizure from its early extreme, in which the employees had been advised to serve "only" the government—Mr. McAdoo's "new era"—to the opposite extreme of serving only the private corporations—a government enforced continuance of "usual duties." This point of view was found chiefly among the civilian war agencies manned by executives borrowed from big business. It found formal expression in a "notice and order" issued by Charles H. Buford, federal manager of railroads in the industrywide seizure of May 17, 1946.

Mr. Buford had been brought from the Chicago, Milwaukee, St. Paul & Pacific Railroad, where he was executive vice-president, to direct the government's industrywide railroad operation. Probably no more able operating executive could have been found, but Mr. Buford's "notice and order" was unusual in several respects. It emphasized the "limited" nature of the government's possession and the freedom of railroad management to carry on as before.

All persons, officers, agents and employees, employed by you in the operation of your transportation system, plants and facilities are called upon to resume or continue the performance of their usual duties and in the customary manner until otherwise ordered. No such officer, agent or employee shall be deemed to be an official or employee of the United States.[17]

How differently this reads from Mr. McAdoo's appeal to the employees of the same railroads 28 years earlier. There is no reference here to the "public interest." Instead, the employees are now expressly advised that their circumstances and duties have not been changed in the slightest by the action of President Truman. It may be significant that these words were not used again in either of the two subsequent industrywide seizures of the railroads by the Department of the Army (in 1948 and 1950–1952).

We may recall in this connection that Mr. McAdoo approached that early railroad seizure with the personal conviction that it should continue indefinitely—a prelude to possible nationalization of the industry—and that Mr. Buford approached the same responsibility a generation later with the conviction that it should be very brief and should interfere as little as possible with the normal routine. Against these two extremes, it may be useful to present the intermediate viewpoint of Secretary of the Interior Ickes, who was called upon to operate the coal mines in 1943 under similar circumstances, and who regarded himself as having a dual responsibility to both public and private interests as the temporary "custodian" of the business.

In Mr. Ickes' regulations for "operation of the coal mines under government control," he described the employees as having a dual status in his order of May 19, 1943.

All personnel of the mines, both officers and employees, shall be considered as called upon by executive order 9340 [by President Roosevelt] to serve the government of the United States, but nothing in these regulations shall be construed as recognizing such personnel as officers and employees of the federal government within the meaning of the statutes relating to federal employment.[18]

This balanced view of the employees' responsibility and status under presidential seizure was adopted in a similar order by Secretary of War Stimson in December of that year in the first industrywide seizure of the railroads by the army. Like Mr. Ickes, Mr. Stimson accepted the paradox of a temporary dual allegiance without explanation and without apology.[19]

LAWS GOVERNING COLLECTIVE BARGAINING

Seizure not only obliges seizing officials to consider which laws govern the individual employees in the seized plants, but it introduces conflicts of methods (and occasionally of policy) between seizing officials and the labor-relations bodies created under our permanent labor laws. Since seizure, by its very nature, is an effort to adjust things quickly, its methods naturally clash with those of the peacetime laws governing collective bargaining, which are designed to facilitate adjustments by a slow and deliberate consideration of the rights of everyone concerned.

During the Civil War and World War I, there were no federal laws regulating collective bargaining. The peacetime policy was fundamentally laissez-faire. Hence the seizures during those major wars involved no conflict of method with permanent labor relations agencies.

In World War II, however, the major emphasis of our permanent labor law had changed from laissez-faire to federal (and state) regulation of employer–employee relations. So the wartime arrangements had to be designed either to replace these temporarily or to fit into them in some manner. The decision was to try to fit the "new wine into old bottles." Both Congress and the president proclaimed that the temporary adjustment procedures of wartime were not to replace or even to modify the permanent legislative framework of collective bargaining, but the temporary procedures were to supplement the others.[20] This proved to be an impractical goal, but it looked good on paper. The new wartime agencies were to fill in the gap not covered by the old ones, or they were to wait until the permanent procedures had been "exhausted." They were to settle disputes over the actual terms of collective bargains and to stabilize the terms of wage agreements. This would leave the permanent agencies free to continue their normal work of regulating the organizational and other procedural aspects of collective bargaining. This separation of jurisdiction was drawn between the permanent and the temporary agencies of adjustment. No such distinction was made between the permanent and the seizing agencies.

Actual experience during the defense period and in the war showed, however, that strikes were as apt to occur over organizational disputes as over contract terms. The slow, deliberate procedures of the permanent National Labor Relations Act (Wagner Act) and of the Railway Labor Act often caused impatient union leaders or employees to strike. These strikes in many cases were perfectly legal alternatives to the proceedings before the National Labor Relations Board and the National Mediation Board, alternatives to proceedings which the employers could (and still can) drag out by appeal through one or two years. In these circumstances, the temporary agencies—the National Defense Mediation Board and National War Labor Board—frequently stepped in and adjusted the disputes promptly, even while proceedings continued. Thus, the clean line of jurisdiction broke down rather early.

The policy of the NDMB toward the permanent NLRB was summarized in its official history. "Where the disputing [rival] unions were not members of one federation, the mediation board took jurisdiction . . . Usually these disputes were over bargaining representation, and they were handled solely for the purpose of expediting a determination by the NLRB as to which union should be the bargaining agent, and of maintaining, or securing resumption of, production pending NLRB action."[21]

The policy of the National War Labor Board (1942) was described by a public member, Wayne L. Morse.

The board in these cases has taken the position that it is not in conflict with or superseding the NLRB. It will give full faith and credit to the decisions which that board renders until such time as its decisions are overturned by a court with jurisdiction. However, where the NLRB has made no decision upon the issue, this board will issue its own order, subject of course to being reversed by the NLRB in that board's own field.

Obviously, the war labor board cannot wait for the NLRB's procedure to run its full course of many months when it is faced with a dispute which threatens war production now. The board is of the opinion that such disputes must be settled immediately, and this board will order such settlement as it deems most satisfactory. The order of the NWLB will remain in effect until the NLRB directs to the contrary. Such a solution will promote continuous industrial operation.[22]

In thus entering the field of the permanent regulatory bodies, the wartime agencies tried to follow the purposes and spirit of the permanent legislation. They sought to arrive at the same result as the NLRB or NMB, but more quickly—through the sacrifice of some of the rights of appeal conferred upon the employers and some of the right to strike assured to the employees.[23] This was not always effective. Some employers refused to comply with the temporary agencies just as they had refused to comply with the permanent ones, and so continued to provoke strikes. Some unions refused to accept defeat by rival unions and so struck against the certification of their competitors by the NLRB or NMB and against the reaffirmation of these rulings by the wartime agencies.

In order to keep war production going without such interruptions, Presidents Roosevelt and Truman turned to seizure. The entrance of the seizing agencies into the war labor picture created a third level of authority and a new area of conflict over adjustment methods. The seizing officials, like the two types of labor boards—permanent and temporary—were direct appointees of the president. But they were appointed under a separate set of laws for a separate purpose. So while the permanent and temporary labor relations boards had jurisdiction in certain subject matters throughout most of the nation, the seizing agencies had jurisdiction within the particular businesses seized on nearly all issues.

The exact scope of the seizing agencies' authority was never fully clarified. Two of the seizure statutes contained provisions requiring literal observance of the cumbersome procedures of all the permanent labor relations acts during government possession. Congress had provided in the seizure section of the Selective Training and Service Act of 1940 (sec. 9) that nothing therein "shall be deemed to render inapplicable existing state or federal laws concerning the health, safety, security, and employment standards of the employees in such plant" (54 Stat. 892); and in the War Labor Disputes Act (which was enacted as an amendment to sec. 9 of the Selective Training and Service Act) that changes in the interim terms and conditions of employment could be made by the seizing agencies only with the approval of the NWLB and the president, and that the NWLB, in ordering such changes, may order any "which it deems to be fair and reasonable and not in conflict with any act of congress or any executive order issued thereunder." (57 Stat. 163, sec. 5.) And yet there were other provisions which gave the president, and the agencies to which he delegated these powers, great discretion in the operation of the seized businesses. The Transportation Seizure Act of August 29, 1916, empowered the president to "take possession," to "control," and "to utilize" any system of transportation. Sec. 9 of the Selective Training and Service Act empowered him to "manufacture" military articles in seized plants. The War Labor Disputes Act extended the authority of the Selective Service Act to all production required or useful in the "war effort." It authorized the president to provide for the "use and operation by the United States or in its interests" of the seized plants, mines, or facilities. Congress required both the continuance of normal procedures and the introduction of emergency ones simultaneously, leaving the reconciliation of these contradictory requirements to the presidents—which meant, in practice, largely to the seizing agencies—and to the courts.

To a great extent, the seizing agencies' authority was whatever they made of it. They usually drafted the executive orders. Thus, each agency developed its own form of executive order to fit its own conception of seizure. The orders therefore appear inconsistent unless examined and classified by agencies. They varied from those asserting the supremacy of the seizing agency over all other federal departments and agencies to those merely directing the agency to observe existing laws and regulations. For example, under an identical law (the Transportation Seizure Act), the executive orders issued to the army have required "all federal agencies" to "comply with the directives of the secretary [of the army] hereunder," while the orders issued to the Office of Defense Transportation merely forbade the ODT itself to act contrary to any "existing state or federal laws" on the labor question.

Most seizing agencies, however, obtained executive orders from the White House commanding "all federal agencies" to "cooperate" with them to the "fullest extent possible." The vagueness of the word "cooperate" led to disagreements between some of the seizing agencies and some of the regulatory bodies, and many of the later executive orders therefore referred to regulatory bodies by name. The navy, for instance, had both the NLRB and the Department of Labor designated in two such orders, requiring them to cooperate with the secretary of the navy "to the fullest extent of their authority" (Ex. Order 9585, 9639, in the Goodyear and oil refinery seizures).

But these orders, in themselves, were mere claims of power. What they were in operation depended upon the interpretation and skill of the individual seizing officers and upon the circumstances of the case. In general, the seizing agencies felt that they were interim industrial managers of the seized firms, substituting their own judgment temporarily for that of the private management. This gave the agencies the right to put NLRB orders into immediate effect, over the objection of the private owners, or to defer the observance of such orders until the owners' appeals had been fully heard and decided in the higher courts. This theory of seizure was upheld by the highest federal courts, as we shall see.

By the time of the Korean War, other changes had occurred in the permanent system of labor regulation. First, the unions had been brought under regulation by the NLRB along with the employers; and so the employers could also bring charges of "unfair labor practices" against the unions. Moreover, provision had been made for the NLRB to obtain injunctions against certain types of strikes, including strikes by raiding unions against the government's certification of rival unions—a form of strike that had required several seizures in World War II. On the other hand, no change had been made that would shorten the long procedure for compelling an employer to cease an unfair labor practice—another important occasion for seizures.[24] These changes, however, had no effect during the Korean War, since the only seizures then were either of railroads to which the National Labor Relations Act does not apply, or of the steel industry in which no question of an unfair labor practice arose. These changes remained on the books, however.

A second change in the peacetime labor law which did cause serious difficulty during the Korean War was the new provision for injunctions in "national emergency" strikes (Taft-Hartley Act, title II, secs. 206–210). This authorized the president to obtain short delays in strike situations by court injunctions but did not authorize him to settle any disputes. With the outbreak of fighting in Korea, Congress authorized the president to hold labor–management conferences preparatory to establishing "effective procedures for the settlement of labor disputes affecting the national defense."[25] Under this authority, President Truman set up a new Wage Stabilization Board and gave it dispute-settlement powers. Congress reviewed the board's work in 1951 and decided to make no changes.

Again, however, Congress failed to reconcile its peacetime and wartime labor policies, merely declaring that nothing should be done under the wartime act "inconsistent with" any of the peacetime acts. This avoidance of responsibility became a source of major difficulty in the steel industry dispute of 1952. President Truman chose to employ the emergency provisions of the new Defense Production Act in preference to those of the Taft-Hartley Act.[26] Although he had already interpreted these rather vague provisions with considerable freedom, he then added seizure to them, much as President Roosevelt had done in the cold war period of 1941.

The Supreme Court did its best to try to make sense out of Congress' inconsistent policies of war and peace, and a majority concluded that the more explicit peacetime statute had sufficient force to exclude seizure as a legal step for the president to take, even in a period of armed hostilities. It was certainly plain that in no statute had Congress expressly authorized seizure of the steel industry. So the court ruled the seizure illegal. It did say, however, that Congress could very helpfully clarify its intentions, as President Truman repeatedly urged. Congress reacted with a series of measures indicating that in this instance it wished the president to use the peacetime provisions of the Taft-Hartley Act, but it did nothing to clarify the statutes.

With this historical review in mind, we can examine certain actual experiences of the seizing agencies in World War II in trying to insure uninterrupted production without doing anything "inconsistent with" the peacetime labor laws guaranteeing the right to strike. We will examine first those seizures involving management's resistance to the organization of employees into unions, and then those seizures involving union rivalry.

Unfair labor practice by management. In this first group of cases, management engaged in activities that are deemed unfair labor practices under the Wagner Act and its revision, the Taft-Hartley Act, or under the Railway Labor Act. One of these activities was refusal to recognize or to bargain with a union legally certified by one of the permanent labor-relations boards under a permanent act of Congress. The company's action usually resulted in a strike and an interruption of war production. Usually, too, the company was contesting the finding of the permanent labor-relations agency in the courts.

The policy of the seizing officials in such cases seems to have turned on whether the company's anti-union conduct had been the main issue leading to seizure or an incidental one. When it was a main issue, the seizing agency nearly always sought to adjust it at once by observing, as the interim terms of labor, the orders of the permanent government agency, regardless of the stage of litigation brought by management. The agencies usually regarded these forcible changes as provisional, subject to correction later if the long procedures of the courts finally yielded a verdict in favor of private management.

The opposite policy was followed in incidental disputes over nonrecognition. The seizing agencies felt that there was no need for hurry in solving these problems. Therefore, they generally continued the company's policy of nonrecognition of the union until the union had carried its fight successfully through the last stage of the normal, peacetime procedure.

It will be noticed that both these policies derived from a basic loyalty to the nation's permanent labor-relations laws—the Railway Labor Act and the National Labor Relations Act. The policy in main issues was looked upon as upholding the authority of the permanent labor-relations agencies until the final decision was reached. Wartime experience indicates the need for temporarily reversing the rule and immediately enforcing the adjustments ordered by competent government boards in emergency situations. Otherwise, the boards of adjustment are made to appear so ineffective that employees and labor unions, confronted with the frequent and rapid changes of market conditions in wartime, are liable to resort to strikes.

There have been seven seizures in which the main issue was the refusal of private management to recognize the certified union or to bargain with it in good faith. The action of the seizing agencies, in five of the cases, was to grant immediate interim rights to the union, although the companies were still contesting the union's status (Air Associates, T.P. & W. R.R., Hughes Tool Co., Ward's in seven cities, and the steel companies owning "captive" coal mines in the coal seizure of 1946–1947). In a sixth case, the seizing agency made no interim changes, but soon persuaded the company to sign a contract with the certified union (Atlantic Basin Iron Works, Inc.). In the remaining case (the Chicago plants of Montgomery Ward), the government failed to support fully the certified union and withdrew hurriedly from its occupancy of the property; but even here it returned after eight months, reseized the property, and gave immediate and full recognition to the union despite the company's continued opposition.

The two most significant cases were those of the Hughes Tool Co., Houston, Texas, and the "captive" coal mines, in which the seizing agencies effectuated certain orders of the NLRB although the company managements were appealing these orders in court. The companies responded to the seizing agencies' action by further petitioning the courts specifically to forbid the agencies to observe the NLRB orders until the court review was completed. But the courts refused the company petitions, and affirmed that the president, through the seizing agencies, had replaced former private managements and so exercised (temporarily) all the prerogatives of the former managements.

In the Hughes Tool case, the War Department observed an NLRB order of May 27, 1944, despite the fact the company was contesting this order in the Fifth Circuit Court of Appeals. The order required the recognition of the United Steelworkers of America as representative of the employees, and forbade certain "unfair" practices, the most significant of which was deducting dues on a voluntary basis for members of a rival union—the Independent Metal Workers. Both the company and the independent union thereupon asked the court to stay the enforcement of the NLRB order by the army until the court had heard the case and had rendered its decision. The court refused, and in its normal fashion proceeded to hear the parties and to issue its judgment, January 22, 1945, upholding the NLRB in part and overruling other parts of its order, including the ban on a voluntary check-off for the uncertified union. The circuit court held that voluntary deduction of dues for the members of another organization did not in any way injure the rights of the certified union (the United Steelworkers). Whereupon, the army withdrew its earlier order and restored the check-off for the independent union.[27]

In the "captive" coal mines case, the court of appeals of the District of Columbia heard a plea to restrain Secretary of the Interior Krug from recognizing the foremen's union in the companies' coal mines then in government possession. The court refused to restrain the secretary of the interior, declaring that the government was free to make any changes that the private employer would have been free to make. "The government, in its capacity as operator of the mines, stands on an equal footing so far as the period of government operation is concerned," said the court (in an opinion dated December 16, 1946).[28]

Thus, we see that three of the seizing agencies—army, interior, and ODT —have not hesitated to change the terms and conditions of employment that had been observed by private management in order to give immediate recognition to an order of the NLRB or NMB. Also, when the actions of the seizing agencies were brought to the courts, they were judged a proper exercise of the administrative discretion bestowed on the government during its temporary possession.

As we have already mentioned, an opposite policy was generally followed by the same seizing agencies in purely incidental instances of nonrecognition of unions by private management. Here the seizing agency usually continued the company's policy without change until the dispute had been finally determined under the permanent labor-relations laws.[29] But this alternative tactic by the government also brought an alternative tactic by the seized companies. Not content with the seizing agencies' acquiescence in the ordinary peacetime procedures in incidental cases, the companies went to court to argue that the seizures by the president dispossessed them of their properties, made the government the employer, and deprived the permanent labor-relations boards of jurisdiction. In effect, they held that seizures made the peacetime legislation inapplicable and that all further proceedings of the permanent labor boards should be deferred until the seizures ended. Obviously the companies had no need to press appeals from adverse NLRB decisions in these cases, so long as the seizing agencies continued the companies' nonrecognition policy and so effectively nullified the NLRB decisions.

A test case was brought by the Glen Alden Coal Co. in the Third Circuit Court of Appeals.[30] Chairman Millis of the NLRB, evidently concerned over the possibilities of this line of argument, asked the top seizing official, Secretary of the Interior Ickes, his position with respect to the requested postponement of all NLRB proceedings during government operation. He then submitted Mr. Ickes' reply to the court.

Mr. Ickes pointed out that, acting under the authority of President Roosevelt, he had designated the private managers as the federal operating managers of the seized companies and instructed them to continue collective bargaining in the normal fashion, provided it did not interfere with production. He added: "Accordingly, despite the fact the government has taken possession of mining properties of Glen Alden Coal Co., the company remains subject to the orders of NLRB. I have at no time indicated that I would have any objection to compliance by the company or the operating manager with the board's order."

The court quoted these words of Mr. Ickes verbatim and concluded:

"This is a determination by the administrator of the extent to which he has exercised the power conferred upon him by the President. Under the circumstance of the case at bar, this determination is binding upon us." The court thereupon examined the order of the NLRB, found it entirely proper, and ordered the company to comply with it.[31]

A protest by the management of another company in the same seizure resulted in the seizing agency relinquishing possession of that firm at once. The company nevertheless continued to maintain, until the highest courts ruled otherwise, that the brief seizure had deprived the NLRB of jurisdiction.[32]

Interunion rivalry. The second group of seizure cases in which the permanent laws governing collective bargaining conflicted were cases of interunion rivalry, leading to strikes over the representation of certain employees or over the jurisdiction of certain jobs. The most frequent situation was a strike by a minority union in protest over the certification of another union by the National Labor Relations Board as a representative in collective bargaining. The strike usually accompanied an effort to win members away from the successful union. Under the more recent Taft-Hartley Act, such a strike is an unfair labor practice, subject to a mandatory injunction,[33] but in World War II it was still perfectly legal. Presidents Roosevelt and Truman, therefore, dealt with such strikes through seizures.

The choice confronting the seizing agencies in these cases was whether to refuse all demands of the raiding union, throwing the full weight of the government behind the certified union, or whether to grant some interim concessions to the dissident organization pending a final settlement of the representational or work-assignment dispute. The problem was particularly troublesome because of the grave possibility that one of the two unions would strike no matter which decision was made. An additional complication was the covert support or encouragement of the raiding union by private management. Thus, to suppress the striking union, the seizing agency might have to fight both management and a minority of the employees; if it did not do so, it might have to fight the certified union and a majority of the employees.

In the circumstances, the agencies showed their independence of the permanent regulatory bodies and even of the temporary war labor boards. In five out of eight known seizures of this type, they made uninterrupted production the goal rather than literal enforcement of peacetime labor-relations laws. They devised interim solutions that saved face for both the unions involved, and thus narrowly prevented strikes.[34]

This meant that concessions were required of the certified unions as well as the uncertified unions. This is not the solution one would expect from a permanent, semijudicial body like the NLRB or NMB. This kind of solution is possible only because the seizing agency is the temporary employer and (unlike the permanent boards) can use either legal or bargaining methods.

Resolving the problem in this fashion is inconsistent with a literal observance of the permanent labor-relations laws, but it did not prevent full restoration of those laws after the war. This sometimes forced the company management to alter decisions—a fact considered minor and coincidental. The primary objective was uninterrupted operation; the second, observance of peacetime rules so far as possible.

In this kind of controversy, we have no court cases; but we find that the seizing agencies did, in practice, substitute their interim decisions for those of the permanent labor relations boards and, in several instances, they adopted policies during government possession that did not fully defend the certified unions. Nevertheless, they did suppress strikes by the raiding unions and, subject to the interim compromises mentioned, caused these unions to abandon the strike weapon and to accept the procedures of the permanent labor acts.

Economic disputes. The third group of seizures in which permanent labor-relations laws were involved were economic—over the terms of labor-management contracts. As we have noted, in this area the permanent legislation during World War II consisted of mediation machinery for the railroad industry (the NMB) and for business generally (the conciliation service), plus the Norris-LaGuardia anti-injunction act, and certain additional provisions in the railroad industry such as national adjustment boards for grievance cases, a procedure for voluntary arbitration of wage and other disputes and for special fact-finding boards whose appointment would delay but not forestall emergency strikes. By the time of the Korean War, the Taft-Hartley Act had introduced emergency procedures for delaying strikes in industry generally. All this legislation meant to create voluntary means of adjustment and compulsory means of delaying certain stoppages without outlawing them. It was obviously inadequate for assuring uninterrupted wartime production.

However, Congress was so zealous that this peacetime labor legislation be preserved for use after the war that it made no alteration in it for the war period, although (a year and a half after Pearl Harbor) it granted to President Roosevelt the seizure power that he had already been exercising, and then required him also to continue to use the permanent legislation. Congress made no effort to reconcile the inconsistencies between the temporary seizure law and the permanent statutes, leaving this unpleasant task to the president, which actually meant to the War Labor Board and to the seizing agencies. This was especially difficult in the railroad industry because so many special, peacetime, adjustment provisions were available.

Let us examine first the conflict of seizure with the peacetime railroad labor laws, then with the anti-injunction act, and finally with the more recent Taft-Hartley Act, in relation to economic (wage) controversies.

The first question was: Should the procedures of the permanent statutes be exhausted before seizure is resorted to? The experience of the government shows that this was done in the great majority of cases. The procedures were ineffective in settling the disputes, although they successfully delayed the threatened stoppages.

The next question was: Should the procedures of the railroad labor laws be used during the period of government possession to adjust grievances, mediate incidental (or even the main) economic disputes, and to delay strikes? The problem is significant principally in lengthy seizures, especially in those that were industrywide. Of the five railroad seizure operations lasting one year or more, one was not subject to the Railway Labor Act (American R.R. of P.R.), two were nationwide (1917–1920, and 1950–1952), and two were individual railroads (T.P. & W. R.R., and the steel company railroads, 1951).

In the railroad case of the First World War, the mediation procedures of the Newlands Act were completely replaced by new ones devised by the seizing agency during government operation. In the T.P. & W. R.R. case, the various procedures of the Railway Labor Act appear to have been replaced, except for some representation elections, by the activities of the National War Labor Board (arbitration) and the seizing agency (mediation and interim changes). These two seizures were both direct operations by the seizing agency.

In the railroad operations of the Korean War, the seizing agency designated the company presidents as federal operating managers and allowed them to conduct business as usual, except that any changes in wages and other conditions of labor had to be submitted to the Department of the Army for approval.[35] This resulted in a normal use of Railway Labor Act procedures in the vast majority of grievance cases and economic disputes that arose coincidentally during the 21 months of government operation. But even under these favorable conditions there were several respects in which the act's procedures were replaced or modified.

Because of strikes—and one lockout—the seizing agency had to intervene directly in several economic disputes that arose coincidentally on individual railroads; and both the army and the White House intervened significantly in the long struggle over the main issue—the wages and hours of operating employees on all the railroads. Furthermore, even when the permanent procedures were followed they were sometimes modified. In appointing three emergency boards during government possession, in disputes in which no such boards had been created prior to seizure, President Truman and the NMB altered methods in such a way as to avoid the necessity of a strike ballot and strike action and to assure the paramount authority of the seizing agency.

During the Korean War, the army referred all labor grievances to "the procedure established in such cases by the Railway Labor Act," which usually meant arbitration by the National Railroad Adjustment Board; but in the one case, where private managers objected to an NRAB award, the army refused to uphold the NRAB (although in several nonrailroad seizures it had carried out decisions of the National Labor Relations Board over the objections of private management).[36]

We may conclude that the seizing agencies showed as much independence in handling economic disputes that were subject to peacetime regulation as they had in handling organizational disputes and interunion disputes. Their authority over the interim terms of employment on the seized railroads gave them great freedom of action; but in the two later cases wherein the rules of the Railway Labor Act were effective, they followed the peacetime procedures of that act to the letter, especially in the disputes arising coincidentally on individual railroads during the seizure of 1950–1952. We also see that there was a variation in policy among the different agencies, and even a variation over time in the same agency.

The conflict of the Railway Labor Act with seizure has been mild, however, compared to that of the anti-injunction act (the Norris-LaGuardia Act of 1932).[37] This act reflects the early trade-union philosophy that the president and the courts ought to be forbidden to intervene in labor disputes because of their tendency to act for management. It was designed in part to ensure that a president would never again be able to obtain a court injunction to halt a major economic strike.[38] Although Congress soon nibbled away at the Norris-LaGuardia Act by authorizing the NLRB to obtain injunctions in organizational disputes (in the Wagner Act, 49 Stat. 449, sec. 10 [h]), it left the area of economic disputes guarded against the injunctive process throughout World War II.

As we have seen, wartime policy necessarily required federal control of nearly all economic matters, including disputes over wages. As a war measure, seizure without the injunction is an alternative means of accomplishing one of the very things the Norris-LaGuardia Act was intended to prevent—the suppression of strikes by presidential intervention, including strikes in economic disputes. Congress seems to have tried to reconcile the contradiction in a technical way (although it could not do so in reality) by authorizing the president to suppress strikes in seized plants through criminal prosecution rather than court injunctions.[39] Although this interpretation is subject to some question, President Roosevelt fully adopted it, refraining from any use of the injunction against unions, either with or without seizure, despite the gravest provocations, including the industrywide coal mine shutdowns of 1943. Hence the letter of the Norris-LaGuardia Act was adhered to, although certainly not its spirit of laissez-faire, through some 60 seizures, starting in 1941 right up until May 1946.

Then in May 1946, in the first complete, nationwide shutdown of the railroads, President Truman asked Congress to authorize him to obtain an injunction in connection with his operation of the roads. This request shows that at that time he regarded the use of an injunction with seizure as a violation of the Norris-LaGuardia Act. The House and Senate rushed approval of this request, together with certain other powers asked by Mr. Truman, but, in view of the speedy retreat of the railroad brotherhoods under this onslaught, the two chambers never reconciled their separate measures, and the injunction power was not granted with seizure.[40]

A few months later, however, the attempt of John L. Lewis to break his contract with the government during the operation of the bituminous coal mines led Mr. Truman to seek an injunction again. This time he applied directly to the courts. The court granted the injunction, fined Mr. Lewis for continuing the strike, and, confusingly enough, the Supreme Court declared that this was not a violation of the Norris-LaGuardia Act.[41] So President Truman became free to obtain injunctions in later seizures, as needed, and did so in three railroad operations, two of which were industrywide. Seizure had won a precarious victory over the Norris-LaGuardia Act.

Seizure was not so successful, however, a few years later when it tangled with the Taft-Hartley Act. This measure attempts to apply delaying rules to industrywide strikes similar to those of the Railway Labor Act. It was adopted in 1947 just as the seizure powers of the War Labor Disputes Act were expiring, and its emergency section was regarded by some of its sponsors as a mild, peacetime substitute for seizure.

The first and only conflict of this act with seizure occurred in 1952 when President Truman seized the steel mills—his first seizure other than of railroads following the expiration of the WLDA. He did not use the emergency features of the Taft-Hartley Act but instead obtained a number of voluntary postponements of the strike by the union and then, when his mediation efforts had failed, seized the industry. The steel companies asked the courts to declare the seizure illegal because the alternative for the handling of emergency disputes provided by Congress in the Taft-Hartley Act had not been employed. Thereupon the Supreme Court granted the companies' plea, finding the seizure illegal, partly because Congress had rejected seizure and adopted the alternative procedure for emergency strikes.[42]

Whether the seizure would have been legal, if President Truman had previously exhausted the procedures of the Taft-Hartley Act, is not yet clear. This is the point which is applicable here. If seizure is otherwise legal, must the president exhaust the procedures of all the permanent regulatory legislation before he uses his valid seizure powers? For example, in wartime, would the president now have to exhaust the many steps of the Railway Labor Act before taking over a railroad under the Transportation Seizure Act of 1916?[43] This is a point that ought to be clarified in future legislation.

The experience cited should convince us that peacetime labor legislation, designed to assure the right to strike against private employers and to regulate the relations between labor and management, cannot be expected to function without change in wartime, nor to serve the public interest effectively during government possession and operation. The conclusion is unavoidable that our wartime and emergency labor legislation needs clarification to assure (at least, in part) the same labor standards during government intervention without necessarily requiring the same procedures.

LAWS REGULATING PRIVATE BUSINESS

The seizure operation has come in conflict with still another group of peacetime laws—a group not connected with labor relations—the federal and state laws for the regulation of private business. This includes the laws for the government regulation of the rates and services of public utilities (natural monopolies), and for the suppression of conspiracies in restraint of trade (artificial monopolies).

The conflicts have been caused by several factors: the sweeping jurisdiction of the president and the seizing agency over the business or industry for the duration of the emergency under most legislation and during nonstatutory seizures, the lack of jurisdiction of the permanent administrative bodies over the president, and the inadequacy of these peacetime laws, providing merely for the encouragement and regulation of a private, competitive economy, to meet the wartime needs for a single, national, productive mechanism under federal control.

The points to be examined with regard to such conflicts are: To what extent has seizure actually interfered with observance of the permanent, federal and state regulatory laws? Does the maintenance of uninterrupted production by seizure actually require such interference with the normal relations between government and business? Let us look for the answers in the two areas of public control just referred to: the regulation of public utilities, including common carriers and electric power companies, and the enforcement of the antitrust laws.

Public utilities. These firms have been involved in 20 of the 71 seizures—in eight individual railroad takeovers, in five industrywide railroad takeovers, three urban transit seizures, two groups of trucking companies, one electric power company, and one industrywide seizure of telephone, telegraph, and cable companies.[44] Most of these utility seizures involved no serious problem, however, because of the brevity of government possession—11 being terminated in less than three months, frequently in a few days or weeks. Nevertheless, seven continued for a year or more, making it impossible to defer or to dodge decisions on jurisdiction with respect to proposed changes in rates and services.[45]

The normal methods of utility regulation were thought to be unsuited for unified, wartime operation of the railroads and the wire systems by the government in World War I. The procedure of rate-making by 48 state commissions plus the Interstate Commerce Commission was regarded as too slow and too diverse in this period.

Congress, therefore, directed that the regulatory authority for the railroads should be divided between the president and the ICC in a fashion which reduced the ICC to an agency for hearing protests against the decisions of the president without any real power to change those decisions.[46] Congress, however, adopted no comparable law respecting the wire systems. President Wilson then proceeded, through his seizing agencies, to increase, and otherwise to change, the rates and services of railroad, telephone, and telegraph systems not only in interstate commerce but in commerce wholly within individual states. Some of the changes were increased rates due to increased wage scales previously authorized by the seizing authorities, but other changes were admittedly efforts at reform of the basic conceptions of rates and services. It seems clear that the normal methods of regulation were almost completely replaced for the period of the seizure operation.[47]

Looking back at this episode, it is difficult to understand the furore created by this aspect of the seizures without noting how different the circumstances were from those of today. The whole conception of federal regulation of public utilities was new, quite limited in application, and subject to much suspicion and attack, especially from the state governments. When President Wilson, at one swoop, took away the bulk of the powers of the railroad and utility commissions of the 48 states, many people were shocked. Their concern was not lessened by the open campaigns then being waged by the heads of the seizing agencies to have the seizures made permanent. Secretary of the Treasury McAdoo, who was appointed director general of the railroads, urged indefinite federal operation of the roads by the government. Postmaster General Burleson, who was designated to operate the telegraphs, telephones and cables, continued his advocacy of a plan to merge these services with the federal postal system. Secretary of the Navy Daniels, who had been given charge of all the wireless stations of the nation (this seizure was not due to a labor dispute), urged Congress to put all wireless communication under the permanent control of the navy.

With the trucking and aviation industries then negligible factors, it appeared that the Wilson administration was urging, and perhaps beginning, the nationalization of the entire transportation and communication industries. It appeared to many that the disputes on the railroads and telegraphs were pretexts for the permanent control and acquisition of these basic services by the federal government.

The state commissions, therefore, attacked the new intrastate rates for the railroad and wire services in both the state and federal courts, holding them to be an unlawful exercise of presidential power. The various cases were carried to the United States Supreme Court, where they were considered together, and the court rendered a series of opinions embracing all the cases on June 2, 1919. The court ruled that the president had taken lawful possession of these industries under express acts of Congress and that his control was limited only by his discretion. His authority over intrastate rates was fully upheld. The state regulatory bodies were completely subordinated.[48]

These decisions of the highest court turned the legal controversy into a political one. The state officials appealed to Congress for a new statute giving back the control of intrastate rates and regulation of the railroads to the 48 states for the remainder of the period of federal possession. Since the control of Congress had changed in 1919 to the opposition party (Republican), the requested measure was passed by both houses, but it was vetoed by President Wilson on November 19, 1919, and was not adopted over his objection. The changes in railroad rates and services thus remained in effect until the same Congress, hostile even to the temporary seizure of the roads, returned them to private hands on March 1, 1920. No comparable effort was made (or needed) to restore state control of the intrastate telephone and telegraph rates because Postmaster General Burleson, under another act of Congress, returned the wires to private hands shortly after the Supreme Court's decisions of June 2, 1919.

Looking at this as objectively as is possible now, with the aid of more than 45 years of historical perspective, we may conclude that the almost complete subordination of the normal regulatory bodies to presidential authority in the two industrywide seizures of 1917–1920 was necessitated by contemporary circumstances, not by anything inherent in the seizure process. The most important of these circumstances were the inexperience of the private managers in cooperating with one another on an industrywide basis (either for rate-making or other policy), the absence of any federal regulatory agency established solely for the telegraph and telephone industries (the ICC had recently been given "jurisdiction" over the interstate wire system), and the reluctance of the only peacetime federal agency, the

ICC, to meet the demands of the times by approving increases in interstate railroad rates sufficient to cover new equipment and higher labor costs. These were compelling reasons in the midst of war.[49]

There was another reason that was far less impressive, but undoubtedly was also influential—the zeal of President Wilson's cabinet to show the country that they could operate its basic industries more efficiently than the private managers (either in war or peace) by integrating them under federal control. To do this, they needed control of the rates. But the weakness of this argument was its failure to distinguish between the circumstances of war and peace. The country might have accepted presidential rate-making more graciously if it had been assured that this was "for the duration" only.

When seizure was again attempted in World War II, great social changes had taken place. Private industry had gained some experience in self-regulation under the National Industrial Recovery Act and the Guffey Act. The federal government had increased the scope and depth of its normal regulatory activities. The ICC had become more flexible. The old crusade for the nationalization of utilities had fizzled, and President Roosevelt's cabinet contained none who openly advocated that cause. While the basic conflict of jurisdiction was still unavoidable in theory, no repetition of the World War I displacement of the normal agencies was proposed or imposed in any of the numerous seizures.

In the three long utility seizures of World War II (Toledo, Peoria & Western R.R.; American R.R. of Porto Rico; midwestern trucking), the seizing agencies took rate matters directly to the state and federal regulatory bodies or participated indirectly with private managements in the preparation of rate cases. During the big railroad seizures of the Korean emergency, the Army Department allowed the carriers to appear before the ICC and state commissions in their normal peacetime manner and to obtain significant rate increases—all without army participation.[50] In none of these cases did seizure interfere with the observance of the permanent federal and state laws for the regulation of public utilities. The World War I example remained in the background, however, as a grim reminder of the vast power available to the federal government.

Antitrust laws. Just as the peacetime regulatory laws were found inadequate in World War I for utility rate-making, so they were found inadequate in that same period for authorizing (and controlling) the temporary pooling and allocating of the services of competitive enterprises.[51] The inexperience of the federal government with the wartime control of the national economy, as well as its inexperience with peacetime regulation of business mergers, led it to turn to seizure. Therefore, seizures for reason of emergency labor disputes also became the means for temporarily suspending the antitrust laws, and for justifying or compelling the cooperation of rival firms.

In World War I, the railroad administration routed traffic as though the roads were a single system. So many of the company executives protested over this forced cooperation—and over other government rulings—that the administration removed all the company presidents and named federal managers.[52] (Yet not one company went into court to object.) At the same time, the Post Office Department combined services and even companies in the telephone industry, acting not only with the hearty support of the American Telephone & Telegraph Company but often at its instigation.[53]

The Post Office Department was not so effective in the telegraph industry, however, where it vainly tried to merge the services and the revenues of Western Union and Postal Telegraph, running up against the firm resistance of Clarence Mackay of the Postal system. Mr. Mackay easily outwitted Postmaster General Burleson, but it is interesting to note that Mr. Burleson's actions were upheld in the U.S. District Court by Judge Learned Hand. The government had complete discretion in its operation of the seized wire systems, the judge ruled, and could temporarily merge services and accounts if it wished. His opinion was appealed to the Supreme Court by Mr. Mackay, but that body ruled the case moot because the postmaster general suddenly returned the cables (which were the immediate subject of controversy) to private control.[54]

By the time of World War II, public policy toward competition among the utilities had changed. No longer did the government try to force an unnatural competition among these natural monopolies. Instead, the railroads, wire systems, and power companies had been accepted as necessarily monopolistic and therefore subject to public regulation. The Federal Communications Commission and the Federal Power Commission had been established. Therefore, a wartime policy was adopted of authorizing the utilities to pool their services and in other ways to cooperate under the joint supervision and control of the established peacetime agencies plus new wartime agencies such as the Office of Defense Transportation and War Shipping Administration.

At the same time, the government also relaxed the enforcement of the antitrust laws against manufacturing and mining firms, but kept control of this situation through the creation of other agencies such as the War Production Board, the Solid Fuels Administration for War, and the Petroleum Administration for War. The manufacturing and mining concerns had benefited from prior experience in industrial self-regulation under federal control during the depression under the NRA and the Guffey Act. The cooperation of the Department of Justice in suspending prosecution under the antitrust laws "for the duration" was an essential part of the semivoluntary arrangement.

Thus the seizing agencies in World War II were able to devote themselves largely to the labor problems that had caused the seizures, leaving the questions of joint action and allocation of production to the specialized wartime agencies. Although some of the labor seizures were assigned to these specialized agencies (ODT, WSA, SFAW, and PAW), the operations were handled as a distinct problem. This was illustrated in the coal mine seizures, which Secretary of the Interior Ickes initially assigned to SFAW but later turned over to a separate agency which he established for the express purpose—the Coal Mines Administration.

Nevertheless, seizure again proved its usefulness as a means of compelling the cooperation of persistent rivals in one labor case of World War II. This was the midwest trucking seizure, in which the ODT forced several trucking firms to adopt joint action plans, and even took over direct operation of one carrier which had stubbornly refused to discontinue a wastefully overlapping route.[55] Two of the concerns which the ODT thus forced into a joint plan became so thoroughly intertwined that they were unable to unscramble their accounts after the war, and formally consolidated. The two firms were Century Motor Freight of St. Paul, and Matthews Freight Service, of Grand Rapids, Minnesota, according to a despatch from Minneapolis in the *New York Times* of April 27, 1952, on p. 48.

On the whole, however, seizing agencies were not concerned with the pooling of services or with the issuing of orders to justify the temporary disregard of the antimonopoly laws in World War II. Indeed, one agency remained so aloof from these matters as to offer no objection (and no cooperation) when the Department of Justice, in normal peacetime fashion, prosecuted one of its seized companies for monopolistic practices. The Philadelphia & Reading Coal and Iron Company was indicted, pleaded *nolo contendere* (no defense), and was fined $5,000, despite the fact that it was in the possession of the Department of the Interior (CMA) as the result of an almost continuous series of labor disputes.[56] This is the only discovered instance of the wholly normal operation of the federal antitrust laws during the labor-dispute seizures.

Clearly the presidents and the seizing agencies have been given great discretion and have shown varied policies in labor seizures. They have allowed firms to compete, and they have forbidden them to do so; they have allowed firms to consolidate, and they have forbidden them to do so; and they have urged them to cooperate temporarily. They have taken the necessary steps in the social environment of the times to assure maximum national output of essential products and services despite the retarding influences of labor controversies and business rivalries. As better methods have been devised for the peaceful adjustment of the labor disputes and for the equitable pooling and allocation of the activities of competing firms, seizure has been used less for these purposes.

The use of presidential seizure in World War I in the railroad and wire disputes, however, left more of an imprint on our antitrust policies than is suggested above. It not only met the wartime need for coordinated operation of our transportation and communication systems in a crude way, giving an impetus to the development of better methods for the emergency pooling and allocation of these services in the future, it also gave a decisive push to the Wilsonian concept that the rail and wire systems should not remain, even in peace, as a series of small, regional services, often duplicating, but should be technically unified to furnish one unbroken service from coast to coast. Although seizure failed to provide a satisfactory political method for such unification, it demonstrated the great economic and technological need for some kind of national coordination in peace as well as war; and it showed the principal obstacle to such coordination to be mistaken insistence on small competitive systems in fields which required large government-regulated (or government-owned) ones.

So it came about that a new pattern for peacetime control of public utilities was set by Congress in the very legislation returning the railroads to private hands on March 1, 1920.[57] Thereafter, consolidations of both railroad and telephone companies became more frequent; government regulation became more centralized in Washington; and self-regulation (as in the nationwide car-service section of the Association of American Railroads) became more accepted. Finally, in World War II, the merger of the two telegraph companies (Western Union and Postal Telegraph) which Postmaster General Burleson had tried in vain to impose by force during government possession of the wires was effectuated permanently by an act of Congress in a far more equitable manner.[58] Thus the idea of unified (or coordinated) national systems of transportation and communication, which had been practiced first during World War I in seizures resulting partly from labor disputes, became a permanent element of our antitrust policy in war and peace.

Chapter 10

Seizure Compared with Other Experience in Required Operations

In this chapter we examine presidential methods other than seizure used in compelling continued industrial production and compare them with the seizure experience. We are not trying to examine the whole range of policy alternatives, nor to make a case for the adoption of seizure or any other device as the exclusive or necessarily predominant tool of public policy. Our aim is to throw light on the actual experience of seizure and other forms of required operations as a contribution to the history of presidential intervention in labor disputes.

The total experience with measures other than seizure has been small—only 23 disputes in 100 years compared to the 71 resulting in seizure. Moreover, this has included several means of coercion, some of which have been utilized only a few times. Nevertheless, some of the techniques have been used simultaneously in disputes, thus increasing the total experience. The various means other than seizure are listed in Table 11, with the number of times each has been the primary means of coercion. The specific disputes and the nine presidents who intervened are identified in Appendix C.

It will be recalled that all these actions but two were improvised by the presidents from statutes intended for other purposes or from their "inherent powers." Table 11 shows that the presidents, when not employing seizure, have relied mainly upon either their own military and administrative powers or upon the cooperation of the courts. The experience with *ad hoc* congressional legislation has been surprisingly brief.

Each of the several means of requiring production, other than seizure, will be examined from the same standpoints used in our study of seizure, although more briefly.

TROOP OR CIVILIAN REPLACEMENTS

The earliest example of required production, as we have seen, was the use of soldiers and of specially hired civilians to load and unload government vessels at New York piers during a strike of longshoremen in June 1863; and this form of action has persisted throughout the years in both war and peace. During the period under review, there have been at least nine disputes in which the Department of Defense has furnished workers, either civilian or military, to help break strikes that were interfering with

TABLE 11
METHODS OF REQUIRING PRODUCTION, OTHER THAN SEIZURE

Means of coercion	Number of uses[a] as primary instrument of coercion			
	War	Recon- version	Peace	Total
Improvised measures				
Temporary troop or civilian replacements	4	3	2	9
Qualified martial law	3	1	—	4
Administrative sanction	1	—	—	1
Prosecution for violating criminal statute, other than physical violence	—	—	3	3
Prosecution for contempt of antistrike injunction	—	1	3	4
Ad hoc legislation				
Substantive terms of employment	—	—	1	1
Compulsory arbitration of specific issues	—	—	1	1
Total[b]	8	5	10	23

[a] The above cases are described in Appendix C.
[b] The comparable totals for seizure cases are: war 41, reconversion 25, peace 5, total 71.

the supply of important military material. The presidents who were involved have been: Lincoln, Wilson, Franklin Roosevelt, Truman, and Eisenhower.

The common characteristic of these disputes is that they have been between the employees and managements of private firms under contract with the armed forces. The workplace has been either company property or a military base. In either situation, the defense establishment was receiving and paying for certain services of the contractor. When these services were interrupted by strikes, the armed forces in most cases temporarily substituted their own personnel, their own equipment, and their own supervision. This has been the recurring practice in New York Harbor during strikes by the longshoremen or the tugboat crews. There have been variants, however. In one case (the San Francisco ship-repair yards, 1941), the navy recruited civilian employees in behalf of its contractors. In another case (spruce production in the Pacific northwest, 1917–1919), the army rented out 10,000 soldiers to the private logging firms which it had under contract. The soldiers worked side by side with civilian employees under terms and conditions specified in the contracts. In two of the New York longshore disputes (1951 and 1954), the army hired hundreds of regular dockworkers, who were not striking, as temporary civil service personnel. In this way, the men transferred from the employ of the stevedoring contractors into direct government service, losing both the obligation and the right to strike. There are probably other instances of the temporary replacement of striking employees of defense contractors.

The effectiveness of this kind of control in an emergency dispute is limited only by the number of replacements available. There is no picketing problem because the presence of military police renders this ineffective. In the cases cited, however, the number of personnel needed (with two exceptions) was never more than a few hundred, and was a type readily available in uniform. It will be noted that all cited cases, except three, pertained to New York Harbor transportation—an area in which the navy and army have special responsibilities and competence. The three exceptions were a laborers' strike in the shipyards of the Bethlehem Steel Corp. in New York in 1944; the loggers' strike, and the machinists' strike in the San Francisco ship-repair yards. Only the last two required unusual recruitment operations.

The standards of public policy observed in the nine cases under examination show little in the way of consistent development. One pattern, however, has been the Lincolnian policy of requiring only partial operations in the New York Harbor strikes. Subsequent presidents have enforced only the movement of military passengers and supplies, leaving the private cargoes and passengers under the strike bans. Generally, the armed services have paid the "going rate," that is, the prestrike rate, to their temporary help when they have used civilians, but there were awkward exceptions in the harbor strikes of 1919; and in one other exception both soldiers and civilian loggers, employed in the spruce forests, were beneficiaries of improved working conditions imposed by the army and enforced against the logging companies with economic sanctions.

The outcome of these disputes has depended on the degree of unity among the strikers, and the degree of firmness in the wage policy of presidential agencies. When the strikers were united against unfavorable decisions of the governmental agencies, they won more favorable rulings (New York Harbor, January 1919, and September 1946). When the strikers and their leaders were divided, the governmental agencies stood firm, and the strikers lost (New York Harbor, October 1919 and March 1954; San Francisco shipyards, June 1941; Bethlehem Steel shipyards, New York, August 1944). In the spruce case, the strikers, although divided (IWW *vs.* AFL), won the eight-hour day and other benefits but not union recognition. This was because the army command, headed by Brigadier General Brice P. Disque, which effectively broke the strike, considered the workers' demands (other than union recognition) to be meritorious.

In the spruce operation, General Disque granted wage increases, instituted the eight-hour day, established a government-sponsored union with a complete grievance procedure (the Loyal Legion of Loggers and Lumbermen), hired civilian workers on an open-shop basis, but suppressed IWW activities and allowed little freedom to the AFL unions. At peak operations, at least 25,000 soldiers and 75,000 civilians were at work under army direction.[1]

This remarkable operation began as an action of army procurement officials but was formalized after some months by Congress' creation of the Spruce Production Corporation, wholly government-owned. Congress deliberately refused to give either the corporation or the War Department authority to seize logging camps and forests, and in so doing left the corporation without coercive powers with which to settle the basic labor dispute which had created the emergency—the eight-hour day. So the corporation had to call upon the Railroad Administration, which did have seizure powers, to help it enforce the eight-hour day against recalcitrant logging firms. The Railroad Administration withheld railroad cars from the noncomplying firms. One firm immediately complied; another chose to go out of business.[2]

A comparison of the nine cases with a half dozen seizures, in which similar replacements were supplied by the armed forces, reveals important considerations.

As related in earlier chapters, soldiers were assigned to run the seized Philadelphia & Reading R.R. in 1864 and the Fairport, Painesville & Eastern R.R. in 1942; soldiers were rented out as truck drivers and dockers in the Chicago trucking strike of 1945; the navy manned seized towboats and furnished some of its own tugs in the New York Harbor strike of February 1946. In addition, the government recruited civilian employees without discrimination as to membership or nonmembership in unions in the Alcoa freighter seizure of 1941 and in the United Engineering shipyard seizure of 1945. Preparations for similar moves were made in a half dozen other seizures.

Here, too, the effect on the disputing parties clearly depended on the policy adopted by the presidential agencies in operating the seized property. The Reading seizure of 1864 was a strike-crusher pure and simple. Nothing so sophisticated as government mediation or arbitration had been developed then. In the others (all in the 1940's), the government was active in arbitrating a settlement, with one instructive exception—the New York Harbor towboat seizure of February 1946. In this the federal and local governments sought only to mediate a solution. The experience of the federal manager, Laurence C. Turner, shows the effect of this policy.[3] Mr. Turner relates that he was summoned to New York City Hall by Mayor William O'Dwyer, who asked if the federal government could not stop using navy crews to run the seized boats, as this was proving embarrassing to him in his mediation efforts. Mr. Turner believed that O'Dwyer wanted more pressure put on the owners and was dismayed to find that the government's replacement of striking crews put pressure only on the strikers. But the Washington policy was to keep the towboats moving, and this was continued. In the end, the parties were persuaded to submit the unresolved issues to private arbitration.

The similarities between the seizure cases and the nonseizure cases are rather strong in this kind of intervention, especially since in all such cases it has been in the interest of company managements to cooperate fully with the government agency supplying replacements. Moreover, if we assume that in all such cases the government will undertake to arbitrate and to determine the dispute and to enforce its findings against the losing party, then seizure might well be the less desirable of the two postures from which to supply replacements for striking employees. The contracting power may often be more direct—that is, less complicated—in controlling procurement of military supplies and services (especially in relation to transportation) than the power of eminent domain. But the seizure weapon remains the more powerful, and therefore the more appropriate in two circumstances: (1) if the employee resistance is extensive, and (2) if the losing party, after arbitration, turns out to be management.

QUALIFIED MARTIAL LAW

No president of the United States has ever declared unqualified martial law in a labor dispute emergency.[4] This extreme measure goes far beyond any requirements of the public interest so far disclosed by a labor dispute. However, there are degrees of martial law, or martial rule, and the presidents and their military commanders have curtailed some of the civil rights of persons directly involved in eight or 10 labor disputes.[5] A survey shows a record of considerable self-restraint by the national government— a record that one wishes had been emulated over the years by the state and local authorities in dealing with the same and other industrial disputes.

The following four cases of martial law concern the essential element in our definition of emergency disputes—the withdrawal of the right to strike. This was carried out by generals of the United States Army without being countermanded by the president and commander in chief.

St. Louis and Louisville, 1864	Gen. W. S. Rosecrans
Tennessee, 1864	Gen. George H. Thomas
Gary, Indiana, October to December 1919	Gen. Leonard Wood
Hawaii, 1941–1944	Gen. Delos C. Emmons

It will be observed that three of these cases occurred during war at the very margin of enemy contacts. Each of them appears to have established a general policy within a limited area. Contrastingly, the fourth case came during a year of reconversion (1919) and was confined to activities in a single key city in a dispute. Out of a hundred years of industrial strife in an expanding national economy, with four major wars, the brevity of this list seems a symbol of the moderation of popular governments.

While other instances of qualified martial law have been found and studied by a generation of scholarly work, no other seems to have been intended to terminate the right to strike. In fact, some of the uses of martial law in peacetime definitely helped the strikers either by protecting them against company guards and sheriffs' deputies (West Virginia coal fields, 1921), or by barring the importation of strikebreakers into the areas (Colorado coal fields, 1914). One borderline example was the use of federal troops in Coeur d'Alene, Idaho, in 1899, to prohibit the re-employment of union miners after a violent strike; but this action of the local commander (Brigadier General H. C. Merriam) was overruled by President McKinley as soon as the protests of union officers reached him.[6]

The most serious employment of martial law was the general denial of collective-bargaining rights and the substitution of military control of wages and employment in the Territory of Hawaii for a period of more than two years in the Second World War. Although the declaration of martial law on December 8, 1941, had the approval of President Roosevelt. the responsibility for the administration of the islands became that of the army commander on the scene; and the use of his authority to regulate wages, punish absenteeism from jobs, bar organization activities by unions, and forbid strikes appeared increasingly unnecessary as the threat of enemy invasion lessened. In fact, Governor Ingram M. Stainback complained that the principal reason for its continuance after the defeat of the Japanese fleet at the Battle of Midway was the desire of business interests in the islands to maintain the system of "labor control" which the military commander had established.[7] It was apparently the pressure of other departments in Washington upon the War Department which brought it to an end in 1944.

The actions of Generals Rosecrans and Thomas in barring strikes and union organizing in parts of Kentucky, Missouri, and Tennessee during the Civil War had the same justification: the areas were in or close to theaters of war; but no such excuse was offered for the action of General Wood in Gary, Indiana, in October 1919. General Wood forbade meetings and parades, arrested strikers, and raided homes and offices in order to break up what he called "Red anarchistic elements." The steel strike was not directly denounced, but it was severely hampered.

In none of these instances was any attempt made by the military commanders or by their superiors in Washington to assure the workers of an equitable adjustment of their disputes. Instead, the firm suppression of the strikes deprived the workers of whatever collective-bargaining power they may have had.

A comparison of these four instances of martial law with the use of seizure is illuminating. It will be remembered that the presidents have entrusted 41 of the 71 seizures to the Army or Navy Departments for administration, and have allowed the use of military personnel in seven other seizures which were primarily administered by civilian agencies. In fact, it may be said more broadly that nearly all the seizures have had the appearance of a military operation conducted by the president "as commander in chief of the armed forces"; and some scholars have classed seizure as a "form of martial rule."[8]

The evidence indicates that seizure and martial law are about equally capable of maintaining national authority in the affected plants or other industrial facilities, but that seizure permits much more flexibility in minimizing the degree of control. For one thing, martial law is not so easily confined to a particular labor dispute; its operation is essentially geographic in definition. For another, only seizure gives the president and his military subordinates managerial authority in plants and therefore the direct ability to assure equitable wages and working conditions during the period of control, and to bring a variety of pressures to bear upon the parties to coax them to agreement. Finally, seizure, because of its more limited scope, permits closer supervision of the labor policies of the officers in charge by Washington.

ADMINISTRATIVE SANCTIONS

So far we have considered two coercive measures by which the presidents, without calling upon the aid of the courts, have repressed strikes and lockouts over the resistance of one of the disputing parties: martial law and the supplying of temporary replacements. There is one other measure, apart from seizure, which the presidents have had immediately available in labor disputes—administrative sanctions. This term has been employed to designate the imposition of penalties by an administrative agency in circumstances not specifically provided for by law. It has sometimes been called economic sanctions or indirect sanctions, and has been used by Presidents Wilson and Franklin Roosevelt in nonlabor situations as well as in labor disputes.[9]

The following are examples of the use of administrative sanctions in emergency labor disputes (asterisk indicating action supplemented later by seizure):

Wanamaker & Brown management, Philadelphia, 1918 (May-June)
Scotch Woolen Mills management, Chicago, 1918
*Draft-deferred workers in all defense plants, 1941 (June)
*Montgomery Ward & Co. management, Chicago, 1944
*Goodyear rubber workers (URW), Akron, 1945 (July)

These situations involved the use of the government's contracting power (the two clothing firms), its militia power (the defense workers), its postal power (the Montgomery Ward case), and the WLDA-NWLB powers (rubber workers). None of the statutes was originally intended for use in this way, yet no legal test was brought to court.

The first example of the use of this technique was the action of the War Department early in 1918 in holding up renewal of a contract for the procurement of army clothing from Wanamaker & Brown, Philadelphia, until the company ended a lockout of its employees who had joined the Amalgamated Clothing Workers Union. The action ended the shutdown but had to be renewed a few months later when the company sought to evade the terms of settlement imposed by the labor division of the Quartermaster Corps (then headed by Professor William Z. Ripley). However, a repetition of this action in Chicago was unsuccessful, resulting only in a big anti-union firm, Scotch Woolen Mills, giving up its government contracts. This, of course, meant that the government lost this source of supply.[10]

In the other examples of administrative sanctions, during the 1940's, the penalty failed to bring compliance with procedures or decisions established by the presidents for the adjustment of emergency disputes, and so was followed by seizure and operation of the industrial facilities. One of these cases was the order of Selective Service Director Lewis B. Hershey in June 1941 to all local draft boards to cancel the draft deferments of striking workers employed in defense production.[11] The inadequacy of this order to end the strike at North American Aviation in Los Angeles led to the seizure of that plant a few days later. The other two uses of administrative sanctions were similarly unsuccessful. One was President Roosevelt's controversial order withdrawing the special post office facilities which had been operative for 30 years at the Chicago mail-order house of Montgomery Ward & Co.—an inept maneuver that was followed later by seizure (May

1944). The second was an order of the National War Labor Board in July 1945 to the Goodyear Tire & Rubber Co., releasing it from the board's previous requirement of shift premiums, paid vacations, and other fringe benefits for the company's Akron employees—a mild penalty against the union which was soon followed by seizure of the Akron plant.[12]

In defense of this technique, two points have been made. First, the method provides for consideration of labor standards, as well as of the public interest, since by definition it is a means for enforcing decisions of federal agencies. Second, the method is moderate in some respects, since its penalties are economic. It sends no one to prison, for example. However, the method is subject to attack on two grounds of considerable importance. First, it has seldom been effective as a means of public control against either employees or managements. Second, it violates "the accepted doctrine that Congress alone may enact penalties and that no one may be subjected to a penalty that was not duly enacted by Congress prior to his alleged offense."[13]

In comparing seizure with administrative sanctions, it may be noted that when the administrative measures failed, seizure was frequently resorted to. However, if we look further, we find that in several instances, when seizure was not going too well, the seizing authorities supplemented their new managerial prerogatives by imposing administrative sanctions. For example, draft deferments were canceled, referral to other war work was denied, and gasoline rationing privileges were withdrawn as sanctions against striking employees in a half dozen seizures. Again, the army canceled its procurement contracts with a seized firm (S. A. Woods Machine Co., Boston) and threatened to do so during several other seizure cases.

Without recounting details, it seems clear that effective public control can be achieved over an uncooperative management by the withholding of procurement contracts only if the firm is heavily dependent on them. Otherwise, the firm will shift its business to the private market. This was avoided in the S. A. Woods case by condemning the firm's properties and turning both the contracts and the properties over to another company for the balance of the war. In the Ward case, the postal boner was followed by a bungling seizure, from which the president's prestige was barely rescued by a second seizure under the direction of the War Department.

The effectiveness of seizure control is greater than that of ordinary administrative sanctions because of the larger number of penalties and pressures available when the property is possessed and directly managed, and because of its well known face-saving effect. In addition, seizure is more moderate toward owners, because of the availability of "just compensation" for any resulting losses.

When it comes to sanctions against strikers, the use of the draft and other manpower controls has an uncertain record. The mere threat of it by President Wilson in the great machinists' strike at Bridgeport, Connecticut, ended the workers' resistance to a NWLB decision. Yet in certain other cases, its actual use has proved too slow and selective to be effective. In seizure cases it also has a varied history, but in one seizure (the San Francisco machinists' case) the application of manpower sanctions worked so well in ending the strike that the federal courts compelled the government to moderate its procedures when the strikers appealed for relief to the judiciary.[14]

CRIMINAL PROSECUTION

The presidents, through the attorney general, have arrested private employees and union officials for unlawfully striking in connection with eight emergency disputes, other than seizure cases. These cases have consisted of (1) prosecution in criminal courts for allegedly violating statutes construed as forbidding strikes, and (2) citation in courts of equity for contempt of court in violating antistrike injunctions. Although in some of these cases the presidents used troops to suppress outbreaks of physical violence, they were seeking in these court actions to establish the unlawfulness of concerted and peaceful withdrawals from work. The presidents involved were: Hayes, Cleveland, Wilson, Harding, and Franklin Roosevelt.

Six of these disputes resulted in the indictment, trial by jury, and conviction of strike leaders for violations of criminal statutes, as follows (asterisk indicates action supplementary to antistrike injunction):

Boston & Maine R.R., 1877 (February) *obstructing mails*
*Major railroads, 1877 (July) *obstructing mails*
*Major railroads, 1894 *obstructing mails and interstate commerce; also violating Sherman Antitrust Act*
Major railroads, 1920 *violating Sherman Act and Lever Act*
*Major railroads, 1922 *obstructing mails*
S.S. *Algic,* 1937 *violating mutiny-statute of 1790 and Merchant Marine Act of 1936*

It should be noted, first of all, that none of the statutes relied on had been adopted with strikes or labor disputes in mind. Nevertheless, the application of these statutes to strike situations (incidentally, all of them in transportation and all of them in peacetime), was upheld in every case in which it was challenged in the courts.[15] In the second place, it may be noted that the use of statutory prosecutions in strikes appears to have been discontinued since 1922, except for the mutiny case and, as we shall see, wartime seizure cases.

The effect of these criminal prosecutions was to hamper the strikers and ultimately to bring about a termination of the stoppages, but in no case except the mutiny case was the transportation operation immediately restored by the arrests. In fact, in three of these cases, the government had to supplement the criminal arrests by obtaining antistrike injunctions and prosecuting simultaneously for contempt of court. Thus, the record of this device is only fair with respect to keeping essential services going. It is especially weak in large industrywide shutdowns.

It is even less satisfactory with respect to the other questions we are asking. In the first three cases, the government took no position on the dispute, other than to declare the strike unlawful and to punish its leaders. Nor did the government seek to mediate a settlement. The result was complete victory for the managements.

On the other hand, in the fourth case, the yardmen's strike of 1920, rank-and-file workers were defying an agreement between President Wilson and the brotherhoods, reached just prior to the termination of wartime seizure. In this case, the governmental action, like the disciplinary measures of the labor organizations, had the effect of enforcing presidential terms. In 1922, the railroad shopmen's strike continued for many months with varying effectiveness on different lines, despite the criminal prosecution and the injunction which was also in effect—while President Harding sought vainly to mediate a settlement. The outcome reflected the president's policy—temporizing at first but later working against the unions—and the strike on many lines was lost.

The lesson of all these experiences surely is that statutory prosecution in strikes works only in one direction—to crush the strikes—and that sometimes slowly. In itself, prosecution ranges the governmental power fully on the side of management. However, if the prosecution is in support of a judgment on the merits by the president or by a presidential board, then it becomes a form of enforcement of a public, instead of a private, owner's decision.

During the Second World War, Congress ruled that all strikes in plants seized by the president would be unlawful. The theory of this provision in the War Labor Disputes Act was that, in seizure, the president was in a position to enforce equitable terms of settlement recommended by the National War Labor Board, and so this whole procedure was being substituted for strikes and lockouts during the war. Under this provision, we find that strikers were arrested and tried in criminal courts in four seizures—three coal mine seizures (May 1943, November 1943, and 1945) and the Philadelphia Transportation case. In these, the strikers were defying the recognized union as well as the government, although they were the beneficiaries of determinations found by the president to be equitable and in the public interest.

ANTISTRIKE INJUNCTIONS

In addition, the presidents have prosecuted union officials and individual employees for contempt of court because of defiance of antistrike injunctions. There have been only four such cases, apart from seizure. All but one were in time of peace, and that one occurred during the economic turmoil of reconversion from war to peace (soft coal, 1919). (Asterisk indicates concurrent statutory prosecution.)

*Major railroads, 1877 (July) *carriers in federal receivership only*
*Major railroads, 1894 *all carriers in interstate commerce; injunction also based on Sherman Antitrust Act*
Soft coal, 1919 *no basis for injunction stated by court; government request based on Lever Act*
*Major railroads, 1922 *injunction based on Transportation Act of 1920 and on Sherman Act*

In this litigation, as in the statutory prosecutions, the presidents claimed the strikes to be unlawful, and again relied on legal concepts that were improvised for the occasions. The presidents moved from the concept of protecting property that had been temporarily entrusted to the federal courts in receivership cases to the protection of commerce in general, using the courts (rather than Congress) as an avenue for proclaiming the strikes unlawful and for forbidding all measures in support of the stoppages.

In the Pullman railroad strike of July 1894, President Cleveland established the basic doctrine. In effect, the right to strike involved the fallacy of composition. A stoppage in a single firm or railroad might be consistent with the public interest and entirely lawful, while a stoppage of many railroads might threaten the very continuance of commerce among the states and with foreign countries and therefore constitute an unlawful conspiracy. This view was upheld, in its essence, in the case of *In re Debs,* the only test of this form of public control ever to reach the Supreme Court.[16] In this case, the court upheld President Cleveland partly on the theory of the government's general responsibilities and powers for the protection and regulation of commerce and partly on the basis of the Sherman Antitrust Act of 1890.

This technique was applied by the presidents in three widespread railroad strikes and in one industrywide coal strike. Then the method was abolished, not by the courts but by Congress. In 1932, Congress enacted the Norris-LaGuardia Act, with the approval of President Hoover, which denied the federal courts jurisdiction to issue injunctions in labor disputes.[17] The act made no distinction between injunctions obtained by the President of the United States and those obtained by private employers. The act clearly was aimed at both, and, in view of one of its sponsors, Professor Felix Frankfurter (afterward associate justice of the Supreme Court), it was aimed more especially at ending presidential intervention by this means.[18]

In reviewing the experience with this technique, it is evident that the antistrike injunction was a powerful instrument of control. Both Debs and John L. Lewis have testified to its efficacy. The injunctions put strike leaders in jail for contempt of court in 1877 and again in 1894. In December 1919, the arrest of Lewis for contempt was followed almost immediately by the ending of the strike, and the charges were then dropped without a trial. Although in the railroad shopmen's strike of 1922 the government did not arrest the strike leaders, it did prosecute numerous individual strikers and their sympathizers. The FBI aroused special resentment against the injunction by arresting and prosecuting such sympathetic third parties as barbers who refused to shave nonstriking railroad workers, and landladies who refused to rent rooms to strikebreakers.

The standards of public policy followed in these cases were generally negative, but President Wilson's handling of the soft coal strike of 1919 was a notable exception. Wilson considered that the coal mines were still under government regulation, during the reconversion from war to peace, with both wages and prices still subject to government control. Lewis maintained that normal collective bargaining had been (or should have been) re-established as soon as hostilities had ceased on the Western Front. This strictly legal issue was decided by a federal judge in favor of the government, and the union significantly did not appeal.[19]

Instead, the economic issues were fought with economic and political weapons. The miners remained away from work in spite of the injunction and so brought economic pressures against both the government and the operators. The president's subordinates finally settled the dispute by mediating an agreement which gave the miners a 14-per cent wage increase without requiring a rise in the price of coal. However, the administration was slow in pressing its citations for contempt, and so had to mediate the settlement under the pressure of a widespread stoppage. Lewis said later that the chief hardship had been the union's inability to pay strike benefits. In any event, the public went without coal until the dispute was settled, not by the court but by the executive arm of the government.

The episode illustrates three points about antistrike injunctions: they are almost ineffectual unless backed by punishment for contempt; the courts are not equipped to settle economic and political controversies such as the determination of the wage and price structures of key industries; and the injunctions are automatically biased against the strikers, except when they are used in support of presidential procedures for the equitable determination of the merits of the disputes.

So the antistrike injunction was abolished as an instrument of public policy in 1932, and Franklin Roosevelt had to turn to other measures in the labor dispute emergencies of World War II. During the defense emergency of 1941, which included the undeclared naval war with Germany, Roosevelt acted five times to compel the continuance of military production—once by recruiting civilian replacements (San Francisco shipyards) and four times by seizing and operating the industrial property. Even after Pearl Harbor, the president still carefully avoided the injunction, experimenting with many other forms of coercion. We have already noted the use of qualified martial law in the Hawaiian Islands, and the use of troop replacements in a shipyard tieup in 1944. There were 34 seizures—all of which followed the wartime examples of Lincoln and Wilson. But when John L. Lewis in 1943 defied the seizing authorities and continued his coal strikes, even as he had defied Wilson's injunction of 1919, there was no personal penalty available such as a citation for contempt. So Roosevelt turned uncertainly from one possible remedy to another in a vain effort to compel Lewis to keep the miners at work. He first offered the miners the protection of troops (but assigned none); then made secret preparations to draft all miners who disregarded his personal "order" to resume work (none was ever drafted); levied "fines" against some of the strikers, that is, deductions from their pay (but immediately rescinded this); and then asked Congress to extend the age limit for the military draft so that he could draft miners up to age 65 for duty at the mines (which Congress refused to do).[20]

At this juncture, Congress enacted the War Labor Disputes Act which made strikes in seized plants and facilities, including mines, a federal crime.[21] But Lewis was not arrested. It was said later that he took no overt action to aid or encourage further stoppages while the mines were in government possession, so he had not violated the statute. However, local union officers who led bands of roving pickets were arrested, pleaded *nolo contendere,* and were given six-month suspended prison sentences with three years' probation.[22] Roosevelt finally turned to the idea of a national service law, under which all strikes by essential workers would have been unlawful. But Congress rejected this proposal.[23] So Lewis won his terms, coal was mined (despite frequent interruptions), and "government by injunction" was avoided.

It was Harry Truman who in 1946, faced with the extensive strike wave of the reconversion period, boldly advocated and then revived the use of the injunction in emergency labor disputes by combining it with seizure. As we have mentioned, during the rail crisis of May 1946, although the railroads were in federal possession, two of the rail brotherhoods shut them down in the most extensive railroad stoppage of our history. The brotherhood chieftains avoided arrest as Lewis had done, by taking no overt action in support of the strike.[24] The president asked Congress for additional powers to enable him to uphold federal authority and to maintain operations in seized properties.[25] Among the powers requested was the injunction. To permit its use, the president requested modification of the Norris-LaGuardia Act. The two houses of Congress approved different bills, but the injunction was in both. Before the two bills could be reconciled, however, the rail brotherhoods capitulated and accepted the president's terms, and the strike was over. The president's legislative proposals did not become law.

This experience clearly shook Congress and the public, however, and Congress proceeded to enact strong antilabor legislation. The two houses approved and sent to the president a measure (the Case bill) which, among other things, would have modified the Norris-LaGuardia Act to permit private employers to obtain injunctions in antitrust actions against labor organizations. In vetoing the legislation, Truman explained his position on labor injunctions.

> The labor injunction is a weapon to which no private employer should be entitled except within the careful restrictions laid down by that act [the Norris-LaGuardia Act]. We should not invite the return to the practice of issuing injunctions without notice or hearing and a revival of the other abuses that tended to discredit our courts and give rise to the widespread popular denunciation of "government by injunction."
>
> Injunctions requested by the government itself, and designed to restrain strikes against the government in cases where refusal to work for the government has produced a condition of national emergency, are, to my mind, an essential element of government authority. This authority, however, should not be available to private employers under the vast variety of conditions contemplated by section 11 of this bill.[26]

Within a few months, the need for presidential action to require production arose again—this time in the soft coal crisis of October 1946. Although the mines were in federal possession, Lewis closed them down. Lewis was engaged in a dispute with the government over the terms of its wage controls, as he had been in the reconversion period of 1919. The dispute was not with private management, but the mines were in government possession and subject to the antistrike provisions of the War Labor Disputes Act. As he had in the struggle with Roosevelt, Lewis avoided arrest under the criminal provisions of that act by taking no plainly overt steps to call or support the strike.

Once more President Truman turned to the injunction as the instrument of public control; but this time he did not ask Congress to modify the Norris-LaGuardia Act. Instead he sent Attorney General Clark into court and asked for an injunction. In effect, the president argued that Lewis had, by the use of "code words," unlawfully called a strike in federally operated mines, and should be required by the court to cancel the strike order and secure the resumption of mining. Judge T. Alan Goldsborough issued the requested order. Lewis again ignored the injunction, but the government did not repeat the mistake of delaying Lewis' citation and trial for contempt. He was tried, found guilty, and fined $10,000, and the union itself was fined $700,000.[27]

In due course, the Supreme Court, by the close vote of five to four, upheld the president's action as not constituting a violation of the Norris-LaGuardia Act, since that act did not apply to federal employees.[28] The mine workers were considered by the court's majority to have become temporary employees of the government. Lewis was obliged to comply with the court's order and ended the strike on the president's terms. Thus the antistrike injunction and contempt proceedings again became available, if used with seizure, as an instrument of public control in emergency labor disputes.

Thereafter, the combination of seizure with injunction was successfully applied by President Truman to two nationwide railroad seizures (1948 and 1950–1952); the method was upheld by the lower courts as lawful, partly on the basis of the mine workers' case, partly on the Debs' case, and partly on more general grounds of public security.[29] In these two cases, one in peace, the other in the Korean War, Truman established full national control over not only the operation of the roads but over the terms and conditions of employment, and then won acceptance of the government's terms by both labor and management. While this went on, collective bargaining and private management continued with only minor interference. Although Truman's terms of employment were criticized by some observers, actually only the 1950–1951 terms involved any significant concessions to the striking labor organizations; and, after yielding these, the president stood firm against repeated pressures for a second round.

Thus the Truman policies in the railroad disputes of 1946, 1948, and 1950–1952 afforded an instructive contrast with the policies of the earlier presidents in the railroad disputes of 1877, 1894, and 1922. Although the presidents in all six cases relied similarly upon the injunction with prosecutions for contempt, the standards of public policy in the three seizure cases were broader—taking account of the interests of labor as well as of management and reconciling this, so far as possible, with the public interest in wage-price stability.

LEGISLATIVE ACTION

Up to this point, we have examined the impromptu measures which the presidents have devised using legislation intended for other purposes or using their full powers as chief executive and commander in chief. We now turn to the steps taken by the presidents to seek new legislation.

We find three examples enacted to avert specific stoppages of production. The disputes which led to this legislation all concerned the railroad operating brotherhoods and related, in turn, to wages, to the eight-hour day, and to work-rules affecting crew sizes. A stoppage on all eastern railroads was threatened in the first case, and nationwide stoppages in the others. All of the disputes were in peacetime.

The legislation adopted was the Newlands Act, which established a new voluntary-arbitration procedure for railroad workers, approved July 15, 1913, by President Wilson; the Adamson Act, which required a reduction in basic working hours to eight per day with no reduction in pay for all train and engine employees, approved September 3, 1916, by Wilson; and a joint resolution approved August 28, 1963, by President Kennedy, which forbade a strike over work-rules for six months and created a special board of arbitration to settle the two key issues in the dispute, with the award to be made mandatory for two years.

It is significant that the first of these measures, which was adopted at the request of both parties, was effective for less than three years. In 1916, when the eight-hour dispute arose, the parties were unwilling to rely on the voluntary procedure which the industry itself had sponsored, and the president was obliged to seek coercive legislation. Similarly, half a century later, other parties in the same industry rejected the voluntary procedures of another railway labor act, together with numerous supplementary procedures offered by the president, and forced President Kennedy and Congress to make arbitration of the work-rules dispute compulsory.

The operation of these two compulsory statutes deserves examination— first, as to their effectiveness as a means of public control; and, second, as to the standards of public policy observed in imposing these controls. With regard to the first point, there are interesting parallels between the two statutes. While each resulted in prompt postponement of the threatened strike, each was followed within a year by a renewed, nationwide strike threat, requiring dramatic intervention by the president. Moreover, each was delayed in its application by a legal attack carried to the highest court by one of the disputing parties. Nevertheless, each was ultimately held to be constitutional and became effective. Let us see how this came about in each case.

In the eight-hour dispute, Wilson asked Congress not only to make an eight-hour pay-base compulsory but to back the new statute with standby seizure powers. However, Congress refused to grant the seizure powers, except for use in case of war. When the railroad managements challenged the constitutionality of the act, the dispute remained unresolved; and the brotherhoods renewed their plans to shut down the railroads. Wilson again asked for seizure powers (December 1916) and was again refused but obtained a postponement of the strike. In March 1917, with American vessels being torpedoed by the German government, and war imminent, the brotherhoods again pressed a strike date. Wilson urged the carriers to accept the provisions of the Adamson Act, regardless of its constitutionality, as a means to labor peace. After a weekend of continuous mediation, conducted by a board headed by Secretary of the Interior Lane, the carriers gave in at daybreak on Monday, March 19, 1917. Later in the day, the Supreme Court announced its decision that the law was constitutional.[30]

In 1963, when Kennedy followed the Wilsonian precedent, he requested a two-year ban against strikes over work-rules, and asked that all unresolved points in the dispute be given to the Interstate Commerce Commission for binding interim decisions. But Congress, heeding the pleas of the railroad brotherhoods, reduced the ban on striking to only six months, and the scope of arbitration to two "key issues"—the use of firemen in freight and yard service, and the size of train crews. The brotherhoods struck after six months. To prevent a nationwide stoppage, President Johnson, early in his administration, was obliged to bring the parties to the White House and to coax and to pressure them into accepting the recommendations of the latest in a long line of distinguished mediators.[31] This merely settled the "other issues." For the Railroad Arbitration Act, unlike the eight-hour law, was made effective for a limited time only. The award of the compulsory arbitration board was to be effective for only two years, which meant, after the initial delays, until March 30, 1966. Under the statute, the brotherhoods were left free after that date to put the carriers, the president, and the country again under the pressure of a nationwide strike threat over "key issues."

This indicates the uncertainty of the public controls set up under the special legislation, especially the act of 1963. Now what kind of labor standards were followed in imposing these controls to keep production going? The Adamson Act, or eight-hour law, gave train employees an immediate increase in pay for their first eight hours of work each day and established eight hours as the permanent basic day's work for such employees thereafter. Once the measure was held constitutional, it was accepted by both sides. The subject was succeeded by other disputes in the following years.

The Arbitration Law of 1963 appears to have settled nothing. True, it called attention to the balanced principles embodied in the previous recommendations of the Presidential Railroad Commission and of the special emergency board, but, like the president's plan, it called only for a temporarily imposed governmental solution and then proposed a return to traditional collective bargaining, with the right to strike.

In these circumstances, the brotherhood most directly concerned, the Brotherhood of Locomotive Firemen and Enginemen, quite naturally proclaimed that it would seek by every lawful means to overturn and reverse the award of the arbitration board—first by appeal to the courts, and then by resort to the strike as soon as the two-year compulsory period came to an end.[32] After the act was upheld, the award of course went into effect; many firemen's positions were discontinued; the most recently hired men were discharged; and the redundant veteran employees were given the special protections provided for in the award. Thus the interim effect of the act was to alter forcefully the status quo ante, shifting the relative bargaining strengths of the two parties toward the side of management. Moreover, the act temporarily effectuated the balanced principles for equitable adjustment of automation disputes that had been enunciated by the Presidential Railroad Commission and by Kennedy himself. Yet the act provided no ultimate means of settlement except the strike. Unlike the act of 1916, the act of 1963 deferred the final resolution of an already long-deferred question.

While the above experience is too brief for systematic comparison with seizure, it clearly establishes that other legislative solutions are available which also embody powerful public controls and equitable policy standards, although the effectiveness of such measures certainly will depend, as is true of seizure, on the detailed provisions of the law, on the interpretations given by the courts, and on the manner of administration. So far, the nonseizure legislation appears to have been as liable to litigation as the seizure legislation. One notable difference in seizure cases is the protection given to property owners for losses that may be attributed to the government's possession and control. This results, as we have seen, from the constitutional guarantee that "just compensation" shall be paid whenever private property is taken for public use. By contrast, property is not "taken" simply because its value declines when Congress lowers tariffs, or raises taxes, or fixes minimum wages, or requires compulsory arbitration; hence no compensation is paid in such cases.[33]

Although the nonseizure experience includes only a small number of presidential appeals to Congress, there has been a larger number of such appeals in connection with the use of seizure. These have consisted of requests that Congress grant the seizure power, or that it strengthen the controls available during seizure, or that it provide alternative controls in lieu of indefinite continuance of government possession. These will now be compared with the nonseizure requests.

Here is a list of 13 proposals by four presidents for legislative action in particular labor disputes. It will be observed that all but the first called for compulsory measures. (Asterisk indicates strike threat and legislative proposal during presidential possession.)

Wilson

Eastern railroads, 1913. Request for new voluntary-arbitration procedure; granted. (Newlands Act; 38 Stat. 103.)

Major railroads, 1916 (Aug.). Request for statutory eight-hour day for train crews, with standby seizure powers; eight-hour day granted. (Adamson Act; 39 Stat. 721.) Congress also authorized transportation seizure in case of war. (39 Stat. 619, 645.)

Major railroads, 1916 (December). Renewed request for peacetime railroad-seizure powers; refused.

Telegraphs and telephones, 1918. Request for seizure powers; granted. (Joint resolution of July 16, 1918; 40 Stat. 904.)

*Major railroads, 1919. Request for permanent wage-adjustment machinery (with mandatory cost-plus rule for ICC); refused.

Roosevelt

"Captive" coal mines, 1941. Request for seizure powers, transmitted through conferences at White House; later (in effect) withdrawn.

*Coal mines, 1943. Request for statutory seizure power with penalties, followed by request for draft of strikers into army; seizure power granted. (War Labor Disputes Act; 57 Stat. 163.)

*Major railroads, coal, and steel, 1944 (January). Request for national service legislation; refused.

Truman

*Major railroads, 1946. Request for increased penalties during seizure: injunctions and draft of strikers into army; Congress speeded favorable action on injunctions, rejected draft. Strike called off; proposal lapsed.

Soft coal mines, 1950 (March). Request for seizure powers; Congress speeded favorable action. Dispute settled; proposal lapsed.

*Major railroads, 1952 (April). Request for temporary continuance of wartime transportation-seizure powers; granted. (Emergency Powers Interim Continuation Act; 66 Stat. 54, 96, 137, 296.)

Steel mills, 1952 (June). Request for seizure powers; refused.

Kennedy

Major railroads, 1963. Request for ICC powers to settle work-rules dispute. Congress established special board of compulsory arbitration to settle dispute. (Joint Resolution of August 28, 1963; 77 Stat. 132.)

The above record indicates that Congress and the president have tended to prefer seizure legislation. The presidents have asked for seizure powers in eight of the 13 proposals. Congress has responded favorably to five of the eight seizure proposals and to three of the others.

Since the adoption of legislation is the joint responsibility of Congress and the president, the initiative may be taken by either branch; and, in either event, the conducting of hearings by congressional committees is a valuable contribution to public understanding. Nevertheless, it is a fact that every piece of antistrike legislation adopted during the existence of labor emergencies has been at the president's initiative. Perhaps this is not so much a sign of presidential aggressiveness as it is a reflection of a national labor policy, long upheld by Congress, of not forbidding strikes in the negotiation of union contracts except when the presidents determine that they have created national emergencies.

Of the six pieces of antistrike legislation adopted during emergency situations, four authorized the use of seizure in wartime: the transportation-seizure statute of 1916, still in effect; the telephone and telegraph resolution of 1918, which expired at the end of the First World War; the War Labor Disputes Act of 1943 (Smith-Connally Act), which expired at the end of the Second World War; and the Emergency Powers Continuation Act of 1952, effective for only a few months near the end of the Korean War. As we have seen, the two nonseizure measures adopted were the Adamson Act and the Railroad Arbitration Act, both enacted in peacetime.

The country seems to have relied very little on *ad hoc* legislation for dealing with emergency disputes, yet this is a method by which most of the requirements of the public interest may be met. Its chief drawbacks are the tendencies to supply the president with too little authority to be effective, or to spread the authority over too wide an area (as when permanent regulations are legislated for an entire industry in order to settle a particular dispute). Nevertheless, further experimentation by Congress in the area of emergency disputes would be valuable.

SOME CONCLUSIONS REGARDING EMERGENCY DISPUTES

The national experience with both seizure and nonseizure techniques for compelling the continuance of production points to the conclusion that a rather consistent national policy has emerged, in which unions and managements are allowed, under procedural regulations, to use the strike and the lockout in negotiating the terms of agreements, except in particular situations where a stoppage would adversely affect the operations of the national government or the national economy; and in which the designation of the exceptional cases and of the means of control to be substituted for the right to strike and to lock out is considered to be the responsibility of the president, subject to veto by either the Supreme Court or Congress.

This policy has developed, historically, from three kinds of presidential intervention in emergency labor disputes: first, the use of troops to protect life and property in cases where management's insistence upon the right to continue production with replacements has led to violence, but where the government allows the strike if conducted peacefully; next, the use of a variety of techniques to require the continuance of production where public policy finds the strike or lockout unacceptable and either disputing party insists upon a stoppage; and third, presidential efforts, through mediation, voluntary arbitration, or public recommendations, to induce a full agreement between the parties in circumstances wherein presidential pressures are limited to something short of required production.

As we have seen, each of these forms of intervention, including mediation, has involved the application of some kind and degree of pressure upon the parties by the president, and has therefore modified, to a lesser or greater degree, the probable market determination of the terms of employment. Each act of intervention has constituted some degree of public control.

With increasing experience, there has evolved a set of policy standards with which the presidents and their subordinates have sometimes moderated and guided the use of these controls. This has been especially true in the use of seizure. However, the policy standards have been more frequently administrative determinations than statutory provisions, since Congress has (probably wisely) not encumbered its emergency labor legislation with detailed regulations. Therefore, the policies followed have not always been consistent, and there is no assurance that these standards would again be adopted in any future presidential intervention. Indeed, the lack of any central agency for administering presidential labor controls has meant that no central record of such experience exists, and no central formulation of basic policy standards has ever been made.

Therefore, the following is an attempt to synthesize the standards of public policy that have evolved in a century of presidential intervention in emergency disputes.

Suppressing violence. When the president intervenes to suppress violence, the troops should be controlled directly from Washington, not turned over to the state or local authorities, nor to any private organization. Particularly, decisions regarding picketing and the use of strikebreakers should be made at the White House. The importation of strikebreakers from outside the local area should probably be forbidden.

Requiring production. When the president intervenes to require the continuance of production, he should moderate his use of coercive measures by observing standards of public policy such as those developed in the seizure experience, including the continued attempt to mediate a settlement, the insistence upon terms of settlement that are equitable to the private parties and consistent with the national requirements of wage and price stabilization, and the minimizing of interference with permanent market relationships. Above all, the inequitable, partly fictional standard of freezing the terms of employment during required production should be discarded for the equitable standard and operational flexibility of presidential control over the work operations he has commandeered.

Mediating settlements. When the president intervenes to mediate or otherwise bring about a settlement, he should uphold the standards of industrial equity and national price stability referred to, and should also have in reserve sufficient powers to ensure that the effects of presidential mediation will neither be random nor biased. Conversely, if a purely market (bargaining) solution is desired, the government should refrain from intervening.

The following axiom has been a theme running through the three sets of standards: just as any intervention to establish controls may be biased and oppressive unless moderated by standards, so any intervention to impose standards may prove ineffective unless supported by adequate controls.

This suggests that the standards observed in emergency disputes may be as important a consideration for public policy as the choice of the specific machinery of control. It may be as desirable to assure the private parties of fairness and the public of stability as to choose among injunctions, compulsory arbitration, seizure or creative mediation.

A FEW CONCLUSIONS REGARDING SEIZURE AND REQUIRED PRODUCTION

It is unfortunate that some critics of the presidency have overemphasized the use of improvisation in emergency disputes. The record of improvisation (11 seizures, 21 other instances of compulsion) constitutes only one-third of the whole. It reflects the experimental approach of the presidents to a new and little-understood problem, as well as a reluctance to risk disapproval of their actions by Congress and the public. One seldom finds reference by these critics to the fact that even the improvisations were upheld by the courts (with one exception), and that Congress itself has authorized the use of seizure in four statutes and of other forms of required production in two statutes. Instead, we find irrelevant attacks on seizure as a kind of presidential "usurpation," including the implication that a president who used seizure without specific authorization to protect the public from a major strike was somehow more "dictatorial" than one who used the injunction without such authorization. We conclude that it is time now for attention to turn from the question of the availability of power to the question of how the power is used.

The century of experience with required production has been one of controversy and experiment but also one of marked growth of federal influence in the resolution of major labor-market impasses. It is noteworthy that the bulk of this experience has been concentrated in two industries—transportation and defense production (Table 1). Hence the problem of emergency labor disputes could be largely solved if suitable means of wage determination, without resort to strike and lockout, were devised for these industries. Until this is done—either by voluntary industry-union agreement or by congressional adoption of some form of required arbitration or government wage board—the presidents should be excused if they step in, on an *ad hoc* but recurring basis, to protect the public interest.

Controls. The effectiveness of public controls in keeping production going in the face of private resistance has depended not only upon the concurrence of the three major branches of government in their specific use, but also upon the adroit and vigorous application of the controls. As we have seen, the legislative and judicial branches have normally responded favorably to the president's initiative, but their reviews and investigations have affected the outcome in two ways: they have delayed the settlement of the disputes until the propriety of the president's actions has been established; and they have sometimes influenced the outcome of the settlements by altering the nature of the controls imposed.

In addition, we should note the importance of certain technical requirements in connection with each method of control. For example, to be effective, the supplying of replacements must be accompanied by the protection of either the local police or the armed forces or both; the antistrike injunction must be enforced against defiant individuals and unions by prompt citation and trial for contempt of court; *ad hoc* legislation must include specific procedures of enforcement; and the statutory designation of criminal offenses, to be meaningful, must be followed up by the indictment and trial of violators.

Similarly, in the use of seizure, there are important technical requirements for effective control: (1) the ability of the president to change or to forbid change in the terms of employment that are effective during government possession and operation; (2) the placing upon the president of the responsibility and power to determine when the property should be returned to private operation—a decision to be based either upon a finding that the dispute has been fully settled (hence the property can be returned without a stoppage occurring) or upon a finding that uninterrupted operation is no longer essential to the national interest; and (3) the right of the president, notwithstanding the Norris-LaGuardia Act or any other act of Congress, to petition the federal courts, through the attorney general, for injunctive relief against strikes, lockouts, or other resistance to his directives in the operation of seized property. If any one or more of these requirements is denied by Congress or the courts, or is left out of consideration by the president, seizure becomes something different from what it has been in the usual case, and it ceases to be an instrument of unbiased public control.

Let us see what would happen if the president had to conduct seizure without these accompanying powers. Suppose he were forbidden to alter the terms of employment during the period of public possession. The effect of seizure would then be similar to that of an antistrike injunction. It would aid the disputing party which favored continuance of the status quo ante, and would weaken the party seeking change. In this form, seizure would have a built-in bias, normally favorable to employers. This is why some employer interests have urged that seizure, when it is authorized by law, should be accompanied by a freezing of the previously existing conditions of employment.

Now let us see what the effect would be of denying the president the second of the powers named above—the power to determine when the property should be returned. There have been proposals that the president should be authorized to seize property and to keep it operating for a specified time, such as 60 or 80 days, during which further efforts would be made to mediate a settlement. These proposals usually also require a continuance of the status quo. The effect of this type of seizure upon the dispute would be the same as that of the cooling-off periods under the Taft-Hartley Act and under sec. 10 of the Railway Labor Act. The stoppage would be postponed, but would be lawful at the end of the specified period.

Again seizure could be very different if the Norris-LaGuardia Act were allowed to prevent the president from obtaining court injunctions against strikes and lockouts in seized plants, mines, and transportation facilities. So far, although Congress has not acted to modify the Norris-LaGuardia Act to permit such injunctions, the Supreme Court has interpreted the act as not barring such injunctions, since the employees in seized plants are, in effect, temporary government employees. But a different interpretation by the court, without further action by Congress, would leave the president virtually helpless against large industrywide shutdowns even in commandeered properties.

We conclude from the experience of seizure, both with and without these supplementary controls, that the first two supplements are necessary to enable the president to exert pressures upon the parties to settle their disputes on terms consistent with the public interest; and that the third is necessary, in some situations, in order to keep production going.

Standards. In seizure cases, as we have seen, the administrative officials have developed a rather systematic set of policy standards which they have applied to labor relations during the period of public control. Although these standards were never formalized (*The Army Seizure Manual* of 1944 being the closest approximation), considerable uniformity arose because of the influence of the army's Industrial Personnel Division and the navy's Emergency Plants Operation Section in guiding the remaining agencies that were entrusted with seizure.

In practice, the seizing agencies (with a few exceptions) have assumed responsibility not only for keeping production going but also for assuring equitable industrial relations during the period of government control and for seeking (whenever practicable) a full settlement of the basic dispute in order to permit an early termination of presidential possession. The evident intent has been to use the government controls in such a way as to achieve a balance among all the public and private interests involved.

In so doing, the agencies have devoted special attention to the following four aspects of labor relations and to the indicated policy standards:

1. The ability of the disputing parties to strike or to lock out during government control: Did the government's action terminate (or thwart) the stoppage, and keep production going? Did it avoid the extremes of national service and confiscation of property?

2. The degree to which the parties were required to accept terms of employment set by the government: Did the government enforce the president's terms during the period of control, or, in the alternative, did the government protect the public interest in the terms of final settlement negotiated by the parties (as by requiring, in either case, terms consistent with stable prices and with equitable working conditions)?

3. The ability of the parties to negotiate mutually satisfactory settlements during compulsory operations: Did the government provide a method of settlement free of systematic (built-in) bias toward either labor or management; and did it succeed in obtaining full settlements of the disputes?

4. The continuity of basic practices and institutions: To what extent did the government's action interfere with (or endanger) the normal operations of business management, collective bargaining, and governmental regulation?

Public standards have also been applied by the presidents and their subordinates in several of the nonseizure cases we have examined; for example, the spruce production case of 1917–1919, the army's cancellation of a procurement contract in 1918, the soft coal injunction of 1919, and the *ad hoc* railroad legislation of 1916 and 1963. However, there has been no equivalent development of systematic rules of practice, aimed at balancing all public and private interests. There has been a notable absence of standards in the one-sided criminal prosecutions and the other injunction cases. Hence the relatively abundant seizure experience can be credited with having made a unique contribution to the history of public intervention in labor disputes—the deliberate, systematic moderation of public controls in such cases.

Equally notable is the fact that only seizure of all the means of requiring continuance of production protects property owners from any loss of income attributable to public intervention. The exact amount of compensation for the temporary public use of their property is subject to negotiation and, if necessary, to court litigation; but this does not delay the government's occupation and control of the property. So effective is this constitutional protection that the owners of seized firms often have made out quite handsomely, even in company noncompliance cases.

However, there is nothing in the seizure technique, nor in any other technique of compulsory production, that ensures the observance of moderation or standards of equity in their use. We have no assurance that any one of these techniques will operate in the future as it has in the past. Each technique will affect the outcome of the dispute in some way; but, in the absence of conscious guidance by the president and his subordinates, the outcome will depend upon the market circumstances in which it is applied, upon the skill of the disputants in adapting to it, and upon the particular details of the controls adopted. The consequences of unguided controls will either be random (unpredictable in a given case), or biased (certain to favor the same side in every case); but they will not be neutral (without impact upon market forces). So the history of seizure as well as of other means of required production suggests the need for conscious guidance by the presidents in the use of these extreme forms of control.

This rule has special relevance to seizure cases because of the special protection given to property owners by the Constitution. Although the unions in these cases have often urged that the owners' right to "just compensation" be balanced by "seizure of the profits," the experience with compensation suggests that the government's retention of the profits (after payment of a fair rental) has not been a sufficient economic or strategic counterweight, and sometimes also has been inexpedient. The most effective standards to offset the owners' special position have been found to be the president's twin controls over the interim terms of employment and over the date for terminating possession.

So long as our public policy continues to be that the government may suspend the right to strike and to lock out only in emergency situations—

that is, on a case-by-case basis—surely it is important that such suspensions be carried out with due regard for their effects upon industrial relations and upon the national economy. An outstanding lesson of all experience in emergency disputes is that the public interest will not automatically be safeguarded by some selected technique of intervention. Only through conscious policy—through the sophisticated study of the conflicting interests involved—can the presidents control the new forces created in the market-place when they intervene. If the government is to continue to use force in particular cases to restrain businesses and unions from exercising their full market power in labor disputes, certainly this public use of force should be restrained. Naturally, we expect the government to act in the national interest, broadly conceived, without bias toward either party, without permanent impairment of the rights of collective bargaining or of private property, and with a minimum of interference in the day-to-day operations of unions, business, and government. The subject of standards should receive as full consideration as the subject of techniques. Indeed, the observance of standards may be as important a goal, in a free society, as keeping production going.

Chronological List of 71 Presidential Seizures with Historical Data

SYMBOLS FOR APPENDIX A

a, b, c, etc.	Phases of a single seizure (extension of control to additional property)
AAC	Army air corps
AAF	Army air forces
A	Existing management served as government agent (indirect control)
D	Direct control by government agency throughout possession
D—	Direct control by government agency for only part of the period (or of only some of the firms)
L	Labor noncompliance case
M	Management noncompliance case
U	Unadjudicated dispute (no governmental recommendation or order upon the merits, prior to seizure)

Dates of seizure refer to actual occupation by federal officials.

The notes are at the end of the appendix, beginning on p. 282.

Administration of Abraham Lincoln
Period of the Civil War, 1861–1865.

Administration of Woodrow Wilson

Period from declaration of war by Congress, April 6, 1917, to the Armistice of November 11, 1918.

Property Seized	Date Seized	Date Returned	Seizing & Operating Agency	Authority for Seizure	Reason for Seizure
1. Philadelphia & Reading Railroad, eastern Pa. (anthracite carrier)	July 11, 1864	July 20, 1864	War Dept.[1] (D)	Act of Jan. 31, 1862; ex. orders Feb. 11 and May 25, 1862[2]	Strike by members of the Brotherhood of the Footboard (U)
2. Transportation systems:					
a. The railroads: 385 major lines and subsidiaries, nationwide; 220 switching and terminal lines; 1,434 plant-facility roads[3]	Dec. 28, 1917	Mar. 1, 1920[4]	Railroad Admin. (D—)	Acts of Aug. 29, 1916; Mar. 21, 1916; June 30 and Nov. 19, 1919; proc. of Dec. 26, 1917[5]	a. Strike threats by railroad brotherhoods (independent) and shopmen's unions (AFL)[6] (U)
b. 855 independent short-line railroads, nationwide	Dec. 28, 1917	Mar. 1, 1920[7]	Railroad Admin. (D—)	Same as above	b. Same as above

(Continued on next page.)

Property Seized	Date Seized	Date Returned	Seizing & Operating Agency	Authority for Seizure	Reason for Seizure
c. 4 independent coastal steamship companies, Atlantic coast[8]	Apr. 13, 1918	Dec. 6, 1918	Railroad Admin.	Same statutes; proc. of Apr. 11, 1918[9]	c. Seized to coordinate service with rail-owned steamship companies
d. Pullman Co., nationwide	July 3, 1918	Mar. 1, 1920	Railroad Admin. (D)	Same as a	d. Seized to coordinate service with railroad companies
e. Cape Cod Canal	July 25, 1918	Mar. 1, 1920	Railroad Admin.	Same statutes; proc. of July 22, 1918[10]	e. Seized to dredge canal
f. American Railway Express Co., nationwide	Nov. 18, 1918[11]	Mar. 1, 1920	Railroad Admin. (D)	Same statutes; proc. of Nov. 16, 1918[12]	f. Seized to clarify and strengthen the government's control of its new unified express service[13]
g. 10 tugboats, New York Harbor	Mar. 17, 1919[11]	Apr. 19, 1919	Navy Dept.[1] (A)	Probably act of June 15, 1917[14]	g. Strike by Marine Workers' Affiliation of Port of New York (AFL unions)
3. The wire systems: a. Land lines of 14 telegraph and 17,792 telephone companies, nationwide[15]	July 31, 1918	Aug. 1, 1919[16]	Post Office Dept.[17] (D—)	Joint res. of July 16, 1918; act of Oct. 29, 1918; proc. of July 22, 1918[18]	a. Western Union Telegraph Co.'s noncompliance with recommendation of NWLB I[19] (M)

b. Cable lines and terminals of 7 companies, New York, Miami, San Francisco, Canada and Great Britain[20]	Nov. 20, 1918[11]	May 2, 1919	Post Office Dept.[21] (D—)	Same statutes; proc. of Nov. 2, 1918[22]	b. Seized to assure control of traffic between Washington and Paris during peace conference
4. Smith & Wesson Co. Springfield, Mass. (pistols)	Sept. 13, 1918	Jan. 31, 1919	War Dept.[22a] (D)	Sec. 120, act of June 3, 1916[23]	Company's noncompliance with recommendation of NWLB I (M)

Administration of Franklin D. Roosevelt

Period from proclamation of defense emergency, May 27, 1941, to declaration of war by Congress, December 8, 1941.

5. North American Aviation, Inc., Inglewood plant, Los Angeles (company 29% owned by General Motors Corp.)	June 9, 1941	July 2, 1941	War Dept. (AAC) (A)	General powers; Ex. Order 8773 (6 F.R. 2777)	Strike by Local 683, United Automobile Workers (CIO), in violation of agreement with NDMB (U)

(Continued on next page.)

Property Seized	Date Seized	Date Returned	Seizing & Operating Agency	Authority for Seizure	Reason for Seizure
6. Federal Shipbuilding & Dry Dock Co., Kearny, N.J. (subsidiary of United States Steel Corp.)	Aug. 25, 1941	Jan. 6, 1942	Navy Dept. (D)	General powers; Ex. Order 8868 (6 F.R. 4349)	Company's noncompliance with recommendation of NDMB (M)
7. 3 freighters of Alcoa Steamship Co. at Weehawken, N.J. (subsidiary of Aluminum Co. of America)[24]	Sept. 18, 1941	Nov. 9, 1941[25]	Maritime Commission[26] (A)	Sec. 902, act of June 29, 1936[27]	Strike by Seafarers' International Union (AFL) (U)
8. Air Associates, Inc. (aircraft parts)					
a. Main plant, Bendix, N.J.	Oct. 31, 1941	Dec. 29, 1941	War Dept. (AAC) (D)	General powers; Ex. Order 8928 (6 F.R. 5559)	a. Company's noncompliance with recommendation of NDMB (M)
b. Branch plants in Calif., Tex., Mo., Ill., and N.J.	Nov. 7, 1941	Dec. 29, 1941[28]	War Dept. (AAC) (D)	Same as a, plus pres. approval Nov. 4, 1941[29]	b. Seized to coordinate operations with main plant

Administration of Franklin D. Roosevelt

Period from declaration of war by Congress, December 8, 1941, to adoption of the War Labor Disputes Act, June 25, 1943.

	Date of seizure	Date of return	Agency	Authority	Reason
9. Toledo, Peoria & Western Railroad, Ill.	Mar. 22, 1942	Oct. 1, 1945	ODT (D)[29a]	Act of Aug. 29, 1916; Ex. Order 9108 (7 F.R. 2201); Ex. Order 9320 (8 F.R. 3687); Ex. Order 9572 (10 F.R. 7315)	Company's non-compliance with directive order of NWLB II to arbitrate dispute (M)
10. General Cable Corp., Bayonne, N.J. (connected with American Smelting & Refining Co.)	Aug. 14, 1942	Aug. 20, 1942	Navy Dept. (A)	General powers; Ex. Order 9220 (7 F.R. 6413)	Noncompliance by members of International Brotherhood of Electrical Workers (AFL) with directive order of NWLB II (L)
11. S. A. Woods Machine Co.					
a. Privately owned shell plant, South Boston	Aug. 19, 1942	Aug. 31, 1945	War Dept.[30] (D)	General powers; Ex. Order 9225 (7 F.R. 6627)	Company's non-compliance with directive order of NWLB II (M)
b. Plant making woodworking machinery, South Boston	Aug. 20, 1942	Aug. 31, 1945			

(Continued on next page.)

Property Seized	Date Seized	Date Returned	Seizing & Operating Agency	Authority for Seizure	Reason for Seizure
c. Government-owned shell plant, Natick, Mass.	Sept. 28, 1942	Aug. 31, 1945			
12. Fairport, Painesville & Eastern Railroad, Ohio (carrier of magnesium and chlorine)	Nov. 7, 1942	Nov. 10, 1942	War Dept.[1,30a] (D)	General powers and act of Aug. 29, 1916; Ex. Order 8972 of Dec. 12, 1941 (6 F.R. 6420)[31]	Strike by local of District 50, United Mine Workers of America (U)
13. The anthracite and bituminous coal mines:					
a. 3,400 soft coal mining companies and 400 hard coal mining companies, 22 states	May 1, 1943	Oct. 25, 1943[32]	Interior Dept. (A)	General powers; Ex. Order 9340 (8 F.R. 5695)	a. Noncompliance by United Mine Workers of America with directive order of NWLB II (L)
b. 150 hard and soft coal companies	June 28, 1943	Aug. 24, 1943[33]	Interior Dept. (A)	Same as a	b. Seized because "unintentionally omitted" in May
14. American Railroad of Porto Rico (operating agent for Spanish owning firm)	May 17, 1943	July 1, 1944	ODT[34] (D)	Act of Aug. 29, 1916; Ex. Order 9341 (8 F.R. 6323)	Strike by Union of United Railroad Workers of Puerto Rico (U)

Administration of Franklin D. Roosevelt

Period from adoption of War Labor Disputes Act, June 25, 1943, to April 12, 1945.

	Date seized	Date returned	Agency	Authority	Cause
15. Atlantic Basin Iron Works, Inc. Brooklyn, N.Y. (ship repairs)	Sept. 4, 1943	Sept. 22, 1943	War Shipping Admin. (A)	WLDA (act of June 25, 1943, 57 Stat. 163); Ex. Order 9375 (8 F.R. 12253)	Company's noncompliance with directive order of NWLB II (M)
16. The anthracite and bituminous coal mines; 3,400 soft coal and 400 hard coal mining companies, 22 states	Nov. 1, 1943	June 13, 1945[35]	Interior Dept. (A)	WLDA; Ex. Order 9393 (8 F.R. 14877)	Noncompliance by United Mine Workers of America with directive order of NWLB II (L)
17. 13 tanning companies, members of Massachusetts Leather Manufacturers Assn., Salem, Peabody and Danvers	Nov. 24, 1943	Dec. 14, 1943	War Dept. (A)	WLDA; Ex. Order 9395B (9 F.R. 16957)	Strike by National Leather Workers' Union (U)
18. Western Electric Co., Point Breeze, Md. (subsidiary of American Telephone & Telegraph Co.)	Dec. 19, 1943	Mar. 23, 1944	War Dept. (A)	WLDA; Ex. Order 9408 (8 F.R. 16958)	Noncompliance by Point Breeze Employees Assn. with decision of FEPC and directive order of NWLB II (L)

(Continued on next page.)

Property Seized	Date Seized	Date Returned	Seizing & Operating Agency	Authority for Seizure	Reason for Seizure
19. The railroads: 750 companies (major lines, subsidiaries, short lines, terminal companies, express and parlor-car companies), nationwide	Dec. 27, 1943	Jan. 18, 1944	War Dept. (A)	Act of Aug. 29, 1916; Ex. Order 9412 (8 F.R. 17395)	Noncompliance by Brotherhood of Locomotive Firemen & Enginemen, Order of Railway Conductors, and Switchmen's Union of N.A. (AFL), with recommendation of Railway Labor Act emergency board and presidential offer of arbitration (L)
20. Berkshire Fine Spinning Associates and 6 other textile firms, Fall River, Mass.	Feb. 7, 1944	Feb. 28, 1944	War Dept. (A)	WLDA; Ex. Order 9420 (9 F.R. 1563)	Strike by Loom Fixers Union, Drawing-In Knot-Tiers & Work Tenders Assn., and Slasher Tenders & Helpers Assn. (U)
21. City of Los Angeles, Department of Water & Power, operating in southern Calif. and Nev.	Feb. 23, 1944	Feb. 29, 1944	War Dept. (A)	WLDA; Ex. Order 9426 (9 F.R. 2113)	Strike by Local B-18, International Brotherhood of Electrical Workers (AFL) (U)

22. Jenkins Bros. (valves)					
a. Plant and office, Bridgeport, Conn.	Apr. 14, 1944	June 15, 1944	Navy Dept. (D)	WLDA; Ex. Order 9435 (9 F.R. 4063)	a. Company's non-compliance with directive order of NWLB II (M)
b. Main office, New York City, and branch offices in Mass., Pa., Ga. and Ill.[36]	Apr. 17, 1944	June 15, 1944	Navy Dept. (D)	Same as a	b. Seized to assure control of all receipts and expenditures
23. Ken-Rad Tube & Lamp Corp.					
a. Main plant, Owensboro, Ky.	Apr. 14, 1944	May 25, 1944	War Dept. (D)	WLDA; Ex. Order 9436 (9 F.R. 4063)	a. Company's non-compliance with directive order of NWLB II (M)
b. Branch plants in Ky. and Ind.	Apr. 19, 1944	May 25, 1944	War Dept. (D)	Same as a	b. Seized to coordinate operations with main plant
24. Montgomery Ward & Co., main office and retail facilities in Chicago	Apr. 26, 1944	May 9, 1944	Commerce Dept.	WLDA and general powers; Ex. Order 9438 (9 F.R. 4459)	Company's noncompliance with directive order of NWLB II (M)
25. Montgomery Ward & Co., Hummer manufacturing division, Springfield, Ill. (aircraft parts)	May 21, 1944	July 2, 1945	War Dept. (AAF) (A)	WLDA; Ex. Order 9443 (9 F.R. 5395)	Company's non-compliance with directive order of NWLB II (M)

(Continued on next page.)

Property Seized	Date Seized	Date Returned	Seizing & Operating Agency	Authority for Seizure	Reason for Seizure
26. Philadelphia Transportation Co. (citywide transit system, partly city-owned)	Aug. 3, 1944	Aug. 17, 1944	War Dept. (A)	WLDA and act of Aug. 29, 1916; Ex. Order 9459 (9 F.R. 9878)	Noncompliance by PRT Employees Union and members of Transport Workers Union (CIO) with decisions of FEPC and WMC and directive order of NWLB II (L)
27. Midwest trucking firms:					
a. 103 member firms of Midwest Operators Assn. (engaged in business west of the Mississippi)	Aug. 12, 1944	Nov. 1, 1945[38]	ODT[39] (D—)	WLDA and act of Aug. 29, 1916; Ex. Order 9462 (9 F.R. 10071)	a. Companies' noncompliance with directive order of NWLB II (M)
b. 2 terminal companies in Minneapolis-St. Paul[37]	Unknown	Unknown	ODT[39a]	Same as a	b. Seized to coordinate operations with trucking companies
28. Uptown machine shops of California Metal Trades Assn., San Francisco:					

a. 5 companies	Aug. 14, 1944	Sept. 14, 1945	Navy Dept. (A)	WLDA; Ex. Order 9463 (9 F.R. 9879)	a. Noncompliance by Lodge 68, International Assn. of Machinists (AFL) with directive order of NWLB II (L)
b. 99 companies	Aug. 20-21, 1944	Sept. 14, 1945[539b]	Navy Dept. (A)	WLDA; Ex. Order 9466 (9 F.R. 10139)	b. Seized to forestall extension of strike action
29. Philadelphia & Reading Coal & Iron Co., Pa. (29 anthracite mines)	Aug. 23, 1944	Apr. 16, 1945	Interior Dept. (A)	WLDA; Ex. Order 9469 (9 F.R. 10343)	Strike by workers of United Mine Workers of America (U)
30. International Nickel Co., Inc., Huntington, W.Va. (subsidiary of International Nickel Co. of Canada, Ltd.)	Aug. 29, 1944	Oct. 14, 1944	War Dept. (A)	WLDA; Ex. Order 9473 (9 F.R. 10613)	Strike by members of United Steelworkers of America (CIO) (U)
31. 74 bituminous coal mines of 34 companies in Pa., W.Va., and Ky.	Sept. 1, 1944				
a. Mines of Ford Collieries Co. and Rochester & Pittsburgh Coal Co.		Feb. 24, 1945	Interior Dept. (A)	WLDA; Ex. Order 9474 (9 F.R. 10815)	a. Strike by foremen's division of District 50, United Mine Workers of America (U)

(Continued on next page.)

Property Seized	Date Seized	Date Returned	Seizing & Operating Agency	Authority for Seizure	Reason for Seizure
b. Mines of additional companies	Sept. 4, 6, 13, 15, 19, 1944	Feb. 24, 1945	Interior Dept. (A)	WLDA; Ex. Order 9476, 9478, 9481, 9482, 9483 (9 F.R. 10817, 11045, 11387, 11459, 11601)	b. Seized because of extension of strike to other mines after WLDA strike votes
32. Cleveland Graphite Bronze Co., Cleveland (ball bearings)	Sept. 5, 1944	Nov. 8, 1944	War Dept. (A)	WLDA; Ex. Order 9477 (9 F.R. 10941)	Noncompliance by Mechanics Educational Society of America (CUA), with directive order of NWLB II (L)
33. Hughes Tool Co., Houston, Tex.: main plant (oil well drills) and aircraft strut plant	Sept. 6, 1944	Aug. 29, 1945	War Dept. (AAF) (A)	WLDA; Ex. Order 9475A (9 F.R. 10943)	Company's noncompliance with directive order of NWLB II (M)
34. Twentieth Century Brass Works, Inc., Minneapolis (bushings)	Sept. 9, 1944	Feb. 17, 1945	War Dept. (D—)	WLDA; Ex. Order 9480 (9 F.R. 11143)	Company's noncompliance with directive order of NWLB II (M)
35. Farrell-Cheek Steel Co., Sandusky, Ohio (castings)	Sept. 25, 1944	Aug. 28, 1945	War Dept. (A)	WLDA; Ex. Order 9484 (9 F.R. 11731)	Company's noncompliance with directive order of NWLB II (M)

36. Willys-Overland Motors, Inc., and 7 machine shops, Toledo, Ohio	Nov. 4, 1944	Nov. 6, 1944	War Dept. (A)	WLDA; Ex. Order 9496 (9 F.R. 13187)	Sympathetic strike by Mechanics Educational Society of America (CUA) (U)
37. Cudahy Bros. Co., Cudahy, Wis. (meats)	Dec. 8, 1944	Aug. 31, 1945	War Dept. (A)	WLDA; Ex. Order 9505 (9 F.R. 14473)	Company's noncompliance with directive order of NWLB II (M)
38. Montgomery Ward & Co.					
a. 3 mail order houses, 10 retail stores, and other retail facilities in Chicago, New York, Detroit, St. Paul, Denver, Portland (Ore.), San Rafael (Cal.)	Dec. 28, 1944	Oct. 18, 1945	War Dept. (D—)	WLDA and general powers; Ex. Order 9508 (9 F.R. 15079)	a. Company's noncompliance with directive order of NWLB II (M)
b. Additional retail facilities in Detroit	Jan. 2, 1945	Oct. 18, 1945	War Dept. (D)	Same as a	b. Seized to coordinate operations with other Detroit facilities
39. Cleveland Electric Illuminating Co. (subsidiary of North American Co.)	Jan. 13, 1945	Jan. 15, 1945	War Dept. (A)	WLDA; Ex. Order 9511 (10 F.R. 549)	Strike by Local 270, Utility Workers Organizing Committee (CIO) (U)

(Continued on next page.)

Property Seized	Date Seized	Date Returned	Seizing & Operating Agency	Authority for Seizure	Reason for Seizure
40. Bingham & Garfield Railway, Utah (subsidiary of Kennecott Copper Corp.)	Jan. 26, 1945	Aug. 29, 1945	War Dept. (A)	WLDA and act of Aug. 29, 1916; Ex. Order 9516 (10 F.R. 1313)	Noncompliance by Brotherhood of Locomotive Firemen & Enginemen with recommendation of Railway Labor Act emergency board (L)
41. American Enka Corp., Asheville, N.C., textiles (subsidiary of the Dutch "Enka")	Feb. 18, 1945	June 6, 1945	War Dept. (A)	WLDA; Ex. Order 9523 (10 F.R. 2133)	Noncompliance with directive order of NWLB II by both the company and Local 2598, United Textile Workers of America (AFL) (L-M)
42. The anthracite and bituminous coal mines: a. 218 soft coal mines of 154 companies (many serving steel mills) in Pa., Ohio, Ky., Va., Ind., Tenn., and Ala.	Apr. 11, 1945	June 23, 1945[40]	Interior Dept. (A)	WLDA; Ex. Order 9536 (10 F.R. 3939)	a. Noncompliance by members of United Mine Workers of America with directive order of NWLB II (L)

Description	Date seized	Date returned	Agency	Citation	Reason
b. 363 hard coal companies in eastern Pa., 2 more in Va., Md.	May 4, 8, 1945	June 24, 1945	Interior Dept. (A)	WLDA; Ex. Order 9548 (10 F.R. 5025)	b. Noncompliance by United Mine Workers of America with directive order of NWLB II (L)
c. 30 soft coal mines of 20 companies in Pa, Ohio, Ky., W.Va., Ill., and Tenn.	May 8, 1945	June 24, 1945[41]	Interior Dept. (A)	Same as a	c. Noncompliance by miners with new directive order of NWLB II (L)

Administration of Harry S Truman

Period from April 12, 1945, to V-J Day, proclaimed September 2, 1945.

Description	Date seized	Date returned	Agency	Citation	Reason
43. Cities Service Refining Corp., Lake Charles, La., refinery and government-owned butadiene plant (subsidiary of Cities Service Co.)	Apr. 18, 1945	Dec. 23, 1945	PAW (A)	WLDA; Ex. Order 9540 (10 F.R. 4193)	Secondary strike by members of Lake Charles Metal Trades Council (AFL unions) over housing rentals (U)
44. United Engineering Co. Ltd., San Francisco, ship repairs (subsidiary of Matson Navigation Co., Ltd.)	Apr. 25, 1945	Sept. 5, 1945	Navy Dept. (A)	WLDA; Ex. Order 9542 (10 F.R. 4691)	Noncompliance by Lodge 68, International Assn. of Machinists (AFL) with directive order of NWLB II (L)
45. Soft coal mines: a. Carter Coal Co., W.Va. (3 mines)	May 4, 1945	Mar. 28, 1946	Interior Dept. (A)	WLDA; Ex. Order 9536 (10 F.R. 3939)	a. Company's noncompliance with directive order of NWLB II (M)

(Continued on next page.)

Property Seized	Date Seized	Date Returned	Seizing & Operating Agency	Authority for Seizure	Reason for Seizure
b. 3 mines of 3 Ky. companies[41a]	May 8, 1945	Oct. 23, 1945	Interior Dept. (A)	Same as a	b. Same as a
46. Cocker Machine & Foundry Co., Gastonia, N.C. (textile machinery)	May 19, 1945	Aug. 31, 1945	War Dept. (A)	WLDA; Ex. Order 9552 (10 F.R. 5757)	Company's noncompliance with directive order of NWLB II (M)
47. 1,700 trucking firms in Chicago and vicinity:					
a. All struck firms	May 24, 1945	Aug. 16, 1945	ODT (A)	WLDA and act of Aug. 29, 1916; Ex. Order 9554 (10 F.R. 5981)	a. Noncompliance by Local 705, Chicago Truck Drivers, Chauffeurs & Helpers Union (indep.) & members of International Brotherhood of Teamsters (AFL), with directive order of NWLB II (L)
b. All other firms having contracts with either union	June 16, 1945	Aug. 16, 1945	ODT (D)	Same as a	b. Seized to cope with extension of strike after WLDA strike vote

	Date	Date	Agency	Authority	Cause
48. Gaffney Manufacturing Co., Gaffney, S.C., textiles (connected with Deering, Milliken & Co.)	May 28, 1945	Sept. 9, 1945	War Dept. (D)	WLDA; Ex. Order 9559 (10 F.R. 6287)	Company's noncompliance with directive order of NWLB II (M)
49. Mary-Leila Cotton Mills, Inc., Greensboro, Ga.	June 1, 1945	Aug. 30, 1945	War Dept. (A)	WLDA; Ex. Order 9560 (10 F.R. 6547)	Company's noncompliance with directive order of NWLB II (M)
50. Humble Oil & Refining Co., Ingleside, Tex. (near Corpus Christi) (subsidiary of Standard Oil Co. [N.J.])	June 6, 1945[42]	Sept. 10, 1945	PAW (A)	WLDA; Ex. Order 9564 (10 F.R. 6791)	Company's noncompliance with directive order of NWLB II (M)
51. Pure Oil Co., Cabin Creek oil field, Dawes, W.Va.	June 7, 1945	Sept. 10, 1945	PAW (A)	WLDA; Ex. Order 9565 (10 F.R. 6792)	Company's noncompliance with directive order of RWLB V (M)
52. Scranton Transit Co., Scranton, Pa.	June 16, 1945	July 8, 1945	ODT (A)	WLDA and act of Aug. 29, 1916; Ex. Order 9570 (10 F.R. 7235)	Strike by Division 168, Amalgamated Assn. of Street, Electric Railway & Motor Coach Employees (AFL) (U)
53. Diamond Alkali Co., Painesville, Ohio	June 19, 1945	July 17, 1945	War Dept. (A)	WLDA; Ex. Order 9574 (10 F.R. 7435)	Strike by District 50, United Mine Workers of America (U)

(Continued on next page.)

Property Seized	Date Seized	Date Returned	Seizing & Operating Agency	Authority for Seizure	Reason for Seizure
54. The Texas Company, Port Arthur, Tex.; refinery, terminal, and case and package plant	July 1, 1945	Sept. 10, 1945	PAW (A)	WLDA; Ex. Order 9577A (10 F.R. 8090)	Strike by members of Local 254, and threatened strike by Local 23, Oil Workers International Union (CIO) (U)
55. Goodyear Tire & Rubber Co., Akron; private rubber plants and government-owned synthetic rubber plant	July 5, 1945	Aug. 30, 1945	Navy Dept. (A)	WLDA; Ex. Order 9585 (10 F.R. 8335)	Strike by Local 2, United Rubber Workers (CIO) (U)
56. Sinclair Rubber, Inc., Houston, Tex., operating government butadiene plant (subsidiary of Sinclair Refining Co.)	July 19, 1945	Nov. 19, 1945	PAW (A)	WLDA; Ex. Order 9589A (10 F.R. 8949)	Strike by Local 227, Oil Workers International Union (CIO) (U)
57. Springfield Plywood Corp, Springfield, Ore. (subsidiary of Washington Veneer Co. and Weyerhaeuser Timber Co.)	July 25, 1945	Aug. 30, 1945	War Dept. (A)	WLDA; Ex. Order 9593 (10 F.R. 9379)	Noncompliance by Local 2787, Lumber & Sawmill Workers Union (AFL) with directive order of WCLC (L)

No.	Company	Date seized	Date returned	Agency	Authority	Reason
58.	United States Rubber Co., Detroit	July 30, 1945	Oct. 10, 1945	War Dept. (AAF) (A)	WLDA; Ex. Order 9595 (10 F.R. 9571)	Strike by members of Mechanics Educational Society of America (CUA) (U)
59.	Illinois Central Railroad and its subsidiary, Yazoo & Mississippi Valley Railroad, 11 midwestern states	Aug. 24, 1945[43]	May 27, 1946	ODT (A)	WLDA and act of Aug. 29, 1916; Ex. Order 9602 (10 F.R. 10957)	Noncompliance by Brotherhood of Locomotive Firemen & Enginemen with recommendation of Railway Labor Act emergency board (L)

Administration of Harry S Truman

Period from V-J Day, proclaimed September 2, 1945, to termination of hostilities, proclaimed December 31, 1946.[44]

No.	Company	Date seized	Date returned	Agency	Authority	Reason
60.	49 oil refineries and 4 pipe lines in 15 states (29 companies)	Oct. 8-13, 1945	Aug. 3, 1946[45]	Navy Dept. (A)	WLDA; Ex. Order 9639 (10 F.R. 12592)	Strike by Oil Workers Internat. Union (CIO) (U)
61.	Capital Transit Co., Washington, D.C. (affiliated with North American Co.)	Nov. 21, 1945	Jan. 8, 1946	ODT (A)	WLDA and act of Aug. 29, 1916; Ex. Order 9658 (10 F.R. 14351)	Strike by Division 689, Amalgamated Assn. of Street, Electric Railway & Motor Coach Employees (AFL) (U)

(Continued on next page.)

Property Seized	Date Seized	Date Returned	Seizing & Operating Agency	Authority for Seizure	Reason for Seizure
62. Great Lakes Towing Co., Cleveland and other Great Lakes ports	Nov. 29, 1945	Dec. 18, 1946	ODT (D—)	WLDA and act of Aug. 29, 1916; Ex. Order 9661 (10 F.R. 14591)	Lockout by company management, followed by strike of Tug Firemen, Linemen, Oilers & Watchmen's Protective Assn. of International Longshoremen's Assn. (AFL) (U)
63. Meat-packing firms: 150 meat-packing facilities of 18 companies, 5 union stockyards of 4 companies, in 32 states and D.C.					
a. 131 facilities of 18 packing companies and 2 stockyards companies	Jan. 26, 1946	May 23, 1946[46]	Agriculture Dept. (A)	WLDA; Ex. Order 9685 (11 F.R. 989)	a. Strike by United Packinghouse Workers (CIO), Amalgamated Meat Cutters (AFL), and members of National Brotherhood of Packinghouse Workers (CUA) (U)

b. 9 more facilities of same companies and 1 additional stockyards company	Jan. 27, 1946	May 23, 1946[46]	Agriculture Dept. (A)	Same as a	b. Same as a
c. 10 more facilities of same companies and 1 additional stockyards company	Feb. 3, 1946	May 23, 1946	Agriculture Dept. (A)	Same as a, plus Ex. Order 9690 (11 F.R. 1337)	c. Reason obscure, but probably seized because of extension of strike to other facilities
64. 91 harbor towing companies, New York Harbor	Feb. 6, 1946	Mar. 3, 1946[46a]	ODT (D)	WLDA and act of Aug. 29, 1916; Ex. Order 9693 (11 F.R. 1421)	Strike by United Marine Division of International Longshoremen's Assn. (AFL) (U)
65. Major railroads: 337 companies, nationwide	May 17, 1946	May 26, 1946	ODT (A)	WLDA and act of Aug. 29, 1916; Ex. Order 9727 (11 F.R. 5461)	Noncompliance by Brotherhood of Locomotive Engineers and Brotherhood of Railroad Trainmen with recommendation of Railway Labor Act emergency board (L)

(Continued on next page.)

Property Seized	Date Seized	Date Returned	Seizing & Operating Agency	Authority for Seizure	Reason for Seizure
66. The bituminous coal mines:					
a. Mines of 2,600 companies in 24 states	May 22, 1946	June 30, 1947[47]	Interior Dept. (D—) (mostly navy personnel)[48]	WLDA; Ex. Order 9728 (11 F.R. 5593); Ex. Order 9758 (11 F.R. 7927)	a. Strike by United Mine Workers of America (AFL) (U)
b. 5 additional companies in Ky.	May 27, 1946	Unknown but not after June 30, 1947	Interior Dept. (A)	Same as a	b. Same as a
c. 71 additional companies in 13 states	Aug. 5, 1946	June 30, 1947	Same as a[49]	Same as a	c. Seized because "inadvertently omitted" in May
67. Monongahela Connecting Railroad, Pittsburgh (subsidiary of Jones & Laughlin Steel Corp.)	June 14, 1946	Aug. 12, 1946	ODT (A)	WLDA and act of Aug. 29, 1916; Ex. Order 9736 (11 F.R. 6661)	Noncompliance by members of Brotherhood of Railroad Trainmen with recommendation of Railway Labor Act emergency board as modified by the president (L)

Administration of Harry S Truman

Period of continued technical state of war with Germany and Japan, marked by cold war with Soviet Russia, January 1, 1947 to June 25, 1950.

68. Major railroads: 207 companies, nationwide	May 10, 1948	July 9, 1948	Army Dept. (A)	Act of Aug. 29, 1916; Ex. Order 9957 (13 F.R. 2503)	Noncompliance by Brotherhood of Locomotive Engineers, Brotherhood of Locomotive Firemen & Enginemen, and Switchmen's Union of N.A. (AFL) with recommendation of Railway Labor Act emergency board (L)

Administration of Harry S Truman

Period of hostilities from Communist invasion of South Korea, June 25, 1950, to January 20, 1953.[50]

69. Major railroads: a. Chicago, Rock Island & Pacific Railroad, 14 midwestern states	July 8, 1950	May 23, 1952[51]	Army Dept. (A)	Acts of Aug. 29, 1916, and April 14, 1952, as extended; Ex. Order 10141 (15 F.R. 4363)[51a]	a. Noncompliance by Switchmen's Union of N.A. (AFL) with recommendation of Railway Labor Act emergency board (L)

(Continued on next page.)

Property Seized	Date Seized	Date Returned	Seizing & Operating Agency	Authority for Seizure	Reason for Seizure
b. 194 major railroad companies, nationwide	Aug. 27, 1950	May 23, 1952	Army Dept. (A)	Same statutes; Ex. Order 10155 (15 F.R. 5785)[51a]	b. Noncompliance by Brotherhood of Railroad Trainmen and Order of Railway Conductors with recommendation of Railway Labor Act emergency board (L)
70. Steel company railroads:					
a. 3 subsidiaries of Jones & Laughlin Steel Corp. in Pa. & Ohio	Jan. 21, 1951	May 23, 1952	Army Dept.[1,51b] (A)	Acts of Aug. 29, 1916, and April 14, 1952, as extended; Ex. Order 10155 (15 F.R. 5785)[51a]	a. Strike by members of Brotherhood of Railroad Trainmen on Monongahela Connecting Railroad; strike threats by members of B.R.T. on Cuyahoga Valley Railway and by United Railroad Workers (CIO) on Aliquippa & Southern Railroad (U)

b. Newburgh & South Shore Railway, Ohio (subsidiary of United States Steel Corp.)	Jan. 22, 1951	May 23, 1952	Army Dept.[1,51b] (A)	Same as a	b. Strike threat by members of BRT and BLFE (U)
71. United States Steel Co. (subsidiary of United States Steel Corp.) and 70 other steel manufacturing or fabricating firms, 18 states[52]	Apr. 9, 1952	June 2, 1952[53]	Commerce Dept. (A)	General powers; Ex. Order 10340 (17 F.R. 3139)	Companies' non-compliance with recommendation of WSB III (M)

(Notes to Appendix A begin on next page.)

NOTES TO APPENDIX A

1. Seized under a general delegation of authority by the president; no specific presidential order was issued.

2. 12 Stat. 334 (Railroad and Telegraph Control Act). *Official Records, War of the Rebellion,* III, II, 69; III, V, 67–68, 974 (executive orders and official report). The 2 executive orders placed all the railroads of the nation at the disposal of the War Department. Text of Major General Cadwalader's seizure order is in *New York Times,* July 19, 1864, p. 2.

3. Seizure of the major railroads and their subsidiaries brought under government control many nonrailroad properties that were railroad-owned, including about 25 coastwise and Great Lakes steamship companies, many docks and wharves, ferries and harbor tugboats, grain elevators, waterworks, and the Delaware and Raritan Canal.

4. The plant-facility roads were returned almost immediately after seizure.

5. 39 Stat. 619, 645 (Army Appropriation Act for fiscal year 1917); 40 Stat. 451 (Federal Control Act); 41 Stat. 34, 359 (other acts); 40 Stat. 1733 (seizure proclamation). The Act of Aug. 29, 1916 (Army Appropriation Act) authorizes the president to seize and operate "systems of transportation" in time of war.

6. In addition to threatened strikes, other reasons for seizure were: to unify control and allocate the use of transportation facilities during the war; to furnish government capital for new railroad equipment; to permit the pooling of railroad services despite the antitrust laws; and to test economies of consolidated operations for possible continuance in peace.

7. All of the short-line railroads were returned on June 29, 1918, but subsequently the Railroad Administration entered into agreements with 225 of them to retain them under indirect controls. The agreements treated the 225 as if they had been in continuous government possession since Dec. 28, 1917.

8. Clyde Steamship Co., Mallory Steamship Co., Merchants & Miners Transportation Co., Southern Steamship Co.

9. 40 Stat. 1769.

10. 40 Stat. 1808.

11. Seized after the Armistice of Nov. 11, 1918.

12. 40 Stat. 1888.

13. The individual express companies had been merged in June 1918, at the government's request, into the new American Railway Express Co., which then entered into a contract with the Railroad Administration.

14. 40 Stat. 182 (Deficiency Appropriations Act); section entitled, "Emergency Shipping Fund."

15. Includes Western Union Telegraph Co.; Postal Telegraph-Cable System (a subsidiary of the Mackay Companies); the American Telephone & Telegraph Co.; 36 Bell companies (subsidiaries of A.T. & T.); 7,830 small "class D" commercial telephone companies; and 8,981 "mutual," noncommercial, telephone lines.

16. The "mutual" noncommercial lines were "released from supervision and control" on Nov. 18, 1918.

17. Postmaster General Burleson placed an "operating board" in control of the wires from Jan. 1, 1919, to June 5, 1919. On Mar. 22, 1919, he removed the top officers of the Postal Telegraph System and appointed Arthur F. Adams, an independent telephone man, as federal manager of Postal's land wires. This arrangement was discontinued June 5, 1919.

18. 40 Stat. 904, 1017 (Wire Control Acts). 40 Stat. 1807 (seizure proclamation).

19. In addition to Western Union's noncompliance, other reasons for seizure were: to assure government control of wire traffic during the war; to strengthen military secrecy; and to test economies of consolidated operations for possible continuance in peace.

20. Includes Commercial Cable Co. (a subsidiary of the Mackay Companies), and the cables of Western Union Telegraph Co. The seizure of property in foreign countries drew protests to the U.S. secretary of state.

21. Postmaster General Burleson on Dec. 13, 1918, removed the officers of the Commercial Cable Co. and appointed Newcomb Carlton, president of Western Union, as federal manager of all the cables.

22. 40 Stat. 1872.

22a. The Army Ordnance Department operated the plant through its own dummy private corporation, called the National Operating Corp.

23. 39 Stat. 166, 213 (National Defense Act). See President Wilson's letter of Sept. 13, 1918, to striking Bridgeport employees, stating his approval of the seizure of Smith & Wesson, and the War Department's seizure statement of the same date, both in the Committee on Public Information's *Official Bulletin* of Sept. 14, 1918.

24. *Alcoa Banner, Alcoa Scout, Alcoa Trader,* seized for one voyage each.

25. *Alcoa Banner* was returned Oct. 30, 1941; *Alcoa Trader* Nov. 6, 1941; *Alcoa Scout* Nov. 9, 1941.

26. The Maritime Commission was directly empowered by Congress to requisition any vessel documented under U.S. laws during a national emergency proclaimed by the president. (See next footnote.) Text of the MC seizure statement is in the *New York Times,* Sept. 20, 1941, p. 8.

27. 49 Stat. 1985, 2015 (Merchant Marine Act of 1936).

28. The branch plant in Missouri was returned about Nov. 11, 1941, as non-essential.

29. F.D.R. "noted his approval" on letter to him from Acting Secretary of War Patterson dated Nov. 3, 1941. (Ohly MS., p. 62 and app. J-5.)

29a. The War Department seized the T.P. & W.R.R. from the ODT on Dec. 27, 1943, when it took possession of all the railroads, and inadvertently returned the T.P. & W. to its owners with the rest of the railroads on Jan. 18, 1944. The ODT, however, claimed that it had never relinquished possession of the T.P. & W., and on June 15, 1945, President Truman issued a new executive order affirming this position (Ex. Order 9572).

30. The War Department cancelled its shell contracts with the Woods Co. on Sept. 29, 1942, and transferred them to the Murray Co., of Dallas, Texas. The new contract with the Murray Co. provided that it assume management of all the Woods properties.

30a. The War Department's seizure statement is summarized in *Railway Age,* Nov. 14, 1942, p. 791. Full text in Ohly MS., app. N-5.

31. Because President Roosevelt was "unavailable" on short notice, the War Department was unable to obtain a specific executive order for this seizure. It relied, therefore, on an earlier executive order which authorized and directed the secretary of war (or secretary of the navy), whenever he deemed it necessary or desirable, to establish military guards and patrols and to take other appropriate measures to protect national defense materials, premises, and utilities. If the seizure had lasted more than a few days, however, an executive order was to be issued under the Act of Aug. 29, 1916. (Ohly MS., pp. 125–127 and app. N-4.)

32. 11 companies which reached agreements with the Progressive Mine Workers of America to extend existing contracts were released on May 31, 1943. 2 mines of

the Commonwealth of Pennsylvania were released on June 11, 1943, because no strikes had occurred. Subsequently (and prior to Oct. 12, 1943), the mines of 953 other companies were returned to their owners as follows: 28 because mining operations had been abandoned prior to seizure; 35 because mining operations had ceased since seizure; 400 because no strikes had occurred under government possession and control; 490 because "productive efficiency" prevailing prior to seizure had been "restored" (strikes had ceased). On Oct. 12, 1943, Secretary of the Interior Ickes ruled that the "productive efficiency" of all remaining mines had been "restored" and ordered them returned as soon as the owners executed releases waiving claims against the government.

33. Seizure of these companies was "revoked" by the secretary of the interior's order no. 1850 (8 F.R. 11758), which declared that no notice of the takings had been issued to the companies and that nothing had been done to implement the seizure.

34. Governor Tugwell of Puerto Rico assumed control of the railroad from noon of May 12, 1943, to the evening of May 14, 1943, after which local officers of the ODT, acting on advice from Washington, attempted to direct operations. Officials from the Washington office of ODT arrived and formally took control on May 17, 1943.

35. During the first months of government possession (prior to May 31, 1944), a number of companies were returned as follows: an unknown number because mining operations had been abandoned prior to seizure; 11 because mining operations had ceased since seizure; 69 because daily production was less than 50 tons; 343 because no strikes had occurred under government possession and control; 52 because agreements had been executed with the Progressive Mine Workers of America; 8 because of other agreements with their employees (mostly unorganized). On May 31, 1944, Secretary of the Interior Ickes terminated possession of bituminous coal mines in 9 production districts because they had executed agreements with the United Mine Workers of America. Between May 31 and June 21, 1944, additional companies were released as they signed the agreement. On June 21, the secretary ordered the release of all companies, both bituminous and anthracite, then remaining in government possession, with one exception, as soon as they should execute the agreement with the UMWA. These remaining companies apparently signed and were released by Aug. 16, 1944. The exception, Jewell Ridge Coal Corp., of Tazewell, Va., was retained until June 13, 1945, while it tested the validity of portal-to-portal payments in the federal courts.

36. The navy also took control of a subsidiary sales corporation in New York City.

37. Triangle Terminal Co. and Hi-Way Freight Terminal, Inc.

38. Between Sept. 1944 and early Aug. 1945, the ODT returned 25 firms which had reached agreements with the International Brotherhood of Teamsters (AFL) accepting the NWLB order. The remaining firms were released during Sept. and Oct. 1945 without such agreements.

39. The ODT took 8 firms under direct control after several weeks of indirect control—3 for refusing to carry out orders of the federal manager of motor carriers systems (Midnite Express, Inc.; Wilson Storage & Transfer Co., Healzer Cartage Co.) and 5 because their operations were unprofitable and liable to be discontinued (Janke Transfer Co.; Century Motor Freight; Matthews Freight Service, Inc.; R-B Freight Lines, Inc.; Toedebusch Transfer, Inc.).

39a. The Department of Justice argued before the Motor Carrier Claims Commission that these firms had not actually been "taken possession of" by the government, but the MCCC found that they had and awarded them compensation.

39b. 3 companies were returned on Oct. 31, 1944, and a fourth on Aug. 15, 1945, as unessential to the war effort.

40. The mines were returned as their owners reached agreement with the United Mine Workers of America—209 companies on June 13, 1945, the remaining 9 on June 23, 1945.

41. One company was returned May 12, 1945; 26 more on June 13, 1945; and 3 on June 24, 1945.

41a. The 3 Kentucky mines were the Blue Gem, Mount Ash, and Mammoth Blue Gem of the Gatliff Coal Co.; Jellico Coal Mining Co.; and the Ester and Effie Croley Co., respectively.

42. The PAW posted notices and formally seized the Humble plant on June 6, 1945, but was restrained a few hours later by a federal district court. The PAW refused to remove its notices or to concede that it was not in possession. When the restraining order expired on June 22, 1945, PAW commenced active supervision of operations.

43. The Illinois Central seizure is classed by some as a "postwar" seizure (NWSB, *Research & Statistics Report No. 2;* and appendix to Associate Justice Frankfurter's opinion, *Youngstown Sheet & Tube Co.* v. *Sawyer,* 343 U.S. 579), but this classification ignores that: the labor dispute arose, and the strike date was set, during active hostilities; plans for seizure of the railroad were made during active hostilities; the Japanese military forces did not surrender, and V-J Day was not proclaimed by the president, until Sept. 2, 1945. The earlier "victory" celebrations in mid-August occurred during the surrender negotiations and prior to the American landings in Japan. The later seizures were truly "postwar" not only because they occurred after the official V-J Day, but because they concerned disputes which arose after V-J Day over wages to be effective in the reconversion period.

44. Under the terms of the War Labor Disputes Act, the authority granted to seize war plants and facilities expired at the termination of hostilities as proclaimed by the president Dec. 31, 1946, and the authority to operate plants and facilities previously seized terminated 6 months later, on June 30, 1947.

45. An oil supply company, seized in error, was returned Oct. 12, 1945. 2 refining companies and one plant of another (all in Ohio) were returned Nov. 10, 1945—the OWIU having won its demands from one and having withdrawn its pickets from the others (where it held no bargaining rights). Then on Dec. 17, 1945, the navy relinquished possession of 9 refineries and a pipe line belonging to Sinclair Refining Co. after mediating a company-union agreement. Thereafter other companies were released as they reached agreements with the union—usually along the lines of the Sinclair formula and the subsequent fact-finding board's recommendations. By Apr. 12, 1946, all except one plant, the Toledo refinery of the Gulf Refining Co., had been turned back.

46. One small company, seized in error, was returned Jan. 26, 1946. About 50 plants of the 3 largest packers (Armour, Swift, and Wilson) were relinquished in Feb., apparently because of local agreements between the employees and companies. Commencing Mar. 13, 1946, the companies were returned as they reached agreements with the unions along the lines recommended by the fact-finding board. Between Mar. 13 and Apr. 10, 10 small packers were returned. On Apr. 30, 1946, the "big 5" packers were returned (Armour, Cudahy, Morrell, Swift, and Wilson); and on May 23, 1946, the four stockyards companies were returned.

46a. One towing company was returned on Feb. 19, 1946, because no strike had occurred during government possession.

47. The mines of 20 companies in Illinois, which reached an agreement with the Progressive Mine Workers of America, were returned on May 25, 1946; and the mines of the Alabama Fuel & Iron Co., which reached an agreement with the Asso-

ciated Miners, were returned on June 1, 1946. 2 days later, all companies not subject as of Mar. 31, 1946, to the national bituminous coal wage agreement of Apr. 11, 1945, with the United Mine Workers of America, were returned. It is not known how many firms were in this group, but the Carter Coal Co., of West Virginia, claimed to be one of them and later had to be reseized (Ex. Order 9758). In July 1946, a few more companies were returned, 10 on July 5, and 13 more on July 27, presumably because they had reached agreements with their employees; but the remaining mines, the vast majority, were retained in government possession until the expiration of the War Labor Disputes Act on June 30, 1947.

48. One of these firms, the Carter Coal Co., of West Virginia, was taken under direct control on Dec. 31, 1946, due to the refusal of private management to observe the terms and conditions of employment required by the government. All the other firms were controlled indirectly through agreements with private management.

49. One of these firms, the Fox Coal Co., of West Virginia, was taken under direct control on Jan. 7, 1947, due to the refusal of private management to observe the terms and conditions of employment required by the government. All the others were controlled indirectly.

50. This period was marked by a proclamation of national emergency "due to Communist aggression" on Dec. 16, 1950, and by acts of Congress terminating the technical state of war with Germany and Japan on Oct. 19, 1951, and Apr. 28, 1952, respectively. The "defense emergency" proclaimed by President Roosevelt on May 27, 1941, as a result of German aggression was also terminated by President Truman on Apr. 28, 1952. In sum, the United States ceased being in a technical state of war on Apr. 28, 1952, although it remained in a state of national emergency under the proclamation of Communist aggression and was engaged in hostilities with Chinese and North Korean forces. In order to permit continued government possession and control of the railroads after Apr. 28, 1952, Congress continued the authority, a few weeks at a time, until July 3, 1952. Hostilities in Korea were terminated by an armistice on July 27, 1953, during the administration of President Eisenhower.

51. This dispute was settled on Sept. 21, 1950, but the Department of the Army continued in possession of the Rock Island because of the trainmen's and conductors' dispute with the Rock Island and other major railroads. The 2 disputes were closely related, both dealing with the 40-hour week and both being subject to the same recommendations of the same emergency board.

51a. The transportation-seizure provision of the Act of Aug. 29, 1916 (39 Stat. 619, 645), which applies only in time of war, was extended for 30 days after the formal end of World War II (Apr. 28, 1952) by sec. 1, a (34) of the Act of Apr. 14, 1952 (Emergency Powers Interim Continuation Act, 66 Stat. 54). This authority was further extended by 3 joint resolutions until July 3, 1952 (66 Stat. 96, 137, 296).

51b. Ex. Order 10155 authorized the secretary of the army to take possession and assume control of any transportation system of any carrier by railroad in the continental United States, whenever he found it necessary or appropriate. This authority was subdelegated by Secretary Pace to Assistant Secretary of the Army (General Management) Karl R. Bendetsen, who effected these seizures. (Army Department, *Army Operation of Rail Transportation Systems,* Report of Undersecretary of the Army, Sept. 15, 1952, p. 11 and app. B, table 8; *Railway Age,* Sept. 2, 1950; Mar. 19, 1951, p. 74; and Apr. 2, 1951, p. 64.)

52. In accordance with the executive order, Secretary of Commerce Sawyer took possession only of companies which had a labor dispute with the United Steelworkers of America (CIO) and seriously affected defense production. Although the executive order listed 86 companies, Mr. Sawyer took possession of only 71. (See his order

no. 1, 17 F.R. 3360; H. Doc. 534, 82nd Cong., 2nd sess., p. 22.) He omitted the vast holding company United States Steel Corp., but took its new manufacturing subsidiary, United States Steel Co., and 12 of the latter's subsidiaries; also other basic steel manufacturers and several firms fabricating instruments, wire, oil well machinery, and so forth.

53. Between Apr. 11 and 25, 1952, Secretary of Commerce Sawyer reduced the number of firms in government possession from 71 to 51 by lumping the correspondence with all 12 United States Steel Co. subsidiaries into one package and handling them through U.S. Steel Co. itself, releasing 8 other companies because the labor dispute had been settled locally. Certain plants of the seized companies were also released because the employees were found to be represented by another union than the USW-CIO.

Additional historical information about many of these seizures will be found in the following published tables: Bernard Yabroff and Daniel P. Willis, Jr., "Federal Seizures in Labor-Management Disputes, 1917–52," *Monthly Labor Review,* June 1953, pp. 611–616; omits seizures 1, 7, 12, 70. Associate Justice Felix Frankfurter, concurring opinion in *Youngstown Sheet & Tube Co.* v. *Sawyer* (1952), app. II (343 U.S. 579); omits seizures 1, 7, 12, 31, 70. NWLB, *Termination Report* (Washington, 1948–1949), vol. II, app. J-39(a), pp. 704–727; lists about 40 seizures of World War II. About 58 seizures are listed in the Ohly MS., app. A, B, D, and AA-1.

Federal Laws Authorizing Seizure

This appendix lists 24 acts and resolutions of Congress authorizing the president or other executive agencies of the government to seize industrial property in national emergency situations. Although only four of the statutes were adopted by Congress during labor-dispute emergencies, with the evident intention that they would be applicable in such crises (6, 12, 19, 24), at least seven others have been applied by the government to labor-dispute emergencies—three in actual seizures (1, 5, 15), and four more in threats or plans for seizure (2, 9, 11, 21). These 11 items are marked in the appendix by asterisks.

I am indebted for this list of statutes primarily to appendix I of the concurring opinion of Associate Justice Felix Frankfurter in *Youngstown Sheet & Tube Co.* v. *Sawyer* (decided June 2, 1952), entitled: "Synoptic Analysis of Legislation Authorizing Seizure of Industrial Property" (343 U.S. 579). To it I have added six other statutes which have come to my notice (2, 3, 4, 7, 15, 24), together with certain historical material.

*1. *Railroad and Telegraph Act of 1862* (12 Stat. 334). Enacted Jan. 31, 1862, amended July 14, 1862 (12 Stat. 625). Authorized president to take possession of telegraph lines and railroads, to prescribe rules for their operation, and to place all officers and employees under military control. Duration of Civil War only. Relied on in seizure of Philadelphia & Reading Railroad during strike in July 1864 (seizure 1).

*2. Sec. 6 of *Railroad Construction Act of 1862* (12 Stat. 489, 493). Enacted July 1, 1862; amended July 2, 1864 (13 Stat. 356). The act created the Union Pacific Railroad Co. and the Central Pacific Railroad Co. and authorized them to construct a railroad and telegraph line from the Missouri River to the Pacific Ocean. Sec. 6 established the condition that the railroad companies "shall at all times transmit despatches over said telegraph line, and transport mails, troops, and munitions of war, supplies, and public stores upon such railroad for the government, whenever required to do so by any department thereof, and that the government shall at all times have the preference in the use of the same for all the purposes aforesaid (at fair and reasonable rates of compensation, not to exceed the amounts paid by private parties for the same kind of service)." No time limit. Relied on by Major General John M. Schofield in threatening to seize trains of the Union Pacific in 1885 to move troops to Rock Springs, Wyoming, to suppress riots in the face of a threatened sympathetic strike by the railroad brotherhoods; by President Cleveland in 1894 in ordering the army to re-establish railroad communications with the Pacific coast during the Pullman strike.

3. Sec. 11 of *Railroad Construction Act of 1864* (13 Stat. 365, 370). Enacted July 2, 1864. The act created the Northern Pacific Railroad Co. and authorized it to construct a railroad and a telegraph line from Lake Superior

to Puget Sound on the Pacific coast. Sec. 11 provided that the new railroad, "or any part thereof, shall be a post route and a military road, subject to the use of the United States, for postal, military, naval, and all other government service, and also subject to such regulations as Congress may impose restricting the charges for such government transportation." No time limit. Relied on by President Cleveland in 1894 in ordering the army to re-establish railroad communications with the Pacific coast during the Pullman strike.

4. Sec. 2 of *Radio Communication Act of 1912* (37 Stat. 302, 303). Enacted Aug. 13, 1912. Authorized the president to close any licensed radio station or to authorize its use or control by any department of the government, in time of war, public peril, or disaster.

*5. Sec. 120 of *National Defense Act of 1916* (39 Stat. 166, 213). Enacted June 3, 1916. Authorized the president to seize plant of any army contractor who refused a compulsory order for war materials and to operate the plant through the Army Ordnance Department. Applies in time of war or when war is imminent. Relied on in seizure of Smith & Wesson Co. (4).

*6. *Army Appropriations Act for Fiscal Year 1917* (39 Stat. 619, 645). Enacted Aug. 29, 1916. One paragraph of sec. 1 authorizes the president, in time of war, "through the secretary of war, to take possession and assume control of any system or systems of transportation, or any part thereof, and to utilize the same, to the exclusion as far as may be necessary of all other traffic thereon, for the transfer or transportation of troops, war material and equipment, or for such other purposes connected with the emergency as may be needful or desirable." No time limit. Relied on in numerous seizures of railroads, streetcar lines, shipping lines, towboat companies, and trucking firms in labor disputes.

7. *Naval Appropriations Act for Fiscal Year 1917* (39 Stat. 556, 604). Enacted Aug. 29, 1916. One provision further amended sec. 6 of the Interstate Commerce Act of Feb. 4, 1887, to strengthen the requirements of preferential treatment for military traffic laid on all railroad carriers in interstate commerce, making the provisions applicable in time of peace as well as war or threatened war. Relied on by the U.S. Railroad Administration in seizure 2 (USRRA, *Bulletin No. 4,* Revised, p. 5).

8. *Naval Emergency Fund Act of 1917* (39 Stat. 1168, 1192). Enacted Mar. 4, 1917. One provision authorized the president to seize the plant of any naval contractor who refused a compulsory order for ships or other naval material and to operate the plant. Applies in time of war.

*9. "Emergency Shipping Fund" section of *Deficiency Appropriations Act of 1917* (40 Stat. 182). Enacted June 15, 1917. Authorized the president to seize any shipbuilding yard, including one whose owner refused a compulsory order or refused to accept a fair price, and to operate the yard through such agency as he might name; or to seize any ship or any ship under construction for use and operation by the government. World War I only. Relied on by U.S. Shipping Board to threaten seizure of ships and shipyards in several labor disputes.

10. 1918 amendments to "Emergency Shipping Fund" section of *Deficiency Appropriations Act of 1917* (40 Stat. 535; 40 Stat. 1020, 2022). Enacted Apr. 22, 1918, and Nov. 4, 1918. The first amendment authorized the president to take possession of any street railroad if necessary for transporting employees to shipyards building ships for the government. The second authorized the president to extend any seized shipyards and to requisition land for use in extensions. World War I only.

*11. Secs. 10, 12, and 25 of *Food and Fuel Act of 1917* (40 Stat. 276, 279, 284). "The Lever Act." Enacted Aug. 10, 1917. Sec. 10 authorized the president to requisition foods, fuels, feeds, and storage facilities. Sec. 12 authorized the president to take over any factory, packing house, oil pipe line, mine, or other plant where any necessaries are or may be produced, and to operate the same. Sec. 25 authorized the president to seize the property of any producer or dealer in coal or coke and to operate it through an agency of his choice. World War I only. Relied on by U.S. Fuel Administration to threaten seizure of midwestern coal mines in wage-price dispute; and by President Wilson to threaten seizure of Alabama coal mines in similar dispute.

*12. *Joint Resolution of July 16, 1918* (40 Stat. 904). Authorized the president to take possession and control of any telegraph, telephone and marine cable or radio systems and to operate them as necessary in connection with the war. World War I only. Relied on in seizure of wire systems (3).

13. Sec. 16 of *Federal Water Power Act of 1920* (41 Stat. 1063, 1072). Enacted June 10, 1920. Authorized the president to take possession of any project, dams, power houses, or transmission lines, constructed or operated under a license from the Federal Power Commission, and to operate them, whenever the safety of the United States demands it. No time limit.

14. Sec. 606 of *Communications Act of 1934* (48 Stat. 1064, 1104). Enacted June 19, 1934. Authorized the president to take over the use or control of any licensed radio station through any department of the government in the following emergency situations: war or threat of war; public peril or disaster or other national emergency; when it is necessary to preserve the neutrality of the United States. No time limit.

*15. Sec. 902 of *Merchant Marine Act of 1936* (49 Stat. 1985, 2015). Enacted June 29, 1936. Authorized the Maritime Commission to requisition any vessel documented under the laws of the United States during any national emergency proclaimed by the president. No time limit. Relied on in seizure of three Alcoa freighters in labor dispute (7).

16. Sec. 8(b) of *National Defense Act of 1940* (54 Stat. 676, 680). Enacted June 28, 1940. Authorized the secretary of the navy, under the president's direction, to take over and operate any plant which the secretary deems necessary for the national defense and with whose owner he is unable to reach agreement for its use or operation. No time limit; but repealed in less than three months, Sept. 16, 1940 (54 Stat. 865, 893).

17. Sec. 9 of *Selective Training and Service Act of 1940* (54 Stat. 865, 892). Enacted Sept. 16, 1940. Authorized the president to seize any plant

capable of manufacturing supplies for the defense effort whose owner refused to fill a compulsory order or refused to accept a reasonable price. Expired March 31, 1947. This act balanced compulsory military service and compulsory orders for military supplies, and so was the basis for later amendments extending the seizure power to labor disputes (see WLDA, below). It was often cited with the WLDA in executive orders for labor-dispute seizures.

18. Amendments to *Communications Act of 1934* (36 Stat. 18). Enacted Jan. 26, 1942. Extended president's authority to seize radio stations to include: war or threat of war proclaimed by the president; when the president deems it necessary in the interest of national security and defense; but limited the power to "not later than six months after the termination of such state or threat of war" or than a date set by concurrent resolution of Congress. No time limit.

*19. *War Labor Disputes Act of 1943* (57 Stat. 163). "The Smith-Connally Act." Enacted June 25, 1943. Sec. 3 authorized the president to take immediate possession of any plant, mine, or facility equipped for the manufacture, production, or mining of any articles or materials which may be required or may be useful for the war effort, if there is an interruption of production on account of a labor dispute. This section constituted an amendment to sec. 9 of the Selective Training and Service Act of 1940. Sec. 5 provided a means for the orderly change of terms and conditions of employment in plants, mines, or facilities seized by the president. Sec. 6 made strikes and lockouts unlawful in plants, mines, or facilities seized by the president. World War II only. Relied on in nearly every labor-dispute seizure from its adoption on June 25, 1943, until its expiration with the official termination of hostilities on Dec. 31, 1946.

20. Title VIII, "Repricing of War Contracts," of *Revenue Act of 1943* (58 Stat. 21, 92). Enacted Feb. 25, 1944. Authorized the president to take possession of any plant whose owner refused to furnish articles or services required by a federal department at a price deemed reasonable by the secretary of the department. World War II only.

*21. Sec. 18 of *Selective Service Act of 1948* (62 Stat. 604, 625). Enacted June 24, 1948. Authorizes the president to take possession and to operate any plant, mine, or other facility engaged in supplying articles or materials for the armed forces or the Atomic Energy Commission whenever the owner refuses or fails to give precedence to a compulsory order, or refuses or fails to fill the order properly. No time limit. Words "or fails" inserted to permit seizure in strikes. Relied on in preparation for seizure in several labor disputes which were settled before seizure became necessary.

22. Sec. 201(a) of *Defense Production Act of 1950* (64 Stat. 798, 799). Enacted Sept. 8, 1950. Authorized the president to seize equipment, supplies, or facilities for the manufacture of equipment and supplies whenever he determined that their use was needed for national defense. Korean emergency only.

23. Sec. 102(b),2, of *Defense Production Act Amendments of 1951* (65 Stat. 131, 132). Enacted July 31, 1951. Restricted the president's power under

sec. 201(a) of Defense Production Act of 1950 in the main to personal property, but authorized court condemnation of real property and immediate possession by the government whenever the president deems it necessary in the interest of national defense. Korean emergency only.

*24. *Emergency Powers Interim Continuation Act of 1952* (66 Stat. 54). Enacted Apr. 14, 1952. Sec. 1(a),34, extended the president's power to seize systems of transportation under the Army Appropriation Act of Aug. 29, 1916 (39 Stat. 619, 645), until June 1, 1952, notwithstanding the impending termination of the state of war with Japan, and authorized the president to exercise his authority through such officers or agencies as he might designate. Sec. 5 stated that nothing therein should be construed to authorize seizure by the government, under any act therein extended, of any privately owned plants or facilities which were not public utilities. This extension of authority was further extended by amendments until July 3, 1952 (66 Stat. 96, 137, 296). Relied on in seizures of major railroads and steel company railroads (69, 70).

Cases of Required Production, Other Than by Seizure (chronologically arranged)

Abraham Lincoln

1. Federal troops, together with civilians hired by the government, were used to load and unload government vessels at New York piers, during a strike of longshoremen, June 1863. See B. L. Lee, *Discontent in New York City, 1861–65* (Washington, 1943), pp. 99–102. E. D. Fite, *Social and Industrial Conditions in the North During the Civil War* (New York, 1911), p. 203.

2. Qualified martial law was proclaimed by General W. S. Rosecrans in St. Louis, Missouri, and Louisville, Kentucky, to suppress strikes by mechanics, May 1864. (Lee and Fite, in works cited.)

3. Similar use of qualified martial law by General George H. Thomas in Tennessee, 1864. See Fite, *Social and Industrial Conditions.*

Rutherford B. Hayes

4. Criminal trial and conviction of six members of the Brotherhood of Locomotive Engineers for conspiring to obstruct the mails during a strike on the Boston & Maine Railroad, February 1877. (*U.S.* v. *Stevens,* 27 Fed. Cas. 1312.)

5. Trial and conviction of several strikers on railroads then in federal receivership for contempt of court in violating antistrike injunctions obtained by the federal receivers, July 1877. (*Secor* v. *Toledo, Peoria & Warsaw Ry.,* 21 Fed. Cas. 968, 971; *King* v. *Ohio & Mississippi Ry.,* 14 Fed. Cas. 539.) Concurrent criminal trial and conviction of strikers on the Lehigh Valley Railroad, which was not in receivership. The accusation was obstructing the mails. (*U.S.* v. *Clark,* 25 Fed. Cas. 443.)

Grover Cleveland

6. Trial and conviction of leaders of the American Railway Union for contempt of court in violating antistrike injunctions that had been issued at the request of U.S. Attorney General Olney during the Pullman railroad strike, December 1894. The injunctions had been based on provisions of the Sherman Antitrust Act of 1890 and the government's general powers over interstate commerce. (*In re Debs,* 64 Fed. 724; upheld in 158 U.S. 564.) Also one trial and conviction for contempt of court on a railroad under federal receivership, the Cincinnati, New Orleans & Texas Pacific. (*In re Phelan,* 62 Fed. 803.) Criminal trials were held concurrently in Los Angeles and San Francisco for conspiracy to obstruct the mails and to obstruct interstate commerce, and for violating the Sherman Act, resulting in a guilty verdict in Los Angeles and a split jury in San Francisco. (*Clune* v. *U.S.,* 62 Fed. 798, 834; upheld in 159 U.S. 590; *U.S.* v. *Cassidy,* 62 Fed. 840; 67 Fed. 698.)

Woodrow Wilson

7. Congress averted a nationwide railroad strike by legislating the eight-hour day for operating employees at the president's request, August 1916. The terms were not satisfactory to either side, but were accepted as law, after the Supreme Court had upheld the constitutionality of the statute. (Adamson Act, 39 Stat. 721; upheld in *Wilson* v. *New,* 243 U.S. 332.)

8. Federal soldiers were used in two ways to obtain spruce lumber in the Washington and Oregon woods for construction of army aircraft during a long loggers' strike, October 1917 to late in 1918: (a) assigned to logging camps under contract with private firms; and (b) constructed and operated a logging railroad and a giant sawmill, financed at first by the War Department, then by a specially chartered government corporation, the Spruce Production Corp. See A. M. Bing, *War-Time Strikes and Their Adjustment* (New York, 1921), pp. 53–57, 270–272. War Department, Office of the Secretary of War, *Report of War Department Activities in the Field of Industrial Relations* (Washington, 1919), pp. 44–50.

9. The War Department held up renewal of its contracts with Wanamaker & Brown, of Philadelphia, for the manufacture of army uniforms until the firm agreed to end its lockout of union employees and to continue production under labor standards set by the War Department, May-June 1918. Matthew Josephson, *Sidney Hillman* (New York, 1952), p. 169.

10. Government-operated towboats were used to move troopships and military cargo vessels in and out of New York Harbor, and, for a time, also to move coal barges to supply Manhattan Island traction and power companies, during strikes by the Marine Workers Affiliation of the Port of New York, January 9–11, 1919, and March 4 to April 19, 1919. The *New York Times, passim,* especially Jan. 12, 1919, pp. 1, 20; Mar. 18, 1919, p. 5; Mar. 25, 1919, p. 1; Mar. 30, 1919, p. 14, col. 6.

11. Qualified martial law was proclaimed and maintained by General Leonard Wood in Gary, Indiana, from October 6 to late in December, 1919, during the industrywide steel strike. The army forbade parades and mass meetings by the strikers, except in a few instances and only in the presence of troops. Intelligence agents of the army, working with agents of the Department of Justice, raided the homes of several strike leaders, and took some of them into custody for varying periods. Bennett M. Rich, *The Presidents and Civil Disorder* (Washington, 1941), pp. 156–158, 210.

12. U.S. soldiers were used to load and unload government vessels, mostly troopships with returning soldiers of the A.E.F., at New York piers during a wildcat strike by longshoremen, October 1919. The *New York Times,* Oct. 10, 15, 20, 21, and 22, 1919, all on p. 1.

13. Leaders of the United Mine Workers of America were arrested on a charge of contempt of court for allegedly violating an antistrike injunction that had been issued at request of U.S. Attorney General Palmer during an industrywide soft coal strike, December 1919. The government's request for an injunction had alleged that the union officers were conspiring to withhold

"necessaries of life" (coal) contrary to the Food and Fuel Act of 1917. The strike was ended a few days after the arrests, and no trial was ever held. Edward Berman, *Labor Disputes and the President of the United States* (New York, 1924), pp. 177–193. Selig Perlman and Philip Taft, *A History of Labor in the United States, 1896 to 1932* (New York, 1935), pp. 469–479.

About the time of the federal arrests, the governors of Missouri, Kansas, and North Dakota seized a number of mines and attempted to operate them. Perlman and Taft, *History of Labor,* pp. 473, 474; Cecil Carnes, *John L. Lewis, Leader of Labor* (New York, 1936), pp. 41–42.

14. Leaders of a wildcat strike by railroad yardmen in the Chicago area were tried and convicted on criminal charges brought by Attorney General Palmer, August 1920. The men were accused of conspiring to limit the facilities for transporting and distributing necessaries of life in violation of the Lever Act. *U.S.* v. *Chicago Yardmen's Association,* cited in Annual Report of Attorney General for 1920, p. 43. Perlman and Taft, *History of Labor,* pp. 452–456; Berman, *Labor Disputes and the President,* pp. 193–199.

Warren G. Harding

15. On September 1, 1922, Attorney General Daugherty obtained from the federal courts an injunction outlawing a nationwide strike by railroad workers belonging to the shopcraft unions of the AFL. The strike had begun July 1. The antistrike injunction was based upon a contention that the strikers were conspiring to obstruct interstate commerce in violation of the Sherman Act, and in addition were refusing to comply with provisions of the Transportation Act of 1920. Although none of the leaders of the striking unions appears to have been arrested, many striking railroad employees were arrested and punished for contempt of court. A number of persons who were not employees were also prosecuted for contempt, for aiding and abetting the strikers. Several other strikers were tried and convicted on criminal charges of obstructing commerce and the mails. *U.S.* v. *Employees' Department of AFL,* 283 Fed. 479; 286 Fed. 228; 290 Fed. 978; text of restraining order in Felix Frankfurter and Nathan Greene, *The Labor Injunction* (New York, 1930), app. IV. *Clements* v. *U.S.,* 297 Fed. 206; cert. denied, 266 U.S. 605. Max Lowenthal, *The Federal Bureau of Investigation* (New York, 1950), chap. 25. Berman, *Labor Disputes and the President,* pp. 226–248.

Franklin D. Roosevelt

16. The U.S. Maritime Commission, headed by Joseph P. Kennedy, ordered the captain of the government-owned, privately operated *S.S. Algic* (American Republic Lines) to arrest members of the crew who remained on strike while the ship was at anchor in Montevideo Harbor, September 10, 1937. The men returned to work when notified of the commission's order, but the Department of Justice subsequently prosecuted 14 of the men under the mutiny provisions of the Act of 1790 as well as the Merchant Marine Act of 1936. They were found guilty and punished. *Rees et al.* v. *United States,* 9 Fed. (2d) 784.

17. The Navy Department for several weeks transported members of non-striking unions through picket lines of other unions into ship-repair yards of the San Francisco Bay area, during a wildcat machinists' strike, May and June 1941. By the end of the strike, the navy also had begun recruiting civilian workers for the shipyards. Samuel H. Ordway, Jr. (ed.), "United States Naval Administration in World War II, Office of the Secretary of the Navy, Civilian Personnel," 1946, 3 vols., typescript (vol. I, pp. 429, 464–466), in the Office of Naval Records and History. J. L. Blackman, Jr., "Navy Policy Toward the Labor Relations of Its War Contractors," Part I, *Military Affairs,* Winter 1954, p. 183.

18. Qualified martial law was proclaimed in the Hawaiian Islands by General Delos C. Emmons, with the approval of the president, after the Japanese naval air attack, and was used thereafter to forbid strikes and collective bargaining, and to control wages and employment, December 8, 1941, to mid-1944. J. P. Frank, "Ex Parte Milligan v. The Five Companies," *Columbia Law Review,* Sept. 1944, vol. 44, esp. pp. 653–657. A. J. Garner, *Hawaii Under Army Rule* (Palo Alto, Calif., 1955), esp. pp. 41–45. Clinton Rossiter, *The Supreme Court and the Commander in Chief* (Ithaca, N.Y., 1951), pp. 54–59.

19. Details of soldiers and sailors, totaling about 250, were assigned for several days to the task of cleaning out debris from government vessels in the ship-repair yards of the Bethlehem Steel Corp. in Hoboken, New Jersey, and Brooklyn, New York, during a walkout of laborers affiliated with the Industrial Union of Marine and Shipbuilding Workers of America, August 1944. The removal of the inflammable material was necessary before welding could begin. The *New York Times,* Aug. 18, 1944, p. 15; Aug. 19, 1944, p. 13.

Harry S Truman

20. During a nationwide strike by AFL seamen (SIU and SUP), in September 1946, sympathetic walkouts were conducted by AFL longshoremen and New York tugboat crews (both ILA), tying up even military shipping in all ports. In New York, army tugs brought at least three transports with servicemen, war brides, and children, into pier 11, Staten Island; there soldiers, including MP's, handled the mooring lines and gangways, in the absence of longshoremen. Other transports were docked without tugboats but with the aid of soldiers on the piers. At the request of the Maritime Commission, 11 Navy LCM's brought ashore 887 passengers from a government transport anchored in the harbor, disembarking them at a picketed Hudson River pier. In Boston, sailors from the *U.S.S. Missouri,* using handlines, moved a strike-bound cargo ship which obstructed the battleship's departure and then pulled the cargo vessel back to her original position. The *New York Times,* Sept. 9, 10, 11, and 12, 1946, details within strike stories beginning on p. 1. For background, consult H. M. Sturm, "Postwar Labor Relations in the Maritime Industry," in Colston E. Warne (ed.), *Labor in Postwar America* (Brooklyn, N.Y., 1949), pp. 478–481.

21. Although the president urged longshoremen in the Port of New York, in the interest of the national defense effort, to give up a wildcat strike that had

closed the port in October 1951, he did not proclaim an emergency nor invoke emergency provisions of the Taft-Hartley Act; hence the men continued on strike. However, the army hired laborers, clerks, and checkers under temporary civil service rules, and put them to work at the six army terminals in New York. The replacements were escorted through picket lines by MP's and city police, and in at least one case evaded pickets by being ferried to work on army tugs. On the fifteenth day of the strike, more than 500 nonprofessional civil service employees were at work on 13 MSTS vessels, aided by several hundred nonstriking members of the ILA. On this day, the strike leader, John J. (Gene) Sampson, offered to withdraw all pickets from army terminals if the army would abandon the use of civil service workers, and the offer was accepted. The *New York Times,* Oct. 27 to Oct. 31, 1951, all on p. 1. For background, see Daniel Bell, "The Racket-Ridden Longshoremen," in Galenson and Lipset (eds.), *Labor and Trade Unionism* (New York, 1960), pp. 249–250, 255–256.

Dwight D. Eisenhower

22. The army again hired dockworkers in the open market, as temporary civil service employees, to load and unload troop and cargo ships in the Port of New York, beginning March 16, 1954, during a strike of longshoremen and other harbor workers who belonged to the International Longshoremen's Association (independent). The union was then engaged in a fight for existence against a rival "clean union" sponsored by the AFL. As in 1951, the army employed dockworkers directly as government employees rather than indirectly as the (private) employees of stevedoring contractors. This made any strike at army piers unlawful. A. H. Raskin, "Government Sets Tough Pier Policy," the *New York Times,* Mar. 16, 1954, p. 1. *National Emergency Disputes Under the Labor Management Relations Act, 1947–62,* BLS Report No. 169, Washington, revised 1963, p. 13. For background, see Daniel Bell, "Some Aspects of the New York Longshore Situation," *I.R.R.A. 7th Annual Proceedings 1954* (Madison, Wis., 1955), pp. 298–304.

John F. Kennedy

23. In August 1963, at the request of the president, Congress forbade any strike or lockout for 180 days on the nation's railroads over the unresolved work-rules dispute that had originated in 1959–1960. The action was taken on the eve of a scheduled strike. Although the president recommended that Congress require settlement of all outstanding issues by the ICC, Congress created a special board of arbitration to make a final determination of the two key issues (the firemen issue and the crew-consist issue) and directed the parties to resume collective bargaining over the remaining matters in controversy. The award of the arbitration board was made final and binding for two years. Railroad Arbitration Act, 77 Stat. 132; upheld in *Brotherhood of Locomotive Firemen* v. *Certain Carriers,* and *Brotherhood of Locomotive Engineers* v. *Certain Carriers,* 331 Fed. (2d) 1020; cert. denied, 377 U.S. 918. Theodore C. Sorensen, *Kennedy* (New York, 1965), pp. 441–443.

APPENDIX D

Enforcement of Contested Rulings in 49 Seizures[a]

Management noncompliance cases

(Rulings issued prior to seizure, except as indicated by[d] in column 3)

Case no.	Property seized	Source of ruling	Subject of ruling[b]	Seizing and operating agency	Ruling observed during govt. poss.	Ultimate compliance[c]
	1918					
3	Wire systems (Western Union noncompliant)	NWLB	Sec.	P.O.	Ineffective	No
4	Smith & Wesson	NWLB	Sec.	War	Yes	No
	1941					
6	Federal Shipbuilding	NDMB	Sec.	Navy	No	No
8	Air Associates	NDMB	Sec.	War	Yes	Yes
	1942					
9	T.P. & W. R.R.	NWLB	Sec.-Wa.-Wk. load	ODT	Largely	No[e]
	T.P. & W. R.R.	NWLB[d]	Sec.-Wa.-Wk. load (M)	ODT	Largely	No[e]
	1943					
11	Woods Machine	NWLB	Sec.	War	Yes	No
	1944					
15	Atlantic Basin Iron	NWLB	Sec.	WSA	Yes	Yes
22	Jenkins Bros.	NWLB	Wa.	Navy	Yes	Yes

(Continued on next page.)

Case no.	Property seized	Source of ruling	Subject of ruling[b]	Seizing and operating agency	Ruling observed during govt. poss.	Ultimate compliance[e]
23	Ken-Rad Tube & Lamp	NWLB	Wa.-Sec.	War	Yes	Modified
24	Montgomery Ward (Chicago)	NWLB	Sec.	Commerce (War)	No	No[e]
25	Montgomery Ward (Hummer mfg.)	NWLB	Sec.-Wa.	War	Yes	Modified
27	Midwest trucking firms	NWLB	Wa.	ODT	Largely	No[e]
33	Hughes Tool	NWLB	Sec.-Rep.	War	Largely	No[e]
34	Twentieth Century Brass	NWLB	Wa.-Sec.	War	Yes	Modified
35	Farrell-Cheek Steel	NWLB	Sec.-Wa.	War	Yes	No
37	Cudahy Bros.	NWLB	Sec.	War	Yes	Modified
38	Montgomery Ward (7 cities)	NWLB	Sec.-Wa.-Gr.	War	Largely	No[e]
	Montgomery Ward (Chicago)	NWLB[d]	Gr. (M)	War	(Yes)	(Yes)
	1945					
45	Carter Coal, et al.	NWLB	Wa. (bitu.)	Interior	Yes: Carter (No: 3 smaller firms)	No[e] (No)
46	Cocker Machine	NWLB	Sec.	War	Yes	No
48	Gaffney Mfg.	NWLB	Sec.	War	Yes	No[e]
49	Mary-Leila Cotton	NWLB	Sec.	War	Yes	No
50	Humble Oil (Ingleside)	NWLB	Sec.	PAW	Ineffective	No[e]
51	Pure Oil (Cabin Creek)	V RWLB	Sec.	PAW	Ineffective	No[e]

Labor noncompliance cases
(Rulings issued prior to seizure, except as indicated by[d] in column 3)

	WSB	Wa.-Sec.	Commerce		
1952					
71 Steel mills	NWLB	Wa.	Navy	No	No[e]
1942					
10 General Cable (Bayonne)	NWLB		Interior	No	Yes
1943					
13 Coal mines (May)	NWLB	Wa. (bitu., interim)	Interior	Yes	No[e]
Coal mines (May)	NWLB[d]	Wa. (L) (bitu.)	Interior	Yes	No[e]
16 Coal mines (Nov.)	NWLB	Wa. (bitu.)	Interior	Largely	Modified
Coal mines (Nov.)	NWLB	Wa. (anth.)	Interior	Largely	Modified
Coal mines (Nov.)	F-F bd.[d]	Wa. (L-M) (travel time)	Interior	(No)	(No)
18 Western Electric (Point Breeze)	FEPC & NWLB	Gr. (race)	War	Largely	Modified
19 Railroads	Emerg. bd. (Stacy) & pres.	Wa. (BLFE, ORC, SUNA)	War	(No)	(Yes)
Railroads	Emerg. bd. (Shaw)	Wa. (non-ops)	War	No	Modified
1944					
26 Phila. Transportation	FEPC & NWLB	Gr. (race)	War	Yes	Yes

(Continued on next page.)

Case no.	Property seized	Source of ruling	Subject of ruling[b]	Seizing and operating agency	Ruling observed during govt. poss.	Ultimate compliance[e]
28	San Francisco machine shops	NWLB	Hr.	Navy	Yes	No[e]
32	Cleveland Bronze	NWLB	Gr.	War	No	Modified
	1945					
40	Bingham & Garfield Ry.	Emerg. bd.	Gr. (wk. load)	War	Yes	No
42	Coal mines	NWLB	Wa. (bitu., interim)	Interior	(Yes)	(Yes)
	Coal mines	NWLB[d]	Wa. (L) (bitu.)	Interior	No	Yes
	Coal mines	NWLB	Wa. (anth., interim)	Interior	(No)	(No)
	Coal mines	NWLB[d]	Wa. (L) (anth.)	Interior	No	Yes
44	United Engineering Co., Ltd.	NWLB	Gr. (jur.)	Navy	Yes	No[e]
47	Chicago trucking firms	NWLB	Wa.	ODT (War)	Yes	Yes
57	Springfield Plywood	WCLC	Gr. (rep.)	War	Effectively	Yes
59	Illinois Central R.R.	Emerg. bd.	Gr. (jur.)	ODT	No	No
	1946					
65	Railroads	Emerg. bd.	Wa. (BLE, BRT)	ODT	No	Modified by pres.

Railroads	Bd. arb.	Wa. (BLFE, ORC, SUNA)	ODT	No	Modified by pres.
Railroads	Bd. arb.	Wa. (non-ops)	ODT	No	Modified by pres.
67 Monongahela Connecting R.R.	Emerg. bd. & pres.	Wa. (BRT)	ODT	Yes	Yes
1948					
68 Railroads	Emerg. bd.	Wa. (BLFE, BLE, SUNA)	Army	No	Effectively
1950					
69 Railroads	Emerg. bd.	Wa. (SUNA)	Army	No	Modified at White House
Railroads	Emerg. bd.	Wa. (BRT, ORC)	Army	No	Modified at White House
Railroads	Emerg. bd.	Wa. (RYA)	Army	No	Modified at White House
Railroads	Emerg. bd.[d]	Wa. (L) (BLFE)	Army	(No)	(Yes)

Both labor and management noncompliant
(Ruling issued prior to seizure)

1945					
41 American Enka	NWLB	Gr. (wa.)	War	No	Modified

(Continued on next page.)

Cases initially unadjudicated
(Rulings in main disputes, issued and defied during seizure)

Case no.	Property seized	Source of ruling	Subject of ruling[b]	Seizing and operating agency	Ruling observed during govt. poss.	Ultimate compliance[c]
	1917					
2	Railroads	R.R.[d] Wage Comm.	Wa. (L-M) (shopmen)	RRA	Largely	No[e]
	Railroads	Pres.[d]	Wa. (L) (shopmen)	RRA	(Yes)	(No)[e]
	1943					
17	Mass. tanneries	NWLB[d]	Gr. (rep.) (L)	War	Yes	Yes
	1944					
31	Soft coal mines (foremen)	NWLB[d]	Sec.-Wa. (L)	Interior	Yes	No[e]
	1945					
62	Great Lakes Towing	NWSB[d]	Gr. (hr.)- Wa. (M)	ODT	Largely	No[e]
	1946					
63	Meat-packing	F-F bd.[d] & NWSB[d]	Wa. (M)	Agric.	Yes	Yes
66	Soft coal mines	NWSB[d]	Wa. (L-M) Sec. (M)	Interior (Navy)	Yes	No[e]

a Each ruling in this table was rejected by one or both of the parties to the dispute, and so could not be effectuated, except by coercive action. The word "ruling" covers any decision on the merits by an emergency board or by the president, whether issued as "recommendations," "directive order," or other. Each ruling relates to the main dispute only. Where inconsistent results were obtained with regard to two or more rulings in the same seizure, the less significant result is enclosed in parentheses and is disregarded in statistical summaries of the table.

b Abbreviations: Sec. = union recognition and/or security; Wa. = wages and other compensation; Rep. = union rivalry over representation of employees; Jur. = union jurisdictional rivalry over work assignments; Hr. = hours of labor; Gr. = employee grievances under existing contract.

c "Ultimate compliance" is defined as settlement of the dispute during government possession in accordance with the contested ruling. A ruling is described as "modified" when its terms have been changed by the issuing authority or by the president, and agreed to by the parties, during government possession.

d This ruling was issued during government possession. Whether defying party was labor (L), management (M), or both (L-M), is indicated by the letters.

e A strike over the same dispute occurred within a short time after the return to private operation.

APPENDIX E

Emergency Disputes Fully Settled during Presidential Possession[a]

Case no. and classification[b]	Property seized	Agency ruling on the merits[c]	Agency mediating during govt. poss.	Seizing and operating agency	Subject of disputed	Length of govt. poss. in days[e]
	1864					
1 U	Phila. & Reading R.R.	None	None	War	Wa.	10
	1941					
5 U	North American Aviation	NDMB[f]	War	War	Wa.[g]	23
7 U	Alcoa freighters	NDMB[f]	MC	MC	Wa.[g]	52
8 M	Air Associates	NDMB	War	War	Sec.	59
	1942					
10 L	General Cable (Bayonne)	NWLB	Navy	Navy	Wa.	7
12 U	F.P. & E. R.R.	NWLB[h]	War & NWLB	War	Gr. (Rep.)	3
	1943					
14 U	American R.R. of P.R.	NWLB[f]	NWLB	ODT	Wa.	415
15 M	Atlantic Basin Iron	NWLB	NWLB	WSA	Sec.	18
16 L	Soft coal mines, Nov. (excluding Jewell Ridge Coal Co., which refused to accept settlement until approved by U.S. Supreme Court)	NWLB (mod.)	Interior	Interior	Wa.[g]	289
	Anthracite mines (Nov.)	NWLB (mod.)	Interior	Interior	Wa.[g]	

17 U	Mass. tanneries	NWLB[f]	War	War	Gr. (rep.)	20
18 L	Western Electric (Point Breeze)	NWLB & FEPC (mod.)	War	War	Gr. (race)	94
19 L	Railroads	Emerg. bd. (Stacy) & pres.	Pres. & War	War	Wa. (BLFE, ORC, SUNA)	23
	Railroads	Emerg. bd. (Shaw) (mod.)	Emerg. bd. (Shaw)	War	Wa. (non-ops)	
	1944					
20 U	Mass. textile mills	NWLB[f]	War	War	Gr. (jur.)	21
22 M	Jenkins Bros.	NWLB	Navy	Navy	Wa.	31
23 M	Ken-Rad	NWLB (mod.)	War	War	Wa.-Sec.[g]	41
25 M	Montgomery Ward (Hummer mfg.)	NWLB (mod.)	War	War	Sec.-Wa.	407
26 L	Phila. Transportation	NWLB & FEPC	War	War	Gr. (race)	14
30 U	International Nickel (West Virginia)	None	War	War	Gr.	46
32 L	Cleveland Bronze	NWLB (mod.)	War	War	Gr.	64
34 M	Twentieth Century Brass	NWLB (mod.)	War	War	Wa.-Sec.	161
36 U	Toledo machine shops	War[f]	War	War	Gr. (rep.)	3
37 M	Cudahy Bros.	NWLB (mod.)	War	War	Sec.	266

(Continued on next page.)

Case no. and classification[b]	Property seized	Agency ruling on the merits[e]	Agency mediating during govt. poss.	Seizing and operating agency	Subject of dispute[d]	Length of govt. poss. in days[e]
1945						
39 U	Cleveland Electric	None	War	War	Gr.	2
41 L-M	American Enka	NWLB (mod.)	War	War	Gr. (wa.)	108
42 L	Soft coal mines	NWLB & NWLB[f] & Sup. Ct.[f]	NWLB	Interior	Wa.[g]	74
	Anthracite mines	NWLB & Sup. Ct.[f] & NWLB[f]	Interior	Interior	Wa.[g]	(49)
47 L	Chicago trucking	NWLB	NWLB	ODT (War)	Wa.	84
52 U	Scranton Transit	None	ODT & RWLB III	ODT	Wa.	22
53 U	Diamond Alkali (Painesville, Ohio)	None	War	War	Gr.	28
55 U	Goodyear Rubber (Akron)	Arb.[f] & umpire[h]	Navy & NWLB	Navy	Gr.	56
57 L	Springfield Plywood	WCLC	War	War	Gr. (rep.)	36
58 U	U.S. Rubber (Detroit)	None	War	War	Gr. (rep.)	72
60 U	Oil refineries	F-F bd.[f]	Navy	Navy	Wa.	303
61 U	Capital Transit	Bd. Arb.[f]	ODT	ODT	Wa.	48
1946						
63 U	Meat-packing firms	F-F bd.[f] & NWSB[f]	Agric. & F-F bd.	Agric.	Wa.[g]	116

64 U	N.Y. Harbor tugboats	Bd. arb.[h]	Labor & mayor	ODT (Navy)	Wa.[g]	25
65 L	Railroads (excluding the Hudson & Manhattan, Monongahela Connecting, and a number of smaller lines, on which one party refused to accept the national agreement)	Emerg. bd. (mod. by pres.)	Pres.	ODT	Wa.[g] (BLE, BRT)	9
	Railroads	Bd. arb. (mod. by pres.)	Pres.	ODT	Wa.[g] (BLFE, ORC, SUNA)	
	Railroads	Bd. arb. (mod. by pres.)	Pres.	ODT	Wa.[g] (non-ops)	
	1948					
67 L	Monongahela Connecting R.R.	Emerg. bd. & pres.	ODT	ODT	Wa. (BRT)	59
68 L	Railroads	Emerg. bd.	Pres.	Army	Wa.[g] (BLFE, BLE, SUNA)	60
	1950					
69 L	Railroads	Emerg. bd. (mod. by pres.)	Pres.	Army	Wa.[g] (SUNA)	684
	Railroads	Emerg. bd. (mod. by pres.)	Pres.	Army	Wa.[g] (RYA)	

(Continued on next page.)

Case no. and classification[b]	Property seized	Agency ruling on the merits[c]	Agency mediating during govt. poss.	Seizing and operating agency	Subject of dispute[d]	Length of govt. poss. in days[e]
	Railroads	Emerg. bd. (mod. by pres.)	Pres. & NMB	Army	Wa.[g] (BRT, ORC)	
	Railroads	Arb.[f]	NMB	Army	Rules (BRT)	
	Railroads	Emerg. bd.[f]	Pres. & NMB	Army	Wa.[g] (BLFE)	
1951						
70 U	Steel company railroads; Aliquippa & Southern	Bd. arb.[f]	NMB	Army	Wa. (URW)	487
	Monongahela Connecting	Army[f]	NMB & Army	Army	Wa. (BRT)	
	Newburgh & South Shore	None	NMB	Army	Wa. (BRT, BLFE)	

[a] The term "fully settled" means that the disputing parties agreed during government possession either upon specific terms of labor or upon a peaceful method of settlement; that the president then relinquished possession, and the parties continued operations without interruption.

[b] Classification of seizures: M = management noncompliance; L = labor noncompliance; L-M = both parties noncompliant; U = unadjudicated at time of takeover.

[c] The federal agency ruled on the merits of the main dispute, either as a directive order, or a "recommendation," or as a judicial decision. If the ruling was prior to government possession, no letter follows the agency's abbreviation. "Mod." (modified), when used alone, indicates that the agency, during seizure, modified a ruling it had made before seizure. "Mod. by pres." means during seizure.

d Abbreviations: Wa. = wages and other compensation; Sec. = union recognition and/or union security; Gr. = employee grievances under existing contract; Rep. = representation of employees; Jur. = jurisdiction over jobs.

e In multifirm seizures, duration of possession was computed from date of seizure of the first firm to date of relinquishment of the last one. The median number of days was 50 and mean 108, for the 40 seizures listed.

f The ruling was during government possession.

g The wage settlement was accompanied or followed by compensatory increases in price ceilings, in approved utility rates, in terms of procurement contracts, or in government subsidies.

h The ruling was after termination of possession.

APPENDIX F
Emergency Disputes Not Settled during Presidential Possession[a]

Case no. and classification[b]	Property seized	Agency ruling on the merits[c]	Agency mediating during govt. poss.	Seizing and operating agency	Subject of disputed[d]	Length of govt. poss. in days[e]
	1917					
2 U	Railroads	R.R. Wage Comm.[f] & R.R. Adm.[f] & pres.[f] & R.R. lab. bd.[h]	Pres. & Congress	R.R. Adm.	Wa.	794[g]
	1918					
3 M	Wire systems (Western Union)	NWLB & P.O.[f]	None	P.O.	Sec.	365
4 M	Smith & Wesson	NWLB	None	War	Sec.	140
	1941					
6 M	Federal Shipbuilding	NDMB & NDMB[f]	Navy	Navy	Sec.	134
	1942					
9 M	T.P. & W. R.R.	NWLB & ODT[f] & NWLB[f]	ODT & NWLB	ODT	Sec.-Wa.- Wk. ld.	1,289[g]
11 M	Woods Machine Co.	NWLB	War	War	Sec.	1,107

Code	Company					
	1943					
13 L	Soft coal mines (May)	NWLB & NWLBf	Pres. & NWLB & Interior	Interior	Wa.	177g
	Anthracite mines (May)	None	NWLB	Interior	Wa.	
	1944					
21 U	Los Angeles Power (municipal)	None	War	War	Wa.	7
24 M	Montgomery Ward (Chicago)	NWLB & NLRBf	Pres.	Commerce (War)	Sec.	13g
27 M	Midwest trucking	NWLB	ODT	ODT	Wa.	446g
28 L	San Francisco machine shops	NWLB & Navyf	Navy & NWLB	Navy	Hr.	396g
29 U	Phila. & Reading Coal	None	None	Interior	Gr. (wa.)	236
31 U	Soft coal mines (foremen)	NWLBf	None	Interior	Sec.-Wa.	176g
33 M	Hughes Tool	NLRB & NWLB & CCA-Vf	War	War	Sec.-Rep.	357g
35 M	Farrell-Cheek Steel	NWLB	War	War	Sec.-Wa.	337
38 M	Montgomery Ward (7 cities)	NWLB & NWLBf	None	War	Sec.-Wa.-Gr.	294g
	1945					
40 L	Bingham & Garfield Ry.	Emerg. bd.	War	War	Gr. (wk. ld.)	215g
43 U	Cities Service Refinery (Lake Charles, Louisiana)	None	None	PAW (War)	Housing rentals	249
44 L	United Engineering Co., Ltd.	NWLB & NWLBf	None	Navy	Gr. (jur.)	133g

(Continued on next page.)

Case no. and classification[b]	Property seized	Agency ruling on the merits[c]	Agency mediating during govt. poss.	Seizing and operating agency	Subject of disputed[d]	Length of govt. poss. in days[e]
45 M	Carter Coal, et al.	NWLB	None	Interior	Wa.	328[g]
46 M	Cocker Machine	NWLB	War	War	Sec.	104
48 M	Gaffney Mfg. Co.	NWLB	War	War	Sec.	104[g]
49 M	Mary-Leila Cotton	NWLB	War	War	Sec.	90
50 M	Humble Oil (Ingleside)	NWLB	None	PAW	Sec.	96[g]
51 M	Pure Oil (Cabin Creek)	V RWLB	None	PAW	Sec.	95[g]
54 U	Texas Co. (Port Arthur)	None	NWLB	PAW	Wa.	71[g]
56 U	Sinclair Rubber	None	None	PAW	Sec.-Rep.	123
59 L	Illinois Central R.R.	Emerg. bd.	None	ODT	Gr. (jur.)	276
62 U	Great Lakes Towing	NWSB[f]	Labor	ODT	Gr. (hr.)-Wa.	394[g]
1946						
66 U	Soft coal mines	NWSB[f] & umpire[f]	Interior (Navy)	Interior (Navy)	Wa.	404[g]
1952						
71 M	Steel mills	WSB	Pres. & WSB & Commerce	Commerce	Wa.-Sec.	54[g]

a The "emergency disputes" are those which induced the seizures. In the longer seizures other disputes arose coincidentally, and were in most cases fully settled.

b c d Same as Appendix E.

e The median number of days of government possession was 215, and the mean 290, for the 31 seizures listed.

f The ruling was during government possession.

g A strike over the same dispute occurred shortly after the return to private operation.

h The ruling was after termination of possession.

SEIZURE AND OTHER FORMS OF CONTROL
IN EMERGENCY DISPUTES

1. The Great Northern R.R. was "offered" to the government by its president, James J. Hill, during the strike of July 1894; and General Wesley Merritt, commanding the Department of Dakota, threatened to seize trains of this road to move his troops. See *Annual Report of Secretary of War for 1894*, pp. 126–128. Members of the United Mine Workers of America urged President Wilson to seize the Colorado coal mines in Sept. 1914. B. M. Rich, *The Presidents and Civil Disorder* (Washington, 1941), pp. 148–149; *New York Times*, Oct. 24, 1914, p. 10; Nov. 25, 1914, p. 12. President Wilson asked Congress twice in 1916 to grant him power to seize the railroads in case of a nationwide strike, but Congress refused to grant this, except in war (addresses before Congress Aug. 29, 1916, and Dec. 5, 1916). In the rail crisis of July 1963, President Kennedy informed Congress that he had rejected the use of seizure "as unjustified in the circumstances of this case." 109 Congressional Record 13004. The 1902 seizure threat is described later in this chapter.

2. See Rich, *The Presidents and Civil Disorder;* F. T. Wilson, *Federal Aid in Domestic Disturbances* (Washington, 1922), S. Doc. 263, 67th Cong., 2d sess.; and Major General J. M. Schofield, *Forty-Six Years in the Army* (New York, 1897), chap. 28.

3. This earliest known presidential intervention in a labor dispute was discovered by Prof. Richard B. Morris of Columbia University. See his "Andrew Jackson, Strikebreaker," in *American Historical Review*, Oct. 1949, pp. 54–68.

4. Edward Berman, *Labor Disputes and the President of the United States* (New York, 1924), Columbia University Studies in History, Economics and Public Law No. 249, pp. 90–91.

5. Basil L. Lee, *Discontent in New York City, 1861–1865* (Washington, 1943), pp. 99–102.

6. Emerson D. Fite, *Social and Industrial Conditions in the North During the Civil War* (New York, 1910), pp. 203, 211. *War of the Rebellion; Official Records* (Washington, 1880–1901), series III, vol. V, pp. 67–68. Jay V. Hare, "History of the Reading," *The Pilot* (monthly publication of the P. & R. Ry. department of the YMCA), Jan. 1911, pp. 5–6 (made available to the author by Douglas M. Klink of Philadelphia).

7. Charles E. Smith to Major General George Cadwalader, July 18, 1864, in National Archives, U.S. Army Command, Department of Susquehanna, Letters Received (RG98). Text of letter in full in Chapter 7 of this volume.

8. Philip Taft, *Organized Labor in American History* (New York, 1964), pp. 58–59.

9. *U.S. v. Stevens et al.*, 27 Fed. Cas. 1312–1321, No. 16392. See also Taft, *Organized Labor in American History*, p. 76.

10. Repeated in 1919, 1946, 1951, and 1954.

11. Railroad and Telegraph Control Act, approved Jan. 31, 1862 (12 Stat. 334). Executive orders of Feb. 11, 1862, *War of Rebellion; Official Records,* series III, vol. V, p. 974; and May 25, 1962, *War of Rebellion,* series III, vol. II, pp. 69–70. See also interpretation of these executive orders in "Annual Report of Secretary of War for 1862," *War of Rebellion,* series III, vol. II, pp. 905–906, and explanations by Quartermaster General Meigs in his annual reports to secretary of war for 1862 and 1864.

12. Executive order of July 7, 1894, placing transcontinental railroads under military protection, and *Annual Report of Attorney General for 1896 (sic),* appendix p. 230 (H. Doc. 9, 54th Cong., 2d sess.). Also proclamation of July 9, 1894, ordering all persons to cease unlawful obstruction of the railways.

13. 54 Congressional Record 16, 31 (also H. Doc. 1384, 64th Cong., 2d sess.).

14. Among the best studies of presidential mediation and voluntary arbitration in wartime are A. M. Bing, *War-time Strikes and Their Adjustment* (New York, 1921); Joel Seidman, *American Labor from Defense to Reconversion* (Chicago, 1953); Chalmers, Derber, and McPherson (eds.), *Problems and Policies of Dispute Settlement and Wage Stabilization During World War II,* BLS Bulletin, no. 1009 (Washington, 1950); and George W. Taylor, *Government Regulation of Industrial Relations* (New York, 1948), chaps. 3, 4. Among the best studies of presidential mediation, and of the less frequent use of voluntary arbitration by presidential boards, in peacetime are Berman, *Labor Disputes and the President;* Bernstein, Enarson, and Fleming (eds.), *Emergency Disputes and National Policy* (New York, 1955); Herbert R. Northrup and Gordon F. Bloom, *Government and Labor* (Homewood, Illinois, 1963), chaps. 10–13, 15; and David L. Cole, *The Quest for Industrial Peace* (New York, 1963), chap. 2. In most of these studies, the use of required production is alluded to, without systematic and comprehensive treatment in a separate category.

15. Samuel Yellen, *American Labor Struggles* (New York, 1936), reissued 1956, p. 162.

16. Mark Sullivan, *Our Times, vol. II: America Finding Herself* (New York, 1927), pp. 430–435.

17. Sullivan, *Our Times,* pp. 435–438. Theodore Roosevelt, *Autobiography* (New York, 1913), pp. 504–518, esp. p. 514.

18. Sullivan, *Our Times,* pp. 438–443. Yellen, *American Labor Struggles,* pp. 167–170.

19. For example, Jacob J. Kaufman, "Emergency Boards Under the Railway Labor Act," *Labor Law Journal,* Dec. 1958, pp. 910–920, 949; and Thomas J. McDermott, "Use of Fact-Finding Boards in Labor Disputes," *Labor Law Journal,* Apr. 1960, pp. 285–304.

20. Northrup and Bloom, *Government and Labor,* pp. 368–369; James J. Healy (ed.), *Creative Collective Bargaining* (New York, 1965), pp. 202–205, 213–216; Joseph P. Goldberg, George W. Taylor and John Perry Horlacher, articles in the *Annals of the American Academy,* Jan. 1961.

21. Wilson's public statements of Aug. 25, 1919, and Oct. 24, 1919. Berman, *Labor Disputes and the President,* pp. 161, 179; Bing, *War-time Strikes,* pp. 93, 99.

22. The nonseizure statutes were upheld in *Wilson* v. *New,* 243 U.S. 332 (1917), and in *BLFE* v. *Certain Carriers* and *BLE* v. *Certain Carriers,* 331 F.2d 1020, cert. denied, 377 U.S. 918 (1964). The seizure statutes were upheld in *State of North Dakota* v. *Northern Pacific Railway Co.,* 250 U.S. 135 (1919), *State of South Dakota* v. *Dakota Central Telephone Co.,* 250 U.S. 163 (1919), *Ken-Rad Tube & Lamp Corp.* v. *Badeau,* 55 Fed. Supp. 193 (1944), and other cases cited in App. C of my unpub. diss., Harvard Univ., 1957.

23. Clinton L. Rossiter, *Constitutional Dictatorship* (Princeton, N.J., 1948), p. 245.

24. *Missouri Pacific* v. *Ault,* 256 U.S. 554, at 559, 561 (1921). Also, Justice Frankfurter in *U.S.* v. *United Mine Workers,* 330 U.S. 258, at 320–321 (1947).

25. *North Carolina R.R.* v. *Lee,* 260 U.S. 16 (1922).

26. "Seizure in Emergency Disputes," in Bernstein, *Emergency Disputes and National Policy,* p. 228.

27. John H. Ohly, "History of Plant Seizures During World War II . . . by the War Department" (1946), MS., chap. 8, in Office of Chief of Military History, Department of the Army. Cited hereafter as Ohly MS.

28. *The Constitution of the United States of America—Analysis and Interpretation* (Washington, 1953), S. Doc. 170, 82d Cong., 2d sess., p. 494.

29. *Youngstown Sheet & Tube Co.* v. *Sawyer,* 343 U.S. 579. Harry S Truman, *Memoirs, vol. II: Years of Trial and Hope* (Garden City, N.Y., 1956), chap. 29.

30. Unsuccessful appeals are cited in Chapter 10.

CHAPTER 2

THE RESISTANCE OF LABOR AND MANAGEMENT
TO SEIZURE CONTROL

1. This belief in the prompt acceptance of the president's authority by the disputants in seizure cases is found mostly in textbooks, but it may have been encouraged by former officials of the second National War Labor Board. See, for example, the board's *Termination Report* (Washington, 1947–1949), vol. I, p. xxix; also, *Problems and Policies of Dispute Settlement and Wage Stabilization During World War II, BLS Bulletin,* no. 1009 (Washington, 1950), p. 59, wherein the authors, while granting several exceptions, let rosy generalizations prevail.

2. At least 105 instances of obstruction occurred in the 46 seizure cases referred to. Of the 105 instances, 76 were due to labor's resistance, and 29 to management's.

3. The number of seizures in which some or all employees resisted the president's authority at the outset (by refusing to end the strike, for instance)

was 24, and the number in which some or all of the company executives resisted at the outset (by refusing to serve as agent of the government) was 16. This includes two seizures in which some elements of both labor and management refused to cooperate—American R.R. of Porto Rico, and the second Montgomery Ward seizure (Dec. 1944).

4. Of the 105 situations of resistance referred to in Note 2, 68 related to the main disputes and 37 to coincidental ones. The resistance over the main disputes occurred in 45 of the 46 seizure cases involving resistance. (The exception was Farrell-Cheek Steel.) By contrast, the resistance over coincidental matters was confined to 11 of the 46 seizures, because of the tendency for these to occur in multifirm operations. Of the 11 seizures, six were industry-wide and two were regional.

5. Seizure cases nos. 1, 5, 7, 12, 13, 16, 18, 20, 26, 28, 36, 42a, 44, 45, 47, 63, 64, 66, 69, and Ward's St. Paul store in no. 38. (Seizure numbers are identified in Key List and Appendix A.)

6. Seizures 42a, 65, 68, 70.

7. One or more firms in each of seizures 2, 3, 13, 16, 17, 28, 31, 35, 38, 66, 69, 71, and sit-downs in 6 and 55.

8. Lockouts were effective for a time in seizures 6, 45 (three Kentucky mines permanently closed), 66 (some mines in Iowa), 70 (Moncon R.R.), 71 (after Judge Pine's decision). Attempts to close down were unsuccessful in seizures 23, 27 (Wilson S. & T. Co.), 48, 66 (Carter Coal Co.).

9. Seizures 3, 17, 28, 31, 36, 47, 51, 55, 56, 69.

10. 39 Stat. 619, at 645. The court cases upholding the president were: *U.S.* v. *Switchmen's Union*, 97 Fed. Supp. 97; and *U.S.* v. *Brotherhood of Locomotive Firemen & Enginemen et al.*, 29 Labor Relations Reference Manual 2536 (hereafter referred to as LRRM); preliminary injunction 21 Labor Cases par. 66,895, and 104 Fed. Supp. 741; held moot, 343 U.S. 971 (June 9, 1952).

11. Independent union, Point Breeze (Maryland) plant, Western Electric Co., 1943; Lodge 68, IAM, in San Francisco machine shops and at United Engineering Co., Ltd., in 1944; Mechanics' Educational Society in Toledo machine shops, 1944; Chicago truck drivers' Local 705 (independent), 1945; and the railroad trainmen and engineers in 1946.

12. See, for example, *New York Times*, May 17, 1945, p. 20; June 26, 1945, p. 34.

13. See George W. Taylor, *Government Regulation of Industrial Relations* (New York, 1948), p. 155; Rear Admiral Harold G. Bowen, report to Undersecretary of Navy Forrestal, Sept. 25, 1944 (processed), pp. 8, 12, in Naval Records Management Center, Arlington, Va., Job no. 1666; the same report is drawn upon in Admiral Bowen's *Ships, Machinery and Mossbacks* (Princeton, 1954), pp. 287–289, 293–294.

14. *New York Times*, May 30, 1946, p. 5; *U.S. News*, June 7, 1946, pp. 71–74; A. F. Whitney, *Railroad Rules-Wage Movements in the U.S. 1944–46* (Cleveland, July 1, 1946), pp. 84–91. The ODT had formally requested the brotherhoods to call off the scheduled strike, and the brotherhoods had refused,

when the president asked them to postpone it. ODT, *Civilian War Transport*, (Washington, 1948), p. 278.

15. *New York Times,* Sept. 2, 1944, p. 13; Sept. 8, 1944, p. 32; Sept. 10, 1944, p. 33.

16. The rail seizure of 1950–1952.

17. This view of Lewis' tactics is widely held. C. E. Warne says, "Lewis was anxious not to violate the Smith-Connally act; thus he was establishing grounds for voiding his contract." *Labor in Postwar America* (Brooklyn, N.Y., 1949), p. 375. President Truman wrote in his personal diary on Dec. 11, 1946: "Mr. Lewis called his strike by a subterfuge in order to avoid prosecutions under the Smith-Connally act [WLDA]. But he will be prosecuted nevertheless." Wm. Hillman (ed.), *Mr. President* (New York, 1952), pp. 128–29. First the U.S. District Court and then the U.S. Supreme Court ruled that Lewis' letter of Nov. 15, 1946, to the miners was an illegal strike notice. (19 LRRM 2082; 330 U.S. 258.) The text of Lewis' letter may be found at 19 LRRM 2082, 2123, and in 70 Fed. Supp. 45.

18. The words quoted are from the findings of Judge T. Alan Goldsborough in the contempt case against Lewis, Dec. 3, 1946 (19 LRRM 2082), and repeated in his opinion accompanying the preliminary injunction, Dec. 4, 1946 (19 LRRM 2121, 2124), but the same idea is expressed, less crisply, in the temporary restraining order of Nov. 18, 1946 (19 LRRM 2059).

19. The text of Judge Goldsborough's temporary restraining order of Nov. 18, 1946, and his accompanying opinion will be found in 19 LRRM 2059. The order alone is available in *U.S.* v. *United Mine Workers and John L. Lewis,* 330 U.S. 258 (footnote on p. 5 of Chief Justice Vinson's opinion), and in E. A. Wieck, *The Miners' Case and the Public Interest* (New York, 1947), p. 81.

20. Text of Judge Goldsborough's opinion in the contempt case is at 70 Fed. Supp. 42, 45, and 19 LRRM 2079. Text of his judgment and sentences at 19 LRRM 2086.

21. *U.S.* v. *United Mine Workers of America and John L. Lewis,* 330 U.S. 258. On Lewis' compliance with the Supreme Court order, see Wieck, *The Miners' Case and the Public Interest,* pp. 36–39.

22. See 19 LRRM 2082 (Judge Goldsborough) and 330 U.S. 258, at 290 (p. 28 of Chief Justice Vinson's opinion). The majority report of the Senate Committee on Labor and Public Welfare of the 80th Congress also termed Lewis' actions "undoubtedly a breach of the criminal provisions" of the WLDA. S. Rept. 105, 80th Cong., 1st sess. (Apr. 1947), pp. 14–15; quoted in Irving Bernstein *et al.* (eds.), *Emergency Disputes and National Policy* (New York, 1955), p. 102.

23. See report of House Committee on Education and Labor, H. R. 7408, June 30, 1952: H. Rept. 2368, 82d Cong., 2d sess.

24. Despatch from Chicago in *New York Times,* Feb. 8, 1951.

25. Despatch from Chicago in *Christian Science Monitor,* Feb. 7, 1951.

26. (96 Fed. Supp. 428–437, oral and written opinion; 27 LRRM 2308, oral opinion; *New York Times,* Feb. 10, 1951, p. 1, excerpts from oral opinion.) The first plea of guilty was entered in the District of Columbia Federal Court

before Judge Edward A. Tamm on Feb. 19, 1951, when fines of $75,000 were imposed (95 Fed. Supp. 1019; 27 LRRM 2358; *New York Times,* Feb. 20, 1951, p. 1). The second plea of guilty was entered in the federal court at Cleveland on Feb. 26, 1951, but sentence was not imposed until Oct. 15, 1951. The Cleveland sentence was $1,000 and one year's probation. (Dept. of the Army, Office of the Undersecretary, *Army Operation of the Rail Transportation Systems, Pursuant to Ex. Orders 10141 and 10155:* Report prepared by Office of the Undersecretary of the Army [Karl R. Bendetsen], Sept. 15, 1952 [processed], p. 49 and appendix A, p. 7. Cited hereafter as *Bendetsen Report.*)

27. Saul Alinsky, *John L. Lewis: An Unauthorized Biography* (New York, 1949), p. 303.

28. Samuel I. Rosenman (ed.), *Public Papers and Addresses of Franklin D. Roosevelt,* 1943 vol. (New York, 1950), pp. 265–266.

29. A slowdown in the riveting and welding shops at the Federal shipyard was overcome, but slowdowns on the Hudson & Manhattan R.R. and the Monongahela Connecting R.R., and at Universal Cyclops Steel Corp., won concessions.

30. Draft report of Admiral Bowen to Secretary of the Navy Knox in Navy Records Management Center, Arlington, Va., Job no. 1666. See also Admiral Bowen's *Ships, Machinery and Mossbacks,* pp. 209–210.

31. *New York Times,* June 3, 1946, p. 11.

32. Alinsky, *John L. Lewis: An Unauthorized Biography,* p. 330.

33. *Coal Age,* July 1945, p. 134.

34. National Mediation Board, closing digest of case no. A-3596; *Bendetsen Report,* p. 60; *Pittsburgh Post-Gazette,* Mar. 23, 1951, pp. 1, 11; Mar. 24, 1951, p. 6; *Railway Age,* Apr. 2, 1951, p. 64.

35. AP despatch from Pittsburgh in *New York Times,* May 4, 1952; *Bendetsen Report,* p. 58; *Pittsburgh Post-Gazette,* May 3, 1952, p. 3.

36. Ohly MS., chap. 13 and appendix S; also pp. 270–271.

37. Interview with L. Byron Cherry, former counsel for the Carter Coal Co., in New York City, Sept. 28, 1955.

38. Ohly MS., chap. 17; *Chicago Tribune,* Aug. 2–3, 1945.

39. Insubordination by company executives occurred in seizures 2 (several railroads), 3 (Western Union Telegraph Co. and the Mackay Companies), 4, 6, 8, 9, 11, 14, 23, 24, 27 (Wilson Storage & Transfer Co. and Healzer Cartage Co.), 34, 38, 48, 50, 62, 65 (several railroads), 66 (Carter Coal Co., Fox Coal Co., and a majority of coal mine operators in Iowa).

40. Insubordination by production employees occurred in seizures 2 (certain railroad towboat captains), 6, 11, 25, 28, 33.

41. Since the names of labor leaders (and their unions) who defied the president's authority during seizure operations have been given, it seems only fair to name the corporations and their executives who also refused to obey the president's directives during seizure.

Postal Telegraph-Cable System, New York, N.Y. Clarence Mackay, president. A subsidiary of the Mackay Companies, also headed by Mr. Mackay. (One of the wire systems seized in 3.)

Federal Shipbuilding & Dry Dock Co., Kearny, N.J. Lynn H. Korndorff, president. A subsidiary of United States Steel Corp., Irving S. Olds, chairman. (6)

Toledo, Peoria & Western R.R., Peoria, Ill. George P. McNear, Jr., president and sole owner. (9)

S. A. Woods Machine Co., Boston, Mass. Harry C. Dodge, president and principal owner. (11)

Ken-Rad Tube & Lamp Corp., Owensboro, Ky. Roy Burlew, president and principal owner. (23)

Montgomery Ward & Co., Chicago, Ill. Sewell Avery, chairman. (Chicago facilities in 24; Chicago and six other cities in 38.)

Gaffney Manufacturing Co., Gaffney, S.C. Controlled by Deering-Milliken Co., New York, N.Y. (48)

Humble Oil & Refining Co., Houston, Tex. Harry C. Weiss, president. A subsidiary of Standard Oil Co. (N.J.), Eugene Holman, president. (50)

Fox Coal Co., Morgantown, W. Va. Ralph A. Fox, president and sole owner. (One of the mines seized in 66.)

42. Preliminary and interim reports of the officer in charge, Rear Admiral H. G. Bowen, to the secretary of the navy, Sept. 25, 1944, and Apr. 10, 1945; Bowen, *Ships, Machinery and Mossbacks*, pp. 282–335.

43. *New York Times*, Apr. 5, 1919, p. 24; Apr. 8, p. 8; Apr. 13, p. 14; Apr. 17, p. 1; Apr. 20, p. 13.

44. Interview with Kingsland Dunwoody, vice-president of S. A. Woods Machine Co., in Boston, May 28, 1953.

45. A list of the 17 suits to prevent seizure, together with the disposition of each, will be found in App. C of the author's unpub. diss., Harvard University, 1957.

46. *Humble Oil & Refining Co.* v. *Eighth Regional War Labor Board et al.,* 56 Fed. Supp. 950; reversed, 145 F.2d 462; cert. denied, 325 U.S. 883.

47. The leading cases were: *Baltimore Transit Co.* v. *Flynn,* 50 Fed. Supp. 382; not appealed. *Employers' Group of Motor Freight Carriers* v. *National War Labor Board,* 143 F.2d 145; cert. denied, 323 U.S. 735.

48. Quoted by Court of Appeals, District of Columbia, in *Montgomery Ward & Co.* v. *NWLB,* 144 F.2d 528, 530 note, July 19, 1944.

49. *Montgomery Ward & Co.* v. *NWLB* (facilities at Detroit, Denver, and Jamaica, New York), 15 War Lab. Rep. 719; 56 Fed. Supp. 502; reversed, 144 F.2d 528; cert. denied, 323 U.S. 774 (Nov. 13, 1944); immediately seized (seizure 38).

50. Montgomery Ward, Chicago facilities, Apr. 1944; Hummer manufacturing division, May 1944. Twentieth Century Brass Works, Minneapolis, Sept. 1944. Farrell-Cheek Steel Co., Sandusky, Ohio, Sept. 1944.

51. Cudahy Bros. Co., Cudahy, Wisconsin, strike voted Nov. 22, 1944, seizure Dec. 8, 1944. Humble Oil & Refining Co., Ingleside, Texas, strike voted Nov. 16, 1944, seizure delayed until June 6, 1945.

52. Hughes Tool Co., Houston, Texas, 56 NLRB 981 (Aug. 8, 1944), seizure Sept. 6, 1944. Also see Ohly MS., appendix Z-3-a.

53. *United States Gypsum Co.* v. *National War Labor Board* (plant at Warren, Ohio), 145 F.2d 97; cert. denied, 324 U.S. 856 (March 12, 1945).

54. See note 46.

55. The 12 legal moves involving possible termination of specific seizures, together with the disposition of each case, are listed in the author's unpub. diss., App. C. Eight are designated in notes 57 and 58 below.

56. *Youngstown Sheet & Tube Co. et al.* v. *Charles Sawyer,* 103 Fed. Supp. 569; cert. granted, 343 U.S. 937; affirmed, 343 U.S. 579 (June 2, 1952).

57. Five seizures held unlawful by U.S. district courts: *U.S.* v. *Montgomery Ward & Co.* (seizure 38), 58 Fed. Supp. 408; reversed, 150 F.2d 369; held moot, 326 U.S. 690. *Toledo, Peoria & Western R.R.* v. *Stover* (seizure 9), 60 Fed. Supp. 587; held moot (ODT, *Civilian War Transport,* pp. 232–233). *Humble Oil & Refining Co.* v. *Granger* (seizure 50), unreported; later set aside; affirmed C.C.A. 5 (*Oil & Gas Journal,* June 1945; records of PAW in National Archives). *Fox Coal Co.* v. *Krug* (seizure 66), 70 Fed. Supp. 721; reversed, 161 F.2d 1013. *Youngstown Sheet & Tube Co.* v. *Sawyer* (seizure 71), 103 Fed. Supp. 569; affirmed, 343 U.S. 579.

58. Three seizures held valid by U.S. district courts: *Commercial Cable Co.* v. *Burleson and Carlton* (cables in seizure 3), 255 Fed. 99; held moot, 250 U.S. 360. *Jenkins Bros.* v. *National War Labor Board* (seizure 22), 15 War Lab. Rep. 719; 8 Labor Cases par. 62,128. *Ken-Rad Tube & Lamp Corp.* v. *Badeau* (seizure 23), 55 Fed. Supp. 193; not appealed.

59. *Chicago Daily News,* June 9, 1945, p. 3; June 12, 1945, p. 3; *Chicago Tribune,* June 26, 27, 1945, p. 1.

60. 197 F.2d 582; 343 U.S. 937; H. Doc. 534, 82d Cong., 2d sess., parts I and II, pp. 442–449, 456–561.

61. E. S. Corwin, *The Constitution and What It Means Today,* 8th ed. (Princeton, 1946), pp. 68–69, 120–121; E. S. Corwin, *The President—Office and Powers,* 3d ed. (New York, 1948), pp. 178–182, 307, 350–353; Mark Sullivan, *Our Times* (New York, 1927), vol. II, p. 436.

62. Bowen, *Ships, Machinery and Mossbacks,* pp. 309–310.

63. Records of PAW in National Archives.

64. Press conferences of Apr. 17 and 24, 1952.

65. Letter to Charles S. (Casey) Jones, of Washington Crossing, Pennsylvania, Apr. 27, 1952 (98 Congressional Record 4474); and press conference of May 22, 1951.

66. Harold L. Enarson, "The Politics of an Emergency Dispute," in Bernstein, *Emergency Disputes and National Policy,* p. 67.

67. William H. Davis to Frederick Van Nuys, June 9, 1943, in *Termination Report of NWLB,* vol. II, p. 461.

68. Ohly MS., pp. 397–399, and appendix W-1 through W-8.

69. On the continuance of public criticism and normal elections in wartime, compare S. E. Morison and H. S. Commager, *The Growth of the*

American Republic, 4th ed. (New York, 1950), vol. I, pp. 699–702, 731–733, vol. II, pp. 473–477.

70. Tom Connally, *My Name Is Tom Connally* (New York, 1954), pp. 252–253.

71. *National and Emergency Labor Disputes,* hearings on S. 2999 and S. 3016, 82d Cong., 2d sess., pp. 209–211, 237 (Apr. 22, 1952).

CHAPTER 3

METHODS OF OVERCOMING RESISTANCE
TO SEIZURE CONTROL

1. Ludwig Teller refers to the face-saving effect of seizure in his classic legal analysis, "Government Seizure in Labor Disputes," *Harvard Law Review,* Sept. 1947: "Seizure did in many cases, however, provide a face-saving excuse for terminating a strike or delaying it pending further negotiations or mediation," p. 1054. Joseph L. Miller described it in the following terms at the first annual convention of the Industrial Relations Research Association (Dec., 1948): "Sometimes management and sometimes labor wanted seizures to 'bail them out' when they had taken an untenable position." *Proceedings, IRRA,* p. 96.

2. Admiral Harold G. Bowen's reports to the Navy Department; also, his *Ships, Machinery and Mossbacks* (Princeton, 1954), pp. 209, 223.

3. *National Petroleum News,* Oct. 17, 1945, p. 7; Oct. 24, 1945, p. 6.

4. The military preparations in the railroad seizure are described in Chester Wardlow, *The Transportation Corps* (Washington, 1951), pp. 350–352, and in Ohly MS., pp. 206–211; those in the Los Angeles Water and Power Department in Ohly MS., p. 220.

5. Reports of PAW officials in National Archives, Record Group 253; Ohly MS., pp. 542–543.

6. I am indebted to Commander Joseph L. Miller, USNR, for the information on the seized oil properties in Oct. 1945, and to the *New York Times,* June 15, 1946, p. 12, for the Monongahela seizure.

7. Samuel I. Rosenman (ed.), *Private Papers and Addresses, Franklin Delano Roosevelt,* 1941 vol. (New York, 1950), p. 206; *New York Times,* June 10, 1941, p. 16; Ex. Order 8773, 6 F. R. 2777.

8. The use of the retroactive principle by NWLB II is described in NWLB *Termination Report* (Washington, 1948–1949), vol. I, chap. 14. See "Pre-Determination of Retroactive Date," pp. 173–174.

9. Compare comments of L. K. Reynolds in NWLB *Termination Report,* vol. I, p. xxix and footnote.

10. Francis Biddle, *In Brief Authority* (New York, 1962), pp. 308, 324.

11. Ohly MS., pp. 348–352.

CHAPTER 4

THE EFFECTIVENESS OF SEIZURE
AS A MEANS OF CONTROL

1. Full voluntary cooperation by both labor and management: 25 seizures—10, 15, 19, 21, 29, 30, 32, 37, 39, 40, 41, 43, 46, 49, 51, 52, 53, 54, 56, 57, 58, 59, 60, 61, 67.

2. Presidential control obtained by coercive measures: 32 seizures—1, 4, 5, 6, 7, 8, 9, 11, 12, 14, 17, 18, 20, 22, 23, 25, 26, 27, 28, 31, 34, 35, 38, 44, 47, 48, 50, 55, 62, 64, 65, 68.

3. The three cases were railroads, 1917–1920 (2); Great Lakes Towing Co. (62); and bituminous coal mines, 1946–1947 (66). The management of Monongahela Connecting R.R. also withdrew its cooperation (70) when it found that the seizing agency was not suppressing a slowdown.

4. The 105 situations of resistance are identified in Tables II-4-7, II-4-8, and II-4-9 in the author's unpub. diss., Harvard University, 1957.

5. Initial loss of control has been followed in two seizures by the withdrawal (or reinterpretation) of the economic concessions originally made, and by strict and impartial measures which restored governmental authority. Therefore these cases, Fall River textile (20) and the railroads in 1946 (65), have been classed as successfully controlled.

6. The most extreme case (395 days) was the refusal of numerous employees to pay their union dues under a maintenance-of-membership order at Hummer manufacturing division of Montgomery Ward & Co.

7. Walker D. Hines, the director general of railroads during the postwar wave of strikes (1919), stated in his memoirs that all the strikes occurring in seized railroad property were of the "wildcat" variety, opposed by the national officers of the unions. He described his official policy this way: "Whenever the unauthorized strikes took place, the railroad administration took and maintained the position that the grievance assigned as the cause for the strike would not be considered until the employees returned to work, and that the grievance would then be considered on its merits." *War History of American Railroads* (New Haven, 1928), p. 183. At the time of a sympathy strike of train employees in California in Aug. 1919, Mr. Hines issued a proclamation requiring the men to return to work by a certain deadline or be discharged and replaced. The proclamation stated that "the only course which the government can adopt is to exercise its entire power for the purpose of rendering the public service, and the President [Wilson] has so instructed." Mr. Hines added, in the memoirs: "The proclamation was issued with the personal approval and hearty support of the president." *Ibid.*, p. 184; see also pp. 158–159, 174, 182–184, 309–310.

The most important expression of the concept was by Congress in the War Labor Disputes Act of June 25, 1943 (57 Stat. 163). By sec. 6 of this act, Congress made it illegal for anyone to induce or to participate in a strike in a seized plant, mine, or facility; and by secs. 4 and 5, it provided that no change should be made in the terms of employment during government possession, except by an orderly and peaceful procedure which it provided. Nothing could be clearer than that Congress intended by this law to make it a crime for a union leader to bargain with the president of the United States, or with his representative, over the terms under which he would consent to terminate a strike in seized facilities.

8. Presidential control not fully obtained: 14 seizures—2, 3, 13, 16, 24, 33, 36, 42, 45, 63, 66, 69, 70, 71.

9. Harry S Truman, *Memoirs, vol. I: Year of Decisions* (Garden City, N.Y., 1955), pp. 504–505. Note also John L. Lewis' reference to the situation of June 1943 as close to "rebellion," in his article, "Not Guilty!" in *Colliers*, July 15, 1944, p. 49.

CHAPTER 5

KEEPING PRODUCTION GOING

1. Lockouts occurred in seizures 6, 45, 66, 70, 71. Strikes occurred in initially unadjudicated disputes—1, 2, 5, 7, 12, 14, 17, 20, 31, 36, 55, 63, 64, 66, 70; management noncompliance cases—3, 6, 35, 38, 71; labor noncompliance cases—13, 16, 18, 26, 28, 42, 44, 45, 47, 65, 69.

2. Seizures in which there was resistance, but no stoppages: strikes threatened but averted—8, 33, 68; lockouts threatened but averted—9, 23, 27, 48, 66; no stoppages threatened—4, 11, 22, 24, 25, 34, 50, 62.

3. 58 Fed. Supp. 466 (1944). Harold G. Bowen, *Ships, Machinery and Mossbacks* (Princeton, N.J., 1954), pp. 308–320.

4. Ludwig Teller, "Government Seizure in Labor Disputes," *Harvard Law Review*, Sept. 1947, pp. 1043–1044.

5. Bowen, *Ships, Machinery and Mossbacks*, pp. 293–294. Ohly MS., *passim*.

6. *United States* v. *United Mine Workers of America*, 330 U.S. 258 (1947).

7. *United States* v. *Pewee Coal Co.*, 341 U.S. 114 (1951); *U.S.* v. *UMWA*.

8. Settlement agreement, dated April 27, 1955; records of Alcoa Steamship Co., New York, N.Y.

9. Sewell Avery to Major General David McCoach, Oct. 18, 1945, in Ohly MS., appendix V-41. McCoach to Avery, same date, Ohly MS., appendix V-42. Discussion in Ohly MS., pp. 385–389.

10. Motor Carrier Claims Commission Act, 62 Stat. 1222 (1948).

11. *U. S.* v. *Pewee Coal Co.* (1951); R-B Freight Lines, certiorari denied, 342 U.S. 933 (1952).

CHAPTER 6

ENFORCING PRESIDENTIAL LABOR DECISIONS

1. *Free and Responsible Collective Bargaining and Industrial Peace:* Report to the President from Advisory Committee on Labor-Management Policy, May 1, 1962 (Washington, D.C., 1962), p. 5.

2. The government took no position in cases having the following chronological numbers (see the Key List or Appendix A for identification)—1, 21, 29, 30, 39, 43, 52, 53, 54, 56, 58.

3. NWLB *Termination Report,* vol. I, pp. 51–52, 68–70, 425–426.

4. The contested rulings, which were outstanding in 43 seizures when the seizures began (the noncompliance cases), may be classified as:

Final rulings on the merits: specific grievances—3, 4, 18, 26, 40, 44, 57, 59; status of the union in the terms of contract—6, 11, 15, 25, 35, 37, 38, 46, 50, 51; wages in the terms of contract—10, 16, 19, 22, 23, 27, 34, 45, 47, 65, 67, 68, 69, 71.

Interim rulings on the merits (terms of expired contracts extended): wage terms—13, 42; status of union—24, 33, 48, 49; hours of work—28.

Interim rulings on the merits (final procedures of adjustment established): status of union in the companies' first labor contracts—8, 9; specific grievances —32, 41.

5. Consult A. M. Bing, *War-Time Strikes and Their Adjustment* (New York, 1920), and C. E. Warne (ed.), *Yearbook of American Labor, Volume I: War Labor Policies* (New York, 1945).

6. See study by Joseph W. Bishop, Jr., 1941, in Ohly MS., appendix F-1.

7. *Monthly Labor Review,* Oct. 1918, p. 24; *BLS Bulletin,* no. 287, p. 36. The War Department statement on S. & W. is extensively quoted in *Monthly Labor Review,* Oct. 1918, p. 27; it was published in full in *U.S. Official Bulletin* for Sept. 14, 1918.

8. The Navy Department's arrangements with Jenkins Valve were embodied in an exchange of letters. Company folders in files of general counsel, Navy Department, Washington. The text of the navy letter, or "order," is available in Admiral Harold G. Bowen's *Ships, Machinery and Mossbacks* (Princeton, 1954), pp. 279–282. It is possible that some face-saving arrangement was also worked out by the War Shipping Administration in the Atlantic Basin case, but the details of this seizure are unavailable.

9. John H. Ohly discusses the development of this face-saving technique by the War Department at the Hummer plant of Montgomery Ward & Co., and its subsequent applications and limitations, in his manuscript history of the War Department's seizures, chap. 14, esp. pp. 275–280.

10. Bowen, *Ships, Machinery and Mossbacks,* pp. 284, 289, 323. For further particulars, see "Order No. 3" dated Aug. 14, 1944, and a notice to the managements dated Sept. 26, 1944, in Admiral Bowen's final report to the secretary of the navy, dated Apr. 10, 1945, Records of Emergency Plants Operations Section, Executive Office of the Secretary (EXOS), Job No. 1666,

Naval Records Management Center, Arlington, Va. The NWLB order is in 15 War Lab. Rep. 630.

11. See, for example, W. M. Leiserson, "The Role of Government in Industrial Relations," in *Industrial Disputes and the Public Interest* (Berkeley and Los Angeles, 1947), pp. 38, 47; W. L. Morse, "The National War Labor Board, Its Powers and Duties," *Oregon Law Review,* Dec. 1942, pp. 4, 39; J. P. Frank, "The Future of Presidential Seizure," *Fortune,* July 1952, pp. 70–71; and B. F. Willcox and E. S. Landis, "Government Seizures in Labor Disputes," *Cornell Law Quarterly,* Winter 1948, pp. 159, 167.

12. Louis Ruchames, *Race, Jobs & Politics, the Story of FEPC* (New York, 1953), p. 198.

13. Ohly MS., appendix Z-1-a (JAG narrative).

14. Ruchames, *Race, Jobs & Politics,* pp. 196–198.

15. See Bing, *War-Time Strikes and Their Adjustment,* chap. 9; Vidkunn Ulriksson, *The Telegraphers* (Washington, 1953), chaps. 9–10.

16. National Archives, records of Department of Labor, obtained through courtesy of the late Justice Frankfurter.

17. See his reply to Professor Frankfurter in the *New York Times,* Mar. 21, 1919, p. 11, and his annual report to President Wilson for 1919, p. 55, which probably accounts for the inaccurate record in an able and distinguished work, Edward Berman, *Labor Disputes and the President of the United States* (New York, 1924), p. 145, wherein Mr. Berman says that the discriminatory discharges were soon halted as a result of the postmaster general's orders.

18. Bowen, *Ships, Machinery and Mossbacks,* p. 222. See also draft of final report by Admiral Bowen to Secretary Knox, esp. exhibit 31, which is a copy of the NDMB report, in records of Emergency Plants Operations Section, Executive Office of the Secretary of the Navy, Job No. 1666; consulted at Naval Records Management Center, Arlington, Va.; and Federal Shipbuilding and Dry Dock Co., *Chronological Statement of More Important Events Relating to Labor Situation at Federal Shipbuilding and Dry Dock Co., Kearny, N.J., May 8, 1942,* pp. 10, 13–14, 99–100, 147.

19. See his testimony before the House committee investigating the Montgomery Ward seizure; quoted in *Termination Report,* vol. II, p. 606. The error is repeated in one of the classic legal interpretations of seizure, Ludwig Teller, "Government Seizure in Labor Disputes," *Harvard Law Review,* Sept. 1947, p. 1022, and in Joel Seidman's excellent labor history of the war, *American Labor from Defense to Reconversion* (Chicago, 1953), p. 63.

20. Jesse H. Jones and Edward Angly, *Fifty Billion Dollars* (New York, 1951), pp. 48, 478. See also Bascom N. Timmons, *Jesse H. Jones; the Man and the Statesman* (New York, 1956), pp. 343–345; and Francis Biddle, *In Brief Authority* (New York, 1962), chap. 20, esp. p. 313.

21. *New York Times,* Sept. 13, 1945, p. 12.

22. Press releases PAW-714 (OWI-4509) and PAW-713 (OWI-4511), both for release June 6, 1945.

23. Affidavit in Civil No. 363, *Humble Oil & Refining Co.* v. *Gordon T.*

Granger, in U.S. District Court for Southern District of Texas (Galveston), dated June 9, 1945; copy examined in records of PAW (RG 253) in National Archives. The executive order of President Truman seizing Humble (no. 9564), which Mr. Ide cited, said in part: "The Petroleum Administrator shall operate the said plants and facilities pursuant to the provisions of the War Labor Disputes Act, and during his operation of the plants and facilities shall observe the terms and conditions of the directive order dated Apr. 1, 1944, of the National War Labor Board." (10 F. R. 6791.)

24. Deputy Petroleum Administrator Davies to William H. Davis, Director of OES, June 30, 1945, and July 7, 1945, in National Archives, records of PAW.

25. Correspondence in files of PAW (Record Group 253), National Archives. See *International Oil Worker,* Mar. 11, 1946, p. 11.

26. Ohly MS., 65–66, 69–70. See G. W. Taylor, *Government Regulation of Industrial Relations* (New York, 1948), 114–117.

27. Ohly MS., 103–105; *The Fifth Freedom,* a company pamphlet, 1943, p. 19; *New York Times,* Oct. 31, 1942, p. 17; Nov. 3, 1942, p. 30.

28. 4 War Lab. Rep. 276; minutes of NWLB meetings, Oct. 22 and Nov. 6, 1942.

29. Undersecretary of Navy Forrestal to H. G. Bowen, officer in charge, San Francisco machine shops, Aug. 30, 1944, in preliminary report of officer in charge, Sept. 25, 1944, p. 22; Bowen, *Ships, Machinery and Mossbacks,* p. 301.

30. Memo by John H. Ohly, Jan. 23, 1945, in Ohly MS., appendix T-10-f.

31. Taylor, *Government Regulation of Industrial Relations,* pp. 165–166.

32. Unfortunately, this press conference is omitted by Rosenman from the 220 conferences which he preserves for posterity in stenographic form in the *Public Papers and Addresses,* but it is available in the then customary indirect quotation in the *New York Times,* July 10, 1943, p. 1, and in *Coal Age,* Aug. 1943, p. 121.

33. Ohly MS., chap. 4, on Air Associates; final report of officer in charge to secretary of navy, Sept. 29, 1944, p. 7; and Bowen, *Ships, Machinery and Mossbacks,* pp. 279–282, on Jenkins Bros. The resistance of Jenkins Bros. collapsed after their suit to obtain a court injunction ordering a termination of seizure was denied.

34. See Ohly MS., p. 264, and appendix CC-13 (Ralph F. Gow to Undersecretary of War Patterson, Sept. 29, 1944).

35. Letter from Nellie Lee Bok (Mrs. Curtis Bok), *Survey Graphic,* Nov. 1944, p. 435.

36. The wage-adjustment subsidy was made possible by an increased allocation for meat-subsidy payments in the joint resolution of Mar. 21, 1946 (60 Stat. 57), and was authorized by OES directive 104 of Apr. 9, 1946 (text in *National Provisioner,* Apr. 13, 1946, p. 17) and by Department of Agriculture regulation of Apr. 22, 1946 (summary in *National Provisioner,* Apr. 27, 1946, pp. 7, 15).

37. The seven cases of ultimate compliance, after local modifications, were:

Western Electric, Ken-Rad Tube & Lamp, Hummer manufacturing division of Montgomery Ward, Cleveland Graphite Bronze, Twentieth Century Brass, Cudahy Bros., and American Enka Corp.

38. Ohly MS., pp. 261–262.

39. Taylor, *Government Regulation of Industrial Relations*, pp. 162n, 170; E. E. Witte, "Wartime Handling of Labor Disputes," *Harvard Business Review*, Winter 1947, p. 172.

40. Ohly MS., pp. 266–267 (seizure 23); 284–286 (25); 273 and appendix Z-2-a (34).

41. The influence of the seizure threat in inducing voluntary compliance with the decisions of presidential boards was noted by both National War Labor Boards in their official histories. *NWLB, A History, BLS Bulletin*, no. 287, p. 25; NWLB *Termination Report*, vol. I, pp. 419–420, 424.

CHAPTER 7

SETTLING THE DISPUTES

1. One of the most skeptical statements about seizure was made by the late Professor Sumner H. Slichter in 1948: "Government seizure of plants should be avoided—it settles nothing." *The American Economy* (New York, 1948), p. 48. Professor Slichter, who was the father of Massachusetts' choice-of-procedures law (1947), later adopted a more sympathetic attitude toward seizure. See his *What's Ahead for American Business?* (Boston, 1951), p. 111.

2. For example, Labor Study Group (Clark Kerr, chairman), *The Public Interest in National Labor Policy* (New York, 1961), pp. 101–102.

3. Ex. Order 9603 (3 CFR 1945 Supp. 107; 10 F. R. 10960; 2 Term. Rept. NWLB 88).

4. Ohly MS., appendix H-2; also text of MS., p. 36.

5. Ex. Order 8773 (3 CFR Cum. Supp. 943; 6 F. R. 2777; *BLS Bulletin*, no. 714, p. 158; Samuel I. Rosenman, *Papers of F.D.R.*, 1941 volume (New York, 1950), p. 206. In another early seizure, Roosevelt specified that government operation should continue until a settlement was reached, with NWLB approval (T.P. & W. R.R., 9—Ex. Order 9108, 3 CFR Cum. Supp. 1127).

6. C. J. Potter, deputy coal mines administrator, wrote in the *Annual Report of Secretary of Interior* for 1944 (p. 138): "Under the terms of this law, and under the existing circumstances, the mines were all returned to their owners by Oct. 12, 1943, although no wage contracts for their operation had been concluded." Text of the law is 57 Stat. 163; also in 2 Term. Rept. NWLB 80.

7. 40 Op. Atty. Gen. 306; 13 War Lab. Rep. ix; 12 LRRM 2210.

8. Statement filed with the subcommittee on labor-management relations of the Senate Committee on Labor and Public Welfare; published by the subcommittee as *Wartime Disputes Procedures*, p. 49.

9. Frank M. Kleiler, "Presidential Seizures in Labor Disputes," *Industrial and Labor Relations Review,* July 1953, p. 556; see also p. 553.

10. The theory of "equal pressures" during seizure has been expressed by Joseph L. Miller, "Disputes That Create a Public Emergency," IRRA, *1st Annual Proceedings 1948,* pp. 96–97 (applies "equal pressure" only to the unadjudicated disputes); B. F. Willcox and E. S. Landis, "Government Seizures in Labor Disputes," *Cornell Law Quarterly,* Winter 1948, pp. 175–176 ("hesitantly" balances wage freeze with ban on profits); LeRoy Marceau and Richard A. Musgrave, "Strikes in Essential Industries: A Way Out," *Harvard Business Review,* May 1949, pp. 287–292 (proposes "statutory strikes" embodying financial penalties against both parties, supplemented by seizure if necessary); Charles O. Gregory, "Injunctions, Seizure and Compulsory Arbitration," *Temple Law Quarterly,* Spring 1953, p. 402 (replaces "equal pressures" with compulsory arbitration, if agreement is not reached in specified time).

11. NWLB *Termination Report,* vol. I, chaps. 5, 39; vol. II, appendix J-38, J-39, J-40. The seizure table in the *Monthly Labor Review,* June 1953, pp. 613–615, follows the NWLB practice.

12. Ohly MS., *passim.*

13. Report of Capt. H. K. Clark, USNR, officer in charge, to secretary of navy, Oct. 2, 1945. Also 25 War Lab. Rep. 733; and correspondence with Mr. Simkin.

14. For North American Aviation, see B. M. Rich, *The Presidents and Civil Disorder* (Washington, 1941) chap. 11; *BLS Bulletin,* no. 714, pp. 156–160; Ohly MS., chap. 2. For Alcoa case, see J. P. Goldberg, *The Maritime Story* (Cambridge, Mass., 1958), pp. 199, 202–204; *New York Times,* Sept. 24, 1941, p. 1; Oct. 5, 1941, p. 11; Oct. 10, 1941, p. 45.

15. Letter to the author from E. C. Thompson, secretary of National Mediation Board, Sept. 8, 1955.

16. In the matter of Aliquippa & Southern R.R. Co. and United Railroad Workers of America, CIO, Arbitration 152, case no. A-3524 (March 30, 1951).

17. For Scranton Transit case, see *Scranton Tribune,* June 22–30, 1945.

18. For Philadelphia & Reading seizure, see War Department, *War of Rebellion; Official Records,* series III, vol. V, pp. 67–68; E. D. Fite, *Social and Economic Conditions in the North During the Civil War* (New York, 1910), pp. 203, 211; B. L. Lee, *Discontent in New York City 1861–1865* (Washington, 1943), p. 224.

19. National Archives, Record Group 98, U.S. Army Commands, Department of Susquehanna.

20. Report of Undersecretary of War Bendetsen, Sept. 15, 1952, pp. 11–12, 59–60; NMB, closing digest of case no. A-3596; *Pittsburgh Post-Gazette,* Mar. 19, 1951, pp. 1, 30 (paid advertisement by the company); Mar. 23, 1951, pp. 1, 11; Mar. 24, 1951, p. 6.

21. See NWSB History, pp. 237–242; C. E. Warne (ed.), *Labor in Postwar America* (Brooklyn, N.Y., 1949), articles by E. E. Witte, pp. 502–504, and by John T. Dunlop, p. 19; 1 Lab. Arb. Rept. 333, 636; 60 Stat. 57 (sec. c); *National Provisioner,* Mar. 2, 1946, p. 13; Mar. 9, 1946, pp. 11, 27; Mar. 16,

1946, pp. 35–42; Mar. 30, 1946, p. 23; Apr. 13, 1946, p. 17; Apr. 27, 1946, pp. 7, 15. The author has also benefited from correspondence with the late Professor Witte and with Senator C. P. Anderson.

22. Only toward the end of the rail seizure of 1917–1920 did Wilson try to mediate a settlement of the labor dispute. His recommendation of a Railroad Labor Board to settle the dispute after seizure terminated was incorporated in the Transportation Act of 1920; but this did not settle the disputes between the carriers and brotherhoods.

23. Several discussions of the effects of seizure upon the negotiating process in the settlement of disputes have appeared in articles primarily discussing more inclusive subjects: George W. Taylor, "Is Compulsory Arbitration Inevitable?" IRRA, *1st Annual Proceedings 1948,* pp. 74–76; Willcox and Landis, *Cornell Law Quarterly,* Winter 1948, pp. 160–164, 175–176; Gustav Peck, "Emergency Disputes Settlement," staff report to subcommittee on labor and labor-management relations of Senate Committee on Labor and Public Welfare, Dec. 1952, pp. 34–35; and Archibald Cox in Bernstein (ed.), *Emergency Disputes and National Policy* (New York, 1955), pp. 237–241.

24. *New York Times,* Mar. 13, 1952, p. 30, col. 5.

CHAPTER 8

MINIMIZING THE INTERFERENCE WITH MANAGERIAL AUTHORITY

1. *Missouri Pacific* v. *Ault,* 256 U.S. 554; *North Carolina R.R.* v. *Lee,* 260 U.S. 16; *United States* v. *United Mine Workers of America and John L. Lewis,* 330 U.S. 258.

2. *San Francisco Lodge No. 68, I.A.M.,* v. *Forrestal,* 58 Fed. Supp. 466; *James H. McMenamin* v. *Philadelphia Transportation Co.,* 356 Pa. 88.

3. A basic statement on sec. 4 and sec. 5 provisions for interim changes will be found in the formal opinion by Jesse Freidin, general counsel of the NWLB, dated Aug. 22, 1944, in 19 War Lab. Rep. xi, and 15 LRRM 2578. A brief statement appears in NWLB *Termination Report,* vol. I, p. 427. The seizing agencies responded variously—the navy using indirect language to abrogate private arbitration of grievances in the San Francisco machine-shop case so as to avoid conflict with the freezing provisions of the act (H. G. Bowen, *Ships, Machinery and Mossbacks* [Princeton, 1954], p. 324); the army turned to the Department of Justice in the second Ward case for assurance that the furnishing of wage data to the union would not constitute a change in the terms of employment (Ohly MS., pp. 392–393); and the navy in the Goodyear case consulting the NWLB itself—being assured that changing and tightening shop rules and hours of quitting would not be changes requiring approval of the board under sec. 5 (report of officer in charge, Oct. 2, 1945, p. 16), and that sec. 5 did not authorize appeals to the NWLB from decisions in grievance cases

during government operation. "Sec. 5 has to do only with applications for changes in basic terms and conditions of employment." (Statement of the board, July 12, 1945, in 25 War Lab. Rep. 733.)

4. A list of the personnel required in direct operation of seizure cases is given in the War Department's *Seizure Manual,* prepared during the Second World War. What is termed herein "direct operation" is roughly equivalent to "Situation A" in the Army *Seizure Manual.* War Department, Office of the Judge Advocate General, *Emergency Operation of Industrial Facilities,* ASF-EOIF 44, revised Sept. 23, 1944, pp. 3–4, 23–25. An earlier edition was published in the fall of 1942. About 1949, the Department of Defense prepared the tentative draft of a revision of the Army *Seizure Manual,* and distributed it to certain labor-relations personnel in the armed forces for review and possible emergency use, but did not issue a definitive volume.

5. W. H. Davis, "Collective Bargaining and Economic Progress," *Industrial Disputes and the Public Interest* (Berkeley and Los Angeles, 1947), p. 15; E. C. Gerhart, "Strikes and Eminent Domain," *Journal of American Judicature Society,* Dec. 1946, pp. 116–122.

6. The smaller number of personnel required in an indirect operation is clearly specified in the Army *Seizure Manual* cited in note 4 above (same page references). What is termed "indirect operation" here is roughly "Situation B" in the *Manual.*

7. For the first of these independent actions of the seizing agency, see the statements of W. H. Davis, chairman of NWLB, and of W. L. Morse, member, in NWLB *Termination Report,* vol. III, pp. 591, 593. For the second independent action see the statement of F. M. Vinson, director of economic stabilization, dated May 26, 1944, in 16 War Lab. Rep. xii.

8. Bowen, *Ships, Machinery and Mossbacks,* pp. 329–335, esp. p. 333.

9. Department of the Army, Office of the Under Secretary, *Army Operation of Rail Transportation Systems,* Sept. 15, 1952 (Bendetsen Report), chaps. 6 and 8, esp. p. 57.

10. Ohly MS., pp. 392–393, appendix Z-1-d.

11. Union testimony at hearing conducted by review committee of NWSB, Apr. 24, 1946: verbatim transcript, pp. 95–98, 103 (National Archives, Record Group 202).

12. Interviews with David E. Bell, Cambridge, Massachusetts, Dec. 1, 1953 and Mar. 4, 1954. See also Grant McConnell, *The Steel Seizure of 1952* (Alabama, 1960), pp. 39, 43.

13. Including nationwide agreements by representatives of both labor and management to accept governmental arbitration of wage disputes.

14. The voluntary wage changes occurring during seizure operations (with government permission) include the following: Wage increase by agreement (New England T. & T. Co. and IBEW) following a strike during government operation (seizure 3); two wage reclassifications by agreement—Federal Shipbuilding Co. and IUMSW (6); wage increase by agreement—S. A. Woods Machine Co. and UEW (11); eight-dollar per month increase for nonunion foremen and clerical employees in anthracite mines at company request (16);

nine-cents per hour increase by agreement—major railroads and BLFE, ORC, and SUNA (19); wage changes by agreement—Montgomery Ward & Co., Hummer manufacturing division, and IAM (25); wage changes by agreement—various San Francisco machine shops and craft unions (28); wage increases for nonunion foremen in bituminous coal mines authorized by NWLB in denying recognition to union (31); wage increases by Carter Coal Co. similar to industry but without signing any contract with UMWA (45); $600,000 wage increases by agreement—Texas Co. and OWIU (54); outstanding NWLB order regulating payment of overtime was effectuated by agreement (four big New York City packing plants and IBT) after strike (63); wage increases for nonunion foremen and clerical workers at request of mining companies (66); wage increases by a series of agreements (major railroads and SUNA, RYA, ATDA, "nonoperating" labor organizations, and BRT)—Lake Michigan car ferries and GLLOO, after a strike (69); wage increases for other operating employees of rail subsidiaries of J. & L. Steel Corp. to match army-ordered increase on Mon. Con. R.R. by agreement (70); incentive plan revised by agreement (Universal Cyclops Steel Co., and USWA) after a strike (71).

15. Seizures 9, 13, 14, 16, 22, 34, 35, 47, 48, 49, 66, 70.

16. On postwar developments affecting the American R.R. of Porto Rico, see S. L. Debalta, "The Railroad that the Workers Inherited," *Railway Progress,* Dec. 1950, pp. 24–29.

17. Seizures 2, 3, 4, 11, 23, 27, 38, 62, 63, 69.

18. ODT, *Report of Federal Manager of Motor Carrier Transportation Systems and Properties Concerning Possession . . . of 103 Midwest Motor Carriers, Aug. 11, 1944, to March 5, 1946* (undated, processed, made public July 10, 1946), parts IV and V.

19. *New York Times,* May 9, 1952; *Business Week,* May 24, 1952, p. 90; 30 LRRM 113.

20. Louis Ruchames, *Race, Jobs, & Politics; the Story of FEPC* (New York, 1953), pp. 118, 132–134.

21. Interview with David N. Phillips, vice-president for public relations, and Robert H. Dalgleish, Jr., of operations department, Philadelphia Transportation Co., Sept. 3, 1953.

22. Bendetsen Report, pp. 58–59.

23. Rear Admiral H. G. Bowen. Report of the Officer in Charge, Sept. 29, 1944.

24. Ohly MS., appendix Z-2-a (JAG narrative).

25. Ohly MS., pp. 385–389, appendixes V-30, Y-2.

26. Opinion of Jesse Freidin, note 3 above.

CHAPTER 9

REDUCING CONFLICT WITH NORMAL
REGULATORY AGENCIES

1. For early seizure laws emphasizing presidential military authority, see *Railroad Control Act of 1862* (12 Stat. 334); National Defense Act of 1916 (39 Stat. 166, 213, sec. 120); Transportation Seizure Act of 1916 (39 Stat. 619, 645).

2. See note 48 below.

3. 30 Op. Atty. Gen. 530.

4. General Order No. 8; reprinted in Walker D. Hines, *War History of American Railroads* (New Haven, 1928), p. 305.

5. J. W. Bishop, Jr., official study of Smith & Wesson seizure for the War Department, 1941; text in appendixes F-1 and F-2 of Ohly MS.

6. U.S. Railroad Administration, Division of Labor, *Annual Report . . . for 1918* (Washington, 1919), pp. 8–9; Bishop, study of Smith & Wesson seizure in Ohly MS., appendix F-2, p. 3.

7. *Colliers,* July 15, 1944, p. 49.

8. Order dated Nov. 20, 1943, NWLB *Termination Report,* vol. III, pp. 602–604; also letter, Ickes to Davis, chairman NWLB, Nov. 12, 1943, pp. 598–599.

9. USRRA, Director General of Railroads, *Bulletin No. 4,* revised (Washington, 1919), pp. 31–38; Supplement to *Bulletin No. 4,* revised (Washington, 1920); proclamation of President Wilson of March 11, 1920. See also Federal Control Act, sec. 10 (40 Stat. 451); *Missouri Pacific* v. *Ault* (256 U.S. 554); and *North Carolina R.R.* v. *Lee* (260 U.S. 16).

10. Undersecretary of the Navy Forrestal to president, Federal Shipbuilding, Aug. 6, 1942, in Sec Nav file L13-2(22)/QM; undated draft report of Rear Admiral H. G. Bowen in box no. 36, Job no. 1666; Naval Records Management Center, Arlington, Va. See also U.S. Employees Compensation Commission, *26th Annual Report* (Washington 1943), p. 3.

11. Ohly MS., p. 72.

12. *New York Times,* Apr. 20, 1952.

13. Correspondence of John F. Sloan, Jr., Esq., of Peoria, Illinois, with Attorney General Biddle, Nov. 13, 1944, and Jan. 26, 1945, in records of the general counsel, Office of Defense Transportation, series 106.1, Record Group 219, National Archives.

14. Report of the federal manager of motor carrier transportation systems and properties (midwest trucking seizure), p. 52. This practice was confined to the eight firms directly operated; firms indirectly operated continued their customary methods as "agents" of the federal manager, p. 94.

15. Knox to Altmeyer, chairman of SSB, Sept. 29, 1941, in seizure of Federal Shipbuilding & Dry Dock Co. Previously, Acting Secretary of the Navy Bard, in a letter to the officer in charge, Rear Admiral H. G. Bowen, dated Aug. 23, 1941, had referred to the employees as "former employees"

of the company, saying: "You should notify the former employees of the company employed by you that they will not lose any social security or industrial insurance benefits." (Copies of the two letters in files of general counsel, Navy Department, Washington, D.C.)

16. Ohly MS., p. 72.

17. Federal manager's Notice and Order No. 1, 11 F. R. 5512; summarized in ODT, *Civilian War Transport*, p. 278.

18. 8 F. R. 6655; also 30 CFR, Cum. Supp. 603 (sec. 603.23 [d] [1]).

19. General Order No. 1, signed by Lieutenant General Brehon Somervell, commanding general, army service forces, 8 F. R. 17488 (sec. 5[d]).

20. For wartime distinctions between the permanent and temporary adjustment agencies, see the following laws and executive orders: Wage Stabilization Act of Oct. 2, 1942 (56 Stat. 765); sec. 7 of WLDA of 1943 (57 Stat. 163); Ex. Order 8716, creating the NDMB, par. 2 (6 F. R. 1532; NWLB *Termination Report*, vol. II, p. 48); Ex. Order 9017, creating the NWLB, par. 2 and 7 (7 F. R. 237; NWLB *Termination Report*, vol. II, p. 49); Ex. Order 9250, giving wage controls to NWLB, title VI (7 F. R. 7871; NWLB *Termination Report*, vol. II, p. 75).

21. *BLS Bulletin*, no. 714, p. 5.

22. Address before Oregon State Bar Assn., Sept. 3, 1942: *Oregon Law Review*, Dec. 1942, vol. 22, p. 33.

23. In addition to references in the preceding footnote, see Fred Witney, *Wartime Experiences of the NLRB* (Urbana, Illinois, 1949), chaps. 6, 7; and NWLB *Termination Report*, vol. I, chaps. 3, 6.

24. The Labor Management Relations Act of 1947 (Taft-Hartley Act), 61 Stat. 136, esp. secs. 8(b), 10(j) and 10(l). For a discussion of the new injunction powers given the NLRB by this act, see H. A. Millis and E. C. Brown, *From the Wagner Act to Taft-Hartley* (Chicago, 1950), pp. 485–496, 616–618, 662–663. I am also indebted for helpful discussions on this subject with Dr. A. Howard Myers, former New England regional director of the NLRB; the late Bernard Alpert, then regional director; and Robert E. Greene, of Mr. Alpert's staff, in Sept. 1955.

25. Defense Production Act of 1950, approved Sept. 8, 1950, 64 Stat. 798, title V (secs. 501–503).

26. The effects of these contradictory alternatives upon the steel-seizure case are indicated by Mr. Truman in his *Memoirs* (New York, 1956), vol. II, p. 467. They are discussed in H. L. Enarson, "The Politics of an Emergency Dispute," in Bernstein (ed.), *Emergency Disputes and National Policy* (New York, 1955), pp. 50–53, and in F. H. Harbison and R. C. Spencer, *American Political Science Review*, Sept. 1954, vol. 48, pp. 705–720.

27. *Hughes Tool Co.* v. *N.L.R.B.*, 147 Fed. 2d 69 (Jan. 22, 1945); modified, 16 LRRM 918 (Mar. 14, 1945). See also Ohly MS., pp. 531–532 and appendix CC-20.

28. *Jones & Laughlin Steel Co.* v. *United Mine Workers of America, et al.*, 159 Fed. 2d 18 (Dec. 16, 1946); cert. denied, 331 U.S. 828 (May 19, 1947).

29. Three seizures in which the seizing agencies continued the companies'

nonrecognition policy without change were: coal mining, Nov. 1943 (Glen Alden Coal Co. and West Kentucky Coal Co.); Ken-Rad Tube & Lamp Corp.; and railroads, 1950–1952 (several carriers). It should be noted that only one of these cases involved an agency's refusal to recognize a union after it had been certified by the NLRB (Secretary of the Interior Ickes and the Molders' Union at the foundry of the Glen Alden Coal Co.); in the other instances, the agency merely withheld recognition pending formal certification by the NLRB or NMB.

30. *Glen Alden Coal Co.* v. *NLRB*, 141 Fed. 2d 47, CCA-3, Jan. 31, 1944.

31. All of this is from the court's opinion, cited in the preceding footnote.

32. This normal peacetime proceeding required more than two and a half years from the date of the NLRB examiner's hearing, Nov. 5, 1943, to the final disposition of the matter when the Supreme Court refused to look into it, June 10, 1946. (*NLRB* v. *West Kentucky Coal Co.*, 152 Fed. 2d 198, CCA-6, Dec. 6, 1945; cert. denied, 328 U.S. 866, June 10, 1946.) Incidentally, the property had been in the government's hands only from Nov. 1 to Nov. 17, 1943 (8 F. R. 15867).

33. 61 Stat. 136, sec. 8(b), (4)(C) and sec. 10(l).

34. The five seizures in which the seizing agency acted independently of the permanent labor-relations boards and required concessions by the certified union as well as by the raiding union were: Massachusetts tanneries; Fall River textile mills; Toledo machine shops; Springfield Plywood Corp.; and Illinois Central R.R.

The two seizures in which the seizing agency is believed to have upheld fully the permanent labor agencies in its interim decisions over union rivalry were Hughes Tool Co. and Sinclair Rubber.

35. *Bendetsen Report,* chap. 5.

36. *Bendetsen Report,* pp. 34, 57. The carrier was the Duluth, Missabe & Iron Range R.R., a subsidiary of the United States Steel Corp. See also *Labor Dispute,* hearings before Senate Labor Committee, March 1951, 82d Cong., 1st sess., pp. 661–666.

37. 47 Stat. 70.

38. The three occasions in which the president obtained antistrike injunctions were: the Pullman strike of 1894 (Cleveland); the soft coal strike of 1919 (Wilson); and the railroad shopmen's strike of 1922 (Harding). Although the Norris-LaGuardia Act was intended primarily to bar the federal courts to private employers, Mr. Justice Frankfurter disclosed that "it was these very injunctions secured by the attorney general of the United States under claim of compelling public emergency, that gave the most powerful momentum to the enactment of the Norris-LaGuardia Act" (*U.S.* v. *United Mine Workers of America*, 333 U.S. 258, 315; Mar. 6, 1947, concurring opinion); and Justice Murphy echoed this interpretation (333 U.S. 258, 338, dissenting opinion).

39. War Labor Disputes Act, 57 Stat. 163 (sec. 6).

40. Details and documentation of this episode were given in Chapter 2.

41. *U.S.* v. *United Mine Workers of America and John L. Lewis* (333 U.S. 258).

42. *Youngstown Sheet & Tube Co.* v. *Sawyer,* 343 U.S. 579 (June 2, 1952).

43. Compare Archibald Cox, *Emergency Disputes and National Policy,* Bernstein *et al.* (eds.) (New York, 1955), p. 230.

44. The 20 seizures involving public utilities were individual railroads—1, 9, 12, 14, 40, 59, 67, 69; railroad industry—2, 19, 65, 68, 70; urban transit systems—26, 51, 61; trucking companies—27, 47; electric power company—39; the telegraph, telephone and cable industry—3. It will be noticed that 18 of the 20 were common carriers.

45. The seven public utility seizures lasting a year or more were, in chronological order: the railroads 1917–1920, two years and two months; the wire systems, one year; T.P. & W. R.R., three years and six months; A.R.R. of P.R., one year and one month; midwest trucking firms, one year and two months; C.R.I. & P.R.R., one year and 10 months; the major railroads 1950–1952, one year and nine months.

46. Sec. 9 of Federal [Railroad] Control Act of Mar. 21, 1918 (40 Stat. 451).

47. The Railroad Administration, while retaining almost complete control of railroad regulation and operations, made the minor gesture of turning over to the state regulatory commissions the control of such local matters as spur tracks, railroad crossings, and station facilities, General Order No. 58, early 1919; see W. D. Hines, *War History of American Railroads,* p. 91.

48. *Northern Pacific Railway Co.* v. *State of North Dakota, ex rel. Langer, Attorney General* (250 U.S. 135, esp. at 148–149) and *Dakota Central Telephone Co.* v. *State of South Dakota, ex rel. Payne, Attorney. General* (250 U.S. 163). Justice Brandeis dissented from the second of these cases without a written opinion. These decisions of the Supreme Court allowed the immediate enforcement of about $16,000,000 in deferred telephone rate increases that had been held up by state court injunctions. This compares with $26,000,000 in telephone increases that had gone into effect without court hindrance, N. R. Danielian, *A.T. & T., the Story of Industrial Conquest* (New York, 1939), p. 260, quoting an FCC staff study.

49. Compare J. B. Eastman's address before American Economic Association in Washington, Jan. 21, 1944 (XXXIV, no. 1, part 2), *American Economic Review,* Mar. 1944, pp. 86–87.

50. Sources of this paragraph: "Report of T.P. & W. R.R. Operation" by C. M. Roddewig, May 26, 1944, p. 3, in National Archives, Record Group 219, series 106.1; ODT, *Civilian War Transport,* p. 276; *Report of Federal Manager of Motor Carrier Transportation Systems* (midwest firms), pp. 22–27 and appendix IV; *Bendetsen Report,* p. 35 and docs. no. 20, 21.

51. The difficulties in wartime railroad operation—due to the antipooling provisions of the Interstate Commerce Act of 1887, to the Sherman Antitrust Act of 1890, and to the refusal of President Wilson's attorney general,

T. W. Gregory, to suspend their enforcement—have been well summarized in Hines' *War History of American Railroads,* pp. 1, 14–15, 225.

52. President Wilson, in his statement sent to Congress upon taking over the railroads, Dec. 27, 1917, stressed the need for employing the transportation systems of the country "under a single authority and a simplified method of coordination." Text of Wilson's statement in Hines, *War History of American Railroads,* p. 248; and R. S. Baker and W. E. Dodd (eds.), *Public Papers of Woodrow Wilson* (New York, 1925–1927), vol. 5, p. 147. The actual control of traffic by the Railroad Administration, without regard to the wishes of individual shippers and individual railroads, has been described in many studies. The primary sources are W. G. McAdoo, *Crowded Years* (Boston, 1931), pp. 474–490; and Hines, *War History of American Railroads,* chaps. 4 and 6. An authoritative treatment is that of W. J. Cunningham in the *Quarterly Journal of Economics* (Feb. 1921), vol. 35, pp. 309–327, 332–338.

53. Postmaster General Burleson informed President Wilson in his seizure report of Nov. 1919 that 34 consolidations had taken place during federal control. (S. Doc. 152, 66th Cong., 1st sess., p. 8.) It is believed that virtually all these consolidations were of telephone companies operating in the same or contiguous areas. (See *Official U.S. Bulletin,* Aug. 19, 1918, p. 16.) It may be noticed that President Wilson, in his message to Congress, May 20, 1919, urging a return of the wires to private ownership, asked that provision be made for their "coordination" as a "national system" even in private hands (58 Congressional Record 42).

54. *Commercial Cable Co.* v. *Burleson and Carlton,* 255 F. R. 99, 107, Jan. 10, 1919; held moot, 250 U.S. 360, June 9, 1919. See also Mr. Burleson's report to President Wilson on the seizure (S. Doc. 152, 66th Cong., 1st sess.) and the annual reports of the Mackay Companies and of Western Union for 1918–1920.

55. Federal manager's report, pp. 32, 45–48, 56, 76. The concern which had to be operated directly because of refusal to adopt a joint action plan was the Healzer Cartage Co., Hutchinson, Kansas.

56. Annual report of P. & R. C. & I. Co. for 1944, p. 4.

57. The Esch-Cummins Act, approved Feb. 28, 1920 (41 Stat. 456–499).

58. The Telegraph Merger Act approved Mar. 6, 1943 (57 Stat. 5). See Witney, *Wartime Experiences of the NLRB,* chap. 5 and appendix C.

CHAPTER 10

SEIZURE COMPARED WITH OTHER EXPERIENCE
IN REQUIRED OPERATIONS

1. *History of Spruce Production Division, U.S. Army, and U.S. Spruce Production Corp.* (Seattle, 1920); consulted at library of U.S. National War College, Washington. Files of *American Lumberman,* consulted at Baker Library, Harvard Graduate School of Business Administration. Other sources as in Appendix C, item 8.

2. 66th Cong., 2d sess., *War Expenditures,* Hearings before select committee of House of Representatives (Washington, 1919–1920), serial 2 (subcommittee on aviation), vol. 2, p. 2279.

3. Interview with Laurence C. Turner, Cleveland, July 5, 1961.

4. Bennett M. Rich, *The Presidents and Civil Disorder* (Washington, 1941), p. 209.

5. Rich, *The Presidents and Civil Disorder,* p. 210; also F. T. Wilson, *Federal Aid in Domestic Disturbances,* S. Doc. 263, 67th Cong., 2d sess. (Washington, 1922).

6. Rich, *The Presidents and Civil Disorder,* pp. 115–116.

7. John P. Frank, "Ex Parte Milligan v. The Five Companies," *Columbia Law Review,* Sept. 1944, pp. 639, 653–657.

8. The term "martial rule" was applied to seizure by Clinton Rossiter in *The Supreme Court and the Commander in Chief* (Ithaca, 1951), pp. 42, 59–64.

9. Edward S. Corwin, *The President: Office and Powers, 1787–1957,* 4th ed. (New York, 1957), pp. 246–250.

10. Matthew Josephson, *Sidney Hillman* (Garden City, New York, 1952), pp. 167–171.

11. Albert A. Blum, "Work or Fight," *Industrial and Labor Relations Review,* Apr. 1963, p. 376. Byron Fairchild and Jonathan Grossman, *The United States Army in World War II—The War Department; The Army and Industrial Manpower* (Washington, 1959), pp. 197–198.

12. On Montgomery Ward & Co., see Corwin, *The President: Office and Powers,* pp. 249–250. On Goodyear Tire & Rubber Co., see 25 War Lab. Rep. 274; 27 War Lab. Rep. 792.

13. Corwin, *The President: Office and Powers,* p. 248.

14. 58 Fed. Supp. 466 (1944). Harold G. Bowen, *Ships, Machinery and Mossbacks* (Princeton, 1954), pp. 282–335.

15. See Appendix C, items 4, 5, 6, 14, 15, 16.

16. 64 Fed. 724, affirmed 158 U.S. 564 (1895). See also Corwin, *The President: Office and Powers,* p. 152.

17. 47 Stat. 70.

18. Concurring opinion in *U.S.* v. *United Mine Workers of America,* 330 U.S. 258, at 310, 315 (1947).

19. Edward Berman, *Labor Disputes and the President of the United States* (New York, 1924), pp. 183, 185.

20. Blum, "Work or Fight," pp. 376–378. Herman M. Somers, *Presidential Agency; the Office of War Mobilization and Reconversion* (Cambridge, Mass., 1950), p. 170. Saul Alinsky, *John L. Lewis; an Unauthorized Biography* (New York, 1949), chap. 12.

21. 57 Stat. 163.

22. *New York Times*, Aug. 31, 1943, p. 13. *Business Week*, July 31, 1943, pp. 17–18; Aug. 21, 1943, p. 82.

23. Fairchild and Grossman, *The Army and Industrial Manpower*, chap. 11.

24. Wellington Roe, *Juggernaut* (Philadelphia, 1948), chap. 21. A. F. Whitney, *Railroad Rules-Wage Movements in the U.S., 1944–45–46* (Cleveland, 1946), pp. 84–91; consulted in Littauer Library of Labor Relations, Harvard University.

25. 92 Congressional Record 5752 (May 25, 1946).

26. 92 Congressional Record 6677 (June 11, 1946).

27. 19 LRRM 2059, 2079–2087, 2121–2126; 70 Fed. Supp. 42–53. Harry S. Truman, *Memoirs, vol. I: Year of Decisions* (New York, 1955), pp. 500, 502–505. William Hillman (ed.), *Mr. President* (New York, 1952), pp. 128–129.

28. 330 U.S. 258 (1947).

29. *U.S. v. Brotherhood of Locomotive Engineers*, 79 Fed. Supp. 484 (1948); *U.S. v. Switchmen's Union of N.A.*, 97 Fed. Supp. 97 (1950); *U.S. v. Brotherhood of R.R. Trainmen*, 96 Fed. Supp. 428, 95 Fed. Supp. 1019 (1951).

30. Berman, *Labor Disputes and the President*, pp. 113–121. Frederick Palmer, *Newton D. Baker; America at War* (New York, 1931), vol. I, pp. 97–99. *New York Times*, Mar. 19 and 20, 1917, p. 1.

31. Jacob J. Kaufman, "The Railroad Labor Dispute," *Industrial and Labor Relations Review*, Jan. 1965, pp. 210–211. Jimmy Breslin, "Professional 'Man in the Middle,' " *New York* (supplement to *New York Herald Tribune*), Jan. 31, 1965, p. 13.

32. Kaufman, "The Railroad Labor Dispute," pp. 209–212.

33. John R. Commons and John B. Andrews, *Principles of Labor Legislation*, 4th ed. (New York, 1936), pp. 510–517. Edward S. Corwin, *The Constitution and What It Means Today*, 8th ed. (Princeton, 1946), pp. 168–169.

Index

WERTHEIM PUBLICATIONS IN INDUSTRIAL RELATIONS

PUBLISHED BY HARVARD UNIVERSITY PRESS

J. D. Houser, *What the Employer Thinks*, 1927

Wertheim Lectures on Industrial Relations, 1929

William Haber, *Industrial Relations in the Building Industry*, 1930

Johnson O'Connor, *Psychometrics*, 1934

Paul H. Norgren, *The Swedish Collective Bargaining System*, 1941

Leo C. Brown, S.J., *Union Policies in the Leather Industry*, 1947.

Walter Galenson, *Labor in Norway*, 1949

Dorothea de Schweinitz, *Labor and Management in a Common Enterprise*, 1949

Ralph Altman, *Availability for Work: A Study in Unemployment Compensation*, 1950

John T. Dunlop and Arthur D. Hill, *The Wage Adjustment Board: Wartime Stabilization in the Building and Construction Industry*, 1950

Walter Galenson, *The Danish System of Labor Relations: A Study in Industrial Peace*, 1952

Lloyd H. Fisher, *The Harvest Labor Market in California*, 1953

Theodore V. Purcell, S.J., *The Worker Speaks His Mind on Company and Union*, 1953

Donald J. White, *The New England Fishing Industry*, 1954

Val R. Lorwin, *The French Labor Movement*, 1954

Philip Taft, *The Structure and Government of Labor Unions*, 1954

George B. Baldwin, *Beyond Nationalization: The Labor Problems of British Coal*, 1955

Kenneth F. Walker, *Industrial Relations in Australia*, 1956

Charles A. Myers, *Labor Problems in the Industrialization of India*, 1958

Herbert J. Spiro, *The Politics of German Codetermination*, 1958

Mark W. Leiserson, *Wages and Economic Control in Norway, 1945–1957*, 1959

J. Pen, *The Wage Rate Under Collective Bargaining*, 1959

Jack Stieber, *The Steel Industry Wage Structure*, 1959

Theodore V. Purcell, S.J., *Blue Collar Man: Patterns of Dual Allegiance in Industry*, 1960

Carl Erik Knoellinger, *Labor in Finland*, 1960

Sumner H. Slichter, *Potentials of the American Economy: Selected Essays*, edited by John T. Dunlop, 1961

C. L. Christenson, *Economic Redevelopment in Bituminous Coal: The Special Case of Technological Advance in United States Coal Mines, 1930–1960*, 1962

Daniel L. Horowitz, *The Italian Labor Movement*, 1963

Adolf Sturmthal, *Workers Councils: A Study of Workplace Organization on Both Sides of the Iron Curtain*, 1964

Vernon H. Jensen, *Hiring of Dock Workers and Employment Practices in the Ports of New York, Liverpool, London, Rotterdam, and Marseilles,* 1964

John L. Blackman, Jr., *Presidential Seizure in Labor Disputes,* 1967

STUDIES IN LABOR-MANAGEMENT HISTORY

Lloyd Ulman, *The Rise of the National Trade Union: The Development and Significance of its Structure, Governing Institutions, and Economic Policies,* 1955

Joseph P. Goldberg, *The Maritime Story: A Study in Labor-Management Relations,* 1958

Walter Galenson, *The CIO Challenge to the AFL: A History of the American Labor Movement, 1935–1941,* 1960

Morris A. Horowitz, *The New York Hotel Industry: A Labor Relations Study,* 1960

Mark Perlman, *The Machinists: A New Study in Trade Unionism,* 1961

Fred C. Munson, *Labor Relations in the Lithographic Industry,* 1963

Garth L. Mangum, *The Operating Engineers: The Economic History of a Trade Union,* 1964

PUBLISHED BY MCGRAW-HILL BOOK CO., INC.

Robert J. Alexander, *Labor Relations in Argentina, Brazil, and Chile,* 1961

Carl M. Stevens, *Strategy and Collective Bargaining Negotiations,* 1963

John T. Dunlop and Vasilii P. Diatchenko, *Labor Productivity,* 1964